CHIASMS

SUNY series in Contemporary Continental Philosophy
Dennis J. Schmidt, editor

CHIASMS

————

Merleau-Ponty's Notion of Flesh

edited by

FRED EVANS
and
LEONARD LAWLOR

State University of New York Press

Published by
State University of New York Press, Albany

© 2000 State University of New York

For information, address the State University of New York Press,
90 State Street, Suite 700, Albany, NY, 12207

Production by Marilyn P. Semerad
Marketing by Fran Keneston

Library of Congress Cataloging-in-Publication Data

Chiasms : Merleau-Ponty's notion of flesh / Fred Evans and Leonard Lawlor, editors.
    p.   cm. — (SUNY series in contemporary continental philosophy)
Includes bibliographical references and index.
ISBN 0-7914-4685-9 (HC : alk. paper) — ISBN 0-7914-4686-7 (pbk.: alk. paper)
    1. Merleau-Ponty, Maurice, 1908–1961. 2. Body, Human (Philosophy) I. Evans, Fred.
II. Lawlor, Leonard, 1954–   III. Series.
B2430.M3764 C49 2000
128'.6'092—dc21   00-020253

10 9 8 7 6 5 4 3 2 1

CONTENTS

ACKNOWLEDGMENTS

We have imposed on all the essays collected in this volume a consistent English translation of Merleau-Ponty's term "écart" as "divergence." Certain essays have been published previously. We gratefully acknowledge Editions Flammarion for the essay by Henri Maldiney, *Chair et verbe dans la philosophie de Merleau-Ponty,* and for the essay by Françoise Dastur, *Monde, chair, vision,* both in Collectif, *Maurice Merleau-Ponty, le psychique et le corporel,* edited by A. Tymieniecka, © Aubier, Paris, 1988; Suhrkamp Verlag for permitting the publication of an English translation of Bernhard Waldenfels essay, "Das Paradox des Ausdrucks," in *Deutsch-Französische Gedankengänge,* © Suhrkamp Verlag Frankfurt am Main, 1995; and Routledge for the essay by Gail Weiss, copyright © 1998, from *Body Images* by Gail Weiss. Reproduced by permission of Routledge, Inc.

We would especially like to thank Linda Sadler of the Philosophy Department of the University of Memphis for her organization and formatting of this volume in its manuscript form. We benefited immeasurably from the expertise and patience of Dennis J. Schmidt, editor of the SUNY series in Contemporary Continental Philosophy, and Jane Bunker, acquisitions editor; Marilyn P. Semerad, production manager; and Fran Keneston, marketing manager; all of SUNY Press. We are very grateful for Madame Merleau-Ponty's permission to use the handwriting sample on the front cover of this book.

LIST OF ABBREVIATIONS

TEXTS BY MERLEAU-PONTY

All references are first to the original French translations then to the English texts.

AD   *Adventures de la Dialectique* (Paris: Gallimard, 1955); *Adventures of the Dialectic*, trans. Joseph Bien (Evanston: Northwestern University Press, 1973).

ENF   *Les Relations avec autrui chez l'enfant* (cours de Sorbonne) (Paris: Centre de Documentation Universitaire, 1960); "The Child's Relations with Others," trans. William Cobb, *The Primacy of Perception*, pp. 96–155. For a substantially altered and expanded text see "Les relations avec autrui chez l'enfant," *Merleau-Ponty à la Sorbonne: résumé de cours 1949–52* (Paris: Cynara, 1988), pp. 303–96.

EP   *Eloge de la philosophie* (Paris: Gallimard, 1953); *In Praise of Philosophy and Other Essays*, trans. John O'Neill (Evanston: Northwestern University Press, 1988).

NC   *Notes des cours au Collège de France 1958–1959 et 1960–1961*, preface de C. Lefort, texte etabli par S. Menase (Paris: Gallimard, 1997); all English translations by the individual authors and revised by the editors.

OE   *L'Oeil et l'Esprit* (Paris: Gallimard, 1964); "Eye & Mind," trans. Carleton Dallery, improved by Michael B. Smith in *The Merleau-Ponty Aesthetics Reader: Philosophy and Painting*, ed. Galen Johnson, translations ed. Michael B. Smith (Evanston: Northwestern University Press, 1993), pp. 121–49.

PM   *La Prose du Monde* (Paris: Gallimard, 1969); *The Prose of the World*, trans. John O'Neill (Evanston: Northwestern University Press, 1973).

PP   *Phénoménologie de la perception* (Paris: Gallimard, 1945); *Phenomenology of Perception*, trans. Colin Smith (London: Routledge & Kegan Paul, 1962).

PRI   *Primacy of Perception*, ed. James M. Edie (Evanston: Northwestern University Press, 1964).

RC   *Résumé de cours, Collège de France 1952–60* (Paris: Gallimard, 1968); "Themes from the Lecture Courses," trans. John O'Neill, in *In Praise of Philosophy and Other Essays* (Evanston: Northwestern University Press, 1988).

S   *Signes* (Paris: Gallimard, 1960); *Signs*, trans. Richard McCleary (Evanston: Northwestern University Press, 1964).

SC   *La Structure du Comportment* (Paris: Presses Universitaires de France, 1942); *The Structure of Behavior*, trans. Alden Fischer (Boston: Beacon Press, 1963).

SNS   *Sens et Non-Sens* (Paris: Nagel, 1948); *Sense and Non-Sense*, trans. Hubert Dreyfus and Patricia Dreyfus (Evanston: Northwestern University Press, 1964).

VI   *Le Visible et l'invisible* (Paris: Gallimard, 1964); *The Visible and the Invisible*, trans. Alphonso Lingis (Evanston: Northwestern University Press, 1968).

The Value of Flesh:
Merleau-Ponty's Philosophy and the
Modernism/Postmodernism Debate

FRED EVANS AND LEONARD LAWLOR

By collecting the articles presented here—written by some of the most interesting American and European philosophers—we aim to contribute to the evaluation of Merleau-Ponty's notion of the flesh.[1] Merleau-Ponty introduced his notion of *chiasm*—of the *chiasmic* structure of flesh—in his posthumous work, *The Visible and the Invisible*.[2] He intended this notion to overcome limitations in his earlier *Phenomenology of Perception*—limitations concerning the elucidation of our relation to the world and to each other. Because Merleau-Ponty left this notion in an incomplete state (due to his untimely death), it has stimulated efforts of explication. Moreover, a growing number of philosophers think the notion of the flesh can be extended in promising directions; phenomenologists, poststructuralists, feminists, and ecologists use it to clarify the bond between self, others, and world, and to affirm the positive status of difference and alterity in relation to this bond. Others, however, perceive limitations within the notion of the flesh, especially insofar as both "flesh" and "chiasm" are terms sedimented with religious senses stemming from Christianity (the mystery of the incarnation and the cross).[3] Moreover, Merleau-Ponty sometimes speaks as if the flesh subordinates the individual subjects to a *logos* or "voice" of Being that plays through these subjects and the other inhabitants of the world (VI 203/155).[4]

Because Merleau-Ponty's notion of the flesh still requires explications allowing us to extend it and to consider limitations within it, we believe that it lies at the very center of today's chief intellectual and cultural problem: the debate between modernism and postmodernism. This debate swirls around one question: can we find an order after the announcement that God is dead? Can thought have any credibility at all once the foundations established within

1

modern philosophy are dismantled by the deconstructions and other critical maneuvers of postmodernism? The fortunes of Merleau-Ponty's notion of the flesh lie in the answer to this question. Therefore, Merleau-Ponty's central role in the modernism-postmodernism debate is why we have brought forward these explications, extensions, and limitations of the notion of the flesh, an idea whose time seems to have arrived. The first group of papers in *Chiasms,* "Explications of the Flesh," establishes the notion of the flesh as a consistent concept and unfolds the nuances of flesh that make it the compelling idea that so many readers of Merleau-Ponty have already found it to be. Six of the articles in this group are translations of recent work by leading European scholars (French, German, and Italian), making their efforts more accessible to English-speaking readers. The second group of papers, "Extensions of the Flesh," adds to the force of Merleau-Ponty's idea of flesh by showing how it can be extended to phenomena that Merleau-Ponty did not treat, such as the Internet, virtual reality, invasive technologies, contemporary philosophies of mathematics, the glance, and our experience of cadavers. And the third set, "Limitations of the Flesh," suggests criticisms of Merleau-Ponty from feminist and Levinasian points of view. Throughout the articles in each group, Merleau-Ponty's work is related to important modern and contemporary thinkers.

We hope that this threefold division will place the reader in a better position to appreciate the relevance of Merleau-Ponty's notion of flesh for the modernism-postmodernism debate and thereby to understand our current philosophical and political setting. In this introduction, however, we would like to set up a context which, we hope, will help the reader enter into an engagement with these essays. We are going to establish this framework in three steps. First, we shall review the ideas that so many found and still find important in Merleau-Ponty's earlier *Phenomenology of Perception*: the creative tension between unity and multiplicity, identity and difference, sameness and otherness. Second, we intend to show how these ideas develop into those found in *The Visible and the Invisible*: obviously, the flesh and chiasm. Then, we ourselves would like to suggest two extensions of Merleau-Ponty's notion of the flesh. The formulation of this these two extensions, undoubtedly, does violence to the positions that certain contemporary philosophers hold; but we believe this violence is necessary, if we are going to start to think from today about philosophy tomorrow.

PHENOMENOLOGY OF PERCEPTION AND MODERNISM

Merleau-Ponty's *Phenomenology of Perception* can be seen as the culmination of the humanistic tradition within modernism. Like the works of Descartes, Kant, Hegel, and Marx, it identifies the self or "subject" with reason and pronounces reason to be the basis for knowledge and for our emancipation from forces that would otherwise prevent us from developing and fulfilling our human capacities. But Merleau-Ponty achieves these goals without falling into the pitfalls of the other versions of humanistic modernism. He does not guarantee our freedom by bifurcating reality into the mental and the physical or into the noumenal and the phenomenal. And although he conflates reason with the movement of history, he does not assign history a preordained end or sovereignty over the subjects who participate in it. Rather, we and the world are engaged in a dialogue with each other. This dialogue simultaneously provides and calls for a direction and meaning (*sens*) for the development of both of its poles. Because our realization of this trajectory transforms the situation into a new version of itself, because we and the objects now occur within a new "horizon," we are always called upon to determine once again the sense of our situation and to contribute to the history that carries us forward.

If we reflect phenomenologically on our involvement with our surroundings, we arrive at this conclusion: we are always already engaged with flow objects, and these objects simultaneously transcend us and yet "speak to us of ourselves." The importance of this claim for thinkers who have challenged "mechanism," "scientism," "positivism" and other reductionist tendencies during the past thirty years in America and Europe cannot be overemphasized. In psychology, these tendencies (culminating in the computational theory of mind and the equation of nature with bits of information about the measurable properties of matter) treat subjects as fully determinant objects that *then* act upon the things around them. In contrast, the phenomenological tradition and Merleau-Ponty in particular discover subjects to *be* an opening onto, and an engagement with, their surroundings: "consciousness is always consciousness of something."[5] All attempts, therefore, to isolate and examine subjects initially apart from this engagement, however useful otherwise, are a distortion, a crucial misunderstanding, of these subjects. Similarly, to sever objects from their relationship to subjects, to consider them as fully determinate entities, is to ignore that they are present to us as reflecting our hold upon them (their "immanence") as well as their inexhaustibility in relation to our perception and thoughts about them (their "transcendence").

Affirming the intrinsic relation between subjects and the world, Merleau-Ponty develops the phenomenological version of humanistic modernism in two important ways: he claims that perception is the primary mode in which we engage our surroundings and that we *are* our bodies. In *Phenomenology of Perception*, Merleau-Ponty portrays perception in terms of "physiognomic perception" (PP 153/132). According to "objective thought" (PP 86/71), of which the reductionist tendencies mentioned above are instances, perception either mirrors a fully determinate object (empiricism) or constitutes an object in light of a fully determinate idea (intellectualism). In contrast, physiognomic perception "ranges round the subject a world which speaks to him (sic) of himself, and gives his own thoughts their place in the world" (PP 154/132). Like a dialogue, perception leads the subject to draw together the sense diffused throughout the object while, simultaneously, the object solicits and unifies the intentions of the subject. When the subject's intentions are drawn together by the objects of perception—when they find "their place in the world"—the world, at the same time, is transformed into the objects of perception that the subject has been seeking (PP 467/408). Within this exchange, the subjects and objects gain a fuller degree of unity and definition relative to the guiding direction of the dialogue and thus become a fresh basis for the next wave of perception, another installment of the subject-object dialogue, and a new sense that itself demands to be rendered more definite. In other words, this dialogue provides a direction for the becoming of both subjects and objects and yet retains the degree of indeterminacy or ambiguity required for the creative contributions of subjects and for the surprises that the world harbors. Objective thought is overcome, but stability is preserved and freedom is given a place *in the world.*

Merleau-Ponty identifies subjects with their bodies and views perception as the primary mode of the body—of a body that can be itself only by going beyond itself. The body is not first a unified group of organs that *then* confront the things around them; rather, the body is an integral part of the subject-object dialogue, that is, an openness onto things that allows them to come into fuller presence at the same time that they call upon the body to become more completely the "hold" it already has on them (PP 467/408). The body's slippery hold on things, for Merleau-Ponty, is the place of "communion" (PP 245–46/212, 247/214) and therefore he calls it "primordial faith" (PP 395/343). Here the language of faith intersects with that of dialogue, since essentially faith is a questioning. "Carnality" (PP 186/160) responds to the questions that things have already posed and this interrogation leads the organs and parts of the body to draw themselves together in the activity of determining the latent sense of the surrounding objects in which they participate (PP 115/99, 117/101). Once this sense is determined, once the operative stage of perception or intentionality has passed into the more definite acts that we too quickly identify with the whole of perception and expression, the body acquires new resources and the world is clothed in new sediments of sense (PP xiii/xviii, 478/418, 491/429). On the basis of these acquisitions, the body, or "body-subject," is called upon once more to go beyond itself, to "transcend" itself (PP 197/169), by fulfilling the possibilities of its new horizon and thereby contributing to the sense of itself and its new situation (PP 151/130).

Merleau-Ponty's notion of "primordial faith" comes from Husserl, and he also makes use of the Husserlian notion of *"Fundierung"* (PP 451/394, 147/127; S 218/173). This concept clarifies the relation between perception and the body as well as the sense in which perception is the primary mode in which the body engages its surroundings. According to Merleau-Ponty's version of this notion, the opening of our bodies onto their surroundings, their initial hold on and perception of the world, provides the foundation for the specific and personalized acts that refine our more amorphous grasp of objects. Thus the *Fundierung* relation is a form of asymmetrical reciprocity: on the one hand, the secondary activities of the body-subject follow the lead provided by the founding activity or "operative intentionality" of perception; on the other, perception would not be an opening onto the world, and the body-subject would not be a continuous movement of acquisition and transcendence, if perception and the body were not already becoming the more specific, "secondary," acts that complete this initial movement of transcendence.

The *Fundierung* relation is particularly obvious in the way Merleau-Ponty construes the relation between perception and language in *Phenomenology of Perception*. He argues that language originally symbolizes, indeed, "extracts" or "sings," the "emotional essence" of the world that solicits from us its expression and momentary completion in language (PP 218/187). In performing this extraction of emotional essences, creative speech or *parole parlante* (PP 229/197) breaks the "primordial silence" lying beneath the chatter or *parole parlée* of our more routine modes of articulation (PP 214/184). This silence is not that of a mute or meaningless world, but "the core of sense round which the acts of naming and expression take shape" (PP x/xv; see also 446/389 and 462/403). This core of sense, in turn, is the presence of things to our bodies and to the "pre-predicative life of consciousness" (PP x/xv), that is, the significance or presence that things have just prior to their articulation in language. Because this significance is that of our perception of things, it follows that perception is the founding term (like the sun) and language the founded term (like the revolving planets) in the relationship of linguistic expression that holds between the two. It also follows that even our most abstract concepts, for example, geometrical space and measurable time, ultimately refer back to the hold of our bodies on the world, that is, to the subject-object dialogue and "the primacy of perception." This relation between our bodies and their surroundings, then, is Merleau-Ponty's "Copernican revolution" within phenomenology and philosophy.

Because he assigns priority to perception, Merleau-Ponty explains the prevalence of "objective thought" in terms very different from those of "hermeneuticists of suspicion," for example, Freud, Marx, and Nietzsche.[6] Whereas these wary thinkers view objective thought as an evasion or denial of the uncertainties of existence, Merleau-Ponty portrays it as the result of an "experience error" (PP 11/5; OE 36/130): perception ends in objects, and so, once constituted, these objects, and not the body's creativity or movement of transcendence, appear "as the reason for all the experience of [them] which we have or could have" (PP 81/67; 84/70, 85/71). More specifically, the intrinsic or "natural" direction of perception, its quasi-teleological path toward "solid" objects, saves us from "the vital experience of giddiness and nausea, which is the awareness of our contingency, and the horror with which it fills us" (PP 294/254).

Moreover, Merleau-Ponty does not accept the Freudian view of the body as the site of conflicting, often unconscious, instincts. For example, Merleau-Ponty claims that sexuality is coextensive with conscious perception and that we perceive another person's body as a schema of erogenous zones. But he does not view this sexuality as an instinct whose repression by other forces in the body leads to the sudden disappearance of memories or to the occurrence of other psychological anomalies. In explaining why a man has lost the memory of a book given to him by his estranged wife, and why that memory returns when the man and his wife are reconciled, Merleau-Ponty eschews any reference to unconscious denial on the part of the man. He claims, instead, that the man's conscious rejection of all thought about his wife carries with it the specific objects implicit in the horizon surrounding her presence; when he and his wife are reconciled, that horizon and its implicit objects are once again available to him, and so he can now recall the book and the drawer in which he had originally placed it (PP 189/162). Therefore, Merleau-Ponty's thesis of the primacy of perception permits him to account for the tenacity of objective thought and for psychoanalytic phenomena without appealing to a penchant for self-denial or to desires that work beneath the level of the subject's awareness.

Just as Merleau-Ponty does not allow subjects to become the products of unconscious psychological or biological forces, so he does not permit them to be the epiphenomena of economic structures. In his interpretation of historical materialism in *Phenomenology of Perception* (PP 199–202/171–73), he does not treat economic forces in separation from social relations and cultural productions. Rather, he sees these three elements as different dimensions of "social existence" (PP 199/171). The social existence or historical direction (*sens*) founded on these elements pulls them together into the actualization of their latent and still open sense. In other words, these economic, social, and cultural elements take on the sense that the members of the proletariat will give them when they are finally thrown by these same forces into the realization of their destiny—a destiny never guaranteed or closed as to its specific formation (see also SNS /120–24). Like a novel that is compatible with different endings, but only a few, history creates a space for the inscription of the more particular sense that we will provide it. Thus Merleau-Ponty incorporates into the subject's movement of transcendence and sense determination what orthodox Freudianism (instincts) and orthodox Marxism (the "base-structure") maintain outside and determining of subjects—he "existentializes" or "humanizes" the orthodox (and oversimplistic) readings of Freud and Marx.[7]

These last comments emphasize the way in which Merleau-Ponty's existential phenomenology provides a place for freedom and novelty in the world. But he is equally concerned to ensure, and feels that his phenomenological interrogations establish, a basis for continuity, convergence, and rationality—for a common world and the hope of political community. In support of this balance between novelty and stability, he describes the aim of perception and of the subject-object dialogue in terms of an optimal balance between the maximum richness and maximum clarity of what is presented in perception:

> I run through appearances and reach the real color or the real shape when my experience is at its maximum of clarity [*à son plus haut degré de netteté*] . . . : these different appearances are for me appearances of a certain true spectacle, that in which the perceived configuration, for a sufficient degree of clarity, reaches its maximum richness [*pour une netteté suffisante, arrive à son maximum de richese*]. I have visual objects because I have a visual field in which richness and clarity are in inverse proportion to each other, and because these two demands, either of which taken separately might be carried to infinity, when brought together, produce a certain culmination and optimum balance [*point de maturité et un maximum*] in the perceptual process. (PP 367/ 318; see also 289–90/250, 303/262, 349/302–3, 516/452, 381/330)

Because he believes that all modes of human activity are based on and partially complete perception, he also affirms that this ideal of perception, the optimal balance between maximum clarity and maximum richness, regulates the entire field of human activity and constitutes the stability of our relation to the world: "This maximum sharpness of perception and action points clearly to a perceptual *ground*, a basis of my life, a general setting in which my body can co-exist with the world" (PP 289/250). The hallmark of Merleau-Ponty's philosophy, the balance between unity and plurality, identity and difference, stability and novelty, is therefore reflected and based in the balance between clarity and richness that he finds at the level of perception.

Consistent with this "perceptual ground," Merleau-Ponty claims that the constancy of objects and the world—their objectivity and presumptive unity (PP 381/330, 253/219)—is founded upon the aim for balance between clarity and richness that these objects and the world solicit from body-subjects:

> We can no more construct perception of the thing and of the world from discrete aspects, than we can make up the binocular vision of an object from two monocular images. My experiences of the world are integrated into one single world as the double image merges into the one

thing, when my finger stops pressing upon my eyeball. I do not have one perspective, then another, and between them a link brought about by the understanding, but each perspective *merges into* the other and, in so far as it is still possible to speak of a synthesis, we are concerned with a "transition-synthesis." (PP 380/329, 307/265)

Not only does Merleau-Ponty attribute the unity of the world to the latter's demand for optimal balance; he finds this same demand to be the source of the rationality that he believes to be immanent in the world and history. For example, he declares that "[t]o say that there exists rationality is to say that perspectives blend, perceptions confirm each other, a sense emerges" (PP xv/xix). Indeed, the world and its rationality are identical; each is "the sense which is revealed where the paths of my various experiences intersect, and also where my own and other people's intersect and engage each other like gears" (PP xv/xx). This same movement toward unity and univocal meaning is also manifest in the temporal dimension of the world, in its otherwise often hesitant and equivocal unfolding (PP 481/421). And it further signifies for Merleau-Ponty that body-subjects converge toward the same sense or in the same direction (*sens*) traced out by the world in which they find themselves already engaged. Each body-subject is a different perspective on the *same* world and hence one that holds out the promise of social and political unity without nullifying diversity. Merleau-Ponty therefore concludes that "[t]he idea of a single history or of a logic of history is, in a sense, implied in the least human exchange, in the least social perception" (PRI 8/ 10, also PP 254/219).[8]

In *Phenomenology of Perception* and some of his later articles, espe- cially "Indirect Language and the Voices of Silence," Merleau-Ponty fills out his view of history and society by contrasting philosophy and art. Whereas philosophy and speech seek to obtain a final and univocal truth, to bring history and society to completion, the arts are concerned only to multiply worlds of intimate and self-enclosed significance (PP 221–22/190; S 98–100/ 79–81; OE 14–15/123). In both cases, however, perception is limited by the very *Gestalt* configuration or *sens* that Merleau-Ponty accepts as the basis of sentient activity. Although this *Gestalt* is never fully complete, each object of perception is limited to those of its aspects that are congruent with the direc- tion set down by the level or horizon—the *Gestalt* configuration—in which the object appears to the body-subject. The novelty associated with percep- tion is therefore constrained or stabilized within the subject-object dialogue— the *Gestalt*—of which perception is the founding term.

As the ultimate expression of humanistic modernism, Merleau-Ponty's *Phenomenology of Perception* possesses four virtues. First, it shows us how we may consider existence to embody more than reductive materialism or "objective thought" would permit—and it accomplishes this demonstration without endorsing *separate* realms of the mental and the physical or any other form of supernaturalism. Second, it depicts rationality, *logos*, as an inherent feature of our world: the optimal balance between maximum clarity and maximum richness regulates the relation between subjects and objects and ensures that the movement of perception and history ultimately reflects a balance between unity and plurality, identity and difference, stability and novelty. Third, because *Phenomenology of Perception* notes how each realization of this rationality occurs against a new horizon, it guarantees an openness, an essential incompleteness, to the world's unfolding, that is, a place for human freedom and its task of resuming the rational but not fully delineated path that is laid out before it. Fourth, these conclusions are offered on the basis of careful phenomenological descriptions rather than capricious speculation: Merleau-Ponty claims that he *discovers* the *logos* of the world to be this optimal balance, and only on that basis does he then appeal to this *logos* as a norm for evaluating the affairs of women and men.

THE VISIBLE AND THE INVISIBLE: "FLESH" AND THE LOGOS OF THE WORLD

If Merleau-Ponty provides such satisfying and rigorously supported conclusions about our place in the world, then why did he express grave dissatisfaction with this earlier work and attempt to go beyond it? In his posthumously published and incomplete text, *The Visible and the Invisible*, Merleau-Ponty says that he wishes to overcome his earlier allegiance to the consciousness-object schema of thought—that unless one does so "[t]he problems posed in [*Phenomenology of Perception*] are insoluble" (VI 253/200; see also EP 63/ 54). In particular, he feels that this schema obscures the sense in which events in the "objective order," for example, cerebral lesions, are ways of expressing "an event of brute or Wild being which, ontologically, is primary" (VI 253/ 200). Merleau-Ponty's earlier phenomenology fulfills itself in ontology; and, under Heidegger's influence, the subject-object dialogue becomes interrogation, which is itself the very intentionality of Being. This "ontologization" of the body's slippery hold on things leads Merleau-Ponty to what he calls a "hyperdialectic," a dialectic that appears more devoted to respecting plural worlds than enclosing them within a common direction (VI 128–29/94). These innovations indicate that he wanted to achieve what might appear to be conflicting goals. On the one hand, he wants to close the gap of externality suggested by the consciousness-object distinction—as if the subject-object dialogue links together beings that are otherwise strangers to one another. On the other hand, he desires to free the denizens of the world from the common, albeit partially open, direction to which the notion of dialectic or dialogue in *Phenomenology of Perception* subordinates them. The new notion of the hyperdialectic, in contrast, promises its participants greater alterity or otherness, that is, respects difference more fully than does the older phenomenology. In other words, Merleau-Ponty, in *The Visible and the Invisible*, commits himself to an ontology that strives, perhaps paradoxically, to provide both more intimacy and more alterity among the denizens of the world (among subjects and objects) than presumably his earlier work was able to achieve.

In order to accomplish this Janus-faced goal, Merleau-Ponty incorporates physiognomic perception into his new notion of "flesh," that which has "no name in traditional philosophy to designate it" (VI 183/139). He substitutes this new notion for the earlier relationship between consciousness and the world, and characterizes it in terms of "chiasm"[9] or "reversibility," that is, an always "imminent" coincidence between the seeing and the visible, the touching and the touched, self and other selves (VI 193/147; see also 163–64/122–23, 183/139). Flesh turns back upon itself, sees and touches itself, by dividing itself into the "flesh of the world" and the "flesh of the body," into the "sensible" and the "self-sensing" ("sentient") (VI 304/250). Because this coincidence between the flesh of the world and the flesh of the body is always imminent, we, at once visible and sentient, often feel the "eyes" of trees and rocks upon us just as the latter call upon us to transform them into a spectacle (VI 183/139). The seer and the seen form "a Visibility, a Tangible in itself," and "we no longer know which sees and which is seen" (VI 183/139). The flesh, therefore, for Merleau-Ponty, is a new concept of narcissism (VI 183/139). This narcissism, this flesh that *is* its imminent coincidence with itself, is why, in *The Visible and the Invisible,* Merleau-Ponty repeatedly speaks of "one sole Being" (VI 318/265, 265/211). This univocity of Being is why we think the following comment from Merleau-Ponty's 1956 "Everywhere and Nowhere" concerning "great rationalism" is important:

> The extraordinary harmony of external and internal is possible only through the mediation of a *positive infinite* or (since every restriction to a certain kind of infinity would be the seed of negation) an infinite infinite. It is in this positive infinite that the actual existence of things *partes ex partes* and extension as we think of it (which on the contrary is continuous and infinite) communicate or are joined together. If, at the center and so to speak in the kernal of Being, there is an infinite infinite, every partial being directly or indirectly presupposes it, and is in return really or eminently contained in it. (S 187/148–49)

This infinite infinite, which for modern philosophers like Spinoza represented God, would be a pure plane of immanence.

Merleau-Ponty, however, does not take over the modern concept of an infinite infinite without revision, because he thinks it represents an "in-itself," an absolute invisible, a too high verticality, a transcendent God (VI 223/169).

Therefore, in the notion of the flesh we have an invisible that is of the visible, a transcendence that is of immanence, a verticality that is of horizontality, and a delay that is of imminence. Because the flesh accomplishes its narcissism only by separating itself into two "parts"—because it *is* this "dehiscence"—it cannot see itself seeing, touch itself touching. Here, Merleau-Ponty borrows once more from Husserl (and it seems to us that Husserl is always more important than Heidegger for Merleau-Ponty, despite his criticisms of Husserl).[10] Borrowing from Husserl's descriptions of intersubjectivity in *Ideas II* and in the Fifth Cartesian Mediation, Merleau-Ponty characterizes the invisibility of the visible as "Nichturpräsentierbarkeit" (VI 286/233). The invisible of the flesh is like the soul of the other into which I can never see, onto which I can never hold, and, most important, which I can never know. The other is absent, crossed out. Yet, since the soul has been incarnate, I can still feel it, feel with it, feel into it—*Einfühlung*—and believe. Indeed, what is continuous throughout Merleau-Ponty's writings is primordial faith.

We believe therefore that Merleau-Ponty's notion of flesh increases both the intimacy and the alterity of the primary inhabitants (subjects and sensible objects) of the world. A flesh that *is* its dehiscence ensures that its elements are, and remain, the same and yet are, and remain, fundamentally different from one another. Any attempt to promote one of these values at the expense of the other—sameness at the expense of alterity or alterity sameness—would be an imposition upon and contrary to the balanced way things are. Yet Merleau-Ponty sometimes seems to assert a stronger sense of unity than what we have suggested. He seems—and perhaps this is the fuller meaning that he would have given "hyperdialectic"—to retain a "phantom" goal or *telos* in his description of flesh. He says that the coincidence of flesh with itself is always "imminent" even if unattainable. Hence, "coincidence" still haunts the reversibilities of flesh, functions as an unattainable ideal as well as, in its imminence, a structural feature of the flesh. As if to reinforce this interpretation, Merleau-Ponty also retains the notion of a *Gestalt*, equating it with a "principle of distribution, the pivot of a system of equivalences" (VI 258/205; see also, 262/208-9 and 314-15/261). Using an equivalent notion, he further says that vision itself is a "level" in terms of which "every other experience will henceforth be situated" (VI 198/151; see also 243/189). Thus instability and the possibility of novelty, introduced by the absence of complete coincidence, are reined in by their involvement in a structure or *Gestalt* that places restrictions on divergence from the start: "The flesh (of the world or my own) is not contingency, chaos, but a texture that returns to itself and conforms to itself" (VI 192/146).

Although Merleau-Ponty retains an attenuated notion of *telos* (suggested by his appeal to the notion of "level" and "imminent coincidence"), he integrates it with a type of unity that is affiliated with his notion of the reversibilities or chiasms of the flesh. Not only is this new type of unity based on modern philosophy and phenomenology, but also on Saussure. In Saussure's linguistics, as is well known, the basic elements of any language—signs—are established by their differences from each other rather than by reference to univocal signifieds that exist independently of their signifiers and externally to one another (S 53/42). Merleau-Ponty's appropriation of Saussure's structuralism still preserves a central role for subjectivity and perception and for their creative role in the realization of sense. Thus even when Merleau-Ponty maintains that speech is "a fold in the immense fabric of language" (S 53/42), he describes this new "being" or "synchronic parole"[11] as continually throwing itself out of focus toward a new sense that is already hinted at within the diacritical structure of language and the world caught up in its net (S 55/44). Furthermore, he refers to the obtainment of this new sense as the achievement of a temporary "equilibrium," a "state of perfection which has no model" (S 54/43). Because this equilibrium has to do with the obtainment of the sense toward which language finds itself already thrown, Merleau-Ponty is still employing the *Gestalt* notions that have consistently, though with added nuances, guided his thought. Merleau-Ponty therefore integrates the diacritical theory of language into the subject's perceptual realization of a latent meaning in the world. Because this realization is creative, because it renders the sense it finds more determinant and reflective of the subject's specific contribution, it escapes the fixed grid of Saussure's structuralism. At the same time, Merleau-Ponty's continued emphasis on *Gestalt*-like convergence encapsulates this creative dimension of sense production within a tendency toward stability that is deemed intrinsic to the world and the relationship among its different aspects. But, by continuing to rely on the *Gestalt* and its teleology, Merleau-Ponty seems to us to jeopardize, at least, Saussure's new type of "diacritical" unity in which no term is subordinated to any other.

In *The Visible and the Invisible*, the reversibility characteristic of the flesh includes the relation between language and perception. Merleau-Ponty describes ideality as the emigration of the sensible world's visibility into a "less heavy, more transparent body, as though it were to change flesh, abandoning the flesh of the body for that of language, and thereby would be emancipated but not freed from every condition" (VI 200/153). He seems to equate this "condition" with perception—thereby continuing his primacy of perception thesis—when he adds that "the structure of [the human body's] mute world is such that all the possibilities of language are already given in it" (VI 203/155). Yet a few lines later he completes this thought with a statement that suggests he is ready to replace his thesis of the primacy of perception with a purely reciprocal relationship between language and perception:

> And conversely the whole landscape is overrun with words as with an invasion, it is henceforth but a variant of speech before our eyes. . . . [W]hat we have to understand is that there is no dialectical reversal

from one of these views [perception and speech] to the other; we do not have to reassemble them into a synthesis: they are two aspects of the reversibility which is the ultimate truth. (VI 203/155)

Despite this gesture toward reciprocity between perception and language, it is "visibility," not language, that is transformed into a "less heavy" and "more transparent" body, and it is the reversibility between the "sentient" and the "sensible," not the reversibility between language and perception, that Merleau-Ponty privileges when he speaks of flesh (VI 267/214, 304/250). In what is perhaps his most complete statement on the reversibility between vision and speech, Merleau-Ponty states that vision is converted into speech and the latter becomes a renewed, albeit "mental," vision:

> When the silent vision falls into speech, and when the speech in turn, opening up a field of the nameable and the sayable, inscribes itself in that field, in its place, according to its truth—in short, when it metamorphoses the structures of the visible world and makes itself a gaze of the mind, *intuitus mentis*—this is always in virtue of the same fundamental phenomenon of reversibility which sustains both the mute perception and the speech. (VI 203/154–55)

The equation of speech with a form of vision ("*intuitus mentis*" as opposed to, say, "language games" or "writing") reinforces the impression that the primacy of perception is still at play in this later work. Despite the retainment of this primacy, one might still argue that language is primary insofar as Merleau-Ponty imposes a diacritical structure—a model derived from language—upon the phenomenal field. But Merleau-Ponty would reply that the world is simply present to us in this format; that the linguistic model was only needed to articulate more clearly what was always present to us perceptually (VI 267/213–14).

In *The Visible and the Invisible*, Merleau-Ponty introduces us to the notion of flesh. This notion and its chiasmic structure of reversibilities establish a balance between intimacy and alterity (as well as between identity and difference and between unity and plurality) that Merleau-Ponty apparently feels is even greater than the balance between them intrinsic to the "subject-object dialogue" in *Phenomenology of Perception*. Merleau-Ponty's flirtation with Saussurean linguistics affects the description of both language and the perceptually given; but he integrates it within his emphasis upon the creation of sense and the primacy of both perception and phenomenology. The notion of "imminent coincidence" and some of Merleau-Ponty's remarks about "levels" suggest that Gestalt and quasi-teleological notions still play an important role in *The Visible and the Invisible*. But, of course, we are speaking of a text that Merleau-Ponty neither finished nor approved for publication.

THE VALUE OF FLESH

As we see it, Merleau-Ponty's notion of the flesh lies at the very center of today's chief intellectual and cultural problem: the debate between modernism and postmodernism. The leading question of this debate is: is there an order in "the twilight of the idols"? This question of an order, of an intrinsic "*logos* of the world," is important because it is a commonplace to claim that what is called postmodernism notoriously implies relativism and arbitrariness. Yet, as far as we can tell, postmodernism insofar as it eliminates the last vestiges of superstition—absolute transcendence—is actually something like a hyper-Enlightenment. Yet, this hyperbolization of the Enlightenment seems to consist in two strains. In other words, Merleau-Ponty's "Copernican revolution" toward the flesh—a return to a plane of immanence—can be extended in two directions. For better or worse, it will be clear which extension we believe is more valuable.

On the one hand, immanence can be the immanence *to* a subject, as in phenomenology. Undoubtedly in postmodernism, this dative—"to"—is no longer connected to a transcendental, constituting subject, but to a form of intersubjectivity. Here, the dative signifies a contamination of the subject by the other, and it does not matter whether one uses *autre* or *autrui* as long as one capitalizes the word: Other. Using a nonformal logic, this extension would conceive the Other as a nonpresence, but one that is absolute in its very relation to presence.[12] It is an absolute Other relative to the same, an absolute Invisible relative to the visible, and, the most important characterization, an absolute Transcendence relative to immanence. This extension would take advantage of all of the religious senses attached to Merleau-Ponty's philosophy.[13] Turning the flesh into a specter, the dative would end up being expressed by the phrase "à-dieu." And humans—this religion being a humanism of the other man[14]—would end up believing in the imminence of the Savior. In other words, the trace of the Other would be a verticality from which, on high, a command would come: "Thou shalt not kill!" In the twilight, this commandment would provide order and eliminate arbitrariness and relativism. The Good beyond being would put a break on totality; although dimmed by immanence, this sun would stop us from desiring power. In this extension, Merleau-Ponty's "Copernican revolution" would be heliocentric.

The other extension of Merleau-Ponty's "Copernican revolution" would conceive the plane of immanence without a dative, as in ontology. Devoid of transcendence, this pure plane would produce subjects as signs of presence (not as traces of nonpresence). Here, the production of subjects as signs would amount to the production of interobjectivity (not intersubjectivity). Interobjectivity would arise from folding multiple forces; lower (not higher) than the plane, these forces would be related differentially in a depth of infinite dimensions (in Riemannian space, not a space of contamination of same and other).[15] The interobjectivity resulting from folding forces—what in a moment we are going to call "the interplay of institutions"—would itself consist in a battle between a blind word and a mute vision. This extension would take advantage of all of Merleau-Ponty's reflections on structural linguistics. Turning the flesh into a body without organs, the plane of immanence would end up being expressed by the word "chaos." And humans—this pluralism being a profound Nietzscheanism[16]—would end up believing in the earth.[17] Being true to the earth would liberate the forces from the illusions of transcendence, which put a break on them. Freed from these errors, all things would no longer desire power; they would be machines, which desire to do what they can. In other words, all things would order themselves nomadically across the face of the earth. In the twilight, the earth and the stars would form a chaosmos: universality. And if there were a religious sense to this second extension, it would have to be pantheistic.

We would like to elaborate on this second *geocentric* extension of Merleau-Ponty's "Copernican revolution." Above, we tried to show that even in *The Visible and the Invisible*, Merleau-Ponty holds that perception remains our primary relationship to the world, that it and language still share a relation of asymmetrical reciprocity (*Fundierung*): visibility abandons the flesh of the body for the less heavy, more transparent flesh of language, and that the "landscape" becomes a variant of speech before our eyes. Yet his new emphasis on language in the fifties reminds us that perception by linguistic beings always already takes place within a symbolic or discursive framework. In particular, Merleau-Ponty's appropriation of Saussure's view of language as a diacritical structure suggests that the "phenomenal field" may consist in radically heterogenous viewpoints rather than in differences that are unified or balanced by an intrinsic movement toward an "optimal balance between maximum clarity and maximum richness," or by orienting "levels," or by the "imminent coincidence" of flesh with itself. In his 1953 address to the Collège de France, "In Praise of Philosophy," after claiming that Saussure sketched a "new philosophy of history," he says that "the reciprocal relations between the will to express and the means of expression correspond to those between the productive forces and the forms of production, and more generally, between historical forces and institutions" (EP 64–65/55–56).

One could determine Merleau-Ponty's equivocal use of "institution" and "historical forces" here in the following way. One could claim that the scope of what constitutes an institution includes sets of practices, for example, those of a workplace or a laboratory, as well as linguistic and other more strictly symbolic systems. One could also add that an institution establishes the subject status of those who carry out its practices (speaker/audience, manager/worker, male/female, etc.); determines what will count as the relevant objects and events; specifies the range of possible goals and the most reasonable means of obtaining them; and predisposes us to one or another set of values. The subjective side of institutions consist of the cerebral activities that subjects perform (for example, perception, communication in "natural" or "artificial" languages, and thinking) and subjects' desires and beliefs; the more anonymous or "objective" side of institutions resides in their "internal logic" or "discursive structure." Because perception and language do not exist apart from the internal logic of institutions (anymore than institutions can exist in separation from the subjects that carry out the institutional agendas), the internal logic of institutions, and neither language nor perception, is the primary mode with which we engage one another and the objects that surround us. The internal logic of institutions would be the plane of immanence.

Our experience suggests that the institutions of a society interact with one another or, more strongly, that each is what it is only in relation to the others. For example, rejection of the supernatural is part of the meaning of science (at least as commonly understood in the West), and rejection of materialism is part of the identity of most religions. In their actual exchanges with one another, moreover, institutions incorporate specific practices or terms from each other or otherwise modify themselves in order to continue or evade intercommunication. These modifications often amount to the production of new institutions (for example, mestizo culture in Mexico, the civil rights and women's movements in the United States, poststructuralism in philosophy). Because of the pervasive interrelationships among institutions (or among forces), the production of new institutions entails changes in the identity of the other institutions. The entire network, therefore, is in constant metamorphosis, producing new forms of life. Institutions fold themselves into subjects in conformity to their logic, but the incorporated subjects refold the institutions into an interplay of institutions and the sorts of exchanges that create new institutions and metamorphose the network of institutions. The institutionalized is made subjective and the subjective is made institutionalized. Because of the interwoven relationship among these institutions, any understanding of individual or group behavior (including perception and the use of language) must involve reference to the "location" of that behavior within the interplay of institutions. In other words, it must include reference to its place on earth.

According to this geocentric extension, then, Merleau-Ponty's "flesh" (and also his earlier "world horizon") is the interplay of institutions. The "less heavy, more transparent body" into which the visible "emigrates" is not language, as Merleau-Ponty suggests; it is the interplay of institutions. But with this difference: the interplay of institutions, and not perception, is the *milieu* of our more particular reflections, purposes, desires, experiences, speeches, and other activities. Since it is already "institutionalized" (territorialized), the visible does not emigrate; it "de-institutionalizes" itself and "re-institutionalizes" itself. *The primacy of institutions (the audio-visual battle) replaces the primacy of perception.* This replacement entails that the relation between subjects and their surroundings is not guided by an inherent or natural "*logos* of the world"—by the optimal balance between maximum clarity and maximum richness in the case of the subject-object dialogue, and levels and imminent coincidence in the case of flesh. Rather, the relation between ourselves and objects, as well as rationality itself, is determined by the institutions most prominent in the community or interplay of institutions—the relation between subjects and objects is created by institutions, rather than discovered or conformed to. The substitution of an interplay of institutions for the primacy of perception also entails that phenomenology's role is more limited than it would be for Merleau-Ponty. It has a place (for example, we appealed to our *experience* of institutions interacting with each other) and cannot be eliminated as one of the resources in the struggle among the different institutions for a degree of prominence; but it operates within a particular institution[18] and therefore cannot claim universality. What are universal are the institutions that have no limits, no stops, no halts on them, which, as Nietzsche would say, reach the level of the untimely. We can determine which institutions are universal only by testing them—here we come to experience again, *éprouver*—by taking them to the nth power, by universalizing them. Postmodernism is indeed a project that takes the Enlightenment as far as it can go, and the essays that follow, we believe, demonstrate that Merleau-Ponty's notion of the flesh is invaluable in relation to it.[19]

NOTES

1. Because of the profundity of "flesh" and its relevance to contemporary issues, interest in Merleau-Ponty has revived in the last ten years. Circles devoted to his work have sprung up in France, the United States, Germany, Italy, and Japan, and publications concerning his ideas have multiplied. The circle of Merleau-Ponty scholars in the United States, the "International Merleau-Ponty Circle," has held yearly conferences on Merleau-Ponty's philosophy for the last twenty years. Although it has been around for some time (it was the first of such circles despite its location outside of France), its membership has increased considerably in the last five years. We have included some papers in this volume that were originally presented in the two Merleau-Ponty conferences that we separately hosted (Fred Evans, Duquesne University, 1995, and Leonard Lawlor, University of Memphis, 1996).

2. Merleau-Ponty uses the French word "chiasme" for the Greek "khiasmos," which means "a crosswise arrangement." There are two meanings for "khiasmos" in both French and English. In French, the *rhetorical* meaning of "khiasmos" (for example, "To stop too fearful, and too faint to go," where the second phrase inverts the grammatical order of the first) is designated by "chiasme," Merleau-Ponty's choice, and by "chiasmus" ("chiasmi" for the plural, "chiastic" for the adjective) in English. The French use the word "chiasma" for the *anatomical* meaning of "khiasmos" (the criss-crossing of the optic nerves in the brain); in English, this meaning is also

designated by "chiasma" ("chiasmata" in the plural, and "chiasmatic" for the adjective) or simply by "chiasm." Although Merleau-Ponty chooses the French word that corresponds to the rhetorical employment of "khiasmos"—and does so perhaps because it comes closest to capturing the notion of "reversibility" that is central to his idea of the "flesh" (see below)—the convention among his English commentators has been to assume, evidently, that Merleau-Ponty intended the anatomical rather than the rhetorical meaning (his "chiasme"), and therefore use the English "chiasm" rather than the English "chiasmus." Because overturning conventions can lead to confusion, we will follow the standard translation and use "chiasm," "chiasms," and "chiasmic." One should also keep in mind that both "chiasme" and "chiasma" are connected to the Greek verb "chiazein," which means to mark with a *chi* (X), as in the sign of the cross.

3. Gilles Deleuze and Felix Guattari, *What Is Philosophy?* (New York: Columbia University Press, 1994), p. 178. See also Dominique Janicaud, *Le tournant théologique de la phénomélogie française* (Paris: L'éclat, 1991).

4. Compare Patrick Burke, "The Flesh as *Urpräsentierbarkeit*," in *Écart and Différance: Merleau-Ponty and Derrida on Seeing and Writing*, ed. M. C. Dillon (Atlantic Highlands, N.J.: Humanities Press, 1997), p. 69.

5. For a sustained treatment of how Merleau-Ponty might respond to contemporary computational (computer) models of mind, see Fred Evans, *Psychology and Nihilism: A Genealogical Critique of the Computational Model of Mind* (Albany: State University of New York Press, 1993), esp. chapter 6; see also Francisco J. Varela, Evan Thompson, and Eleanor Rosch, *The Embodied Mind* (Cambridge: The MIT Press, 1991).

6. Paul Ricoeur, *Freud and Philosophy*, trans. Denis Savage (New Haven, Conn.: Yale University Press, 1970), pp. 32–36.

7. For a discussion of Merleau-Ponty in relation to the third hermeneuticist of suspicion, Nietzsche, as well as an elaboration of Merleau-Ponty's thesis of the primacy of perception throughout his works, see Fred Evans, " 'Solar Love': Nietzsche, Merleau-Ponty, and the Fortunes of Perception," *Continental Philosophy Review* 31, no. 2 (1998).

8. For a discussion of the role of reason and the status of unity in Merleau-Ponty's philosophy (the contrast between a "Politics of Understanding" and a "Politics of Reason"), see Fred Evans, "Merleau-Ponty, Lyotard, and the Basis of Political Judgment," in *Resituating Merleau-Ponty: Essays across the Analytic-Continental Divide*, ed. Lawrence Hass and Dorothea Olkowski (London: Humanities Press, 2000); James Schmidt, *Merleau-Ponty: Between Phenomenology and Structuralism* (New York: St. Martin's Press, 1985); Kerry H. Whiteside, *Merleau-Ponty and the Foundation of an Existential Politics* (Princeton, N.J.: Princeton University Press, 1988); and Richard Wolin, "Merleau-Ponty and the Birth of Weberian Marxism," *Praxis International* 5, no. 2 (1988).

9. See note 2.

10. See Renauld Barbaras, *De l'être du phénomène* (Grenoble: Millon, 1991), pp. 89–101; English translation forthcoming by Leonard Lawlor and Theodore Toadvine as *The Being of the Phenomenon*, Humanity Press, 2000.

11. For the application of this term to Merleau-Ponty's incorporation of the Saussurian diacritical model of language within a phenomenologically based theory of speech, see James Schmidt, *Merleau-Ponty: Between Phenomenology and Structuralism*, p. 133.

12. Jacques Derrida, "Violence and Metaphysics: An Essay on the Thought of Emmanuel Levinas," in *Writing and Difference*, trans. Alan Bass (Chicago: University of Chicago Press, 1978), pp. 95 and 127–28. The relation between Derrida and Merleau-Ponty is difficult to determine since Derrida has said repeatedly that he did not read Merleau-Ponty in order to avoid his influence. But, in Derrida's early writings on Husserl, he cites frequently Tran-Duc-Thao and Cavailles who were closely connected to Merleau-Ponty in the forties; moreover, there is the continuous influence of Levinas, who refers often to Merleau-Ponty. So, there is good reason to believe that Merleau-Ponty influenced Derrida indirectly. No matter what, however, it is the question of writing that separates Derrida from Merleau-Ponty; in this regard, see Leonard Lawlor, "Eliminating Some Confusion: The Relation of Being and Writing in Merleau-Ponty and Derrida," in *Écart and Différance*. We feel that the publication of Merleau-Ponty's notes on Husserl's "The Origin of Geometry" might clarify Merleau-Ponty's relation to the question of writing; English translation forthcoming by Leonard Lawlor and Bettina Bergo, *Husserl at the Limits of Phenomenology* (Northwestern University Press 2001). The question of writing will also be at the center of distinguishing between Derrida and Deleuze; see Gilles Deleuze and Felix Guattari, *Anti-Oedipus*, trans. Robert Hurley, Mark Seem, and Helen R. Lane (Minneapolis: University of Minnesota Press, 1977), p. 202.

13. Cf. Jacques Derrida, *Memoirs of the Blind*, trans. Pascale-Anne Brault and Michael Naas (Chicago: The University of Chicago Press, 1993), esp. pp. 52–53.

14. Jacques Derrida, *Specters of Marx*, trans. Peggy Kamuf (New York: Routledge, 1994), p. 74.

15. Gilles Deleuze, *Foucault* (Minneapolis: University of Minnesota Press, 1988), p. 112 for the reference to "audio-visual battle, p. 65 for the reference to "a blind word and a mute vision," p. 13 for Riemannian multiplicity, and p. 110 for the influence of Merleau-Ponty's notion of the flesh on Foucault.

16. Gilles Deleuze, *Nietzsche and Philosophy*, trans. Hugh Tomlinson (New York: Columbia University Press, 1983), pp. 4, 76–77, 106; see also Deleuze, *Foucault*, pp. 83, 71.

17. Deleuze, *What Is Philosophy?* p. 75.

18. It operates within the institution of organic discourse, a type of discourse that seeks to understand the aspects of a phenomenon in terms of a whole that at least partially determines the presence or sense of these aspects; this type of discourse or institution is opposed to analytic discourse, which attempts to understand the same phenomenon in terms of elements that are related causally or in some external fashion. For a systematic exposition of "analytic discourse," and "organic discourse," see Fred Evans, *Psychology and Nihilism*, pp. 50–53.

19. For an elaboration of the relation between Deleuze's notion of the "plane of immanence" and Merleau-Ponty's thought, see Leonard Lawlor, "The End of

Phenomenology: Expressionism in Deleuze and Merleau-Ponty," in *Continental Philosophy Review* 30 (1997); "The End of Ontology: Interrogation in Deleuze and Merleau-Ponty, *Chiasmi International: Trilingual Studies Concerning the Thought of Merleau-Ponty* (Milano: Associazione Culturale Mimesis, 1998); and "Phenomenology and Bergsonism: The Beginnings of Post-Modernism," forthcoming. For an elaboration of the relation between "institution" and "subjectivity" and of the "interplay of institutions" (or "voices"), see Fred Evans, "Bakhtin, Communication, and the Politics of Multiculturalism," *Constellations* 5, no. 3 (1998); and "Voices of Chiapas: The Zapatistas, Bakhtin, and Human Rights." In [title forthcoming], ed. Linda Martín Alcoff and Walter Brogan, volume 25 of The Society for Phenomenological and Existential Philosophy supplement to *Philosophy Today*, 42, 2000; and "Merleau-Ponty, Lyotard and the Basis of Political Judgment," in *Re-reading Merleau-Ponty: Essays Beyond the Analytic-Continental Divide*, ed. Lawrence Hass and Dorothea Olkowski. New York, NY: Prometheus Press, 2000.

PART I

Explications of the Flesh

CHAPTER 1

World, Flesh, Vision

FRANÇOISE DASTUR

One cannot deny that the philosophical problem that oriented Merleau-Ponty's entire approach is, in a sense, the "classical" problem of the relations of the soul and the body. Merleau-Ponty did not encounter this, however, as a "regional" problem, to which he would have devoted the full force of his reflection; rather, he encountered this problem because one of the most general philosophical problems guided his investigations from the start: the relation of consciousness to the world. Already in *The Structure of Behavior*, Merleau-Ponty set himself the task of finding an intermediate position between intellectualism and empiricism, that is, between an insular subject and a pure nature. The world and consciousness, the outside and the inside, are not distinct beings that the full force of philosophical thought must contrive to reunite; rather, they are interdependent, and it is precisely this interdependence that becomes legible in the phenomenon of incarnation. If the "frontal" opposition of consciousness and the world is renounced, then what has to be clarified first is the body, that is, what the philosophical tradition has always left unthought. Several times, Merleau-Ponty defines the Western way of thinking as "surveying thought," which, as such, can only produce a "naive ontology" (VI 240/187), because, wresting the object from the flesh from which it is born (VI 302/248), turns it into the Great Object. It becomes that Sublimated Being whose subjective correlate is, then, nothing other than the Kosmotheoros, that look that comes from *nowhere* and that consequently presents itself as a look dominating and embracing everything. Where does the look come from? How does the for-itself arise? What is subjectivity? These are the questions to which Merleau-Ponty always returns, even though he was led to recognize that the consciousness-object distinction can no longer be considered a valid starting point (VI 253/200). Because the question of the subject cannot be set aside so easily (cf. VI 244/190–91 and 247/193–94), Merleau-Ponty tirelessly interrogates Husserl's texts and particularly those texts where the intentionality of consciousness can no longer simply be

23

understood as "activity." In a certain way, Husserl is the first Western thinker who undertook to dismiss the ideal of the Kosmotheoros by stressing the engagement of consciousness in the world—this is the case, even if, in the end, he does it in order to restore this ideal at the transcendental level through the "project to gain intellectual possession of the world," which is what *constitution* always is (S 227/180). Reading *The Visible and the Invisible* carefully, one notices that the philosophical adversary, the representative of a philosophy of the subject for Merleau-Ponty, is Sartre and his massive opposition of the for-itself and the in-itself, and not Husserl, whose last writings more and more take account of the unconstitutable. It is Sartre, and not Husserl, who identifies subjectivity and activity, and already in *Sense and Non-Sense* Merleau-Ponty notes that what he expected from the author of *Being and Nothingness* was a theory of passivity (SNS 133/77). It is again Sartre who, considering the model of the in-itself (VI 269/216), determines the for-itself according to the same "sacrificial" structure that is already found in Hegelian absolute subjectivity (VI 127/93). Certainly there is no passage to absolute subjectivity in *Being and Nothingness*, and the for-itself's passion remains futile.[1] But, precisely because Being slips away, "the For-Itself is charged with the task of *making it*" (VI 269/216). The "activism" of consciousness cannot be pushed any farther. On the contrary, the "later" Husserl— the Husserl that Merleau-Ponty had read and contemplated since his visit to Louvain in 1939, the Husserl of *Ideas II*, the *Crisis*, and the unpublished manuscripts, who placed himself "at the limits of phenomenology" (RC 159/ 181)—is also the one who gave a greater and greater role to intentionality *without acts*, to *fungierende Intentionalität*, which in an anonymous and hidden manner "produces the natural and prepredicative unity of the world and of our life" (PP xiii/xviii).

THE WORLD AND REFLECTION

As can be ascertained by consulting the detailed chronicle that Karl Schuhmann prepared of Husserl's manuscripts,[2] or by reading Gerd Brand's book which synthesizes part of Husserl's unpublished manuscripts,[3] the problem of the world is at the center of the later Husserl's concerns. Husserl is increasingly sensitive to the "fundamental difference of the manner of being of an object in the world and that of the world itself,"[4] and he speaks of the uniqueness of the world in terms that leave no doubt about the irreducibility of the world to the thing.[5] Is it an accident if certain of those who accompanied his philosophic development during the Freiburg period saw in the privilege granted to the world the indication of a new starting point and the necessity of a surpassing of intentional analysis? Since 1923[6] Heidegger had developed the theme of "being-in-the-world," of that which is no longer consciousness or subject but "Dasein," that is, a being radically different from other beings precisely in that it is "constitutive" of the world. And in 1929, the date that marks the beginning of the *philosophical* break between the two thinkers, in a text dedicated to Edmund Husserl[7] which deals essentially with the being of the world, Heidegger wants to establish that "intentionality is possible only on the foundation of transcendence;"[8] for the original surpassing is not brought about by the subject toward objects, but by Dasein toward the world. Eugen Fink, whom Merleau-Ponty met at Louvain in 1939, and who Husserl said in 1931 was "the only disciple to have remained faithful to him,"[9] during the same period, however, denounced the narrowness of the concept of horizon in Husserl, which cannot take into account the being of the totality.[10] Fink consequently developed what can be termed a "cosmological phenomenology" essentially centered on the "cosmological difference" between the world and intramundane being.[11] However, the unpublished manuscripts, on which Gerd Brand comments, show that Husserl endeavored to think as one "*das Welthabende Ich und das In-der-Welt-seiende Ich*," the ego who has the world and the ego who is in the world.[12] The world is not only the kingdom of the "*Ich kann*," the totality of the potentialities of the ego; it is also *bodengebend*, that which gives to consciousness its very first ground. This is why there can be neither a demonstration nor an induction of the world.[13] The world is not the presumptive synthesis of horizons—it truly seems that Husserl breaks here with the world as an Idea in the Kantian sense—but it is *Totalhorizont*, that is, the originary dimension from which all limited experience is possible.[14] It is in this sense that Husserl speaks of the "transcendence of the world."[15] And Heidegger, when he also invokes the "*Transzendenz der Welt*,"[16] that is, when he invokes the *fact* of a revelation of the world always already achieved before the encounter of intramundane being becomes possible, does not contradict Husserl's idea of a world as *universaler Boden*. Nevertheless, as Fink notes very precisely in one of his conversations with Dorian Cairns, Husserl in *Ideas I*, starting from psychology, directed his attention too unilaterally onto the noetic constitution of the Welt*vorstellung* (the world as *representation*) while neglecting the essential noematic moment of the Welt*konstitution* (the constituted *world*).[17] In other words, while Husserl accentuates the ego's *Welthabe* without attaining sufficient clarification of the ego insofar as it is in the world, Heidegger's central problem in *Being and Time* is precisely to determine the mode of being of this "exemplary"[18] being in which the world constitutes itself. For Heidegger, there is no transcendental ego whose operation remains "hidden" from the empirical ego and that "anonymously" unfolds the horizon of the world "behind the back" of the real ego, which directly devotes itself to its objects; rather, there is a unique "Dasein," which in its very "facticity," is always already a relation to the world and to beings *at the same time* that it is a self-relation. If the constitution of the world and of the alter ego by the transcendental subject remains a constantly interrogated enigma for Husserl, it is precisely because the ego is thought at the same time as transcendental and as mundane. In the final analysis for Husserl, the issue is always to make the world in its totality, as well as other subjects, who are also constitutors of the world, emerge from one thing *belonging to* the world. The only way that one can do this is by "the abstraction of the pure ego" being given as the world's origin; in contrast, for Heidegger, the "place" of the transcendental is not outside but within this privileged being, which *is* in a way entirely different from things.

What remains unclarified in Husserl, therefore, is the relation of the ego and the world, and this is why he is led to repeat the movement proper to all reflective philosophy. Through this movement, reflective philosophy "metamorphoses with one stroke the actual world into a transcendental field" (VI 68/44), with the result that, for it, "there is no brute world, there is only a developed world; there is no in-the-world, there is only a signification 'world' " (VI 73/48). For transcendental phenomenology as well, what we are finally as *naturata* (the empirical mundane ego), we are at first *actively* as *naturans* (the transcendental ego), and "the world is our birthplace only because first we as minds are the cradle of the world" (VI 54/33). It is true that Merleau-Ponty wants to reserve a particular fate for phenomenological reflection" (VI 74 n. 2/49 n) not only because the *Urerlebnis* to which phenomenological reflection leads back can no longer be defined as an activity of consciousness, but also because Husserl is willing to consider as a problem what "the reflective attitude ordinarily avoids—the discordance between its starting situation and its ends" (VI 71/46). In effect, what characterizes phenomenological reflection is precisely the illusion of a reflection *without remainder*, for which the trajectory going from the ego to the world and the trajectory returning from the world to the ego would be one and the same. By saying that every transcendental reduction is also an eidetic reduction, Husserl brings to light the principial "delay" of every reflection on the already-there of the world and shows that to reflect is not to coincide with the flux of intentional life. On the contrary, to reflect is to free kernels of meaning, intelligible articulations, and then to reconstruct the flux "*après coup.*" When, in order to surmount the naïveté of the reflective operation that transforms the world into a noema and the subject into pure thought, Merleau-Ponty calls for a hyper-reflection (VI 61/38, 70/46f.), it is certainly not in order to "surpass" or push aside reflection—and with it, philosophy—in favor of the immediate or the lived (cf. VI 57/35, 235/182). Rather, it is a question of a reflection on reflection itself, which thereby stops being unaware of itself as a retrospective reconstruction and that can no longer set itself up as absolute reflection. But what comes into question then is the very starting point of the reflective conversion: doesn't all reflection come from *the hypothetical nonexistence* of the fact that the world such as it is given in actual sensing and seeing exists? The problem here lies in the reflective rupture between the ego and the world, and, ultimately, in the phenomenological reduction itself. A working note from February 1959 recalls that the phenomenological reduction is "wrongly presented—in particular in the [*Cartesian Meditations*]—as a suspending of the *existence of the world*" (VI 225/171). Husserl himself falls back into the Cartesian defect that he had denounced, the defect of a world negation that "has as an immediate consequence that one misses the transcendental." In this way, one is ineluctably led to confuse the transcendental ego with the *mens sive anima* as the only thing in the world resistant to doubt. But Merleau-Ponty also casts doubt on the Husserlian sense of the epochê, conceived as the neutralization of the belief in the existence of the world and no longer as mere negation. Neutrality can be exercised only in regard to the *in-itself* of the world, but not in regard to the " 'wild' or 'vertical' world" (VI 230–31/177), from which one can never withdraw to a position outside. An "adequate" reduction would not be able to enclose us within the immanence of a false subjectivity, but on the contrary leads to the disclosure of spirit as *Weltlichkeit* (VI 226/172). Heidegger and Merleau-Ponty pose the *same* question to Husserl concerning the *right* of the phenomenological reduction to be completed and the *status* of the "subjectivity" with which it leaves us. *In fact* philosophy cannot definitively tear itself out of perceptual faith and enclose itself in the kingdom of pure significations. There is a structural incompleteness to the reduction (VI 232/178) that defines the philosophical endeavor in its permanent inchoativity. One must not then confound a "complete" reduction, which is the transcendental illusion of all reflective philosophy, and a "radical reflection, which amounts to a consciousness of its own dependence on an unreflective life that is its initial situation, unchanging, given once and for all" (PP ix/xiv). It is such a radical reflection that Merleau-Ponty would like to see at work in *Sein und Zeit* (PP ix/xiv), for what hyper-reflection discovers is the problem of the *double* genesis of the world *and* reflection, of being *and* thought—and not solely the problem of the correlation of thought and the existing object. The problem of the double genesis is not "a superior or more profound degree of philosophy" (VI 71/46), nor is it a residual problem that would be confronted only once the reflective method is put in place; it alone is the philosophical problem *par excellence*.

The field that is opened by what might be called Husserlian reflective honesty is that of subjectivity's *facticity*, insofar as this facticity is not entirely absorbed back into the eidetic invariants through which philosophy describes it (VI 70/45–46f.). This unthought of Husserl, "which is wholly his and yet opens out on something else" (S 202/160), namely, on brute or wild being, on the facticity of the subject, on the "there is" of the world, on "the meaning of first sight, is perhaps only the presentiment—constitutive of the phenomenological process penetrating into what it possesses with a more profound character—of an impossible recuperation of being into meaning, of an irreducible divergence between the silence of experience and philosophical speech.

What must be brought to light, then, is not the *Welthabe* of a wholly active subject, but the *Vorhabe* of an incarnate consciousness, "the prepossession of a totality which is there before one knows how and why" (VI 65/42). Such a prepossession shows that existence is not originally the *thought* of existing (VI 246/192). If philosophy is willing to recognize the divergence, which institutes philosophy as speech, and if it commits itself to accounting for its own genesis, then it owes itself to be "the study of the *Vorhabe* of Being" (VI 257/204). Without this *Vorhabe*, nothing is thinkable; nothing is sayable. The term *Vorhabe*, which appears several times in the working notes (VI 246/192, 255/201, 257/204), is borrowed from Husserl. Nevertheless, one can legitimately compare it to the fore-structure (*Vorstruktur*) that Heidegger discovered at the level of the *understanding*. The understanding is a fundamental *existentiale* of Dasein since it determines Dasein as potentiality-for-being and as project, that is, as existing in a way that distinguishes it radically from the thing of the world. To understand is always to interpret the being *as* this or that; it is *to see* as, but from a prepredicative "sight" that "articulates" the signifiability of the world outside language. The *Vorstruktur* contains three moments: fore-having (*Vorhabe*), fore-sight (*Vorsicht*), and fore-conception (*Vorgriff*). These three bear witness to the fact that there is never an apprehension of immediate givens without presuppositions or prejudices[19]—that, between the ego and the thing, there is no "frontal" relation, no pure and simple "face-to-face." What Heidegger denounces in paragraph 32 of *Sein und Zeit* is precisely the Husserlian idea of a pure perception as an original mode of access to the being, which would give itself "in person," "in flesh and blood," "in the original," and that would not already be an articulation of the world. Now, what Merleau-Ponty always understood by the term "perception" cannot be identified with a *pure* seeing or with an original *knowledge*, which would have a world of pure things for its correlate. In *The Visible and the Invisible*, he even proposes to exclude the term *perception* in favor of perceptual faith, because the one who says "perception" "already implies a cutting up of what is lived into discontinuous acts, or a reference to 'things' whose status is not specified" (VI 209/158). It is true that perception, not in the sense of a sensorial function but as "archetype of the originating encounter," remains at the most basic level of the investigation. But it is possible that this encounter with what is not-us is not the experience of an absence, any more than of an original presence (VI 210/159). Also for Merleau-Ponty, "perception" is a kind of articulation, "*articulation* before the letter, the appearance of something where there was nothing or something else" (VI 168/126). To perceive is always to sketch a figure against the background of the world, to organize an area of the visible, to open oneself to a "Gestalt," that is, to "the contingent arrangement by which the materials begin to have a meaning in our presence, intelligibility in the nascent state" (SC 223/206–7). This is why we can speak about perception in the same way as we do about a language: "I describe perception as a diacritical, relative, oppositional system" (VI 267/213), applying to it the terminology that Saussure had reserved for language. There is certainly a "relative positivity of perceiving," a sensible *world* of *things*, but this is not an objective being, substantial, completed; the sensible is never itself given except in an elusive manner, and it is strictly "ungraspable" (VI 267/214). This is why we can say about perception, and about language, that it surrenders to us only "differences" or "divergences." The thing is made quasi-observable only by the precipitation of *Abschattungen* (VI 245/191), only by the work of the senses, these "apparatus to form concretions of the inexhaustible, to form existent significations" (VI 245/192). But this crystallization of *visibilia* remains illusory, ephemeral, always subject to metamorphoses; "the only thing finally that is seen in the full sense is the totality wherein the sensibles are cut out" (VI 268/214). Thus, the being of the world is "inflated with non-being or with the possible" (VI 234/181), and this is why Merleau-Ponty often uses the expressions "being at a distance" or "transcendence" to define it. The world is essentially understood on the basis of the notion of field and configuration, on the basis of *Gestalt*—not as a closed set but as an open environment, where the "something" (and no longer *die Sache selbst*) is "a principle of distribution, a system of equivalences" (VI 258/205).

But the transcendence of the *Gestalt*, its nonpositivity, does not refer to the prevalence of anything other than the sensible; it does not refer to the invariance of the eidos, because there is a Gestalt, a configuration, a field and world only for a perceiving body inside spatiotemporality. This modulation of time and space gives birth to *pregnant* forms, that is, to concretions of the "there is," to *Wesen* in the verbal sense (VI 256/203, 260/206–7, 262/208), *existing* significations. But the internal cohesion of this modulation refers to a primary explosive and productive power, of which the existing significations are only the crystallization or the cipher.[20] Prior to philosophical speech, there is therefore a logos of the sensible, a logos *endiathetos* of the world, that, even if it calls forth the logos *porphorikos* of philosophy or literature, is still no less the silent origin, the influx of meaning by which the latter is nourished. Now, "we can have an idea [of this meaning] only through our carnal participation," and it is this originary carnal relation with the world which the uttered logos "sublimates" (VI 261/208). The sublimation of the flesh is, in a sense, the whole advent of "culture," this "descent of the invisible into the visible" that can lead to the complete obliteration of the "wild" perception beneath cultural perception (VI 267/213, 266/212), and that has as a consequence that the phenomenal order is denied all autonomy in order to turn it into a simple province of the objective order (VI 263/209). If "culture is perceived," if perception itself is cultural, one sees how hard it is to return to the "immediate" and to the phenomenal. The most striking example of this informing of perception by culture is that of the perception of space and the privilege that falls to Euclidean space and to the pregnancy of geometric forms. Where does the privilege of one perspectival world, of one homogeneous, isotropic, three-dimensional space, of lines, points, and planes (none of which are real) come from? Merleau-Ponty recognizes a "profound suitability" of the idea of Euclidean space to "the classical ontology of the *Ens realissimum*, of the infinite being" (VI 264/210), that is, the divine Kosmotheoros that sees in their juxtaposition and their identity the things that humans know in their encroachment and their reciprocal latency. In "Eye and Mind," he shows that Renaissance perspective is a cultural fact, a moment of painting that makes the mistake of setting itself up as an infallible technique and a fundamental law (OE 48 f./134 f.). Beneath the Euclidean mask, on the contrary, one finds a space of encroachment and envelopment, a topological space including relations of proximity, vectors and centers of forces, space "constitutive of life" that founds "the *wild* principle of the Logos" (VI 264/211). It is a space essentially determined by depth; one can even say in a sense that all of Merleau-Ponty's work is articulated around depth, the dimension of encroachment and latency. Depth is the *spatiotemporal* dimension of distance (PP 306/264–65), since to have something at a distance is to have it in the past or in the future as well as in space. It is therefore the dimension of *simultaneity* or coexistence, and "[w]ithout it, there would not be a world or Being. . . . It is hence because of depth that the things have a flesh: that is, oppose to my inspection obstacles, a resistance which is precisely their reality, their 'opening,' their *totum simul*" (VI 272–73/219).

　　Once recognized, the privilege that falls to Euclidean space, the illusion of a sensible positivity, and the carving of the world into solid things by thought demand to be explained in themselves, because the issue with these is not that of simple historical contingency. In the same way, Heidegger has to explain why the phenomenon of worldhood has been lost from view since the beginning of the ontological tradition and why intra-worldly being has always been understood as being present-at-hand (*Vorhandensein*) and not as being ready-to-hand (*Zuhandensein*). For the dissimulation of *Zuhandenheit* is due neither to an omission nor to a negligence that could be remedied. On the contrary, the dissimulation results from an essential way of being of *Dasein*, from a constitutive "inauthenticity" by which *proximally* and *for the most part* it remains closed to what it properly is, namely, the revelation of the world. Dasein does not see that the world is part of its being; this is why it understands the world and itself on the model of the being of things, as *Vorhandensein*. Fink very precisely defines inauthentic existence as "a clenching onto *ontic* truth and a blindness with regard to the ontological truth, an abstention, a suspension of the 'transcendence' of human Dasein."[21] Merleau-Ponty gives a rather similar response to the question of why the *Lebenswelt* remains concealed and why the reflective tradition has always ignored perceptual faith; he also speaks of "a repression of transcendence" and a tendency of "the universe of immanence" to "make itself autonomous:" *"The key is in this idea that perception qua wild perception is of itself ignorance of itself, imperception,* tends of itself to see itself as an *act* and to forget itself as latent intentionality, as *being at*—" (VI 266–67/213). The key phrase is "of itself": it is a question of a natural and inevitable movement, of a constitutive ignorance of perception. All vision assumes this *punctum caecum* of the eye that renders it possible; all consciousness assumes this blindness with regard to itself by which it becomes the consciousness of an object: "It is inevitable that the consciousness be mystified, inverted, indirect, in principle it sees the things *through the other end,* in principle it disregards Being that prefers the object to it." (VI 302/248). Perception gives itself an author and understands itself as an activity of consciousness, even though it is merely the emergence of a *percipere at the center* of the *percipi,* even though perception is born only out of that attachment to Being which makes it possible. A reflection, which wants to be radical, therefore, should not ignore the blind spot of the mind (VI 55/33). But, for Merleau-Ponty, acknowledging its existence cannot mean fusion and coincidence with the origin of vision. That by which everything begins, "nature" or "the originary," is not *behind* us in a past into which one would have to go in order to rejoin the origin; rather it lies in the *écart* of the present from this past, in the *écart* that is the space of our whole experience (VI 165/124. Cf. also 320/267). It is *today,* in the depth of the lived and in the presence of the flesh of the world that "the originating breaks up, and philosophy must accompany this break-up, this non-coincidence, this differentiation" (VI 165/124). Being is not a plenitude into which one would have to sink and dissolve oneself. On the contrary, it is *"what requires creation of us* for us to experience it" (VI 251/197). Being is not a great Object on which thought should tirelessly work in order to make itself adequate, but that "universal dimensionality" (VI 319/265, 280/227) on which all the dimensions are set apart in advance without any one ever expressing it completely (OE 48/134). Being is that "pregnancy of possibles" (VI 304/250) and that "polymorphism" (VI 306–7/252–53) that would not be exhausted by our representations of it, although they are as much experiences of it. Between the *Lebenswelt* as universal Being and philosophical *creation,* there is no antinomy (VI 224/170) "not only because the philosopher *alone* can disclose the Lebenswelt, as Fink already showed in his famous *Kantstudien* article"[22] but also because the natural attitude and transcendental attitude are not two sets of acts with opposite meanings. The originary relation that we maintain with the world is not an "attitude," that is, not a set of acts, but rather a primordial faith, an *Urdoxa,* as Husserl moreover recognizes as well. And it is for this reason that Fink already proposed in 1931 to replace the term *natürliche Einstellung* with *Weltbefangenheit*—thereby designating in a single term both the world's authority over the "subject," which finds itself included therein and the perplexity of the latter with regard to its own being.

Originary experience is that of an *exchange* between the world and the ego, that of a *delay* of *percipere* on the *percipi* (VI 164/123), and this delay of perceiving on the perceived is what Husserl thematized by emphasizing the importance of operative intentionality in relation to act intentionality. For even before an object is constituted in front of consciousness, there is the first opening of consciousness to its outside by which it institutes horizons and a world. But the development of operative intentionality requires a reversal of the agencies of the perceived and the perceiving, a reciprocity of the intentionality of ego to the world and of the world to the ego, which "phenomenology," as an ontology of the object and of the act, cannot integrate (VI 298/ 244). To think *all* of consciousness as operative intentionality is to reject the privilege that Husserl granted to "objectivating acts" over affective or practical, nonobjectivating intentionalities; it is to stop defining consciousness primarily as knowledge and to put Reason back in the world, to anchor it in the body and in the flesh (VI 292/238–39). Transcendental phenomenology is certainly not ready for such a "reform of 'consciousness,' " which strongly resembles the destruction of the classical subject. However, transcendental phenomenology has opened the way for it at least, a way that leads, *on this side* of the subject-object, activity-passivity opposition, to the "generality of the flesh" (VI 173 n/131 n).

BEING AND THE FLESH

Merleau-Ponty does not, however, intend to *complete* the philosophy of consciousness by adding some things to it, namely, the phenomenon of the body on the side of the subject and the world as field and as horizonal structure on the side of the object. What is at issue is not the need to take account of the contingent fact of a perception that might just as easily have not taken place, nor is what is at issue the unmotivated sudden appearance of a for-itself that the in-itself does not need in order to be. It is not even a question of fabricating the architectonic of the world with elements borrowed from the world. One will never make this lacuna and absence, which is subjectivity, emerge from the positivity of a world that has begun by being given (VI 285/231). Also, rather than start from abstractions such as being and nothingness and attempt to "construct" their union, it would be better to remain at the level of structure and transcendence, of the nascent intelligibility and the segregation of the outside and the inside, and to find one's "starting point where Sartre ends, in the Being taken up by the for Itself" (VI 290/237). By placing negativity *outside* of being, Sartre does not succeed in accounting for the sudden appearance of consciousness and history; he remains at an ontology of the "as if": "*everything takes place as if* the in-itself in a project to found itself gave itself the modification of the for-itself."[23] This is the impasse that

every humanization of nothingness, that every philosophy that places negativity exclusively in humanity runs into, since such a placement amounts to
making a worldly being the agent of the world's revelation. There is truly no
exchange or reciprocity between the for-itself and the in-itself, and the passage from a negation of being *through* humanity to being's *self*-negation *in*
humanity remains something that Sartre cannot realize. Sartre rejects every
compromise with a "continuism" that would distinguish intermediary levels
of being between the being of a thing and the being of consciousness; he
considers what Merleau-Ponty wants to insert between humans and things
nonexistent: the "interworld" called "history, symbolism, truth to be made"
(AD 269/184)[24] But is it any surprise that Merleau-Ponty adopts the task, in
The Visible and the Invisible, of elaborating an "ontology of the inside" (VI
290/237) or an "intra-ontology" (VI 279–80/226–67), which no longer raises
itself out of that causal thought or surveying thought that always opposes the
pure negative to the pure positive (VI 99/69–70, 280/227), but that instead
maintains itself in the inherence to the sensible world and within a "being in
dehiscence"? Must we consider the return to ontology and the use of the word
'being" as philosophy's own temptation, the temptation to which Merleau-
Ponty would have finally succumbed?[25] To neglect, however, the "ontological" references that run through *The Visible and the Invisible* is to make the
"text" unintelligible. Merleau-Ponty does not "fall back" into ontology from
the height of an existential problematic or a philosophy of expression, but he
opens onto this being without which our volubility signifies nothing (and
consequently can not even signify itself) and from which spirit learns that it
does not exist without bonds (VI 275/222). There is certainly a "cult" of
presence that always ends up reestablishing being in a frontal relation and
under the species of the in-itself (even though being envelopes and traverses
us); but, inversely, there is also a pathos of absence that often only disguises
the most unbridled subjectivism. By calling "being" the "dehiscence of the
flesh," Merleau-Ponty frees us from both of these.

The expressions "flesh of the world," "flesh of things," indeed "flesh of
being" (VI 121/88), produce at first sight a certain perplexity; one is tempted
to see only metaphors in them, an effect of style or a play on language, unless
one sees in the notion of the flesh a new name for the being of every being,
a new determination of the common essence of things. Through this term,
however, Merleau-Ponty is really trying to conceive the openness of being,
this coiling of being on itself or this "specular phenomenon" internal to being
by which the reign of visibility is opened. The problematic of the flesh does
not simply take over for that of the lived body by a sort of extension of the
experience of the reversibility of sensed and sentient to everything sensible—
an experience discovered by Husserl at the level of the phenomenal body, as
constitutive of *Leiblichkeit*. Merleau-Ponty's work does not arise from a
hylozoism that consists of "conceptualizing" as animated what is at first

posited as *blosse Sache* and imparting the corporeity proper to a subject to the entirety of materiality (VI 304/250). The flesh of the world is not "identical" to the flesh of the body (VI 213/261); in particular, "[the world's flesh] is sensible and not sentient" (VI 304/250). But if Merleau-Ponty calls it flesh nonetheless, it is because the world's flesh does not arise entirely from the objective order. And, as the "*pregnancy* of possibles, *Weltmöglichkeit*," it is not self-identical, but being that contains its negation in itself, a being in dehiscence, which is *eminently percipi* and "big" with its *percipere* (VI 304/ 250). It is necessary, therefore, to reverse the "natural" order of explanation: "it is through the flesh of the world that in the last analysis one can understand the lived body" (VI 304/250). Likewise, the solution to the "regional" problem of the relations of the soul and the body is not to be found in a new definition of their union but in "the unicity of the visible world and, by encroachment, the invisible world" (VI 286/233). It is not by a generalizing induction and by a projection that one passes from the being of the subject to the being of the world. On the contrary, it is rather the being of the subject that appears as a variant of the being of the world. Merleau-Ponty responds as clearly as one could wish to the objection that would see in the flesh only an anthropological notion unduly projected on a world whose true being would remain unclarified: "Rather, we mean that carnal being, as a being of depths, of several leaves or several faces, a being in latency, and a presentation of a certain absence, is a prototype of Being, of which our body, the sensible sentient, is a very remarkable variant, *but whose constitutive paradox already lies in every visible*" (VI 179/136, our emphasis). The body as sensible sentient only concentrates the mystery of visibility in general and does not explain it. The paradox of a being that is at once one and double, objective and phenomenal body at the same time, is not a human paradox but the paradox of Being itself, insofar as it is the double "dehiscence of the seeing into the visible and of the visible into the seeing" (VI 201/153). What Merleau-Ponty understands by flesh, therefore, does not refer to a "referent" that philosophy would have already identified under other appellations; rather, it "has no name in any philosophy" (VI 193/147; cf. 183/139). The flesh does not arise from a determinate region of being; it is no more substance than matter or spirit. The domain that it inaugurates is that of unlimited visibility (VI 185/140). This is why it is necessary, instead, to conceive it as a "general thing," an "element" that does not have a proper place and is nevertheless everywhere (VI 184/139–40), "the formative medium of the object and the subject" (VI 193/147). But if a stable referent cannot be assigned to the flesh, if, *stricto sensu*, there is no "concept" of the flesh, that nevertheless does not mean that we are concerned with a simple *flatus vocis*, nor does it mean that by its generality it proves resistant to all experience. One does not pass from the experience of the lived body to the experience of the world's flesh by analogy, precisely because the experience of the lived body is already in itself the experience of a *general* reversibility. Rather than folding the subject back onto its private world, this reversibility opens the lived body on the contrary to an "intercorporeity" (VI 185/141), to "a Sentient in general before a Sensible in general" (VI 187/142), and to that "anonymous visibility" that inhabits all seers. The flesh, then, is really that "final notion" that one succeeds in reaching after having traversed every region of being, which is "conceivable by itself"; one does this without supporting oneself on other elements in order to construct the flesh, and also without ever identifying it with an object of thought conceivable by means of something other than itself (VI 185/140–41). The experience of the flesh, therefore, is able to take place only on the terrain of perceptual faith, which is also that of vision in action, the place where perceiving and perceived are still undivided and where things are experienced as annexes or extensions of ourselves. Now, the experience of vision is the place of a strange reversal of the relations of *percipi* and *percipere* for which act intentionality and *Sinngebung* can no longer give an account: "It is through the world first that I am seen or thought" (VI 328/274). The perceiving subject is inhabited by that anonymous visibility, that reflection of the visible that constitutes the perceiving subject by seeing; and this is why the perceiving subject can be, as *ghost* of the thing and *écart* in relation to the thing, only the impersonal subject of the *fungierende Intentionalität*, "the anonymous one buried in the world, and that has not yet traced its path" (VI 254/201). The anonymity and the generality of the perceptual self, which is in reality "no one," does not refer back to the negativity of the Sartrean for-itself, to that *hole* (VI 249/196) that introduces an irreducible heterogeneity into the fabric of being; rather, it refers to "a 'lake of non-being,' a certain nothingness sunken into a local and temporal *openness*" that must be understood as that hollow internal to being from which vision springs (VI 254/201, 193/147). The place where we find vision, and certainly feel it, is an experience of dispossession with which we see ourselves confronted: "the things have us and it is not we who have the things. . . . [L]anguage has us and it is not we who have language. . . . [I]t is being that speaks within us and not we who speak of being" (VI 247/194). One can no longer, then, begin again with the consciousness of being and with the constituting power of the subject; but neither can one reject consciousness without, in the same blow, canceling visibility into the night of the in-itself. To surmount this dilemma, the task remains to conceive consciousness otherwise than as knowledge and as taking possession of things—to conceive it as *Offenheit* (VI 252/198–99), as the *simple* openness that develops from the interior of being and not from the interiority of an ego toward the nonego (VI 268/214–15, 135/99). But if, on the one hand, the experience of vision is the test of the exhaustion of the transcendental subject, it is, on the other hand, the revelation of the universal complicity of beings. Complicity, exchange, encroachment, coupling—these are the terms Merleau-Ponty uses to describe the relation of the ego to things

and to others. Their meeting does not open the space of a face-to-face encounter, because they make their entrance *laterally*, from the same side where
the ego finds itself. Others, in particular, never present themselves frontally,
in the universe of things, but are introduced into the universe of seeing by
breaking in, as the radical calling into question of a private spectacle (VI 109/
78; cf. PM 185 f./133 f.). The other springs from the very "substance" of the
ego by parturition or subdivision (VI 86/59), as a diffusion or propagation of
the sensible sentient that I am. This is why Merleau-Ponty cannot be satisfied
with the Sartrean approach to others, which remains at the level of rivalry and
never opens onto a genuine coexistence (VI 268/215, 322/269). If there is a
relation of being between the ego and others, as Sartre nevertheless would
like, and not solely a reciprocal relation of objectification, it does not suffice
to juxtapose the multiplicity of for-itselves as so many parallels or equivalent
universes. Rather, the for-itselves have to form a "system"; they have to be
open to one another as so many partial perspectives confirmed in the *same*
common world (VI 113/81). This "miraculous multiplication of perceptible
being" (S 23/16), by which the *same* things have the force to be things for
more than one and that makes the *duel* of consciousnesses futile, comes from
the world. And to translate a plurality into a duality is still a simplification
of reflexive thought: "Perhaps it even would be necessary to reverse the
customary order of the philosophies of the negative, and say that the problem
of *the* other is a particular case of the problem of others" (VI 113 n/81 n).
Between the ego and the other, there are always those who count as "thirds,"
a bit like the fact that behind the intentionality of the object, there is the
multiplicity of operative intentional productions, of which act intentionality is
only the simplification. These multiple faces of others are so many variants
of one life which is never my private property but rather a moment of a
syntax or a general system of symbols (VI 114–15/82–83). Certainly, the fact
of seeing in the other less a rival than a twin or a double does not mean that
there is total reciprocity between the ego and others: to reduce what is non-
transferable in my own experience and what is inalienable in the experience
of others would mark "the triumph of a disguised solipsism" (VI 110/78–79).
The life of others, just as they live it, remains for me "a forbidden experience." But the *Nichtpräsentierbarkeit* of others—the fact that they are given
to me originarily as absence, the transcendence and the *écart* that they constitute in relation to myself—is of the same order as that of everything sensible, which is to them also the *Urpräsentation* of what is not *Urpräsentierbar*,
"Being's unique way of manifesting itself without becoming positivity, without ceasing to be ambiguous and transcendent" (VI 267/214, 234/180).[26] Far
from shutting them and me into parallel private worlds, the mystery of others
only refers me back to the mystery that I am for myself insofar as I am
perceptive life (PM 188/135). This is why the problem of the relations of the
ego with others and the problem of the relations of the ego with things are
the same. With things also, there is a lateral relation and *Einfühlung*: "Like

madmen or animals they are *quasi-companions"* (VI 234/180).[26] As others
are "the flesh of my flesh," things are "the extension of my body," which, as
Bergson said, extends unto the stars (VI 83 n. 2/57n. 10). Now, if there is an
"intropathy" *(Einfühlung)* from the perceiving to the perceived, this is not a
hylozoism of the Leibnizian type that would recognize a dormant or dull
consciousness in everything, a pure horizontal consciousness that would not
yet reflect on itself in the form of an ego. Husserl takes his chances with
Leibniz's monadology when he defines consciousness as the unity of a flux
in which the dullness of the ego can interrupt the alertness of consciousness
at different times, for "nothing prevents us from thinking that what is familiar
to us as an interruption of alert consciousness would be extended to infinity."[27]
But, for Merleau-Ponty, intropathy is not the way of access to what, in nature,
is not susceptible to being given in the original, to the *psyche*, which can only
be presentified and not presented originally as is the body. It is not an imperfect modality of evidence,[28] but is intermingled with perception itself insofar
as the latter is always also "imperception" (RC 12/72). What is *Urpräsenz* for
Husserl, namely, spatiotemporal material nature,[29] is never for Merleau-Ponty
anything but the extraction that brings about a vision reduced to a pure
thought, the extraction from the seeing of the flesh of the sensible—which,
as Merleau-Ponty repeatedly takes care to specify (VI 183/139, 191/146), is
not identical with matter. From the ego to the things, there is indeed *intro*pathy
since I feel their unity *from within*. Moreover, on the inside "they exist only
at the end of those rays of spatiality and of temporality emitted in the secrecy
of my flesh" (VI 153/114). *Einfühlung* is the *originary* mode of access both
to the being *within* which we are (VI 302/248), and to the being that we are
also for ourselves—not as the pure intimacy of a self-consciousness but as the
self-presence of that which has a world and a body and that can be self-
present only in self-absence (VI 303/249), as "an original of the *elsewhere*,
a *Selbst* that is an Other, a Hollow" (VI 308/254).

As the principle of differentiation—double dehiscence of seeing into
the visible and the visible into seeing, work of the negative that opens in its
medium the sensible mass to visibility (VI 193/147)—the flesh is a name for
Being. But it is also generality, element, fabric common to all beings and the
principle of indivision, and, as such, it is the name of being as a whole. This
ambiguity of the notion of flesh testifies to the "regional" character of Merleau-
Ponty's work in relation to Heidegger's investigation of a "direct expression of
what is fundamental" (RC 156/179–80). Merleau-Ponty in effect conceives of
ontology only indirectly (VI 233/179) and can apprehend the "verticality" of
Being only by traversing the horizons of the sensible and in contrast to the
natural region and the level of objective being (S 29/20; also VI 325/271–72).
And if, in other respects, it is true that the notion of flesh has no equivalent
in Heidegger's philosophy,[30] this is perhaps less the effect of a lacuna—the
filling of which a "phenomenology of perception" would have had as its
goal—than the effect of a more radical thought of *Weltoffenheit*. Heidegger's

thought of *Weltoffenheit* would be one that does not see in sensible experience an originary mode of access to being and that does not conceive an affect as "presence to the world through the body and to the body through the world," that is, as *flesh* (VI 292/239). Rather, Heidegger sees an effect as a consequence of dependence in relation to the world that is also the revelation of the world (*eine erschliessende Angewiesenheit auf Welt*),[31] a dependence relation that characterizes existence more originally than the phenomenon of incarnation. Moreover, an ontology of Dasein, which no longer conceives openness on the basis of consciousness—"consciousness as *Offenheit*" (VI 252/198)— does not have to reevaluate the psychological in terms of the ontological (VI 230/176) and can perhaps, with good reason, be parsimonious with respect to an ontology of the flesh. In contrast, an ontology of the flesh responds to the paradox of phenomenology, which, as philosophy of evidence and presence, is still led to recognize the undeniable horizonal structure of all intentionality. It is not sufficient to conceive, as Husserl still does, the interior horizon and the exterior horizon of things as a "system of potentialities of consciousness," which remains under the control of a classical infinitism (VI 195/148–49). Instead, one has to recognize more decisively than Husserl himself that the horizonal structure "has meaning only in the *Umwelt* of a carnal subject" (VI 238/185) that is not cut off from a *positive* infinite because of the *fact* of its finitude; but rather, *as flesh* and *by an operative finitude*, it is open to a Being that is for it only *negatively* inexhaustible and infinite. This Being is such because it participates in the carnal subject and is thereby near to the subject and far away at the same time (VI 305/251, 223/169). Heidegger recalls, in a 1928 lecture course,[32] that the word "horizon," from the Greek *horizein*, "is by no means related primarily to looking and seeing but simply means in itself that which encloses within limits, that which closes in, *closure*." To have a horizon therefore means less the capacity for the gaze to overcome what is actually given than "to capture" it from being, "to encompass it" within the openness of the visible (VI 195/149). Merleau-Ponty, who thought of horizons only as those of the flesh and who saw the verticality of existence erupt from the relation of embracing that takes place between the body and the world (VI 324/271), is with this conception nearer to Heidegger—who defines horizon as the limit toward which the temporal ecstasies tend,[33] that is, as a structure of a being essentially outside of itself[34]—than to Husserl, for whom the horizon remains the index of a potential infinity at the center of an actual given whose objective status is not called back into question.

SEEING AND TOUCHING

If the ontological rehabilitation of the body and the flesh, as the unthought of the Western tradition,[35] is also the ruin of classical infinitism, it is nevertheless the case that Merleau-Ponty still found the idea of chiasm in Husserl. In effect, in *Ideas II*, the text that Merleau-Ponty analyzes carefully in "The Philosopher and his Shadow," Husserl shows that the level of *Leiblichkeit* is also the plane where one finds the distinction between subject and object "blurred," since the living body (*Leib*) is the object of a *double* constitution, as physical thing and matter on the one hand, and bearer of localized sensations on the other.[36] Now, Husserl's entire analysis in paragraphs 36 and 37 relies on the privilege granted to touching in the constitution of the living body. If Husserl starts from the particular case where the living body itself is the object of perceptual experience—that is, the object of the experience of the double contact of two hands that touch each other—it is to bring to light, in contrast to visual sensation, the remarkable *double* function of *all* tactile sensation as such. It is the *same* sensation that is apprehended once as perception of an external body and that—"according to another direction of attention," which turns toward the "inside" of the body—furnishes a localized sensation of the lived body. The experience of double contact between two hands that are touching one another is characterized more particularly in that, here, we are dealing with two sensations that are *each* apprehendable in two different ways: the touched becoming the touching and the touching becoming the touched.[37] What reveals this remarkable property of the sense of touch is that, concerning the double constitution of the lived body and of nature, "everything can come into play in the extra-visual sphere."[38] There is, therefore, a "striking" difference between the visible sphere and the tangible sphere, because the eye does not appear visually, nor can the visual sensation of color appear as the localized sensation of the lived body. If there is indeed therefore at least an experience of double contact, a touching-touched, there is not in contrast a similar "reflexivity" of vision nor a seeing-seen. This is why one cannot assimilate seeing and touching by speaking "metaphorically" of a look that would "palpate" things. If the eye is the object of localized sensation, that can only be in relation to the sense of touch, because like all the other organs it originally belongs to touched objects and not to seen objects. The experience of the mirror cannot be invoked as a counter-example, because it is not the eye as *seeing* that is perceived in the mirror: "I see something, of which I judge indirectly, by way of '*Einfühlung*,' that it is to be identical with my eye as a thing (the one constituted by touch, for example) in the same way that I see the eye of an other."[39] The body constitutes itself therefore as lived body, not through the intermediary of the sense of sight, but uniquely through that of touch. And inversely, visible things can refer back to an immediate relation with the lived body only if they can be touched and not by virtue of their visibility. A purely ocular subject could not have a phenomenal body at all, because it would *see* its own body solely as a material thing.[40] What is announced in these paragraphs of *Ideas II* is the collapse of any parallelism between vision and touch as a sense involving an *immediate* relation with the object. Here Husserl refuses to consider vision as a touching at a distance, in contrast to Saint Bonaventure, for example.[41] Vision is not a quasi touching because the reversibility between internal and external is strictly found only in touching, which is thereby the origin of their difference, the difference on the basis of which alone vision can be established. Touching therefore is given an astonishing ontological privilege, especially if we connect it not only to the theme of *Wesenschau* but also to the general importance that falls to sight in Husserlian phenomenology. At least concerning the lived body, the principle of all principles finds itself placed in check: there is no originary giving intuition of the flesh. Indeed, only on the basis of the flesh is there even any "originary" giving intuition—that is, the presentation of the thing "so to speak, in its 'corporeal' reality"[42]—since Husserl shows in *Ideas II* that *carnal* intersubjectivity is the foundation of every apprehension of an objective being.[43] And it is still in relation to knowledge founded on seeing that *Leiblichkeit* appears as the limit-experience of constitution. Because one cannot *see* one's body entirely—neither one's back nor one's head—Husserl says that the lived body "is a remarkably imperfectly constituted thing."[44]

Heidegger showed, as early as 1927 in *Being and Time*, that the entire Western tradition from Parmenides to Husserl had privileged sight as the unique mode of access to beings *and to being*,[45] and that the privilege given to pure intuition on the noetic plane corresponds to that given to subsistent being on the ontological plane.[46] Heidegger specifies, moreover, in explicit reference to Husserlian phenomenology, that "the thesis that all cognition has 'intuition' as its goal, has the temporal meaning that all cognizing is making present,"[47] defining thereby the meaning of being as *presentation* for these philosophers of *consciousness*, Kant and Husserl. Merleau-Ponty, with regard to the exorbitant privilege that is granted to vision, hardly seems to have distanced himself in relation to this long tradition, which seems on the contrary to find its culmination in the unique question that the author of *Eye and Mind* continues to ask from his first to his last book: what is vision?[48] Is it not possible, nevertheless, while remaining the inheritor of the tradition, to put into question *from within* the nonexplicit presuppositions on which the tradition is founded? By interrogating the enigma of vision, Merleau-Ponty wanted to differentiate what the philosophical tradition has always identified: to differentiate "the thought of seeing," that is, a sublimated vision, one extracted from seeing and from its body, one identified with the inspection of the mind, from "active vision," that vision that genuinely takes place, "squeezed into a body—its own body," and "of which we can have no idea except in the exercise of it" (OE 54/136). This vision in fact can no longer be assimilated to the "reading of signs" of which the Cartesian *intuitus mentis* consists, nor to the "vision in general"[49] of which Husserlian intentionality consists. What we discover in active vision is no longer the intentional coincidence of the object and the subject, but rather the reversibility of the flesh, if to look is not

originally the act of a consciousness but "the opening of our flesh immediately filled by the universal flesh of the world" (S 23/16). Vision's enigma lies
in the fact that vision happens in the *midst* of things, "in that place where
something visible undertakes to see" (OE 19/124); it is initiation to "a world
in which all is simultaneous, *homon hên panta"* (S 226/179; cf. VI 270/217):
vision alone "makes us learn that beings that are different, 'exterior,' foreign
to one another, are yet absolutely *together"* (OE 84/146). What the Cartesian
analysis of vision does not see is that "vision is tele-vision, transcendence,
crystallization of the impossible" (VI 327/273): tele-vision in the sense that
it "makes us simultaneously with others and the world in the most private
aspects of our life" (S 24/16); transcendence because it discharges consciousness from its immanence; crystallization of the impossible since every visible
is the union of incompossible aspects and the concretion of something
ungraspable. Vision, then, is no longer a form of *self-presence* or a form of
thought, and seeing is less a *presentation* of the in-itself to consciousness
than "the means given me for being absent from myself, for taking part in the
fission of Being from the inside" (OE 81/145). Because the enigma of vision
is really the enigma of *presence*, but of a "splintered" presence that can no
longer be referred to the unity of an agency of presentation, this enigma is
the mystery of *simultaneity* (OE 84/146)—the mystery of a coexistence of
everything in and through distance, of "this deflagration of being" (OE 65/
140) that Cézanne attempted to paint.

Such a conception of vision leads Merleau-Ponty to restore the parallelism between seeing and touching that Husserl contested, and to discover in
them the same reversibility: "we could not possibly touch or see without
being capable of touching or seeing *ourselves"* (S 23–24/16, our emphasis).
There is not only a "vague comparison" between seeing and touching, but
also a literal, essential identity between flesh and visibility (VI 173 n/131 n):
the look "*envelopes, palpates, espouses* the visible things;" the look is with
the visible things as in a relation of preestablished harmony and according to
a proximity similar to that felt in the tactile palpation "*of which, after all, the
palpation of the eye is a remarkable variant"* (VI 175/133, our emphasis).
Just as the crisscrossing of touching and tangible in my hand opens onto a
tangible being of which my hand is a part, one can say that the body is seeing
(VI 176/133–34); that is, one can say that the body is visible and incorporated
into the whole of the visible (VI 327/273–74), because vision, like touching,
happens in the *midst* of the world and *within* being. This does not mean that
Merleau-Ponty is not conscious of the difference between the visual and
tactile spheres; there are certainly parts of my body that I cannot see—the eye
in particular is not seen—while touch is spread throughout the whole body.
If, however, it is "that same thick reflection that makes me touch myself
touching" and makes "the *same* in me be seen and seer," it is because "*by
encroachment* I complete my visible body" (VI 256/202), because it is visible

for others and "in principle" visible for myself: "it counts in the *Visible* of which *my* visible is a fragment" (VI 327/274). It is, consequently, the same reflexivity—"thick" because it does not enclose into immanence but because, on the contrary, it opens the space of the world—that Merleau-Ponty recognizes in seeing and in touching, and as well, moreover, in the understanding (VI 190/144–45, 310/256). The "senses" are not, according to a "crude delimitation" (VI 176/133), openings to different aspects of the world. Rather, beyond their fundamental incommunicability, they are structurally open to each other, and the parts of the world they reveal are each for themselves a "total part," at once singular and universal, giving themselves "as a *certain* being and as a *dimension*, the expression *of every possible being*" (VI 271/218). There is a universal *Transponierbarkeit* between them, since they are the expressions of one *same* world, the dimensions set up on one same and universal dimensionality. Between the visible and the tangible, there is therefore *reciprocal* encroachment, like two total parts that are nevertheless not superimposable, since, if the visible is cut out in the tangible, the tangible is still however promised to visibility (VI 177/134). This reversibility, which Merleau-Ponty discovers equally in seeing and in touching, is nevertheless essentially incomplete, "always imminent and never realized in fact" (VI 194/147), for if touched and touching, seen and seeing, were exactly superimposable, seeing and touching would not open onto one world. It is the "shift" in the reflection of the body (VI 313/260, 194/148), "the overhanging that exists within each sense" (VI 309/256) that prevents the experience of reversibility from being that of a fusion and a total coincidence that would also be closed within the immanence of an *actual* identity. Because reversibility is always *unsuccessful*, because there is only an identity *in principle* between touching and touched, seeing and seen, it opens onto the "il y a" of the world (VI 313/260). The identity in question here is neither actual-real nor ideal, that is, posited by the mind or consciousness; rather it is a *structural* identity, that of a being that can have many dimensions precisely because it is nothing positive (VI 315/261). If, in order to touch or see the things of the world, it is necessary to be capable of touching *oneself* or seeing *oneself*—that is, it is necessary to be capable of incorporating the living body into the space of the tangible and the visible—then inversely to touch and to see something is always to touch and see "oneself," in a "sort of reflection by Ec-stasy" (VI 308/255); tangible and visible things are extensions of our body, which is visible and tangible like them. The "divergent" reversibility of touching and touched, of seeing and seen, which coincides neither in the body nor in consciousness, refers back to an untouchable and an invisible that are such *in principle* and not only in fact; it refers back to a *true* negative that is not solely an *absent* positive (VI 281/227–28, 305/251, 308/254), but that—in the same way as the *punctum caecum* of consciousness *makes* consciousness be consciousness—makes there be a visible and a tangible through the openness

of a corporeality onto the world and being. This openness is that of a corporeality that participates in the world and being and not that of a consciousness
or a thought that would "survey" them. The untouchable and the invisible,
that at which I cannot be present or that with which I cannot coincide, are this
movement of perception that throws me out of myself toward the things and
that makes me always late in relation to myself, which always makes me exist
in a difference or an *écart* that is the world itself (cf. VI 284/231 and 308/
254–55). This blind spot of reversibility, which is, however, "ultimate truth"
(VI 204/155), is the in-principle latency of all flesh that makes the self, quite
by being open to itself, nonetheless be unaware of itself. Moreover the self
would not be able to coincide with a constituting source of perception (VI
303/249–50), since, for such a being, "self-presence *is* presence to a differentiated world" (VI 245/191), the for-itself never being anything but *derived*
from transcendence. This is why one rediscovers this hiatus at the very level
of the *Urerlebnis,* which Husserl mistakenly understood as coincidence or
fusion of the self with the self in the "living" present of consciousness—even
though all presence is merely partial coincidence of the self with the self in
transcendence, "a Self-presence that is an *absence from oneself,* a contact
with self *through* the divergence with regard to self" (VI 246/192), and even
though every present is an opening of spatiotemporal horizons and not only
the unity of an impressional and retentional consciousness (VI 246/192, 248/
194–95). What marks the limits of intentional analysis, in relation to a philosophy of transcendence that thinks "a dimensional present or *Welt* or Being" (VI 297/244), is that it remains a psychological reflection, and that it
continues to think the being of humanity in the Cartesian way—as "a flux of
individual *Erlebnisse,"* whereas it is "a field of Being" (VI 293/240). Nevertheless, what Husserl correctly grasped in his psychological reflection is
consciousness as absolute *retentional* flux, since with *retention* one is concerned with an adherence of the past to the present that is not *posited* by
consciousness, which is therefore preintentional (VI 245–46/192, 297/243–
44, 248/194–95). The past, then, is no longer a modification of the present of
consciousness, as in memory. Rather, it is "simultaneous" with the present;
the present is constantly prolonged in retention,[50] and retention gives to the
present its "thickness." A philosophy of consciousness cannot even give an
account of this thickness of the present, this simultaneity of the past and the
present, if it describes and thematizes the phenomenon of the temporal flow;
what is primary is not consciousness and the flow themselves, but the
spatializing and *temporalizing* "vortex" of the *flesh* of which the flux of the
Erlebnisse is only the schematization (VI 298/244). It is not enough to recognize the field character of time. Even more, one must not identify *Präsenzfeld*
with immanent consciousness. But one must see, on the contrary, that a
"transcendent consciousness" (VI 227/173) is opened in the field of presence
and in the spatial and temporal dimensions, if, as the *Phenomenology of*

Perception has said so precisely already, "subject and object are two abstract moments of a unique structure which is *presence*" (PP 492/430). If, therefore, we want to stop thinking of subjectivity as pure *actuality* and *instaneity*, if we want to understand it as flesh—for "then past and present are *Ineinander*, each enveloping-enveloped—*and that itself is the flesh*" (VI 321/268, our emphasis)" or inversely to understand time as chiasm, then it is necessary to substitute an instituting subject for the constituting subject (RC 60/108) and the order of *Stiftung* for that of *Erlebnisse* (VI 275/221). The notion of institution is not only "a solution to certain difficulties in the philosophy of consciousness," which would allow "the development of phenomenology into a metaphysics of history" (RC 59/107, 65/113); it is also what gives a more decisive turn to the difficult problem of activity and passivity with which Husserlian phenomenology never stopped struggling.[51] In the final analysis, the main point consists in leaving the opposition of active and passive behind in order to think a simultaneous *Urstiftung* of *time* and *space* that—far from enclosing us in a philosophy of history which is still too "personalistic," because it is too tied to praxis and to individual interiority—leads on the contrary to "grasping the *nexus* of history and transcendental geology" (VI 312/259). That is, it leads to the nexus of human freedom and its *terrestrial* "implantation" in the frame of what is no longer a philosophy of the subject, but in the frame of the world as *Offenheit der Umwelt* (RC 170/191). To think the simultaneity of time and space, of past and future, of subject and object, of positive and negative (RC 62/109), is not only to stop opposing a pure interior light to the impenetrable order of the in-itself (VI 67/43), but is also, as Husserl was already bringing to light, to conceive the *passivity* of our *activity* or the *body* of our *mind* (VI 274/221). If no question truly *goes* to Being, but is really rather *returning* to it (VI 161/120), this means that "new as our initiatives may be, they come to birth at the heart of being," since their field of *inscription* has already been opened, and since we are no more the author of this opening—which nevertheless happens through and with us— than the author of ourselves and of the beating of our hearts (VI 274–75/221). The profound sense of the rehabilitation of the figure of Narcissus and of the mirror experience in *The Visible and the Invisible* is to be found in the fact that our activity is equally passivity (VI 183/139). Only the Cartesian—and Husserl is still this Cartesian—does not see himself in the mirror and considers the specular image to be nothing *of* himself (OE 38–39/131); while, for the one who recognizes the metamorphosis of seeing and of the visible, the mirror only translates and doubles the very reflexivity of the sensible (OE 33–34/129–30) and the specularity of all flesh, because "the flesh is a *mirror phenomenon*" (VI 309/255). This fundamental narcissism of all vision and of all flesh does not, however, refer back to a solipsism, because this "coiling over of the visible upon the visible," which is the flesh, opens for other Narcissus" the field of an "intercorporeity" (VI 185/140–41). Nor does it

refer back to a philosophy of fusion and identity, as there is transcendence
between seeing and visible, that is, identity solely *within* difference (VI 279/
225). It is nevertheless the case that the specularity of being is the last word
of Merleau-Ponty, as it is the culmination of the metaphysics of vision in the
Hegelian dialectic, given that it is "in the grasping of opposites in their unity
or of the positive in the negative, that *speculative thought* consists."[52] Merleau-
Ponty does not purely and simply align himself with the Hegelian dialectic,
however, but on the contrary invokes a "hyperdialectic" that, insofar as it is
a "thought of the situation," would be familiar with only partial and local
sublations. It is a dialectic without synthesis that would not posit the ambiva-
lence of the negative and the positive, and that would rediscover the being
prior to reflection and idealization in the reciprocal *encroachment* of myself
and things, in the *thickness* of the present and the *spatiality* of the world (VI
125–30/91–95, 318/264).

⌘

All things considered, if Merleau-Ponty joins back up with the philosophies of absolute reflection, this occurs by working a displacement at once
both infinitesimal and radical in relation to them.[53] The reflexivity that is at
issue is a structure of the *flesh* and no longer of *spirit*. *All* reflection, here
understood as spirit, is of the type that reveals the experience of double
contact (VI 257/204). This is why our conception of spirit as *reflection* is
borrowed from the specular structure of the relation of our body to the world
(VI 325/271). And the mirror play at issue here is no longer that of spirit
preying solely on itself, but is rather the play of the world and of its metamorphoses. Merleau-Ponty leads us in the direction of such a "cosmology of
the visible" by challenging, as had Anaxagoras,[54] every question of origin,
every evolutionary perspective, since there is no longer anything but "one
sole explosion of Being which is forever" (VI 318/265), no longer anything
but an "existential eternity" in the "vertical" presence to the world and in this
"stabilized explosion" of the outside and the inside, which is the sensible and
Nature (VI 321/267; S 30/21). Neither reflection nor presence have the same
meaning any longer then, and philosophy sees itself forced to make room
within itself for nonphilosophy, for indestructible nature and what Schelling
called his "barbarous principle" (S 225/178). No more are there two separate
worlds, the sensible and the intelligible, than there are two different attitudes,
the natural one of surrender to the world and the other, the philosophical, of
reflective return (VI 94/65). In contrast to Husserl, Merleau-Ponty truly aban-
doned the "dream" of philosophy as a rigorous science.[55] If philosophy is no
longer the *overhanging* of life but rather "the simultaneous experience of the
holding and the held in all orders" (VI 319/266), then it says nothing more
than all literature which, like philosophy, is "the *inscription* of being" (VI

251/197) the inscription of a being that is a sort of ledger open to our creations only because we are inscribed in it; this "ledger," nevertheless, appears as "a treasury ever full of things to say" only for "the one who is a philosopher (*that is, a writer*)" (VI 305/252, our emphasis). To recognize that there is no absolutely pure philosophical speech, and to see in the circularity of Proust's *oeuvre* the model of every philosophical approach (VI 231/177), by no means leads to the abandonment of the philosophical *as such*, but indeed rather to *true* philosophy. That is, it leads precisely to a philosophy for which the world and being are neither just an ideate (VI 254–55/201), nor the "truth" independent of the relation of transcendence that we maintain with the world (VI 239/185):

The true philosophy-apprehend what makes the leaving of oneself be a retiring into oneself, and vice versa.

Grasp this chiasm, this reversal. That is spirit. (VI 252/199)

NOTES

This essay was translated from the French by Theodore A. Toadvine Jr. It first appeared as "Monde, chair, vision" in *Maurice Merleau-Ponty: Le psychique et le corporel*, ed. Anna-Teresa Tymieniecka (Paris: Aubier, 1988), pp. 115–44, © Aubier, Paris, 1988.

1. Cf. Jean Paul Sartre, *L'etre et le néant* (Paris: Gallimard, 1943), p. 708; *Being and Nothingness*, trans. Hazel Barnes (New York: Washington Square Press, 1966), p. 784. It is no doubt on this point that there is a "fundamental incompatibility" between Sartre and Merleau-Ponty. Cf. the interview with Sartre in 1975, "An Interview with Jean-Paul Sartre," in *The Philosophy of Jean-Paul Sartre*, The Library of Living Philosophers, vol. 16 (La Salle, Ill.: P.A. Schilpp, 1982), p. 43.

2. Karl Schuhmann, *Husserl-Chronik* (The Hague: Martinus Nijhoff, 1977).

3. Gerd Brand, *Welt, Ich und Zeit* (The Hague: Martinus Nijhoff, 1955).

4. Edmund Husserl, *Die Krisis der europäischen Wissenschaften und die transzendentale Phänomenologie, Husserliana*, vol. 6 (The Hague: Martinus Nijhoff, 1954), p. 146; *The Crisis of European Sciences and Transcendental Phenomenology*, trans. David Carr (Evanston: Northwestern University Press, 1970), p. 143.

5. Ibid., p. 146/143.

6. In Martin Neidegger, *Metaphysische Aufgangsgründe der Logik im Ausgang von Leibniz* (Frankfurt a. M.: Klostermann, 1978); *The Metaphysical Foundations of Logic*, trans. Michael Heim (Bloomington, Indiana: Indiana University Press, 1984). Also in *Sein und Zeit, Gesamtausgabe*, vol. 2 (Tübingen: Neimayer Verlag, 1963);

Being and Time, trans. John Macquarrie and Edward Robinson (San Francisco: HarperCollins, 1962).

7. Martin Heidegger, *Vom Wesen des Grundes* (Frankfurt a. M.: Klostermann, 1965); *The Essence of Reasons*, trans. Terrence Malick (Evanston: Northwestern University Press, 1969).

8. Heidegger, *The Essence of Reasons*, 16/28–29, 18–20/34–41, 47/112–13.

9. Cf. Dorian Cairns, *Conversations with Husserl and Fink* (The Hague: Martinus Nijhoff, 1976), p. 106.

10. Ibid., p. 98.

11. Cf. F. W. von Herrmann, *Bewusstsein, Zeit und Weltverständnis* (Frankfurt a. M.: Klostermann, 1971), p. 21 f.

12. Brand, *Welt, Ich und Zeit*, p. 17.

13. Ibid., p. 21.

14. Ibid., pp. 11, 14–15.

15. Brand, *Welt, Ich und Zeit*, p. 17.

16. Heidegger, *Being and Time*, p. 364/415 f.

17. Cairns, *Conversations with Husserl and Fink*, p. 66.

18. Heidegger, *Being and Time*, p. 7/27.

19. Ibid., p. 149/189–90 f.

20. Merleau-Ponty, VI 262/208–9. Merleau-Ponty recalls in this working note that pregnancy means, primarily, productivity, fecundity; second, it means the typical character of *la "bonne" forme*. It is the implicit being, the dynamic character of *la bonne forme* that gives to it its stability, which imposes it on the perceiving body.

21. Eugen Fink, *Nähe und Distanz: Phänomenologische Vorträge und Aufsätze*, ed. Franz-Anton Schwarz (Freiburg: Alber, 1976), p. 122: *"eine Versteifung auf die ontische Wahrheit und eine Blindheit gegen die ontologische, als ein Unterlassen, eine Stillegung der 'Transcendenz' des menschlichen Daseins."*

22. Cf. Eugen Fink, *"Die Phänomenologische Philosophie Edmund Husserls in der Gegenwärtigen Kritik"* in *Studien zur Phänomenologie* (Den Haag: Nijhoff, 1966), p. 110 f.; "The Phenomenological Philosophy of Edmund Husserl and Contemporary Criticism," in *The Phenomenology of Husserl*, ed. and trans. R. O. Elveton (Chicago: Quadrangle Books, 1970), p. 104 f.

23. Sarte, *Being and Nothingness*, p. 715/789–90.

24. Sartre denies validity to the type of being invoked by Merleau-Ponty for which "he invokes Heidegger" ("An Interview with Jean-Paul Sartre," p. 43). He refers to his 1961 article, "Merleau-Ponty Vivant," where we find this phrase: "Reading him at times, it would seem that being invents man in order to make itself manifest through

him." *Les Temps Modernes* 17 (1961): 36; "Merleau-Ponty Vivant," in *Situations*, trans. Benita Eisler (New York: George Braziller, 1965), p. 313.

25. Cf. M. Blanchot, *Le "Discours philosophique,"* in *L'Arc* 46: no. 2.

26. On the problem of the significance of *Einfühlung* in Husserl, see Cairns, *Conversations with Husserl and Fink*, 74: "In the end, I got no clear idea whether Husserl thinks of plants as limiting cases of *Einfühlung*, or not. Though he did say perhaps Leibniz was right in saying that the only conceivable being was spiritual being, and the 'things' of the world are really 'sleeping' monads."

27. Edmund Husserl, *Ideen II, Husserliana*, vol. 4 (The Hague: Martinus Nijhoff, 1952), p. 108; *Ideas Pertaining to a Pure Phenomenology and to a Phenomenological Philosophy*, Second Book (Studies in the Phenomenology of Constitution), trans. Richard Rojcewicz and André Schuwer (Boston: Kluwer, 1989), pp. 114–15.

28. Edmund Husserl, *Ideen I, Husserliana*, vol. 3 (The Hague: Martinus Nijhoff, 1950), p. 291; *Ideas Pertaining to a Pure Phenomenology and to a Phenomenological Philosophy*, First Book (General Introduction to a Pure Phenomenology), trans. Fred Kersten (The Hague: Martinus Nijhoff, 1982), p. 336.

29. Husserl, *Ideas II*, p. 163/171.

30. Cf. Claude Lefort, *Sur une colonne absente* (Paris: Gallimard, 1978), p. 110.

31. Heidegger, *Being and Time*, p. 137/177.

32. Martin Heidegger, *Gesamtausgabe*, Band 26 (Frankfurt a.M.: Klostermann, 1978), p. 269.

33. Heidegger, *Being and Time*, p. 365/416.

34. Ibid., p. 329/377.

35. That is, the *Cartesian* tradition; Merleau-Ponty refers to Greek ontology only exceptionally, and essentially remains in dialogue with the philosophy of consciousness.

36. Husserl, *Ideas II*, p. 145/152–53.

37. Ibid., p. 147/155.

38. Ibid., p. 147/154.

39. Ibid., 148 n. 1/155 n. 1.

40. Ibid., p. 150/158.

41. Cf. E. Gilson, *La Philosophie de Saint-Bonaventure* (Paris: Vrin, 1924), p. 335 f.; *The Philosophy of Saint Bonaventure*, trans. Dom Illtyd Trethowan and Frank J. Sheed (Paterson, N.J.: St. Anthony Guild Press, 1965), p. 319 f.

42. Husserl, *Ideas I*, p. 43/44.

43. Ibid., p. 82/87. This text is cited by Merleau-Ponty in a note in S 218/172.

44. Ibid., p. 159/167.

45. Heidegger, *Being and Time*, pp. 147/187, 171/215.

46. Ibid., 147/187.

47. Ibid., 363 n/498n xxiii.

48. Cf. C. Lefort, *"Qu'est-ce que voir?"* in *Sur une colonne absente* (op. cit.), pp. 140–54. First published in *Histoire de la Philosophie*, vol. 3 (Paris: Gallimard, 1974), pp. 692–705.

49. Husserl, *Ideas I*, p. 36/36.

50. Edmund Husserl, *Zur Phänomenologie des inneren Zeitbewusstseins (1893–1917)*, *Husserliana*, vol. 10, ed. Rudolph Boehm (The Hague: Martinus Nijhoff, 1966), p. 28; *Lectures on Internal Time-Consciousness*, ed. M. Heidegger, trans. J. S. Churchill (Bloomington: Indiana University Press, 1964), p. 49.

51. See above all Edmund Husserl, *Cartesian Meditations*, trans. Dorian Cairns (The Hague: Martinus Nighoff, 1973), sections 38 and 39 (111–14/77–81), and Edmund Husserl, *Urfahrung und Urteil: Untersuchungen zur Genealogie der Logik*, ed. Ludwig Landgrebe (Hamburg: Felix Meiner Verlag, 1972), section 23, 116–23; *Experience and Judgement*, trans. James S. Churchill and Karl Ameriks (Evanston: Northwestern University Press, 1973), pp. 106–12.

52. Hegel, *Wissenschaft der Logik, I, Werke* 5 (Frankfurt, a.M.: Suhrkamp, 1969), p. 52; *Hegel's Science of Logic*, trans. A. V. Miller (London: George Allen & Unwin Ltd., 1969), p. 56. On the relation of dialectic and vision, see Heidegger, *Being and Time*, p. 171/215, and *"Hegel und die Griechen"* in *Wegmarken* (Frankfurt a. M., Klostermann, 1967), p. 425.

53. These are the terms by which Derrida expresses his own relation to the Hegelian discourse. Cf. Jacques Derrida, *Marges de la philosophie* (Paris: Edit. de Minuit, 1972), p. 15; *Margins*, trans. Alan Bass (Chicago: University of Chicago Press, 1982), p. 14.

54. Anaxagoras, frag. 17. See Kathleen Freeman, *Ancilla to the Pre-Socratic Philosophers* (Cambridge: Harvard University Press, 1957), p. 85.

55. Cf. Husserl, *Crisis*, p. 508/389. Cf. H. G. Gadamer, *Die Phenomenologische Bewegung*, in *Philosophische Rundshau* (Tübingen: Mohr, 1963), vol. 11, no. 1/2, p. 25 f.; "The Phenomenological Movement," in *Philosophical Hermeneutics*, ed. and trans. David E. Linge (Berkeley: University of California Press, 1976), p. 158 f.

CHAPTER 2

Flesh and Verb in the Philosophy of Merleau-Ponty

HENRI MALDINEY

Throughout his whole life—a life that is an existence—Merleau-Ponty wanted every day to be a philosopher. "To be a philosopher everyday" means to be a philosopher according to the insistent agency of time, according to the time about which Merleau-Ponty said that it is someone. In order to make each given moment something present, it is necessary to make presence itself present (*faire acte de présence*). Not in the trivial sense of the expression, *faire acte de*, but in the rigorous sense of the act of existing. What Hölderlin says about poetry, one can say about existence: that it is the most innocent and the most dangerous occupation of all. The most stubborn aim of Merleau-Ponty's philosophy was to determine the horizon in which the innocence of the being [*l'étant*] and the risk of Being [*d'être*] are joined together again [*se rejoignent*]. Over and over again, the innocence of the being has been in search of a place of Being, a place in which these two ontological dimensions (expressed by the German verbs *ist* and *west*) coincide. In *The Visible and the Invisible* these two dimensions together tend to constitute the same formal circle as the reversibility of event and advent. In "Atmen," one of his sonnets to Orpheus, Rilke gives this reversibility the following poetic formula:

> Breathing, you invisible poem!
> World-space constantly in pure
> interchange with our own being. . . . Counterpoise
> wherein I rhythmically happen[1]

But if the source point of poetic existence is exclamation, the source point of philosophical existence is interrogation. I interrogate what is there, close by to where I am; and without fail, whatever is there teaches me its presence and mine. It never stops teaching me that it is there and that I am there, in the simplicity of a single fold that can only exist or disappear, but not degenerate. I would not know how to interrogate it except on the basis of the fact that I might have learned as well. The convoy is blocked; I have joined together again. However, philosophical interrogation intervenes, and this intervention is the original fault.[2] Philosophical interrogation questions the learning about itself, on the basis of itself, in view of leading it to unveil its being [*son être*].

What is learning? What is it to learn? The German language responds: What is to be learned (*erfahren*) is the world, the object of experience (*Erfahrung*). But to call it an "object" is to introduce an objectifying operation between us and the world, an operation that substitutes itself for an originary preknowing of which the operation is at once a second interpretation and its misunderstanding.

A totalitarian physics that understands "to say what is" by relying on an in-principle adequation "between the operation of science and Being" (VI 36/18) hides an implicit ontology. This ontology presumes to have the right to preempt the being of the world by identifying *a priori* the dimension of being with the form of "objectity."

Psychology too "had wished to constitute its own domain of objectivity; it believed it had discovered it in the structures of behavior. Was there not here an original conditioning that would form the object of an original science, as other less complex structures formed the object of the sciences of nature" (VI 38/20)?

The division between the "subjective" and the "objective" by which elementary physics at its beginning defines its domain, and correlatively, by which psychology also establishes its domain, does not prevent, on the contrary, it demands, that these two disciplines be conceived according to the same fundamental structure; they are finally two orders of objects. But "the 'psychism' is not an object" (VI 41/22). The functional relations established by objective psychology "do not represent a *first stratum* of behavior, from which one could proceed little by little unto its total determination; rather they are a first form of integration, privileged cases of simple structuration, relative to which the 'more complex' structurations are in reality qualitatively different" (VI 27/21). This objectifying integration does not correspond at all to the real integration that behavior itself constitutes in itself. The divisions that this objectifying integration claims to operate in concrete behavior in order to determine fragmented behaviors and elementary structures are not given in phenomenological description, and are not inscribed in the proleptic and signifying articulation of the behavioral field.

Merleau-Ponty intends to show "that the being-object, and also the being-subject, conceived by opposition to it and relative to it do not form the alternative, that the perceived world is beneath or beyond this antinomy, that the failure of 'objective' psychology is—conjointly with the failure of objective physics—to be understood not as a victory of the 'interior' over the 'exterior' and of the 'mental' over the 'material,' but as a call for the revision of our ontology, for the re-examination of the notions of 'subject' and 'object' " (VI 41/22–23).

The ontology he intends to revise is that of the *Kosmotheôros* and of "its correlative: the Great Object" (VI 32/15). The contemplator of the world— of the internal world as well as of the external world—"posits himself as Absolute Spirit over and against the pure object" (VI 32/15) in an act of representation. But the theoretical man arrives too late to be contemporaneous with his origin and with the origin of his world. The being—the one that he is and the one that he is not—is already manifested. Here the thought of Merleau-Ponty agrees with the liminary thought of Heidegger in *The Essence of Reasons:* "all pre-predicative manifestness of the being is such that, at the *primary* level, manifesting never has the character of a mere representing (intuiting), *not even in 'aesthetic' contemplation. We will be inclined to characterize prepredicative truth as intuiting* only if ontic, and presumably authentic truth, is defined as propositional truth, i.e., as a 'combination of representations'. . . . *The proper function of representing is to* objectivize being—which itself must then always be already manifest."[3]

To identify Being with objectity is "to postulate that what is, is not *that upon which we have an openness,* but only *that upon which we can operate*" (VI 35/18). This postulate, which designates a possessive will to power, characterizes, moreover, the formal, speculative thought that develops in its own emphasis on knowledge that surveys, as well as the spirit of the "governmental" rationalization that claims to totalize the world by reducing it to a code or to a picture. Both refuse to admit into themselves something that does not depend on them, illustrating, in a way, Freud's remark in "Negation" that "What is bad, what is alien to the ego and what is external are, to begin with, identical."[4] Hegel calls this alien element simply the unknown. Its in principle exclusion is "usually the first reaction on the part of knowing . . . in order to save its own freedom, its own insight, its own authority, from the foreign authority (for this is the guise in which what is *newly learned* first appears)."[5]

Until it first appeared, what was unknown to us and was nothing for us, and that suddenly approached us—at each moment of the world and of us— perhaps in the unpredictable emergence of the most humble sensation, possesses an authority of presence that to us is all the more foreign as it carries with it the experience of our own otherness. But this otherness is precisely proper to us only because, as foreign, it is at the same time that which is to us the most intimate and the most originary: it belongs to the order of the encounter and of the contact whose event is each time that of our origin. Science and theoretical thought want to know nothing about that: they are constituted such that they can and must forever be unaware of it. But nevertheless, science always hopes to be able "to reintroduce little by little what it first put aside as subjective. . . . It will integrate it as a particular case of the relations and objects that define the world for science. Then the world will close in over itself, and, except for what within us thinks and builds science, that impartial spectator that inhabits us, we will have become part of the Great Object" (VI 31/15).

The hyperbole of the scientific hope has the certainty of speculative thought as its asymptote. The thinking subject who escapes, as such, from the closing of the world is the author responsible for it. And philosophy's own task is then to determine a priori its status as contemplator. Kant says that "*A Kosmotheoros.* . . . creates the elements of knowledge of the world himself, *a priori*, from which he, at the same time, as an inhabitant of the world, constructs a world-vision [*Weltbesc hauung*] in the idea."[6] From both sides thought only intends to learn about those things for which it has predetermined the meaning of Being. This ontology by decree must be called a delirium, more precisely a secondary delirium, organized by the understanding. This ontology by decree constitutes the rationalization—the rationalization after the fact which presents itself as primitive—of a lack in being, of the emptiness which inscribes in it the absence of the experience, which is perpetually originary, of the *il y a*, that it has once and for all repressed or rather excised.

In contrast, the care of this fundamental experience defines phenomenology and justifies its claim of being the only authentic ontology. Phenomenology's task, says Merleau-Ponty, is "to reveal the mystery of the world and the mystery of reason" (PP xvi/xxi). Phenomenology exists only to test *through itself* the indivisibility of these two mysteries. Its own action is *to understand* [*entendre*] the world, in the sense of the German word *vernehmen*, from which the word *Vernunft*—reason—is derived. What we understand of the world is that we learn the world in the world. It is a question, therefore, of learning, and of learning to see. It is true that the eye listens. The gaze of the artist is held in the openness where the world produces itself. The philosopher also is open to the world. But while the artist embodies the apparitional movement in a work that is also itself surprising, "philosophy," Merleau-Ponty says, "must appropriate and understand this initial openness upon the world" (VI 49/28).

"It is a matter of describing, not of explaining or analyzing." Such is "Husserl's first directive to phenomenology in its early stages" (PP ii/viii). Given that the task of philosophy is not to describe but to appropriate and to understand, will there be a fault between the two where the very idea of phenomenological philosophy collapses? Heidegger explains this point in the following way: "the expression 'descriptive phenomenology,' which is at bottom tautological" has a prohibitive sense, namely, to refrain from all non directly legitimate determination.[7]

To gain access to a directly legitimate determination is to understand. What is it to understand? The programmatic meaning of the word "phenomenology" tells us: *legein ta phainomena,* which means *apophainesthai ta phainomena*, which itself means to make the phenomena be seen from themselves, to lead them to the light of their own day. The *phainomenon* is what shows itself. Merleau-Ponty answers the question, "what is there to be disclosed when something shows itself in the patency?" by saying "this patency itself." "[Philosophy] must tell us how there is openness" (VI 49/28). This problem is at the bottom of all of Heidegger's work. Merleau-Ponty also indeed understands that the openness in question opens not onto appearance, but onto Being, including the being of the one to whom this openness gives a *place*, as being-in-the-world. But Heidegger and Merleau-Ponty differ concerning Being.

The link between Merleau-Ponty and Husserl at first appears closer. They both agree in this primary conviction, of which each makes evident in his own way: the reciprocity of the dimensional inner framework of the world and of the thought of horizon. But they differ concerning one decisive point that constitutes a point of inflexion, a point from which the thought of Merleau-Ponty never turns back, a point that puts the very idea of phenomenology back in question.

The philosophical quest has two axes available that make complete sense only within that quest: *to see* and *to question*. They are what determine respectively the style of the philosophies of Husserl and Heidegger. The mode of access to the true is for Husserl a *Sehen*; for Heidegger, at the time of *Sein und Zeit*, a *Fragen*. Merleau-Ponty articulates them in terms of each other: "[Interrogation] is for philosophy the only way to conform itself with the vision we have in fact, to correspond with what, in that vision, provides for thought, with the paradoxes of which that vision is made" (VI 19/4).

The interrogative attitude is the only attitude authentically phenomenological because it is the only one that excludes every theoretical precondition, including what we ordinarily understand by dialectic. The interrogative attitude belongs originarily to the *Dasein* that we are. Merleau-Ponty does not see in the interrogative attitude one of the ways of existence but existence itself actualizing itself on the basis of and in view of itself.

But where does *Dasein* have its "there" that is "common to the natural man and to the philosopher"? In its being-in-the-world experienced and lived as *originary faith*, this perceptual faith that Husserl named *Urdoxa*. Perceptual faith is immanent to a seeing. "We see the things themselves, the world is what we see: formulae of this kind express a faith common to the natural man and the philosopher—the moment he opens his eyes; they refer to a deep-seated set of mute 'opinions' implicated in our lives" (VI 17/3). Philosophy does not have to interrogate this faith from the outside, from another perspective.

"Philosophy is the perceptual faith questioning itself about itself. One can say of it, as of every faith, that it is a faith *because* it is the possibility of doubt." (VI 139/103). "But what is strange about this faith is that if we seek to articulate it into theses or statements, if we ask ourselves what is this *we*, what *seeing* is, and what *thing* or *world* is, we enter into a labyrinth of difficulties and contradictions" (VI 17/3).

Doubt is even closer to the perceptual faith itself. This originary faith, this *Urdoxa* is *para doxan*, that is, in the literal sense, contrary to expectation. The reason for this paradox is inscribed in this expectation, which is itself paradoxical. It is an expectation such that the unexpected alone can fulfill it. The real is essentially what one does not expect, what transcends all that is possible, all recourse to the same. Each time, its appearance exceeds a lack of knowledge. This is why all completely transparent knowledge deceives us, starting with the knowledge of others . . . and self-knowledge. The unexpected, which our vision of the world is expecting to be opposed to its own transparency, this background to our vision of the world that is impossible to resolve into a pure spectacle, is for Merleau-Ponty the very depth of the world; and this infinite depth has its correlate in the infinite interrogation that is philosophy.

"This question raised to the second power . . . its own characteristic is that it returns upon itself, that it asks itself not only 'what is the world?' or better 'what is Being?' but what is it to question and what is it to respond, so that nothing can continue to be as if there had never been any question" (VI 160/119–20).

The interrogative function is an exponential function that has what it precisely tries to determine as its variable: the how of our openness to the world. All our questions take place—the place of Being—in this openness.

"We are interrogating our experience precisely in order to know how it opens us to what is not ourselves. *This does not even exclude the possibility that we find in our experience a movement toward what could not in any event be present to us in the original and whose irremediable absence would thus count among our originating experiences*" (VI 211/159).

Here the point of inflection in Merleau-Ponty's thought is discovered, the point from which the very idea of phenomenology changes; the point is sought and discovered in *The Visible and the Invisible*. This is a title that at the same time announces a new path and denounces the defects of the old [*Phenomenology of Peception*]. We dare to say that phenomenology is short-circuited in its very own dimension, if it does not take into account the invisible. Without taking the invisible into account, phenomenology would be only an empirics or an eidetics of transcendental subjectivity, both implying a positivistic thematization of Being. This would be a positivity not only of facts and essences, but also of intentional life and of the pre-predicative life world.

Where exactly does the break with Husserl start? Nothing is more foreign to Husserl than a positivism of transcendental subjectivity and there is in Husserl's phenomenology a way that is partially opened out upon absence. "I, the 'transcendental ego,' am the ego who 'precedes' everything worldly"[8] "As the subjectivity that has the ultimate role of constituting, I precede this constituted world."[9] This subjectivity is not an *archê* in the sense of a beginning, of a beginning that would be behind all experience, as the element or the principle of which experience would be a later development. This subjectivity is, on the contrary, that in which experience precedes itself. It is before the whole pre-predicative world, which has *pre*-sence only thereby. Transcendental subjectivity is what is at the beginning's imperative; it is the originary of the original. Therefore we have a situation that is without analogue since it is everything, a situation Levinas describes in this way: "The constitution of the object is already sheltered by a pre-predicative world that the subject nevertheless constitutes; and inversely the sojourn in a world is conceivable only as the spontaneity of a constituting subject, without which this sojourn would have been the simple belonging of a part to a whole and the subject would be the simple product of the terrain."[10] This sojourn is never present. The intentionality constitutive of the experience in which the world has the sense of world implies "infinite horizons of undisclosed and unknown determinations."[11] The horizon, which is the siteless place of nonunconcealment, is also the radical place of what is heralded. The horizons of the pre-predicative world supported as they are by "the essential potentiality of the intention"[12] attest that the world's constitutive spontaneity is sheltered by the world that it constitutes.

If this spontaneity is sheltered by the prepredicative world, this world is also constituted by it in a still enveloped state. It is precisely this spontaneity of the constituting subject that Merleau-Ponty rejects, and the importance of this rejection, its scope, rivals that of the thought he rejects. According to Levinas, the *Urimpression* is "at once the first subject and the first object, giver and given."[13] The ego is implicated in the sensible world whose evidence however the ego alone actualizes. The ego is at once *in* the world and *to* the world: this is the dual unity of dependence in and transcendence to which defines the situated subject. My dependence has the sense of being a situation only if it is integrated in a transcendence that makes dependence exist; this is a transcendence that, by going beyond dependence, throws dependence back to itself, as if transcendence were a shock wave less rapid than dependence; this is a transcendence which exists only through dependence as if transcendence were a fleeting trace which dependence is always over coming. It is a transcendence in immanence that can define itself neither by this immanence nor outside of it. "The ego as the *now* is defined by nothing other than itself, that is, it does not define itself. It does not coincide with the heritage of its existence, it extends alongside of nothing, and is still outside of the system."[14] Merleau-Ponty absolutizes this in principle lack of definition that makes it impossible for the ego to determine itself. Literally, "the ego is nothing." It is the absence by which there is presence and this absence "counts in the world."

"Never will one construct perception and the perceived world with these positive terms and relations. The endeavor is *positivist:* with something *innerweltlich,* with traits of the world, to fabricate the architectonics of the *Welt.* It is a thought that acts as if the world wholly positive were given, and as if the problem were to make the perception of the world first considered as nonexisting arise therefrom" (VI 285/231). Quite simply, this economizes on the experience.

Once more the German word *erfahren* tells what experience means: experience is a going across that blazes the lanes [*les voies*] of a depth. To go across is not a change of place, but a journey. We do not go from one fixed point to another point which had been fixed in advance. When we go across, this movement is not the cancellation of an already known distance, but a coming close within the distance and a distance within the coming close. As we are engaged in the world, the world unfolds around us in a sliding continuity of horizons, whose renewal accompanies that of our here, which is thereby transformed. We always arrive at a new landscape of the world. "To arrive at . . . . of . . . ." [*en arriver à*] is not the same as "to arrive at . . . ." [*arriver à*]. As the French expression indicates, *"en arriver à"* is to arrive without having departed. We are always in the situation of *arrival.* And this situation integrates the starting point which is constantly transformed in the situation. This is the very sense of the depth of the world: it cannot be crossed.

Our going across however is not in vain. It unveils a particular direction that is one of the dimensions of the inexhaustible depth of the world, a particular direction that Merleau-Ponty calls the "ray [*rayon*][15] of the world." The perception and the appearance of the world are indiscernible. Each perceptive phase is an apparitional phase. They are one and the same phase. The *il y a* is an *j'y suis.* Theories of perception—aside from some very rare exceptions—only revolve around the moment of appearance, without attempting to understand it or to learn from it. The evidence of appearance is an enigma continually eluded and repressed. Fink says, "the expression 'to appear' has a plurality of meanings consisting in an enigmatic depth. 'To appear' means first the sudden appearance of the being, its coming into the openness between sky and earth. All that is finite comes to appearance by taking place in the intervalents of space and time, by discovering there its fragile stability. . . . But "to appear" can also mean the presentation that the finite being which has already come to appear gives of itself. Nothing essential remains enveloped within it. Each thing relates to others—they are neighbors—and each thing collides with the others as if they were limits. 'To appear' now means being held in relation to other things." This self-presentation acquired a particular sense in the modern period. It is the mode "according to which a thing is presented to a representative subject."[16] Entirely reversing this movement, Merleau-Ponty—like Heidegger before him—goes back to the first moment of appearing. The concern to ascend back up to this first moment is present everywhere in *The Visible and the Invisible*.

The Visible and the Invisible constitutes a new *phenomenology of perception* some of whose sketches were latent in earlier work: the conception of sensing (*sentir*), for example, as access and openness to the world in which a prepersonal ego already has taken sides. In a formula that is luminously simple and that makes a highpoint in the history of psychology, Erwin Straus notes that the openness to the world is "the sense of sense," and that it alone allows us to understand the intermodal communication of sensing. For Merleau-Ponty also, that sense of sense is found in the openness to the world. "Each 'sense' is a 'world' that is absolutely incommunicable to the other senses. Yet, it is constructing a *something* that through its structure is straightaway *open* upon the world of the other senses, and with these senses forms one sole Being" (VI 271/217). "What is proper to the sensible (as to language) is to be representative of the whole, not by a sign-signification relation, or by the immanence of the parts in one another and in the whole, but because each part is *torn up* from the whole, comes with its roots, encroaches upon the whole, transgresses the frontiers of the others" (VI 271/218). Each part, moment, event of the world—the dominant color of a clearing, a field of sunflowers, which is, for Van Gogh, "deep yellow," the sound of a rushing stream, the passing of a person in the distance—"when one takes it for itself, suddenly opens unlimited dimensions—becomes a *total part*" (VI 271/218). The part refers to a depth which is that of everything.

The encroachment—of the perceiving by the perceived, where the appearing of the first is nothing but the modifications of the second—is the most intense that can be, one that is, so to speak infinite. All perception is automovement. We maintain the optical connection with the flight of a butterfly only by movements of the body. V. von Weizsäcker says, "This is the movement that makes the object appear, insofar as the object and its movements appear thanks to the fact that coherence is maintained. Coherence is conserved only under the condition of this series of movements and that gives us the right to call the whole process—to see and to move—*one act*."[17] One act and not two operations. "The movement is not included in the perception as a conditioning factor: the perception *is* auto-movement." The mutual intrication of perception and of movement implies their "reciprocal dissimulation." "By moving myself, I make a perception appear and, by perceiving something, a movement has taken place that is my own. The intrication of the two contains this necessary condition that the activity by which something appears to me does not itself appear; however, on the other hand, insofar as something appears to me, I, myself, am active." Merleau-Ponty brings an ontological foundation to bear upon this relation of uncertainty. What makes visible is not visible; it is an "invisible in principle." The visible and its invisible together are "the pulp of the sensible." "The very pulp of the sensible, what is indefinable in it, is nothing else than the union in it of the 'inside' with the 'outside,' the contact in thickness of self with self—The absolute of the 'sensible' is this stabilized explosion i.e., involving return" (VI 321/268).

The principle of uncertainty is a principle of reversibility. Outside and inside allow neither a third nor middle term. They, themselves, are not "terms" that explicate each other, but each implies the other within it. Simply, they are reversible. "Reversibility ... it suffices that from one side I see the wrong side of the glove that is applied to the right side, that I touch the one *through* the other" (VI 317/263).

Reversibility is the very principle of experience. Perceiving, I am in a situation of "total part" open to the entire world. The reciprocal intrication and dissimulation of the perceptive moment and of the apparitional moment are those of the openness of and openness to the world: essentially insepa- rable and essentially never appearing together. The one is the proper and absolute negative of the other. Even the originary of the negative, by which the depth of the flesh of the world comes to *its* manifestation, is found there.

The circularity, intrinsic to perception, of auto-movement and of ap- pearing means that the perceiving and the world arise together in the same clearing that creates the present in advance of every given moment. Auto- movement alone causes a thing or the structure of the world to appear, be- cause these partial phenomena are not to be considered as positive. They are not "positive *lines* on a neutral *ground* connecting positive *points*" (VI 248/ 230). There is fundamentally only this depth of the world that I haunt under the horizon of my "I can." The most simple perception attests to it. If I fix on a point and then I move my head, on this side of the fixed point the movement of my head produces obvious movements; and beyond the point, the same movement of my head produces other movements in the opposite direction. I do not take seriously these movements that I make appear. This lack of seriousness is not the utterly nonchalant attitude of a world master; it is the flip side of the attitude in that I take the stability of the point seriously, a stability which I maintain by compensating for the oscillations of my head with the movements of the eyes. There, only one single act of overcoming takes place starting from and in view of being-in-the-world. Merleau-Ponty also defines it as transcendence.

"The fixity of the fixed point and the mobility of what is this side of it and beyond it are not partial, local phenomena, and not even a set of phenomena: it is one sole transcendence, one sole graduated series of *diver- gences*—The structure of the visual field, with its near-byes, its far-offs, its horizon is ... the model of every transcendence" (VI 248/231). Turning the transcendence of the thing into the very dimension of its reality, Merleau- Ponty's new Phenomenology of Perception gives another sense to Husserl's ontology and discovers another foundation. These things are not ones that we first perceive, but "the *elements* (*water, air*)," the "rays of the world," things "which are dimensions, which are worlds"; I slide upon these 'elements' and here I am in the *world*. I slide from the "subjective to Being" (VI 271/218). These rays are dimensions of a depth *sui-transitive*, of "radiations [*rayonnement*]." "There are only radiations of (verbal) essences. . . . The sensible thing itself is borne by a transcendence" (VI 313–14/260). This transcendence in which everything has a reason to be is not, of course, an idea; it is the originary unrepresentable. It is through its infinite resistance, through its in principle irreducibility to all representation that the being is. Rooted in the depth, which is the "dimension of the hidden par excellence," things subsist outside of a spectacle. "Depth is the means the things have to remain distinct, to remain things, while not being what I look at, at present" (VI 272/219). The depth is the reserve, which is only appresented, of all the presentations.

Gazes and rays internalize one another, as the "grasped" and as the grasping, in our openness to things. We are grasped by the things in the instant that we grasp them. When Merleau-Ponty says that we first perceive elements—air or water—he situates himself at this primary level, where we are required, grasped by the incomparable modality, at once gratuitous and irrefutable, of a suddenly present element, right in which these unlimited dimensions—liquidity, limpidity, coolness—copenetrate in one sole way of being-there. This experience of "wild being" is *sensing* [*sentir*].

"The sensible is precisely that medium in which there can be *being* without it having to be posited. . . . The silent persuasion of the sensible is Being's unique way of manifesting itself without becoming positivity, without ceasing to be ambiguous and transcendent" (VI 267/214). Ambiguity is as essential to Being as transcendence. This ambiguity is the sign of a divergence: never do the gaze and the ray of the world coincide. "The moment my perception is to become pure perception, thing, Being, it is extinguished; the moment it lights up, already I am no longer the thing. . . . As we never have at the same time the thing and the consciousness of the thing, we never have at the same time the past and the consciousness of the past, and for the same reason: in an intuition by coincidence and fusion, everything one gives to Being is taken from experience, everything one gives to experience is taken from Being" (VI 163/123). The world that understands me, as soon as I understand it, is never fullness. This is where the sensible doubt that Weizsäcker expresses as "Do I see where I am, or am I where I see?" comes from. Merleau-Ponty says, this ambiguity immanent to sense-certainty possesses "an organizing power that is at the foundation of the world of perception."

Merleau-Ponty's definition of transcendence as a "graduated series of divergences" arises again in all its amplitude with this *divergence* between Being and experience (which cannot, however, be opposed to one another). Transcendence and divergence have, in fact, the same gradient just as the depth of being and the nothing of the openness have the same gradient. "All that one gives to Being one takes from experience and all that one gives to experience one takes from Being": this is where the very sense of Being lies, precisely insofar as it makes sense and insofar as it is signified in experience. Its self-presence implies an "irremedial absence," irremedial because its absence is the other side of its presence, implied within its presence.

The best situation for seeing is precisely the one where it seems at first to have total presence. This presence is that of *flesh*, in itself, indefectible and nevertheless in itself implying absence. The revelation of flesh culminates in the caress, where the Being of the flesh and the carnal experience coincide in the felt-Being [*l'être-senti*] of the body of the other which is exactly revealed as flesh. While the tactile exploration of a thing maintains contact with the thing only by renewing the horizon under which the touching is close to the thing—in an alternation of approaches starting from emptiness and turning back to emptiness through distance—the caress is, as Erwin Straus says, an approach without end. In the caress there is not a "beyond" of the other's body starting from which the caress gathers it up, as taking hold of something does. The modifications of the *felt* [*senti*] are connected to one another by sliding, right on felt-Being [*à-même l'être-senti*]. The body of the other insofar as felt does not stop being there. Why then does the caress not stop attempting its approach? Because the unintentional structure of pure contact in the caress shelters from the approach a secret intentionality that inversely tends to be unintentional. According to this intentionality of pure agency from which the caress is suspended, what does the caress intend in its very touching? It intends the *untouchable*: that of the flesh that I will never touch.

The untouchable, and as well the invisible, are an intrinsic dimension of the flesh of the world that I touch and that I see. Merleau-Ponty says that it is the invisible of the world that makes the world visible. The invisible is not added to the visible in order to make with it a total. "The two parts are total parts and yet are not superposable" (VI 177/134). This situation is universal. This situation (which Sartre was experiencing as *en trop*) constitutes the paradox of my presence *to* the world and *in* the world. Merleau-Ponty turns this paradox into the sense of my Being: me, invisible to myself insofar as I see, I am visible insofar as seen, and so that—this is the decisive factor— my seeing assumes my visibility. "He who cannot possess the visible unless he is possessed by it, unless he *is of it*, unless, by principle according to what is required by the articulation of the look with the things, he is one of the visibles, capable, by a singular reversal, of seeing them—he who is one of them" (VI 177–78/134–35). I can see only because I myself am also of this visible world. Visible, I am a part of what is originarily capable of being put on view, a part of what participates with the *Urpräsentierbarkeit*. One of Merleau-Ponty's marginal notes in the "Chiasm" chapter says "*Urpräsentierbarkeit* is flesh." What am I insofar as I am capable of this reversal that makes me something that can see? What must I be in order to see? *Nothing*. This indivisible duality of the flesh of the world and of this nothing, which is its negative, is the ontological dimension of the being.

In a September 1959 working note Merleau-Ponty examines this nothing.

> The perceiving subject, as a tacit, silent *Being-at* [*Etre-à*], which returns from the thing itself blindly identified, which is only a *divergence* with respect to it—the *self* of perception as "nobody," in the sense of Ulysses, as the anonymous one buried in the world, and that has not yet traced its path. Perception as imperception, evidence in non-possession: it is precisely because one knows too well what one is dealing with that one has no need to posit it as an ob-ject. Anonymity and generality. That means: not a *nichtiges Nichts*, but a "lake of non-being," a certain nothingness sunken into a local and temporal *openness*—vision and feeling in fact, and not thought of seeing and of feeling. (VI 254/201)

There is another note that immediately follows this one, in which Merleau-Ponty opens the discussion of the flesh in the same way, and uses the same expression. Merleau-Ponty tries to gain access to it through a perceptual analysis of the cube. But why does Merleau-Ponty choose an object that, all the same, could appear as the most disembodied? This example so often holds Merleau-Ponty's attention, because the transcendence of the thing is shown in its naked and, so to speak, pure state. Merleau-Ponty agrees with Husserl that the transcendence of the thing is its moment of reality but he differs with him on transcendence. In Husserl's sense, the transcendence from the views that I have of the thing to the thing itself is in some way vertical. Consisting of the simultaneity of its six sides, the cube "itself," always given in the sides and never seen altogether, is irreducible to all the perspectives on it. It *is* beyond all its profiles, transcending its mode of appearing; without this "beyond" I would not be able to recognize it as an independent being; it would not be distinguished from a certain multiplicity of conscious lived experiences where it would figure as an index. It *is* therefore only for a gaze without viewpoint, "for an unsituated gaze, for an *operation* or an inspection of mind seating itself at the center of the cube, for a field of *Being*—and everything one can say about the perspectives upon the cube do not concern it" (VI 255/202 emphasis in original).

What is to be taken up from this form of transcendence, which takes note of the infinite divergence between the unilaterality of the perspectives and the integrality of the cube "itself"? What is to be taken up according to Merleau-Ponty is this: "the cube itself *by opposition* to the perspectives—is a negative determination. Here Being is what excludes all non-being, all appearance; the in itself is that is not simply *percipi*. The mind as bearer of this Being is what is nowhere, what envelops every *where*" (VI 255/202). It is not at all certain that this last formula, taken literally, expresses a negative determination. It strangely echoes the "lake of non-being" in the preceding note. In fact, it so liberates this place of "nowhere" from all "being sunk into a place" that it invokes Heidegger's assertion: "the nothing is more original than the 'not' and negation."[18]

What Merleau-Ponty is denouncing here, in a still ambiguous expression, is the ontological primacy of reflexive thought absolutizing its own reflection in the void. We do not learn the real through reflection, but in the wild state. The analysis of the perceived thing—a cube or piece of wax—by reflexive thought consists in a "purification," in a total rarefaction of the sensible that leaves behind the absolute void as a "field for Being." The analysis concludes that we understand through a mental inspection what we believe to see with our eyes. But by doing this it "passes to the side of pre-critical being already there." What is indeed the Being of a cube? "Described by what it is" and no longer "by what it is not," it is the revelation of the flesh. "One has then: an openness upon the cube itself by means of a view of the cube which is a distancing, a transcendence—to say that I have a view of it is to say that, in perceiving it, I go from myself unto it, I go out of myself into it. I, my *view*, are caught up in the same carnal world with it; i.e., my view and my body themselves emerge from the *same* being which is, among other things, a *cube*" (VI 256/202). In contrast to Husserl, one could speak of a horizontal transcendence of flesh to flesh. But my going out into the other, my emergence into the other, is the of same order as our two respective emergences. It is the self-emergence of universal flesh: so these horizontal, or transversal, relations imply a unique vertical transcendence *in depth*. The massive unity of "wild being" would be in turn only a product of reflexive thought, if perception were not originally contemporaneous to it, and if it were not absorbing into itself—such that it lets itself describe—the difficulties and paradoxes of the experience that reflection encounters.

Natural experience is an external experience. It is not external because it is spatial. It is spatial because it is external. "*Consciousness in the mode, giving them-themselv es, precedes* all other modes of consciousness relating to them."[19] The giving of things in external experience is a giving through profiles. Husserl calls them *Abschattungen*, shadows cast, projected from the thing. The thing is given—its style is found there—by giving *views* of itself, of which each calls forth a viewpoint. It is from the thing that this multitude of viewpoints emanates, not from the perceiver who is only one of them. Space is the form of a simultaneity of an infinity of possible viewpoints that can be substituted for one another. The thing is given in its very reserve as an inexhaustible reserve, which is neither the image nor a figurative surface. Its reserve does not consist in a sum or in a system of perspectives or pictures, but in a depth that emerges in each view. Starting from what I see or touch, across this reserve, across this depth, I have access to the hidden parts as if to other entrances that are as real as the parts seen and their perspectives. The cube "itself" is a volumic depth that needs all the resources of art, sculpture, or painting, in order to be rendered *directly sensible* in simultaneity. But, aside from these exceptional resources, I have the experience of such a depth in and through my body.

Merleau-Ponty extends the carnal lesson of my body to the entire world, the carnal lesson that brings with it its being-viewed, its being-touched, its being-felt (*senti*). What does the body teach me about itself? I experience it at once closed in upon itself and exposed to the outside; better still, I experience it being exposed to itself, placing itself outside itself in order to be approached from the inside, enveloped and traversed by the space in which it sees, touches, and hears. Through it and in it I have a view upon a world *in which I am in view* from everywhere. I am in view in my flesh. And because it is flesh, the thing also is in view, is visible. What within the thing appears to me as a givenness through profiles presents itself in me, within my corporeality, as a complete givenness of the thing. Considered by itself, the givenness of the thing is also given completely. In each of its sides, a seer sees the thing itself and sees himself in it. It is in this sense that the seer exists from himself into the thing, while remaining within the same carnal fabric, *even insofar as he is a seer.*"

Here Merleau-Ponty is at his most intense: either the "I," the gaze, is corporeal insofar as saying that it is the flesh, or it is incorporeal in the Stoic sense. Despite the fact that I am feeling [*sentant*] and that the flesh of the world does not feel, our community of sensibles is more radical than this difference. There is a priority of being seen over the seeing. My view, my body, just as much as the cube, participates in the sensible.

> The reflection that qualifies them as subjects of vision is that same dense reflection that makes me touch myself touching, i.e., that *the same* in me be seen and seer: I do not even see myself seeing, but *by encroachment* I complete my visible body, I prolong my being-seen beyond my being-visible for myself. And it is for my flesh, my body of vision, that there can be the cube itself which closes the circuit and completes my own being-seen. It is hence finally the massive unity of Being as the encompassing of myself and of the cube, it is the wild, non-refined, 'vertical' Being that makes there be a cube. (VI 256/202–3)

Merleau-Ponty identifies Being and the being to the point of saying: "there is Being." Yet, what would be more nonsensical, what would go more in the reverse direction of his thought than to define Being and the being as a "what" observable through empirics, as an acquired positivity! The sensible is not the *laying out* of Being for all to see; it is its *manifestation*: the manifestation in which Being "does not cease to be ambiguous and transcendent" (VI 267/214). This ambiguity and this transcendence signifies the intimate duplicity of Being.

"Nothing therefore remains enveloped in its essence; each thing is in relation to others, neighbors."[20] Two different states are not found there.[21] The essence of each thing is the radiation of a depth. Everything possesses the being of this depth; everything, including my body, is a participant in this depth (VI 302/248). Merleau-Ponty's analyses and meditations lead to the level of feeling (*sentir*); they always take feeling back to this pre-predicative evidence: the relation of thing to thing is a relation of flesh to flesh. The relation has its paradigm in the contact of my body with itself: "it touches *itself*, sees *itself*. And consequently, it is capable of *touching or seeing* something, that is, of being open to the things in which (Malebranche) it reads its own modifications" (VI 302/249). "The touching itself, seeing itself of the body . . . is not an act, it is a being at (être à). To touch oneself, to see oneself, accordingly, is not to apprehend oneself as an ob-ject, it is to be open to oneself, destined to oneself (narcissism)" (VI 302–3/249).

But openness is divergence. Being open to oneself "is not to reach oneself, it is on the contrary to escape oneself, the self in question is by divergence, is Unverborgenheit of the Verborgen as such, which consequently does not cease to be hidden or latent—" (VI303/249). This exploding-exploded openness, founding at once proximity and divergence, gives way to the oscillations that resound in Merleau-Ponty's language, which is self-explicating. On the one hand, the feeling body and the felt body are same: "The relation of my body as sensible with my body as sentient (the body I touch, the body that touches) immersion of the being-touched in the touching being and of the touching being in the being-touched" (VI 313/260). On the other hand, they never coincide in experience: "What I see of myself is never exactly the seer, in any case not the seer of the moment" (VI 314/260–61). To get out of the contradiction it is necessary to make experience enter into itself, to resolve it into what it is. Experience is what Being is.

The divergence of touching and touched is the divergence of the same. This "same" does not consist in an identity of pure coincidence. Strictly, the divergence is not noncoincidence in alterity. But the divergence of touching and touched, which are the same, expresses the other dimension of this same which Merleau-Ponty formulates under two forms that mutually explain one another. "The touching is never exactly the touched. This does not mean that they coincide 'in the mind' or at the level of 'consciousness.' Something else than the body is needed for the junction to be made: it takes place in the untouchable. That of the other [d'autrui] which I will never touch." (VI 307/254) and that of me that I will not touch either. The untouchable is not a touchable that is factually inaccessible; it is neither the invisible nor a visible that is out of range. "The experience I have of myself perceiving does not go beyond a sort of imminence, it terminates in the invisible, simply, this invisible is its invisible" (VI 303/249). Between the two, "there is not identity, nor non-identity, or non-coincidence, there is inside and outside turning about one another—" (VI 317/264). "We say therefore that our body is a being of two leaves, from one side a thing among things and otherwise what sees them and touches them" (VI 180/137). However, the metaphors, like Saussurian metaphors of one side and its reverse, risk leading us astray by objectifying the unobjectifiable. Merleau-Ponty comes closest to expressing his thought, his experience, when he defines the untouchable or the invisible as the negative, which is absolutely proper to the touchable or the visible. "The negative here is not a positive that is elsewhere (a transcendent)—It is a true negative . . . in other words, an originary of the elsewhere, a Selbst that is an Other, a Hollow" (VI 308/254).

Flesh carries out the perfect reciprocity of symbolization and concretion. The definition that Merleau-Ponty gives to the symbol is the only one that reveals the secret of its essence, by indicating the sense and the foundation of this unity of power that it is. "Every being can be accentuated as an emblem of Being" (VI 323/270). The constitution of a symbol is "the fixation of a 'character' by investment of the openness to Being in a Being—which, henceforth, takes place through the Being" (VI 323/270). Now flesh is the universal being [l'étant] in which the openness of Being to Being (l'Être à l'Être) universally comes to light: it is the place of the ontological difference. According to Heidegger's ontology, this difference is the absolute divergence between the being (which is blind to its own sense of Being) and the unconcealment of that by which the being is. Merleau-Ponty introduces into the being itself the divergence and the reversibility of the visible and of the invisible. The invisible is an equivalent of nothingness, which for Heidegger is the true name of Being, in which it is a no sent to the being. Merleau-Ponty determines the ontological dimension of the world and my ontological dimension as the invisible of a visible, which is not other than it, but is the other of it.

Merleau-Ponty's philosophy depends less on its convergent analyses than on the fact that the depth-quotient of these analyses depends on a global view of an existing philosopher, who is open right on (à même) his concrete and questioning experience. His affinity with the world (with things, with others, with his own past and with the past of the world) is made less of links than of fibers. His communication belongs to the order of contact; his vision is a palpation. He experiences his participation in the world as if it were one of consubstantiality, as if there was no dualism. But, at the same time he is par excellence the philosopher of interrogation, interrogation being something that wants divergence. When he says "we are standing up in front of the world in a relation of embracing," the embracing refers to the first situation of consubstantiality but the verticality refers to the second of divergence. He has pre-predicative certainty of the world, "of being of it." But here is the question, which is as strong as this certainty: how can I, at once, be of the world and be at the world? How can I be there, in the world in such a way that the world is also there? For if there is the world, this "there" is not in the world.

Without doubt, this "there" is the liminary and ecstatic situation upon the divergence of which the openness, between two adverse poles, of the first philosophical question is produced. Parmenides—whose formula Heidegger takes up in order to say "the miracle of miracles: namely, that the being is"—proclaims that every being, even those that are absent, is in the gaze of the mind, which is simultaneously present: "for you will not cut off what is from holding to what is, in order neither to scatter everywhere in every way according to the order, nor in order to gather everything together."²² But, Parmenides' fragment 16 declares that thought is *one more*, "*to gar pleon esti noêma*."²³ Likewise, Parmenides' fragment 108, "the wise thing is separated from everything," responds to the "all things being one" of Heraclitus's fragment 50.²⁴ The following question bears on the "how" of the revelation of the Being of the being, on the clearing where its explosion breaks through. The very possibility of this question involves that of the question: *who*? Merleau-Ponty responds: *no one (personne)*. "*The I, really, is nobody [personne], is the anonymous.... The named I, the I named [Le Je dénommé, le dénommé Je]*, is an object. The primary I, of which this one is the objectification, is the unknown *to whom* all is given to see or to think, to whom everything appeals, before whom ... there is something. It is therefore negativity—ungraspable in person, of course, since it is *nothing*" (VI 299/246).

"The progress of the inquiry toward the [center] is not the movement ... from the founded unto the Grund: the so-called Grund is Abgrund. But the abyss one thus discovers is not such by lack of ground, it is upsurge ... of a negativity that comes to the world" (VI 303/250). Negativity comes to the world. This expression is ambiguous, belonging to an essential ambiguity. It means at once that negativity comes to pass to the world and that it comes to pass within it. The intertwining is still tighter: negativity comes to pass in the world and it is in negativity that the world comes to pass, that it becomes capable of itself, that it is available to itself according to the dimension that negativity constitutes within it. The sensible, but not sentient, pulp that the world is, has its own negative in the pulp, which constitutes the dimension of felt-Being and perceived-Being in the pulp. "Mind as bearer of this being is what is nowhere, what envelops every where" (VI 255/202). Previously put in the account of reflexive analysis, this formula, suddenly understandable in another sense, is found to express a decisive moment in Merleau-Ponty's thought. This "nowhere" place is no longer a place left empty by the evacuation of the sensible. It is the hollow inverse of the visible, without which there would not have been visibility—no more than there would be music without "music's nihilating hollow." Merleau-Ponty's last phenomenology authentically describes the flesh only insofar as the flesh unconceals what precisely is the condition (which is intrinsic to it) of its unconcealment: namely, the negative. "Negative" has two principal senses where one refers to negation and the other to nothingness. There is no choice here; only the second is originary. "Nothingness is nothing more (nor less) than the invisible" (VI 311/258). "[T]he visible is not an objective positive, the invisible cannot be a negation in the logical sense—" (VI 311/257). "It is a question of a negation-reference (zero . . .) or divergence. This negation-reference is common to all the invisibles because the visible has been defined as dimensionality of Being, i.e., as universal, and because therefore everything that is not a part of it is necessarily enveloped in it and is but a modality of the same transcendence" (VI 311/257).

To be visible is to appear. But, this appearing is not an appearing involving two terms, going from one term to the other—which would turn the appearing itself into a third term, and would lead back to the ternary exteriority held in check by Hegel at the beginning of the Phenomenology of Spirit. The appearing is a simultaneity of absence and presence: their reversibility is the essence. The divergence is what brings and takes with itself the immanent transcendence of the appearing. Flesh opens within itself the field where it takes place. The where envelops everything because it is itself enveloped and is only a "modality of this transcendence." Where is in essence a transpossible. The flesh carries out its own transpossibility or better, its own transpassibility, that is, the very dimension of its sensible Being. It comes to pass by leaving itself, like the depth of a Khmer sculpture right on the face's radiation: "a self-clarifying side."[25] By itself the surface is nothing, but without the surface *there is* no depth, since it lacks the *there* where the flesh can—as people still said in the seventeenth century—"*s'apparaître*."[26]

This situation is nothing but the dimensionality, which involves, which implies a simultaneous crossing from itself into itself. The invisible is *implied* in the visible as temporality is *implied* in the "tense" of verb. It is implied without us having to explicate it in a cosmic time, which is outside, which refers to the present of a *Kosmothereôros*. I am no one. I am inhabited by an anonymous visibility, which is "activity = passivity" (VI 318/265). My openness to the world is a "central nothingness" (VI 317/264), a "day" without a proper "where," a specified void of the openness of the world: *il y a*. Lao-tzu says, "Thirty spokes [rayons] join in a single hub; the emptiness in the chariot permits its usefulness." "Being is what creates advantage, but non-being creates usefulness."[27] At first glance, the resemblance is striking. Here as there, the negative of the visible is its own hollow. "Consciousness of the cock, capacity of the hen—they were the ravine of the world. Being the ravine of the world, they maintain the unity of constant virtue. They had accomplished the return to childhood."[28]

The cock's consciousness, the hen's capacity, reversibles like Yin and Yang: the one is referred to the feeling being (*l'être sentant*), to the *percipere*; the other to the felt being (*l'être senti*), to the *percipi*. The return to childhood is a return to the "unlimited," to the "brute." But this "brute" is not the brute being of which Merleau-Ponty speaks: "the one which also contains its negation, its perceived." In Taoism, in fact, if the reversibility of the passage between Yin and Yang, between *percipere* and *percipi* governs the dynamic law of the Real marked by the full, it is the void that is the functional place where the transformation takes place.[29]

In the thought of Merleau-Ponty, the nothing is really in a sense the functional place of a transformation, if one calls transformation the passage— which is internal to transformation—of flesh to its being-perceived, to its visibility, that is, the *implied* transcendence of the appearing. But in Taoism, the nothing is not one of the two poles of an intrinsic reversibility (as are Yin and Yang): "Things leave from being, being leaves from nothing." Even if this leaving is not becoming but simultaneity, the primacy of the nothing is irrevocably asserted. Despite this difference, the rapprochement with Taoism nevertheless contributes to clarifying one of Merleau-Ponty's major assertions: that flesh is not matter, since it involves dimensionally its own negative. In conclusion, it is still the case for Merleau-Ponty as for Taoism that "activity = passivity," although in Taoism impassibility reigns over activity and passivity without ordering them.

All the relations of the visible and of the invisible converge in the primacy of the *percipi* so that the relation that one might think of first, my body's relation to the world, is inverted: "It is by the flesh of the world that in the last analysis one can understand the lived body—The flesh of the world is of the being-seen, i.e., is a being that is *eminently percipi*, and it is by it that we can understand the *percipere*" (VI 304/250). The primacy of the *percipi* is therefore a law of being, and Merleau-Ponty defines the lived body as "this perceived that we call my body" (VI 304/250). Insofar as it is perceived by itself, my body is perceiving. That is, before being corporeal, my body is flesh holding onto the flesh of the world with which it can participate.

The element of the flesh excludes solipsism, which is in advance foreclosed. It liberates the question of the other from the impasse where it is stuck. The impasse is caused by the reflection that, in order to justify the *position* of others, breaks it down in two moments condemned never to join back up: autoposition of an incomparable ego, solitary sovereign of an egological world, and recognition of other egos and of their world, which I should recognize by leaving myself, therefore by losing knowledge . . . and recognition. Husserl had made the constitution of the other the keystone to the constitution of the world and made its paradoxical allure entirely clear:

> This sphere, the sphere of my transcendental ego's *primordial owness*, must contain the *motivational foundation* for the constitution of those *transcendencies* that are *genuine*, that go beyond it, and originate first of all as "others."[30]

For Merleau-Ponty the question is not in the proper sense transcendental. It is not a question of the *constitution* of the other. On this side of all motivated justification, others are understood in the depth of the world in which I have an openness. If what I see or touch is not only a private world but a world whose anonymous visibility inhabits me, therefore visible and palpable for others inhabited by the same visibility, "what is proper to the visible is to be the surface of an inexhaustible depth: this is what makes it able to be open to visions other than our own" (VI 188/143). "There is here no problem of the *alter ego* because it is not *I* who sees, not *he* who sees, because an anonymous visibility inhabits both of us, a vision in general, in virtue of that primordial property that belongs to the flesh, being here and now, of radiating everywhere and forever, being an individual, of being also a dimension and a universal" (VI 187/142).

The reciprocity of the open lanes (*voies*) within the flesh holds the place that the relation of reciprocal expression of perspectives on the world occupies in Leibniz's philosophy. All of Leibniz's theses concerning the correspondence of the monads—"that each of the views of the world is a world apart, that nonetheless 'what is particular to one would be public to all,' that the monads would be in a relation of expression between themselves and with the world, that they differ from one another and from it as perspectives" (VI 276/222–23)—are, Merleau-Ponty says, to be conserved entirely. However, Merleau-Ponty no longer situates the reason and the origin of the reciprocal expression within God and, instead, he turns it into the dimension of the *in der Welt Sein*. Thus, it is confirmed that the relation to the world, in Merleau-Ponty, is before all else participation. He understands the word "participation" in Szondi's sense: originary projection. "The originary dimension of the ego," says Szondi, "is participation. It is the function that realizes all the integrations between self and world."[31] Through this operation, which transfers to the other all the power of which the world is only the repartitioner, the other "becomes both, that is, all and thereby all powerful."[32] The other is he and I and the whole. By substituting for Leibniz's God the flesh of the world, "pregnant with all possibles" (VI 262/208), exploding from it within it, Merleau-Ponty recognizes in the flesh a matrilineal status and confers to wild Being the radiating passivity of the *percipi*.

❀

It is the error of the semantic philosophies to close up language as if it spoke only of itself: language lives only from silence.

—Merleau-Ponty, *The Visible and the Invisible*

Merleau-Ponty's demanding meditation concerning the Being of the World is accompanied by a meditation on the Being of language. In the *Phenomenology of Perception* this unshakeable conviction is asserted, that language is not only a statement of significations, but that to speak is to say something . . . something of which we can have direct access in the experience of "this consciousness that we are" (PP x/xv); "it is on the basis of this experience that all linguistic connotations are assessed." Without doubt it is true that language calls "separated essences" and ideal objectivities to themselves. It makes them exist "through the combination of words. . . . I form the transcendental attitude, I constitute the constitutive consciousness" (VI 225/171). But this separation of essences is only apparent since, by language, "it joins back to the pre-predicative life of consciousness." "In the silence of primary consciousness can be seen appearing not only what words mean, but also what things mean: the core of primary meaning round which the acts of naming and expression take shape" (PP x/xv). Finally, "it is the experience . . . still mute which we are concerned with leading to the pure expression of its own meaning."[33]

But what can language be in a phenomenology that no longer adopts the perspective of consciousness? And especially, what can language be when the experience it describes is not only mute but enigmatic? If being is enigmatic what saying will communicate it? It is no longer a question of stating a thesis. "Speech can no longer be statement, *Satz*, if it is to remain dialectical [and not thesis, "embalmed dialectic"]; it must be thinking speech, without reference to a *Sachverhalt*, speaking [*parole*] and not language [*langage*]" (VI 229/175). Language [*langage*] is the application of linguistic systems while speech is the founder of such systems. Speech has the same originarity as the *declared* being of the world. Nonetheless, rather than being attached to the explosion of this declaration, Merleau-Ponty is attached to the communicative dimension of speech. Speech "aims at others as a behavior . . . that responds to others before he would have been understood as 'psychism,' in a confrontation that repels or accepts his utterances as utterances, as events" (VI 229/175). This level of language, where speech is effective uttering, is conserved in Chinese. The Chinese word, the monosyllable, does not correspond to a concept, nor is it a sign holding its function and the value of its position in a diacritical system. But—as Marcel Granet says—"it retains the whole imperative energy of the act . . . of which it is the emblem."[34] An emblem involves a divergence; this is the divergence, among others, that makes another's uttered speech appear to me to be meaningful—the lacunae of the other never being mine. Moreover, my own speech is not ruled by a signification over which I would be the absolute master. "Speech constitutes *in front of* me a milieu of signification" (VI 229/175). *"In front* of me," this means outside of my possession. The speaking subject "does not hold before itself the words said and understood as objects of thought or ideates" (VI 255/201). In speech, he is preceding himself, as if he is in the place where he is heading—"that is: it is a certain lack of . . . such or such a signifier, which does not construct the *Bild* of what it lacks" (VI 255/201). This lack of speech makes speech be a saying not a said, a saying headed toward an unavoidable *à dire*,[35] which is irreducible to every thematic signification; it is as deep as the flesh.

The speaking speech implies in its very being an essential inadequation that gives it its truth. It can hold being only if it shares its enigma. Since "the silent persuasion of the [world] is Being's unique way of manifesting itself without becoming positivity" (VI 267/214), a silence that envelopes speech would be necessary. Silence is there to make us hear, as Claude Lefort says; speech is between two silences and as it goes from one to the other speech does not abolish silence. Silence is the horizon and the depth of speech. Speech and silence are reversible like the visible and the invisible. Their reversibility is the essence of the saying.

This operative language "which counts as an arm, as action, as offense and as seduction because it brings to the surface all the deep-rooted relations of the lived experience wherein it takes form . . . is an absolutely universal theme of philosophy" (VI 167/126). But it is also its language, transformed within itself by philosophy, insofar as, by the insistence of its self-interrogation, philosophy turns this utterance into an articulation. "That language that can be known only from within, through its exercise, is open upon the things, called forth by the voices of silence, and continues an effort of articulation which is the Being of every being" (VI 168/126–27).

Philosophy exists in its speech, and philosophy exists from speech. The speech of a philosopher is one specific manifestation of the ambiguous sense of the logos. "Give speech to the mute world," this task of the poet, of which Francis Ponge speaks, is also the philosopher's task. For both, things and words say and say themselves according to Plato's expression in the *Cratylus*. But words signify things to themselves only in the divergence. "In a sense, the signification is always the divergence: what others say appears to me to be full of meaning because his *lacunae* are never where mine are" (VI 241/ 187). This comment holds also in regard to world. There is always and everywhere a reserve of divergence, a moment of this universal divergence that makes ambiguous transcendence of being. The *logos* of the world is not the *logos* of anyone [*personne*] and the philosophical logos is not an intepretation of the world by me nor by man. Instead, it is a revelation of Being in man, a revelation right in an open passivity.

"*The visisble* has to be described as something that is realized through man, but which is nowise anthropology. . . . Logos also as what is realized in man, but nowise as his *property*" (VI 328/274). These two obligations converge: the philosophical logos is the becoming visible of the invisible. This *apophansis* that is the *legein* (in opposition to the Stoics) is a form of *phainesthai*, of the universal appearance that is the immanent transcendance of Being. As Plato says in the *Sophist*, the *apophansis* is a *deloun*: a declarative clearing. The intervention of speech in wild Being accomplishes the visibility of the invisible. This is what Merleau-Ponty's final philosophy was searching for; such is the lesson he left behind. To a person who wants to be a philosopher, Merleau-Ponty makes the same recommendation as Cézanne makes to someone who wants to be a painter: "all his will must be made of silence" . . . of a silence right in a speech that makes this silence be heard. His philosophy is a transphyiscs in which the ambiguous transcendence of *physis* has no other accomplishment than its manifestation. The interrogation that his philosophy has put on the road "in order to come to one of its sides as to me, the mute" counts in the flesh of the world as an ambiguity in the sudden divergence of significations.

NOTES

This essay was translated from the French by Claire E. Katz. It first appeared as "Chair et verbe dans la philosophie de M. Merleau-Ponty" in *Maurice Merleau-Ponty: Le psychique et le corporel,* ed. Anna-Teresa Tymieniecha (Paris: Aubier, 1988), pp. 55–83, © Aubier, Paris, 1988.

1. Rilke, Sonnets to Orpheus, (poem 1 of part 2). M. D. Herter Norton from W. W. Norton and Co. (New York, 1962), p. 71.

2. *"Le convoi est bloqué: j'ai rejoint. Pourtant l'interrogation philosophique intervient: faille originelle."* These sentences refer above to the opening paragraph where Maldiney speaks of Merleau-Ponty's aim as being the determination of the horizon within which the innocence of being and the risk of Being are joined together again. In these sentences, Maldiney is using the word *convoi* literally to suggest the joined (the *con*) ways or lanes—*les voies*—between the *l'étant* and *l'être*. His use of *rejoint* refers to Heidegger's term *"Fuge,"* which is normally rendered in French (and in English) as *jointure*. The idea here is that Being and being—"the convoy"—are "blocked" from joining together: I am what joins them together again; I am the jointure. *However*—we have added this italics to emphasize the contrast with the previous sentence—philosophical interrogation intervenes and blocks the lanes between being and Being: the original fault between or breaking up of the jointure that I am. In other words—to use more Merleau-Pontian terminology—I am the link between eye and mind (or between perception and thinking); however, when I reflect philosophically on this link, then its operation is disrupted, blocked. See below where Merleau-Ponty speaks of lanes in connection with Lao-Tzu. (Note composed by Leonard Lawlor with the help of Valentine Moulard).

3. Martin Heidegger, *Vom Wesen des Grundes,* (Hallé: Max Niemeyer, 1929), p. 20/21.

4. Sigmund Freud, "Negation," *The Complete Works of Sigmund Freud,* vol. 9 (Toronto: Hogarth Press, 1961), p. 237.

5. G. W. F. Hegel *Phenomenology of Spirit,* trans. A. V. Miller, p. 35 (Oxford: Clarendon Press, 1977), emphasis Maldiney.

6. Emmanuel Kant, *Opus postumum,* vol. 21:31 (Cambridge: Cambridge University Press, 1993), p. 235.

7. Martin Heidegger, *Being and Time,* trans. John Macquarrie and Edward Robinson (New York: Harper and Row, 1962), p. 35/39.

8. Edmund Hussert, *Formal and Transcendental Logic,* trans. by Dorion Cairns (The Hague: Martinus Nijhoff, 1969), p. 238/211.

9. Ibid., p. 251/222.

10. Emmanuel Levinas, *En découvrant l'existence avec Husserl et Heidegger* (Paris: Vrio, 1967), p. 133.

11. Husserl, *Formal and Transcendental Logic,* p. 251/222.

12. Levinas, *En decouvrant l'existence,* p. 132.

13. Ibid., p. 132.

14. Ibid., p. 120.

15. *Rayon* also means "spoke" (Lao-tsu) *Trans.*

16. Eugen Fink, *Problèms actuels de la phénoménologie* (Brussels: Desclée de Brouwer, 1952), p. 70–1.

17. Viktor von Weizsäcker, *Der Gestaltkreis* (Frankfort am Main: Suhrkamp, 1997), p. 9.

18. Martin Heidegger, "What Is Metaphysics," *Basic Writings,* ed. David Farrell Krell (San Francisco: Harper, 1993), p. 97.

19. Husserl, *Formal and Trancendental Logic,* p. 209/185–86.

20. Fink, *Problèms actuels de la phénoménologie,* pp. 70–1.

21. Cf. Husserl, *Formal and Transcendental Logic* (Gr. 254, Fr. 381. Eng. 288).

22. Parmenides, frag. 4. See Kirk, Raven, and Shofield *The Presocratic Philosophers* (Cambridge: Cambridge University Press, 1957), p. 262.

23. "For what preponderates is thought." Parmenides, frag. 16, in ibid., p. 261.

24. "Listening not to me but to the Logos it is wise to agree that all things are one." Heraclitus, frag. 50, in ibid., 187.

25. André de Bouchet, *Langue, déplacements, jours* (Paris: Cliveges 1978).

26. Maldiney is referring to an archaic reflexive use of the verb "apparaître." See the entry for "apparaître" in the Littré. The reflexive use of this verb would be rendered in English roughly as "appears itself," like "shows itself." *Trans.*

27. Lao-tzu, chap. 11, in Francois Cheng, *Empty and Full,* trans. Michael H. Kohn (Boston: Shambhala, 1994), p. 48.

28. Lao-tzu, chap. 28, in ibid., p. 47.

29. Cheng, *Empty and Full,* p. 56.

30. Husserl, *Formal and Transcendental Logic,* p. 213/241.

31. L. Szondi, *Ich-analyse* (Bern: H. Huber, 1956), p. 35.

32. Ibid., p. 178.

33. Edmund Husserl, *Cartesian Meditations,* trans. Dorion Cairns (The Hague: Nijhoff, 1960), pp. 38–9.

34. Marcel Granet, *La Pensée chinoise, rééd* (Paris: Albin Michel, 1974), p. 38.

35. With the phrase "à dire"—which resembles "avenir"—Maldiney is speaking of a future saying. *Trans.*

CHAPTER 3

Perception and Movement:
The End of the Metaphysical Approach

RENAUD BARBARAS

The purpose of the *Phenomenology of Perception* is to describe the perceived world, as it appears beneath the idealizations of objective thought, whether empiricist or intellectualist. To this end, Merleau-Ponty tries to return to the true meaning of the perceiving subject: it is not an intellectual subject before which the world is spread out in a transparent way, but an embodied subject opening onto a transcendent world. Thus, in Merleau-Ponty's work, the phenomenological reduction takes the shape of a critique of reflexive thought, relying on the results of Gestalt psychology and Goldstein's physiology.

However, as Merleau-Ponty himself admits in *The Visible and the Invisible*, the viewpoint of the *Phenomenology of Perception* turned out to be inadequate. In fact, what is in question is not the results themselves, that is, the discovery of an original layer of experience, but the way in which they are interpreted: "Results of *Ph.P.*—Necessity of bringing them to ontological explicitation" (VI 237/183). At the time of the *Phenomenology of Perception*, Merleau-Ponty considered being-in-the-world as an embodied *consciousness*: the perceiving subject is immediately interpreted as a consciousness and therefore, the body is finally understood as the "mediator of the world" for this consciousness. The relevant opposition is between a reflexive, or intellectual consciousness, and an embodied one. Yet, in *The Visible and the Invisible*, Merleau-Ponty criticizes the use of this category: "The problems posed in *Ph.P.* are insoluble because I start there from the 'consciousness'-'object' distinction" (VI 253/200). There is no doubt that the insufficiency of the interpretation of the *Phenomenology of Perception*'s results is due to the use of this classical opposition. It appears that the fact of interpreting being-in-the-world and, hence, perception, as the activity of an embodied consciousness, amounts to missing the openness upon the world, the givenness (*donation*) of a transcendence that characterizes perceptual life.

In other words, Merleau-Ponty realizes little by little that the critique he has addressed to the philosophy of reflection concerns any philosophy that relies on the concept of consciousness, Husserlian phenomenology included, and, therefore, that this kind of philosophy refers to a more general and more concealed ontological position. Since the recourse to the concept of consciousness prevents us from properly interpreting the results of the *Phenomenology of Perception*, a genuine philosophy of perception requires the disclosure and the uprooting of the ontological prejudice, which governs every philosophy of consciousness.

In order to understand the movement, which leads from the *Phenomenology of Perception* to Merleau-Ponty's final ontology, I would like to show that this ontological prejudice is rooted in a metaphysical attitude, the characterization and critique of which are borrowed from Bergson. This critique leads to a far more radical interpretation of the phenomenological reduction, a new meaning of the being of the world and, consequently, an original characterization of the essence of perception.

Merleau-Ponty's research after the *Phenomenology of Perception* leads him to emphasize an essential relation between the philosophy of consciousness, whether empiricist or intellectualist, and a usually implicit ontology, which Merleau-Ponty sometimes calls "ontology of the object." From that moment, the relevant opposition for him is not the opposition between a philosophy of reflexive consciousness and a philosophy of embodied consciousness, but between an ontology of the object—to which both of these philosophies refer—and a new kind of ontology, which he must delineate.

This point arises clearly in the chapter entitled "Interrogation and Intuition" as well as in the outline entitled "Preobjective Being: the Solipsist World." This text is particularly illuminating, even if Merleau-Ponty would probably not have kept it. In both of these passages, Merleau-Ponty attempts to define the conditions of a return to perceptual experience, which is required to clarify his own position with regard to phenomenology. This implied a critique of Husserl's conception of essence, which is developed in "Interrogation and Intuition": in short, he shows that phenomenology succeeds in overcoming the natural attitude by changing the beings into their meaning but is mistaken in defining the meaning itself as *essence*, namely, as something fully positive and clearly determined, a plenitude attainable by an intellectual intuition. However, the aim of this passage is not to discuss the first phase of Husserl's work but to show that the core, and also the limit, of phenomenology is the decision to define Being as essence. For objective ontology, the presence of the present thing means the presentation of the thing *itself*: to say that an entity is present amounts to saying that it is given as a positive entity, a plenitude that absorbs, as it were, perceptual presence. In other words, we can perceive something provided that we grasp its essence through the appearance. Thus if it is true that perception implies the intuition of the essential features, the "resistant and stable structure" of the perceived object, perception is synonymous with *knowledge*.

Moreover, insofar as the phenomenological meaning of the perceived thing is the presentation of its own essence, it is necessary to posit a consciousness in front of which the presentation presents, in which the essence rests. The nature of the meaning is the essence, but the condition of the essence, which is also the location of this essence, is consciousness as positive being. A being whose meaning consists in being exposed to full view is dependent on a being whose identity is sight throughout, in other words, a consciousness. Conversely, to approach experience from consciousness implies that the object of this experience is described as essence. As Merleau-Ponty notes, "concepts such as 'subject,' 'consciousness,' 'self-consciousness,' 'mind' . . . involve the idea of a *res cogitans*, of a positive being of thought— whence there results the immanence in the unreflected of the results of reflection" (VI 104/74). The characterization of Being as presentation of the essence is related to the definition of the transcendental as *re-presentation*.

At this point, Merleau-Ponty's path crosses Bergson's. Just as phenomenology, and, broadly speaking, philosophy of consciousness, rests on the primacy of essence, this primacy itself refers to a metaphysical decision that Bergson explicates in *Creative Evolution*. To elaborate a philosophy in which duration is the fabric of reality requires that one understand why philosophy has always tended to consider Becoming as inferior to Being. According to Bergson, the invisible motor of metaphysics lies in the notion of nothingness. In fact, it is a peculiarity of metaphysics that it approaches Being from nothingness, presupposing that each particular existence emerges from nothingness and, therefore, requires a sufficient reason. According to Bergson, the disdain in which metaphysics holds duration comes from the fact that this kind of existence does not appear strong enough to overcome inexistence and posit itself. On the contrary, it is a peculiarity of logical being that it is necessary, in such a way that it cannot not be: since it is impossible for this kind of being to have begun to exist, the question of the reason for its existence cannot even be posed. Thus, metaphysics does not characterize Being from itself but from what, in it, is able to resist nothingness; Being, as it were, needs the plenitude, the positivity of essence, to surmount the threat of nothingness. Being is entirely *what* it is, fully and clearly determined, for the slightest insufficiency, the slightest lack of determination, would entail its absorption by nothingness.

Such is the interpretation of the history of metaphysics that grounds Merleau-Ponty's critique of phenomenology and makes the step toward ontology possible. Indeed, Merleau-Ponty's main objection against Husserl is that, in order to reach the *eidos* and have a positive intuition of it, it would be necessary to be located in nothingness: "in order to really reduce an experience to its essence, we should have to achieve a distance from it that would put it entirely under our gaze, with all the implications of sensoriality or thought that come into play in it, bring it and bring ourselves wholly to the transparency of the imaginary, think it without the support of any ground, in short, withdraw to the bottom of nothingness" (VI 149–150/111). The characterization of transcendental life as consciousness, the definition of Being as essence, and the fact of "withdrawing to the bottom of nothingness" are three expressions of the same metaphysical attitude. Likewise, in the unfinished last chapter, Merleau-Ponty denounces the starting point in nothingness as the root of objectivism and, therefore, as the main obstacle standing in the way of a return to the perceived world: "starting with things taken in their native sense as identifiable nuclei, but without any power of their own, we arrive at the thing-object, at the In-itself, at the thing identical with itself, only by imposing upon experience an abstract dilemma which experience ignores," but, Merleau-Ponty comments, "the thing thus defined is not the thing of our experience, it is the image we obtain of it by projecting it into a universe where experience would not settle on anything, where the spectator would abandon the spectacle—in short, by confronting it with the possibility of nothingness" (VI 215/162).

There is no doubt that the recourse to the principle of sufficient reason, which grounds the metaphysical tradition, appears as the ultimate foundation of the definition of Being as essence and, therefore, as the ultimate foundation of the philosophy of consciousness. Thus, Bergson's interpretation of the history of metaphysics enables Merleau-Ponty to grasp in greater depth the meaning of the natural attitude. It does not merely consist in the naive posit of a world in itself; in fact, the attitude that consists in silhouetting Being against nothingness supports this posit of a world submitted to the teleology of reason. It follows that the phenomenological reduction has to approach Being *directly*, without a detour through nothingness. The move toward ontology in Merleau-Ponty is a step taken from a philosophy that silhouettes Being against nothingness—an attitude underlying all philosophies of consciousness—to a philosophy that begins with Being. In other words, it is a move from a philosophy of the positive thing to a philosophy of *something*. The phenomenological reduction is no longer a neutralization of the existence thesis, but, indeed, a neutralization of nothingness as a precondition of this thesis.

The convergence between Merleau-Ponty and Bergson ends here. Indeed, in Bergson's work, duration is defined as continuity and heterogeneity: he stresses the fact that, consequently, duration is devoid of negativity, is a substantial entity that has as much ontological dignity as the *eidos* did for classical metaphysics. However, by attributing the positivity that characterized logical being to duration, he changes the *content* of Being, but does not change its *meaning*. Even if he criticizes the fact of positing nothingness before Being, he maintains the classical concept of Being as what cannot include any negativity, as what eminently *is*. In this sense, Bergson draws the wrong conclusion from a very profound insight. The justification of the definition of Being as pure positivity, as essence, was the fact that it was supposed to overcome nothingness; therefore, considered in a direct way, without the mediation of nothingness, *Being can include an element of negativity*. The positivity of Being is, as it were, proportional to the nothingness from which it emerges: thus, a being that does not have to resist nothingness does not possess the positivity required by this difficult birth. From this standpoint, Bergson's thought is part of the metaphysical tradition that he himself criticizes.

Merleau-Ponty did not miss this apparent contradiction in Bergson and hints at it in an unpublished note: "Bergson is right in his critique of the idea of nothingness. He is simply wrong not to say or see that the being which fills up nothingness is not the entity."[1] On the contrary, Merleau-Ponty accepts the consequences of Bergson's critique of nothingness. Since the only justification for the positivity of Being was the arbitrary posit of nothingness as what Being had to overcome, an ontology that acknowledges the immediate presence of Being is bound to accept that the meaning of Being includes negativity. He tries to show this with, for example, the following statement: "against the philosophy of the thing and the philosophy of the idea. Philosophy of 'something'—something and not nothing."[2] Being is not something fully positive, a plenitude; it is not nothing in the sense that it is just something other than being nothing: *there is* something and nothing else. As Merleau-Ponty notes in *The Visible and the Invisible*, "what is not nothing is *something*, but: this something is not hard as a diamond, not unconditioned, *Erfahrung*" (VI 146n/109n). "There is not nothing" does not mean Being is a negation of nothingness but, rather, that Being is a pure presence, a "there is" that as such is not yet a definite thing and, in this sense, is a negation of essence. In short, this "something" rigorously signifies the impossibility of an ontological void.

Nevertheless, this negative dimension does not have anything to do with "positive nothingness," which is opposed to Being and "filled up" with it. This negativity, which is not based on nothingness, lies within Being and, ultimately, is not different from its very presence. It precisely designates Being's presence as long as this presence *implies an essential distance*. Negativity here is synonymous with the invisibility inherent in the visibility of the visible. Besides, this is perhaps the only relevant way of giving meaning to the notion of nothingness; as Merleau-Ponty says in an unpublished note, "true nothingness, nothingness which is true, is Being as distant and as not hidden (that is, hidden as well)."[3] Anyway, by going through nothingness, classical metaphysics reaches an abstract notion of Being, which finally refers to an intellectual and objectivist attitude, that of the scientist. In contrast to this approach, Merleau-Ponty's critique of the way of thinking of metaphysics enables him to specify the meaning of Being that characterizes perceptual presence. Thus, to a certain extent, the detour through metaphysics and those speculations that seem so removed from a return to the things themselves play the role of a *phenomenological reduction*. In fact, we should say ontological reduction, for Merleau-Ponty explains that the opacity that is peculiar to the perceived world is no longer a consequence of consciousness embodiment but *a feature of Being itself*. The classical conception of perception attributed the opacity, the depth of the perceived world to its dependence on organs of sense, that is, to consciousness embodiment. This is the reason why perception was considered an inferior mode of knowledge, the mere expression of our finitude, as, for example, in Descartes. Likewise, the fact of referring perception to consciousness, as he does in the *Phenomenology of Perception*, leads Merleau-Ponty to interpret the obscurity of the perceived world as the negation of a possible transparence, of an attainable knowledge. On the contrary, in *The Visible and the Invisible*, the withdrawal of the perceived world is interpreted as an essential feature of Being, which is part of its way of existing. Thus, strictly speaking, it is not because we are embodied consciousnesses that the perceived world is distant; it is rather because perceived being implies an essential distance that our experience is partly obscure, that is, embodied. The finitude of experience is founded on the transcendence of the perceived world or, rather, both of these dimensions are expressions of the same ontological event. In addition, insofar as our finitude is rooted in the transcendence of Being, it cannot be overcome and, consequently, does not involve any negation.

Thus, the transcendence of the perceived world is not a measurable and, therefore, reducible distance between the perceiving subject and the perceived thing: this distance, beneath any measure whatsoever, belongs to Being and is, in a way, an inner distance. Transcendence does not qualify a relation to the subject but, indeed, the way of being of the perceived thing. Consequently, we should say that it is because the perceived thing is intrinsically distant—that is, exists as transcendence—that it makes possible a relation with a perceiving subject: this relation and, thus, the terms of the subject/ object relation, arise from transcendence as the perceived world's way of existing. In other words, it is a "pure transcendence, without an ontic mask" (VI 283/229), namely, a transcendence that does not refer to a transcendent thing. It is no longer the synonym of spatial exteriority but the very element of the perceived world, its own way of appearing: "we have to pass from the thing . . . as identity, to the thing . . . as difference, i.e. as transcendence, i.e. as always 'behind,' beyond, far-off" (VI 249/195). Moreover, it is only by interpreting transcendence in this manner that its ireducibility can be preserved: transcendence is irreconcilable with existence in-itself, for if existence were in-itself it could be attained and thus transcendence would be abolished. But for the same reason, it is also impossible to refer it to a consciousness. As Merleau-Ponty comments in another unpublished note:

"the being-distant of the perceived. It is not something transcendent since, in principle, it is out of the question to posit it out of its own distance, in itself or for itself."[4] The transcendence of the perceived world lies beneath the opposition between objective and conscious existence: it is not objective and, *to that extent*, it is not referred to a consciousness. However, the sensible world's depth involves a subjective way of existing, for that distance is the only way for it to *appear as sensible*. Consciousness is opposed to objective existence but, on the other hand, pure transcendence is the same as sensible appearing (*apparaître*): Being is revealed by its own distance. It is in this sense that Merleau-Ponty often emphasizes that it is qua visible and with a view toward its visibility that the perceived is invisible as well. Transcendence is not a negation but a condition of manifestation.

In other words, transcendence or ontological distance is *the form of sensible presence*: to appear means to appear at a distance. Of course, it is a form in a very specific sense since instead of referring to the finitude of subjectivity, it is part of the content that appears and, to a certain extent, its own being. Rather, its form is what gives rise to a subjectivity in the sense that it is the essence of appearing (*l'apparaître*). Here, Merleau-Ponty overcomes the deep-rooted difference between sensible quality and space: in the original understanding of a pure transcendence, the givenness of space is the same as the perception of a sensible quality. Indeed, we could express the sensible presence by saying it is *there* (*là*); the opacity of this "there" really constitutes the originary meaning of transcendence. Yet, it is not there because it is distant: it is distant because it is there. Thus, the being-sensible of the sensible is a foundation, an unfolding of an original space that is not yet geometrical. That is the reason why it is possible to say as well that the sensible is a presentation of transcendence as such, so that we can state too that it is *the form of ontological transcendence*: as Merleau-Ponty says, "the sensible is precisely that medium in which there can be *being* without it having to be posited; the sensible appearance of the sensible, the silent persuasion of the sensible is Being's unique way of manifesting itself without becoming positivity, without ceasing to be ambiguous and transcendent" (VI 267/214).

Finally, here Merleau-Ponty radically takes account of Husserl's statement according to which transcendence is the essential (eidetic) characteristic of the perceived thing: even for the sight of God, the perceived thing gives itself in sketches, in other words, in an incomplete way. But in Husserl, there is a form of contradiction between that claim and the fact of maintaining the theoretical framework of the object. The sketches disclose an object and even if they are inexhaustible, there is a Kantian Idea of a clear and exhaustive possession of the object, which would finally dissolve transcendence. As opposed to this position, Merleau-Ponty emphasizes, thanks to Bergson, that the essential transcendence of the world can be preserved on the condition that the objectivist way of thinking is given up. For Husserl, perception remains a relation of manifestation between the sensible data and the thing, called *noema*; this relation is performed by a transcendental consciousness and relies on subjective acts. On the contrary, Merleau-Ponty brings to the fore *the relation of manifestation itself*, as the primitive meaning of perceived being: the *reference* of every sketch to the infinite series of other sketches— namely, *the structure of the horizon*—is for Merleau-Ponty the very meaning of Being. The horizon is not "a system of potentiality of consciousness: it is a new type of being" (VI 195/149). Thus, however strange it may seem, the perceived thing is nothing but the movement of transcendence from the sketch to the noema, that is, its own appearing, or its own withdrawal. The perceived thing is no longer what is sketched but the very moment of sketching. This amounts to saying that, like Husserl's sketch, which both gives and conceals the object, the disclosure of the thing is also its disappearance. The perceived appearance merges into the background against which it stands out: it is an identity of transparence and opacity. "Transcendence," Merleau-Ponty writes, "is identity within difference" (VI 279/225), and, consequently, is not different from nothingness, defined by Merleau-Ponty as "difference between identicals" (VI 316/ 263).

What are the consequences of this new approach to transcendence? In the classical account—which was to a certain extent that of the *Phenomenology of Perception*—the starting point was the consciousness that was in charge, as it were, of the appearance and, therefore, gave the object by means of its *eidos*: thus, it inevitably missed the dimension of transcendence. The great progress made in *The Visible and the Invisible* was the realization that the specificity of perceived being, well described in the *Phenomenology of Perception*, ushers in a new meaning of Being. Consequently, in order to account for the perceived world it becomes necessary to accomplish an ontological reform. The perceived is not based on perception as a conscious act: on the contrary, perception is dependent on the perceived being. Perception is, in a way, a moment of Being, proceeding from its inner "distantiation" (*écart*), its essential transcendence: "the flesh of the world is of the being-seen, i.e. is a Being that is *eminently percipi*, and it is by it that we can understand the *percipere*," and, Merleau-Ponty adds, "all this is finally possible and means something only because *there is* Being, not Being in itself, identical to itself, in the night, but the Being that also contains its negation, its *percipi*" (VI 304/ 250–51). Thus conscious being is no longer the condition of the perceived as a phenomenal layer; it is rather the perceived as Being that allows us to account for consciousness as phenomenon. Whereas for the classical viewpoint, the positivity of the object, as essence, was related to a consciousness as positive being, in Merleau-Ponty, subjectivity *takes over the negativity* that characterizes perceived being as transcendence. Consciousness is really "a Self-presence which is an *absence from oneself*, a contact with self *through* the divergence (*écart*) with regard to Self" (VI 246/192), and consequently an absence of Self. The moment of experience, namely subjectivity, refers to the "difference" or "distantiation" (*écart*) that characterizes the perceptual transcendence and nothing else. As Merleau-Ponty states, in a very radical way, "the for-itself itself as an incontestable, but derived, characteristic: it is the culmination of separation (*écart*) in *differentiation*—Self-presence *is* presence to a differentiated world. . . . To be conscious—to have a figure on a ground—one cannot go back any further" (VI 245/191).

Nevertheless, this is not sufficient. I have criticized the positivity of consciousness and shown that the subjective moment is dependent on Being's structure as transcendence. In this way, we have really overcome the transcendental viewpoint that considers the world as constituted by consciousness. But the fact remains that there is a perceiving being whose meaning has to be clarified. In other words, we have to deal with the meaning of the being of embodied consciousness, knowing that it is neither a consciousness nor an objective body. The question concerns the being of subjectivity as *essentially* embodied, for subjectivity accomplishes phenomenalization insofar as it is on the side of the world, rooted in it. Thus subjectivity is a negativity in the sense that it is not an entity supporting the "appearing" (*l'apparaître*) of the world, but an openness onto a transcendence. However, on the other hand, it remains impossible to define subjectivity as pure nothingness, as Sartre did. A subjectivity of this kind, as Merleau-Ponty showed at length, would not change anything in relation to the philosophy of essence: the perceived world's meaning would be missed because it would be reduced to a mere in-itself. Sartre's thought is an abstract reconstitution of the relation between consciousness and Being and not a true contact with the perceived world. In fact, subjective negativity includes some positivity in the sense that it is a *concrete* subjectivity. Instead of reducing, in a very abstract fashion, subjectivity to nothingness, we must ask the following question: of what does the kind of positivity of subjective negativity consist, what is the concrete way of existing of a consciousness defined as absence of Self? In short, what kind of being is likely to perform the openness of the world, to be the carrier of a pure transcendence without being transcendent, and lastly to reconcile transcendence in the subjective meaning and transcendence as exteriority?

I commented above that the sensible is essentially distant, for transcendence is the very form of its presence qua sensible. But, for this reason, the transcendence of the sensible thing is not a spatial distance, a measurable space between two points: it is a length that is not unfolded yet, a depth irreducible to another spatial dimension. Our issue then becomes: what can be the foundation of that ontological distance that is the very openness of space? Merleau-Ponty comments that "the idea of being-at-a-distance correlatively requires an idea of *noesis* as constellation of possible paths, of sketched out itineraries. Sensation lies at the end of these paths."[5] This unpublished note relates to the following published note: "the perceived world (like painting) is the ensemble of my body's routes and not a multitude of spatio-temporal individuals" (VI 300/247). In other words, the essence of perception *consists of movement*. As a matter of fact, his critique of the positive thing as well as his rejection of philosophy of consciousness leads Merleau-Ponty to question the deep-rooted idea that perception is the province of knowledge, a mode of knowing. If perception is really the disclosure of a pure transcendence, it cannot be knowledge and, consequently, knowledge itself has to be grounded on another kind of relation with the world. The transcendence of perceived being, which Merleau-Ponty calls the "invisible," cannot be correlated with a conscious being, for this would reduce it to a positive meaning that would abolish the transcendent dimension. For this reason, only a being exceeding itself, existing outside of itself and, as it were, different from itself would be in a position to ground the transcendence of the world.

Subjective movement, or Self-movement, meets these requirements. Of course, it cannot be confused with objective movement, which presupposes objective space as pure exteriority and inherits the features of this exteriority. Indeed, it involves an excess in relation to itself that does not become a duality, an irreducible difference with itself that remains an identity, in other words, a pure potentiality that does not rest on a positivity and, therefore, cannot be abolished. It is this "lack" that is a lack of nothing and thus cannot stop its movement, this negativity characteristic of movement that bears the depth of the invisible as something not different from the visible. It is the peculiarity of movement to accomplish its own identity by exceeding itself, by differing indefinitely from itself, in the same way that transcendence is characterized by identity within difference: in a way, the active negativity, and the dissatisfaction, which are peculiar to lived movement, are the subjective reverse of the invisible transcendence of the visible. The being of movement, as something essentially unaccomplished, is the only possible mode of presence for an irreducible absence, the concrete form of the negativity that is peculiar to perceived transcendence. To perceive means to encroach upon the depth of the world, impelled by a motion toward (*avancée*) that never stops, never exhausts itself: self-movement is the sole possible foundation for the inexhaustible plenitude of perceived being.

Even if Merleau-Ponty did not clearly express this point, we think that when he died, he was heading for that understanding of the perceiving being. Anyhow, in the last notes, he appears to identify perception with movement; what stands in the way of my seeing myself is first something that is a *de facto* invisible, namely, my eyes, but, beyond this invisible, there is a *de jure* invisible: "I cannot see myself in movement, witness my own movement. But this *de jure* invisible signifies in reality that *Wahrnehmen* and *Sich bewegen* are synonymous: it is for this reason that the *Wahrnehmen* never rejoins the

Sich bewegen it wishes to apprehend: it is another of the same. But, this failure, this invisible, precisely attests that *Wahrnehmen* is *Sich bewegen*, there is here a success in the failure" (VI 308/254–55). In other words, it is impossible for perception to witness movement because it is essentially movement: movement cannot be an object of perception because it is the ultimate subject of perception.

We are now in a position to understand to what extent the Merleau-Pontian philosophy of perception and its development into an ontology is dependent on an interpretation of the history of metaphysics. By understanding the real root of the objective attitude, which grounds both intellectualism and empiricism, Merleau-Ponty manages to overcome the limitations of the *Phenomenology of Perception.* This insight, borrowed from Bergson, consists of a specific way of thinking the relation between Being and nothingness. To the extent that Merleau-Ponty rejects the fact of silhouetting Being against nothingness, he discovers a new meaning of Being which he defines as an irreducible transcendence, of which Being and nothingness are abstract dimensions. From this point on, Merleau-Ponty was in a position to renounce any conception of subjectivity as a positive entity and to inquire into a new meaning for it as correlated with that transcendence. My hypothesis is that Merleau-Ponty, when he died, was about to give up completely the philosophy of representation and consciousness, on which he had remained dependent, and, therefore, was about to elaborate a far more radical conception of perceiving subjectivity as self-movement, a conception that would have referred, ultimately, to a conception of the Self as desire.

NOTES

1. English translation by R. Barbaras.

2. *La nature,* Notes du Cours du collège de France (Paris: Seuil, 1995). English translation by R. Barbaras.

3. English translation by R. Barbaras.

4. English translation by R. Barbaras.

5. Unpublished note. "L'idée de l'être-á-distance exige corrélativement une idée de la *noesis* comme constellation de chemins possibles, d'itinéraires esquissés. La sensation est au bout de ces chemins." English translation by R. Barbaras.

CHAPTER 4

The Paradox of Expression

BERNARD WALDENFELS

THE APORIA OF EXPRESSION

The ambiguous, equivocal phenomenon Merleau-Ponty calls the paradox of expression echoes one of Husserl's statements, which the French phenomenologist often cites in the form of a motto. Section 16 of the *Cartesian Meditations*, which concerns the proper beginning of a phenomenologically oriented psychology, says: "The beginning is the pure and, so to speak, still mute experience, which now it is the issue to bring to the pure expression of its own sense."[1] In this statement, Husserl is opposing the position that substitutes sense-data or global forms for experience instead of interrogating experience for the sense intended in it. To the phenomenologist, nothing appears more obvious than this beginning; still, an aporia is hidden here. Husserl carefully limits his demand: experience is, so to speak, still mute. In fact, if it were fully mute, it would only allow something to be said *about it*, without experience finding its own sense. With the first word that violates the innocence of experience, it would already be defiled, since it would have an alien sense imputed or inserted into it. An entirely mute experience could only impose silence. If, in contrast, experience itself were already persuaded to speak, it itself would enunciate *itself*. "Pure enunciation" would fundamentally say nothing that had not already been spoken. Thus, speaking either would get tangled up in its own linguistic "overcoat" and would not go beyond language's own designs and constructions, or it would sink back into the murmur of Being itself.

In a type of reading that brings everything to a head, Foucault, in his *L'ordre du discours*,[2] has brought phenomenology to a point where it must burst to pieces, unless it takes refuge in a "lazy" mediation. Foucault distinguishes three leading themes under which traditional "logophobia," or (as we could also say) the forgetting of discourse, comes together. First, there is the founding subject who animates with his breath the "empty forms of language" and who "penetrates the inertia of empty things." Second, an originary experience appears that sustains a "primary complicity" with the world: "the things already murmur a sense, which our language has merely to extract." The third and last possibility is the theme of a *universal mediation*, which allows us at all times to rediscover the movement of the Logos; discourse becomes the mere "shimmering of a truth about to be born in its eyes." If, in the course of a process of universal mediation, everything is language, discourse is not so much lost; but as "discourse already in operation," it degenerates into an echo of itself. To be sure, Foucault is alluding to typical themes here, without mentioning specific books or authors. Thus he resists the temptation to divide up his phenomenological contemporaries into Fichteans, Schellingians, and Hegelians, and likewise we should not dwell upon this possible, but ultimately useless game. What really matters is to take a look at the enigma of the things themselves.

Merleau-Ponty himself, to whom Foucault's thought of language owes more than Foucault ever admitted, is not a master tailor, but rather a master of gradations and nuances, of gradual variations. When he cites Husserl's statement noted above, he does it in his own way. He quotes it in an abbreviated form: "C'est l'expérience . . . muette encore qu'il s'agit d'amener à l'expression pure de son propre sens." The careful "so to speak" has vanished; the problematic of the beginning of experience recedes into the problematic of the passage of experience into expression. With Merleau-Ponty, we find ourselves already on a third way. This third way presents itself as a passage, as a transition, which leads neither to a beginning nor an end. At the same time, it is to be noted that Merleau-Ponty cites Husserl's guiding statement in the most varied contexts.

In the preface to the *Phenomenology of Perception*, this statement emerges in a passage where Merleau-Ponty considers the eidetic reduction. Agreeing with the later Husserl, Merleau-Ponty here characterizes the way through the ideality of essences as an indirect way to the facticity of lived experience. "Husserl's essences are destined to bring back all the living relationships of experience, as the fisherman's net draws up from the depths of the ocean palpitating fish and seaweed" (PP x/xv).[3] One might object that the net fishes this "palpitating life" out of its life-supporting element. But here, Merleau-Ponty already has clearly in view an essence of things, which adheres to the things, a type of essence that recalls Proust rather than Plato. In one of his later lecture courses, Merleau-Ponty writes, "What has been called Proust's Platonism is the attempt to give an integral expression of the perceptual- and life-world" (RC 40/93). This reference of essences back to experience is opposed to a logical positivism that not only begins from a "ready-made language" (VI 168/126) but also severs the meanings of words from their genesis and thereby amputates the word from the thing. Merely speaking about experience silences the things, instead of helping them reach their expression.

Husserl's statement takes on a practical, even a political coloring, when we encounter it again in Merleau-Ponty's *The Adventures of the Dialectic*. In a long note, Husserl's sense-genesis is treated as a praxis that, in contrast to the "absolute, rootless initiative" of Sartrean doing, continues a movement "which has already begun in experience" (AD 186/130). Thus here, it is praxis that contributes to bringing experience to expression by passing through a "between-world" of symbols and by surrounding itself with a "landscape of praxis" (AD 268/199).

In the later *The Visible and the Invisible*, in which the landscape of praxis is found to be condensed into an "ontological landscape" (VI 137/ 101), we come once again upon our so-called guiding statement, and, indeed, in a crucial passage. It is in the chapter ("Interrogation and Intuition") where Merleau-Ponty develops a philosophy of experience that remains on this side of essences and facts and that, as interrogative thinking, begins and ends in silence; he concludes this chapter by characterizing philosophy as "the reconversion of silence and speech into one another . . . : 'It is the experience . . . still mute which it is the issue to bring to the pure expression of its own sense' " (VI 171/129). Again the reproach is raised against the deficiency of "semantic philosophies to close up language as if it spoke only of itself: language only lives from its silence" (VI 167/126). Thus the same statement guides Merleau-Ponty as a leitmotif in the early *Phenomenology of Perception*, through a philosophy of historical praxis, up to the later ontology's turn to the philosophy of language. The initial paradox is not defused at all; on the contrary, it is intensified and becomes a "paradox of being," a paradox that in no way lets itself be traced back, like a mere "paradox of man" (VI 180/136), to our epistemological failures.[4]

EXPRESSION AND CREATIVITY

Conforming to Husserl's "guiding statement," Merleau-Ponty continuously speaks of a "paradox of expression," of the event of expression as a "paradoxical activity," a "paradoxical undertaking." Similarly, speech is a "wonder" (merveille, prodige), a "circle," an "enigma," or a "mystery" of expression.[5] We have to ask what this paradox refers to, what is to be understood by the word "paradox" or "wonder," and how Merleau-Ponty handles this paradox.

The paradox of expression lies first of all in the act of expression and in the event of expression itself; therefore, the paradox lies in the relation between the actual expression and *what is yet to be expressed*, in other words, between what is yet to be expressed and its means, ways, forms, in short, the "ready-made expressions," in which something *is already expressed*, whether it be in a determinate language or in a sort of pre-language (*pré-langage*) prior to every determinate language (VI, 168/126). Expression is to be understood here in a broad sense, including also bodily expression, and even the expressive content of things. This paradox originates in an inner tension of the expressive event, an event that is neither homogeneous nor reducible to its components. The paradox comes together, for Merleau-Ponty, in *creative expression*, to which he attributes a universal range, going from the first attempts of children to express themselves to the public sphere of expression in politics and to the language of poetry and the other arts, and finally to the formal models of science. "Expression is everywhere creative, and what is expressed is always inseparable from it" (PP 448/391). If, instead of a creative expression, we speak of an expressive creation, then expression and creation become two sides of the same coin.

As in Husserl's "guiding statement," two extremes become impossible here, namely, to regard an event of expression either as pure action and pure creation of newness or, in contrast, as pure passion and pure reproduction. The event of expression can to a greater or lesser extent approach either of these extremes of pure innovation or pure repetition, but cannot reach either of them. From the standpoint of linguistics, one could characterize pure creation as a *saying without a said*, as an *énonciation* that would be completely exempt from the order of the said, while pure reproduction would correspond to a *said without a saying*, a pure *énoncé* that would still integrate the very event of saying into the repertoire and the order of the said. Purely creative discourse would say *nothing*; purely repetitive discourse would have nothing *to say*.

Characterizing creative expression as a paradox means that the phenomenon in question exhibits contradictory aspects and contradictory determinations that can neither be converted into a unified determination nor be sublated in a more comprehensive or higher determination. As already indicated, in the case we are considering it is a question of contradictory determinations of action and passion, of the future and the past, of new and old, of beginning and end. If one conceives of the event of expression as an activity of expression that presumes an actor, then one can see the contradiction as an antithesis between the "who" and the "what," between the expressing subject and the expressed object. This paradox differs from logical paradoxes because we cannot reduce it to a simple problem that can perhaps be solved by distinguishing between objective language and metalanguage, by the distinction with which the paradox of the lying Cretan is clarified. The paradox belongs, rather, to "the things themselves." In this regard, Merleau-Ponty follows in Kierkegaard's footsteps, who separated the antinomy of temporality and eternity, of the finitude and infinity from all speculative mediation. The *how* of an existentially concerned thinking would not be able to find room in the *what* of the thought. For Merleau-Ponty, the event of expression is embodied in a *doing* (*faire*) (PM 59/41). In expression, something happens, something comes to pass, something comes into expression, a threshold is crossed. The unity is not thought, but is made (*est faite*) in the form of a transition-synthesis, which remains in transition and is not propelled to another position. If we go back to the well-known difference of "something as something," the event of expression means precisely *that* something emerges as something, that is discovered as sense *in statu nascendi.* That this founding event is characterized further as "wonder," "enigma," or "mystery" has nothing to do with some form of irrationalism, but instead with a "Suprarationalism" that avoids sacrificing the *fact* of the reason to "ready-made" reason. Even an arch-rationalist like Leibniz speaks of the *miracle de la raison,* and Husserl takes up this formula when he invokes "the wonder of rationality" or the pure Ego and pure consciousness the "Wonder of Wonders."[6] When Merleau-Ponty speaks of the wonder of language, this wonder remains as astonishing as it did at its first appearance. As the "first fact" and the "ultimate fact," it cannot be derived from any other, neither by means of an empirist explanation that traces the new meanings back to the meanings already at hand, nor by means of an intellectualist explanation that appeals to an absolute knowledge "immanent to the first forms of knowledge" (PP 447/ 390). While the empiricist explanation is linked to causal thinking in which the sense is ultimately turned into a mosaic of data and a sequence of facts, the intellectualist variant terminates in ontological-logical implications, in an unfolding of what was already there in an enfolded form. The unsaid ends up coinciding with the not-yet-said. If we posit a psychical inner life as the domain from which the act of expression starts, then expression is reduced completely to a mere ex-pression that makes inner impressions emerge on the outside. The event of expression would be split apart between such forms of exteriorization and interiorization. Against these, Merleau-Ponty insists upon one originary fact: "There is expression," just as we can say "there is meaning" (PP 342/296) or "there is rationality" (PP xv/xix). A thought that, as expressive thought, always remains distant from itself refers to a "fundamental obscurity of what is expressed" (PP 449/392). This "fundamental obscurity" is reminiscent again of Proust, who in *Remembrance of Things Past* demands from "real books" that they "should be the offspring not of daylight and casual talk but of darkness and silence."[7] What comes to light does not stand in the light, rather a zone of shadow still surrounds it.

EXPRESSION AND AMBIGUITY

We still have to discover how we can deal with this paradox without resolving it, how we can welcome it into our thought as a "positivity" of thought that results neither in a new positivism nor even in a phenomenological positivism. Here we find ourselves before an ambiguity that no one has recognized better than Merleau-Ponty, when he distinguished between a "good" and a "bad" ambiguity. His philosophy of ambiguity was first a negative philosophy of "neither-nor." Just as the living body (*Leib*) is neither mind nor body (*Körper*), neither idea nor fact, the event of expression can be reduced neither to facts of experience nor to mental forms. If one tries to recast this negative philosophy as a positive philosophy of the "not-only-but-also," there will still be a "bad ambiguity," that is, a "mixture of finitude and universality, of interiority and exteriority."[8] Just like Descartes's *permixtio* of soul and body, this mixture would still adhere to heterogenous principles such as Reason and Nature; the novelty would merely be a composition of the old, of the already given. Here we cannot examine in detail whether this accusation or self-accusation is worth anything or really justified. In any case, there appears in the early Merleau-Ponty a certain tendency to diminish the enigma of expression in favor of an *anteriority* of experience, in favor of a *passivity* of the event. The hypostatization of an initial experience, which risks opening out onto a traditional form of "First Philosophy," is always prevented by *circular* determinations turning as if in a house of mirrors. Some examples from the *Phenomenology of Perception* can illustrate this. One can read for example that "the sensible gives back *to me* only what *I* have lent to *it*," or "*We* choose our world, and the world chooses *us*" (PP 248/214, 518/454, my emphasis).

The project that Merleau-Ponty presents in 1952 in his prospectus for the Collège de France likewise makes it clear that he sought to escape from a certain impasse. In this connection it is the phenomenon of expression itself that opens up a way out. For Merleau-Ponty, a "good ambiguity" lies in the phenomenon of expression, "that is, a spontaneity which accomplishes the seemingly impossible, to take separated elements into consideration, and bring together a multitude of monads into a single web of past and future, nature and culture." Expression itself takes on the form of a transitional phenomenon. *The transition takes place as expression*, as much in the synchronic as in the diachronic view; nature is transformed into culture, the past into the future, the alien into one's own and vice versa. In this way the "logos which shall bring a hitherto mutely lived world into speech" meets a "logos of the perceptual world."[9] The translation of one Logos into another, namely, as Merleau-Ponty calls it later, the transition from an "internal Logos (λ`$\gamma o\varsigma$ $X\nu\delta\iota V\theta\varepsilon\tau o\varsigma$)" into an "external Logos ($\lambda$`$\gamma o\varsigma$, $\pi\rho$ $o\pi o\rho\backslash\chi o\varsigma$)" (VI, 224/170), takes place in expression. This change indicates no "Kehre" in the sense in which this word is now used, rather Merleau-Ponty tries to repeat his own beginnings more radically. The importance that falls to the phenomenon of expression in this process of thinking through is further emphasized by Merleau-Ponty's self-critique in *The Visible and the Invisible*. This singular critique is concentrated upon a significant theme, namely, the tacit cogito, a concept that leads us to understand not how language is possible, but why it is not impossible. "There remains the problem of the passage from the perceptual meaning to the language meaning, from behavior to thematization" (VI 229/176). Precisely, this passage occurs in expression.

MERLEAU-PONTY'S OPERATIVE CONCEPTS OF EXPRESSION

In order to keep the paradox of creative expression from decomposing into heterogeneous components or from dissolving into a forced unity, the event of expression must be differentiated in itself and from itself. The paradox results from a play of multiple differences to which we can attribute determinate expressive movements. Here we discover a series of operative concepts in Merleau-Ponty that articulate the expressivity of expressions and thus indirectly also the phenomenality of phenomena.

1. Divergence (*déviation, écart*). As Merleau-Ponty always stresses, every creative expression proceeds indirectly, laterally, not directly and frontally. All formations are embedded in fields of expression, within which they are contrasted more or less with other formations. They deviate from a certain level of expression in the shape of a "coherent deformation," as Merleau-Ponty formulates it echoing Malraux and the Russian formalists. Divergence can take on larger or smaller dimensions. The event of expression vacillates between the relatively new and the relatively old, depending on whether the deviation holds up a pregiven frame or modifies and bursts open this frame. The absolutely new and the absolutely old can be thought of only as limit-values to represent the contrasting determinations of the old and the new. The deviations that transform the whole are in fact rather minimal and imperceptible, as when a foundation is washed out or a stone breaks free. Their mere insignificance allows them to slip away from being classified and thus can open a new world within them. This is just like what happens in Proust: the feel of the cobblestones under his feet makes Proust's narrator recall the Guermantes way and makes a forgotten world reemerge right before his eyes.

2. Translation. The idea that the expression of experience itself signifies the work of translating or deciphering is also found already in Proust. This "inner book," experience, is not to be invented by the writer, but translated by him. "The duty and task of an author are those of a translator."[10] In one of his lecture courses at the Collège de France, dealing with the problem of discourse, Merleau-Ponty refers explicitly to Proust when he states: "Surely no one has brought the *circulus vitiosus*, the wonder of speech, to expression like Proust: speech and writing mean to *translate* an experience which is first made into a text by the word experience itself calls forth" (RC 41/94; cf. also PP 445/380). Merleau-Ponty cites the passage from *Recherche* where the reading of the "inner book" of experience itself is interpreted as an act of creation. The paradoxical character of this creative translating and creative reading rests on the fact that the reading neither simply finds an original text nor simply produces a text. An expression that would owe everything to what is to be expressed would no longer be a *creative* expression, while a creation that would owe nothing at all to what is to be expressed would no longer be a creative *expression*. The event of expression always moves between two

extremes. Just as translation leads from a source language to a target language without closing the abyss between the two, expression converts the alien into one's own, without effacing the alienness. A perfect translation, which would make the original be forgotten, would no longer be a translation. Here a bridge may be built to Walter Benjamin's conception of language, which grew out of the spirit of translation.[11]

3. *Après coup* (*Nachträglichkeit*, delayed effect). If *something* preceded it, like a prior phase or a fundamental strata of experience, the event of expression would again be reduced to something that it is not. The paradox of expression means that the event of expression precedes *itself*, that it is younger and older than itself. *Present and past* do not follow one another but are entangled within one another. Merleau-Ponty occasionally describes this relation in hyperbolic terms, as when he attributes a "communication before communication" or a "reason before reason" to the efforts of modern painting that depend upon no pregiven nature (PM 79/56). This anteriority, which finds its expression "après coup," refers to an "unreflective ground," an "original past, a past which has never been present" (PP 280/242). Furthermore, it presupposes a reverse movement of truth or its retrofiguration, a "mouvement rétrograde du vrai," as Bergson already calls it. Merleau-Ponty interprets Bergsonism as the passage from a philosophy of impression to a philosophy of expression, the passage from an expression appearing only "après coup." "What I say of the sensible world is not in the sensible world, and yet it has no other meaning than to say what the sensible world means. The expression antedates itself and postulates that being comes toward it" (EP 49/29).[12] The antedating and retroactivity of expression excludes that there is a first expression, a "first word," because there is nothing before it, no "murmur of things"; speech, however, precedes itself and reaches back into a zone of "prehuman silence" (PM 60f./42f.). This withdrawal of the origin, which moves it back into an unsublatable (author term) prehistory, recalls much of what Derrida and Levinas come to speak of under catchwords such as "après coup," trace, or anarchy.

4. Excess. The event of expression not only precedes itself, it also remains behind itself; what comes to expression is sketched in the movement of expression itself as an "excess" of what is intended in relation to the said and of the said over what is intended, as "a determinate void that is filled in with words" (S 112/90). The void can increase to a "vertigo of the void" emanating from the whiteness of the page, as in the case of the aphasiac who does not possess the normal words or in the case of the poet who renounces the normal words, deferring constantly, like Mallarmé, the writing of his book (PM 201/145). Corresponding to the past that never was present is a future that will never be present. Thus *future and present* are also intertwined in one another. Just as there is no first word, there is no final word. A complete or exhaustive expression, which would say all there is to say, would inevitably

have to become master of its beginnings and be faithful to an "original text" of experience; only in this way could it become master of its own end. The wonder of language is that language itself is greater than the existing, ready-made language. "The marvel that a finite number of signs, forms, and words should give rise to an indefinite number of uses, or that other and identical marvel that linguistic meaning directs inward something beyond language, is the very prodigy of speech, and anyone who tries to explain it in terms of its 'beginning' or its 'end' " (PM 59/41).

EXPRESSION AS RESPONSIVE

An event of expression, which differentiates itself from itself, is never entirely meaningful nor does it ever reach its full potential; it is never completely at home and up to a certain point is always alien to itself. If it cannot refer to something that would be absolutely external to itself, then this externality must intrude into the expression itself. A philosophy indebted to such an expressive event has "its own alienness" (EP 50/30); this alienness does not come from the external, but from our own interiority. This means not only that our discourse and action are limited by factual conditions, but also that they are inhabited by a passivity and a passion that we cannot conceive as we used to do it according to Aristotle or Descartes, as contrasted against *energeia* or action. This brings us to a final question, which turns out to be the most difficult. How does the expressive event start up and and stay in motion? What is at stake in the experience, whose "proper sense it is to bring to expression"? What is at stake in the "determinate void which is to be filled with words"? What does this gerundive—"die zu bringen ist"; "qu'il s'agit d'amener"; "that it is the issue to bring"—mean that overflows the mere play of expressive possibilities and leads Merleau-Ponty to think together in a new way the wonder of expression and the origin of truth. In the preface to *Signs* we read: "there is that which is *to be said* and which is as yet no more than a precise uneasiness in the world of things-said" (S 27/19, my emphasis). Where does this uneasiness, which is never missing from the *vérité à faire*, derive from?

It must not surprise us if Merleau-Ponty leaves the answers to this question somewhat open. It is no different with the "vérité à lire" and the "réalité à exprimer" with which Proust confronts his author (*Recherche*, vol. 3, pp. 878, 882; *Remembrance*, vol. 3, pp. 912, 916). One answer is offered by the customary *vouloir-dire,* that "will or wanting to say," that meaning, which refers back to Husserl's meaning-intention and that is embedded in a desire to speak and a desire to express. In that case, beneath the paradox of expression would stand an "intention" that exceeds the given meaning and available linguistic significations (PP 445/389), a "will to express" as Merleau-Ponty calls it elsewhere (EP 88/55).[13]

In this conception, however, a counterweight is already built in, inasmuch as the saying in the "vouloir-dire" is taken completely seriously beyond the mere intention (cf. S 112/88–89). An intention realizing itself as a wanting *to say* still depends on "what the words want to say" (PP x/xv). The meaning-intention takes the form of an indirect, "broken" intention, broken like the stick in the water, immersed in an alien medium.

Living speech—*Leib*—which is realized in the medium of an operative living language and is dependent on the expressive means of a "physical" language—*Körper*—leads finally to a reversal. In the words, "what the things want to say" (PP x/xv) comes to be expressed. The living body—*Leib*—whose spontaneity is defined precisely by the fact that *it begins with me before I began* leads to a partial dispossession and disempowering of the *sujet parlant*. The *vouloir-dire* extends to a prelanguage in which both the things and elements participate. The simple "I speak" does not change into an "it speaks" or a "language speaks," and yet it finds itself decentered: "Speech transcends us, and yet we are speaking" (PP 459/401). All we need to do is twist a bit the formula from the introduction to *Signs* in order to make Merleau-Ponty sound like Heidegger: "The things *are said* and *are thought* as though [*comme*] by a speech and by a thought which we do not have but which has us" (S 27/19). That *"comme"* keeps Merleau-Ponty from a genuine *Kehre*.

All of these issues are bound up with Merleau-Ponty's passage, taking place at the end of the forties and the beginning of the fifties, from a *"leiblich"* existential apprehension of language to its *"leiblich"* structural apprehension. The new apprehension culminates in the postulation of a *creative expression* that does not merely realize given possibilities, but takes and takes up again some determinate possibilities and leaves aside and relinquishes others. This selective form of expression presents itself as a "warlike expression," which always has moments of *violence*, because, in fact, the realization of these determinate possibilities has no sufficient reason on its side that could justify it completely (Cf. PM 183/131, 195/140, 197f./142). The violence of expression is the reverse side of its contingency. This insight says a lot, but not everything. A mere multiplication of possibilities would bring us close to Foucault or Deleuze. The question concerning the motor of the event of expression would really be resolved if the motor were referring to a play of forces, which would amount to saying that it would not be truly resolved, since a "gay positivism" would cut off all further questions.

But, another aspect of Merleau-Ponty's concept of expression, which will take on more importance, stands out immediately. Expression has the form not only of a creative, but also of a *responsive expression*. Specifically, in the ontological reinterpretation of phenomenology where the paradox of expression is mentioned, we find the following concise formula: "in the patient and silent labor of desire, begins the paradox of expression" (VI 189/144). *Désir* is not *volonté*, beneath desire there is no desiring subject that would be its origin. Desire does not exist without another desire that keeps it in motion, and without a law that keeps it in check. The allusion to Lacan and perhaps already to Levinas is not to be overlooked. The intention of the will-to-say (*vouloir-dire*) is crossed by something that is to be said (*quelque chose à dire*). What is to be said means a demand that is not something that simply can be realized and will be realized, but something that is to be realized. The activity of artists already surpasses the simple testing of possibilities: "the same tireless demand arises from every lived thing (at times trifling), namely, the demand to be expressed" (PM 106/ 75). In the above mentioned passage, where Merleau-Ponty alludes to Proust, experience itself does not seize upon the word, but rather experience *awakens* the word. One of the working notes from *The Visible and the Invisible* says, "The amorphous world of perception . . . , which thus in no way entails an expressive style, nevertheless evokes and provokes everything in general which re-awakens with every painter a new effort of expression,—this perceptual world is at bottom Being in Heidegger's sense, which . . . appears as containing everything that will ever be said, and yet leaving us to create it (Proust): it is the λ`γος XνδιVθετος which calls for the λ`γος, πρ ονορ\χος (VI 223/170). Again we meet a peculiar "desire" in things, a "claim" (*revendication*) or a "demand to appear" (*interpellation*), as it is called elsewhere. Creative expression becomes responsive expression in that it takes up not only those possibilities that offer themselves, but acquiesces to the demands of others that provoke it. *Violence* here means not only that possibilites are sacrificed, but also that claims are always infringed upon. Here it is no longer a matter of a past that was never present, it is much more of an "irrevocable absence," (VI 211/159) that never can be present without forfeiting its claim. It does not follow from this that an existing law, a general rule, or an ideal consensus stands behind what comes to expression and seeks its response. If this were the case, expression would be reduced to a mere fulfillment of the law; the order that serves as a purpose would, simply, be replaced by a legal order.

Now, with a glance to Levinas, one could wonder whether the demand awoken by this creative response is truly inexorable and inescapable. One has to concede that the demand proceeds from something else, not from the other or others as in Levinas. In Merleau-Ponty, there is a dimension of otherness that we cannot get around. The problem that comes to light here, and that Derrida raises in his early essay on Levinas, cannot readily be reduced to a "humanism of the other man." Leaving this aside, we still have to find out whether the demand that proceeds from the other is inexorable and inescapable. One could reproach Merleau-Ponty for moving predominantly in the sphere of a simple aesthetics. Outside of the fact that Merleau-Ponty throughout considers other regions,[14] we should beware of speaking of a "simple aesthetics" when it has to do with forms, colors, and tones. Is there not in writing, as in thinking, an *ethos*, to which Proust appeals in his *Recherche*, when he makes the author confront a *devoir* and a *vocation*? It is not Bergotte's hedonistic life but his death that causes Proust's narrator to speak of the "unknown laws" that have left their marks behind in us; without these laws, we could not understand why an artist comes to be possessed by a bit of a yellow wall, by a musical phrase, or by a memory.[15] As Merleau-Ponty suggests in the previously cited passage (RC 41/94), it is certain that speech and writing cannot be a way of life that would be necessary and sufficient, as if literature were "the only life . . . really lived" (*Recherche*, vol. 3, p. 895; *Remembrance*, vol. 3, p. 931); nevertheless, speech and writing surely produce a certain way of life that places specific demands upon and also benefits those whose company we are deprived of. Merleau-Ponty belongs to that group of philosophers who remain skeptical in regard to every explicit ethics. Yet it is possible that there are implicit forms of ethics that are amalgamated with all the forms of expression. Certainly, a series of questions remains open here. The current demarcation between ethics and aesthetics completely misses the event of expression that lies submerged below the most diverse ways of life and expression. Inasmuch as Merleau-Ponty's thought is attentive to the paradox of expression, it resists not only the extreme forms of fundamentalism and constructivism but also the more moderate forms of linguistic pragmatism and hermeneutical or pragmatic traditionalism, to say nothing of the postmodern nonsense. In a late lecture course on Husserl and phenomenology, Merleau-Ponty says: "Every production of spirit is a response and an appeal, a coproduction" (RC, 166/187). But what do spirit, production, coproduction mean when every production is to be thought of as expression and when every expression is to be thought of as creative-responsive expression? Here the expressive work, like all radical expressive work, even rises up against its own results. It does not stop short of the ego. So reads one of the thoughts from *Monsieur Teste*: "The ego is the momentary answer to every partial incoherence—which presents an impulse."[16] The paradox of expression consists in the fact that an expression is really much more an expression the more vigorously it is moved, incited, and claimed by others.

NOTES

This essay was translated from the German by Chris Nagel. It originally appeared in *Deutsch-Französische Gedankengänge* (Frankfurt, Suhrkamp, 1995), pp. 105–23, © Suhrkamp Verlag Frankfurt am Main, 1995. I have also consulted the French translation of this essay by Alain Pernet in *Merleau-Ponty Notes de cours sur L'origine de la géométrie de Husserl suivi de Recherches sur la phénoménologie de Merleau-Ponty,* sous la direction de R. Barbaras (Paris: Presses Universitaires de France, 1998), pp. 331–48.

1. Cf. Edmund Husserl, *Cartesian Meditations*, trans. Dorion Cairns (The Hague: Nijhoff, 1960), p. 38 f. Husserl's statement in its original German is: "Der Anfang ist die reine und sozusagen noch stumme Erfahrung, die nun erst zur reinen Aussprache ihres eigenene Sinnes zu bringen ist." I have modified Cairns's translation—"stumme" as "mute"; "zu bringen ist" as "it is the issue to bring"; "Aussprache" as "expression"—in order to agree with the French translation of *Cartesian Meditation* by Gabrielle Pfeiffer and Emmanuel Levinas (Paris: Vrin, 1947): "Le début, c'est l'expérience pure et, pour ainsi dire, muette encore, qu'il s'agit d'amener à l'expression pure de son propre sens" (pp. 73–74). Merleau-Ponty always seems to follow their translation. *Trans.*

2. Michel Foucault, *L'ordre du discours* (Paris: Gallimard, 1971), pp. 47–53. English translation: "The Discourse on Language," trans. Rupert Swyer, in *The Archaeology of Knowledge* (New York: Pantheon, 1972), pp. 227–29.

3. On the motif of speech- and expression-events, cf. PM 66/47; VI 158/118 f. Also Marcel Proust, *Recherche* 1, p. 179; *Remembrance of Things Past,* trans. C. K. Scott Moncrieff and Terence Kilmartin (New York: Random House, 1981), p. 195 f. (hereafter cited as *Remembrance*).

4. In Royaumount, Merleau-Ponty says explicitly that Husserl had set for phenomenology a "hard, nearly impossible task," with the demand "to bring the still mute experience to the expression of its own sense." What stands out between the silence of things and the word of philosophy "is not a kind of accord or pre-established harmony; it is a difficulty and a tension" Edmund Husserl, *Cahiers de Royaumount* (Paris: Editions de Minuit, 1959), p. 157 f. On the gradual change of meaning the "little phrase" from Husserl's *Cartesian Meditations* undergoes over the course of Merleau-Ponty's thought, see the minute interpretation by J. Taminiaux, *Le regard et l'excédent* (The Hague: Nijhoff, 1977), chap. 6.

5. See especially: PP 445/389, 448 f/391 f; EP 54/32; PM 51/35, 59/41, 61/43, 160/113; RC 41/83, 23/71; VI 189/144.

6. Edmund Husserl, *Husserliana* vol. 7, p. 394; ed. H. L. Van Breda (The Hague: Martinus Nijhoff, 1950–   ); *Husserliana* vol. 5, p. 75; ed. H. L. Van Breda (The Hague: Martinus Nijhoff, 1950–   ).

7. Proust, *Remembrance,* vol. 3, p. 934.

8. "Un inédit de Merleau-Ponty," (*Revue de métaphysicque et de morale,* no. 4, 1962), p. 409, PRI 11.

9. "Un inédit," p. 408 f; PRI 10 f.

10. Proust, *Recherche* vol. 3, p. 890; *Remembrance,* vol. 3, pp. 926, 932.

11. Cf. A. Hirsch, *Dialog der Sprachen. Studien zum Sprach- und Übersetzungsdenken Walter Benjamins und Jacques Derridas* (München: W. Fink, 1995).

12. See also Proust's "Ars poetica," *Recherche,* vol. 3, p. 880; *Remembrance,* vol. 3, p. 914.

13. See also Proust, *Recherche,* vol. 3, pp. 855, 867; *Remembrance,* vol. 3, pp. 886, 899.

14. On the connection between creativity and responsibility in Merleau-Ponty's practical-political philosophy, see Martin W. Schnell, *Phänomenologie des Politischen* (München: W. Fink, 1995).

15. See Proust, *Recherche* vol. 3, p. 188; *Remembrance,* vol. 3, p. 186f.

16. "Le MOI est la réponse instantanée à chaque incohérence partielle—qui est *excitant*" (Paul Valéry, *Oeuvres,* vol. 2 [Paris: Gallimard, 1957], p. 69). Obviously Valéry grasped the psychological vocabulary of his time; just as obviously he is troubled to extract for himself a deep dimension for example when he plays ever more with the contradiction of excitation and nourishment (see *Cahiers,* vol. 2 [Paris: Gallimard, 1973], p. 373) or when he writes "Nietzsche is no nourishment—he is a stimulant" (Valéry, *Cahiers,* vol. 1, p. 486). It may be noted at this point that Merleau-Ponty was as ardent a reader of Valéry as he was an intensive reader of Proust.

CHAPTER 5

"In Praise of Philosophy": A Hermeneutical Rereading

JEAN GREISCH

The back cover of the French edition of *Signs*, Merleau-Ponty's last collection of articles, states: "Signes, c'est-à-dire non pas un alphabet complet, et pas même un discours suivi. Mais plutôt de ces signaux, soudains comme un regard, que nous recevons des événements, des livres et des choses."[1] Could philosophical hermeneutics, which is the theory of the operations of understanding implied in the reading and interpretation of texts, subscribe to these lines? It all depends on one's idea of hermeneutics. Those who see the sign as a coherent discourse, made up of elaborate messages, will find it difficult to cope with the disruptive and heterogenous character of Merleau-Ponty's "signals," preferring instead to speak immediately of symbols. Nevertheless, because of how philosophy has developed in the second half of this century, we must adopt the task of trying to recontextualise Merleau-Ponty's "philosophy of ambiguity" with respect to some topics of hermeneutical philosophy. In other words, supposing that the emergence of a new figure of reason, "hermeneutical reason," is one of the typical features of twentieth-century philosophy, how can we situate Merleau-Ponty's position regarding this trend? I will try to sketch a possible answer to this question through a "hermeneutical rereading" of the famous "Inaugural Lecture" "In Praise of Philosophy," delivered on 15 January 1953 at the Collège de France.

One should be well aware of the difficulties that such an attempt at a "hermeneutical" rereading of this famous text entails. In fact, Merleau-Ponty would not seem to be concerned at all with the two really fruitful periods, which shaped the intellectual profile of twentieth-century hermeneutical philosophy. The first took place during the twenties. In his early Freiburg lectures, Heidegger sketched the program of an "hermeneutics of factical" life, which eventually was converted into the existential analytic of *Sein und Zeit*. In order to describe the relation both intimate and accidental between hermeneutics and

Husserlian phenomenology, Ricoeur frequently uses the metaphor of a "graft." Using the same metaphor, one might say that Heidegger's hermeneutics of facticity "grafts" Dilthey's notion of "understanding" onto Husserl's notion of intuition. The offspring of this graft—a stillborn bastard for some orthodox phenomenologists—is the notion of a "hermeneutical intuition," which appears as early as 1919 in Heidegger's teachings. We should add to this discussion of Heidegger that recent research has shown very clearly that, in Heidegger's eyes, this first hermeneutical foundation of phenomenology under the form of a hermeneutics of factical life (author's term) was intended to be a phenomenological reply to the then current philosophy of life, with Nietzsche, Dilthey, and Bergson as the main proponents. But focusing the whole discussion on Heidegger's contribution to this first phase would be an error. However widespread this error may be, one must also take into account the original way Georg Misch attempts to take up Dilthey's project at the beginning of the thirties. The 1994 publication of his monumental attempt to ground logic on the basis of a philosophy of life[2] is an important intellectual event, which perhaps we are not yet able to evaluate correctly.

Regarding the development of hermeneutical philosophy, the second fruitful period is the sixties with the publication of important works such as Hans-Georg Gadamer's *Truth and Method* in Germany, Ricoeur's *Symbolique du Mal, De L'interprétation,* and *Le Conflit des Interprétations* in France, Luigi Pareyson's *Verità e interpretazione* in Italy, and others. In the background, the Castelli Conferences in Rome played an important role in the internationalization of a strain of thinking that, in most countries and most notably in France, could not rely upon a long previous intellectual tradition, in contrast to the German tradition.

No wonder then if, for Merleau-Ponty, as well as for almost any other French philosopher, hermeneutics was a *terra incognita.* Concerning the first period, only recently have we been able to read Heidegger "from the start"[3] and thereby discover the genealogical importance of his hermeneutics of facticity. None of the texts regarding this period was accessible during Merleau-Ponty's lifetime. As for the second period, his untimely death in 1961 prevented him from taking part in a philosophical discussion, the progression of which he could, of course, not have foreseen.

Does this mean that a hermeneutical rereading of his own thinking is doomed to be a futile academic exercise without any real impact on contemporary philosophical issues? Although I am well aware of the risks involved in such an attempt, I think that it is justified under two conditions. First, we would have to establish from a historical viewpoint that precisely Merleau-Ponty's philosophy has largely made possible the promotion of an idea of language, which a hermeneutical philosophy cannot but adopt. Second, from a more systematic viewpoint, we would have to show that nothing better than the confrontation with Merleau-Ponty's "philosophy of ambiguity" can help hermeneutical philosophy articulate its own project and, perhaps also, become conscious of some possible errors. The following reflections will mainly be made in this second, more "systematic" perspective.

There are two possible ways of dealing with this problematic. Either we could try to give a complete analysis, as well as a critical discussion of the reception of Merleau-Ponty's thinking within the hermeneutical tradition developing at the beginning of the sixties until our times. What we could assemble with this kind of inquiry would take us far beyond the limits of the present paper. Or, assuming the risk of interpretation I have already mentioned, we could try a kind of "free-lance" "philosophical meditation," which would consist in exposing one's own hermeneutical convictions to the challenge of Merleau-Ponty's texts. This is the strategy I will adopt in this paper, because I think that it suits better the "philosophical meditation" that "In Praise of Philosophy" was obviously meant to be.

My first draft of such a rereading was developed in a paper entitled "Éloge de la philosophie herméneutique."[4] In this short article, my starting-point was the following statement made on the last pages of the "Inaugural Lecture" "Philosophy turns towards the anonymous symbolic activity from which we emerge and towards the personal discourse which develops in us, and which, indeed, we are. It scrutinizes this power of expression, which the other forms of symbolism exercise only in a limited way. In touch with every kind of fact and experience, it tries rigorously to grasp those fecund moments, in which a meaning takes possession of itself. It recovers this meaning, and also pushes beyond all limits the becoming of truth which presupposes and brings it about that there is only one history and one world" (EP 67/57–58).

Although this statement does not use the word "hermeneutics," it implies at least three central motifs, which directly concern an hermeneutical philosophy.

First, it displaces the most classical definition of human being: the *animal rationale,* that is, the ζον λογον εχον, in Aristotle's definition appears now, to quote a formula of Ernst Cassirer's *Essay on Man,* as an "animal symbolicum." But symbols imply necessarily some form of opacity, of nontransparency, of cultural and historical contingency. Only through a difficult labor of interpretation, which may take a very long time, will philosophy be able to integrate the richness of meaning tranported by these symbols into a deeper self-understanding. Thus human beings become what Charles Taylor calls "self-interpreting animals."[5]

The *second* striking feature of this statement is the dialectical construction of human experience and its expressivity. On the one hand, we have to deal with "the anonymous symbolic activity from which we emerge" and, thus we could add, which is still supporting us, under the form of the unconscious that delimits a specific semantics of desire, the structure of language, social codes, historical traditions, and so forth; on the other hand, we have the "personal discourse" developing from all these data. The fundamental wager of hermeneutics is that choosing one side of this polarity against the other: *structure* against *event*, la *langue* against la *parole*, *code* against *message*, *logos* against *chronos,* and so forth, is impossible What might look like a dichotomy, must become a living dialectic.

The *third* interesting point is that Merleau-Ponty stresses "those fecund moments, in which a meaning takes possession of itself." This is what hermeneutics calls the "task of appropriation." But what are "those fecund moments"? Alluding to Ricoeur's writings, I would say that those are the moments when we become able to invent living metaphors that enable us to understand reality more profoundly, or when we configure narrative plots that give time a specific human meaning—consisting in the "synthesis of the heterogenous" or in "discordant concordance"—and that also sketch the "narrative identity" of a self who is no longer reducible to a permanent substance or an immutable character. "Trying rigorously to grasp those fecund moments, in which a meaning takes possession of itself": hermeneutics refuses to consider human beings as prisoners of the system of language, although it has to admit that the individual speaker is not the inventor of the system of instituted signs. If in each moment, however, we are producing with the old words and the same grammar new meanings, new meanings never yet spoken, hermeneutics will have to show, following Merleau-Ponty, how this grasping of fecund moments can be done *rigorously.*

Granted that my first hermeneutical commentary did not then and does not now betray what Merleau-Ponty has in mind, let us try to go through the entire lecture, in order to discover behind its disconcerting, paradoxical, and even disturbing formulas several other motifs that concern directly a hermeneutical philosophy. The general structure of the "Inaugural Lecture" is well known. It starts with a short *captatio benevolentiae* under the form of an homage to the spirit of free investigation proper to the Collège. This leads to a first definition of the identity and the vocation of a philosopher: "The philosopher is marked by the distinguishing trait that he possesses *inseparably* the taste for evidence and the feeling for ambiguity" (EP 10/4). This definition is obviously the germinal cell of the whole lecture. Moreover, it sums up, in an almost emblematic manner, a conception of philosophy that has precisely been defined as a "philosophy of ambiguity." Because "the feeling for ambiguity" plays such a fundamental role here it implies also a critical task: "to distinguish good and bad ambiguity" (EP 10/5). The lecture moves forward to a long critical discussion, which is also a form of homage regarding two very clear philosophies, for which the fundamental motive is the taste for evidence. Nevertheless they were not able to eliminate every feeling for ambiguity: Louis Lavelle and Henri Bergson. After that, the moving recollection of the figure of Socrates allows us to push the meaning of "good ambiguity" farther, that is, the kind of ambiguity philosophy must not and cannot get rid of, because it is inseparable from the philosopher's style of existence.

Ambiguity means first of all finitude. This is why the polemic part of the Lecture discusses two major figures of absolute knowledge: God and History. What is the status of philosophy at the end of the double "labor of mourning," renouncing the theological and the historical figure of absolute knowledge? Philosophy, having become aware of its weakness, is justified, but only under a limping form. This limping has to be taken up as a virtue.

Notwithstanding its strong contextual aspects, the Lecture can be read as a progressive unfolding, pushed ever further, of the philosophical meaning of the "feeling for ambiguity." If this is true, a hermeneutical rereading will have to identify the moments of this unfolding that speak directly to hermeneutical consciousness, and that, thereby, put it sometimes into question. Or, to express the same idea through an image that suits well the Socratic undertone of the whole lecture: just as Socrates presented himself to the Athenians as a gadfly, in order to prevent them from falling to sleep, Merleau-Ponty's "In Praise of Philosophy" might have the same effect on a hermeneutical philosophy that is tempted to lock itself within its own certainties.

"THE TASTE FOR EVIDENCE
AND THE FEELING FOR AMBIGUITY"

Let us start with meditating on the initial gesture: refusing to separate "the taste for evidence and the feeling for ambiguity." Is this not exactly what philosophical hermeneutics is about? From the tradition of reflexive philosophy, going from Descartes to Husserl, passing through Fichte and Jean Nabert, it has inherited the "taste for evidence," an evidence that of course is much more than a mere affaire de goût!" On the other hand, it must recognize, quoting Ricoeur's well-known formula, the historical contingency, the semantic equivocity, and the plurality of possible interpretations of symbols, which provoke one to think ("donnent à penser") only if their ambiguity is accepted. Hermeneutics must therefore hold together both links of the chain: the taste for evidence (that is, the requirements of reflection) and the feeling for ambiguity. Therefore it cannot avoid either the critical task of "distinguishing good and bad ambiguity." Nothing illustrates better the difficulties and the uneasiness of this task than Heinrich Rombach's philosophy. Although he himself is grounded in the phenomenological tradition, he suspects that Gadamer's hermeneutics still makes too many concessions to the Apollinian taste for evidence to be able to admit the powerful feeling for ambiguity that characterizes Apollo's brother Hermes. Therefore Rombach suggests that hermeneutical philosophy must convert to a philosophical "Hermetik" of an entirely new brand, which would have nothing in common with the esoteric traditions of the past, because it would be entirely grounded in phenomenology.

FROM IMMEDIATE PRESENCE TO HERMENEUTICAL INTUITION: THE PROBLEMATIC STATUS OF INTUITION

Regarding hermeneutics itself, one may ask whether Heidegger, introducing the notion of hermeneutical intuition in his early 1919 lecture,[6] was not trying to find the just balance between the (phenomenological) taste for evidence and the (hermeneutical) feeling for ambiguity. I have elsewhere tried to show, analyzing the characteristic features of his hermeneutics of facticity, that this is indeed the case. Of course, in 1953, Merleau-Ponty's interlocutors were not exactly the same as Heidegger's in 1919, with one exception: Bergson. His attempt to show that there can be a good ambiguity, which instead of being reduced to an opaque equivocity that annihilates every "taste for evidence," and shatters all certitude, "contributes to establishing ("fonder") certitudes, rather than menacing them" (EP 10/5). In his mind this possibility had to be justified through a critical dialogue with his great predecessors: Louis Lavelle's philosophy of the spirit and Henri Bergson's and Édouard le Roy's philosophy of life. Even if this tribute to the great ancestors is typical of the conventional "genre littéraire" of an inaugural Lecture at the Collège de France, Merleau-Ponty's discussion of this double heritage is important for our purpose. In fact, at the end of this double confrontation, the reader is supposed to understand much better how exactly "the taste for evidence" and "the feeling for ambiguity" can cooperate and not exclude one another.

Lavelle's "descending dialectic" attempts to anchor the taste for evidence directly in the miracle of Being, in the name of a philosophy of participation and total presence. But even here, the totally positive relationship with Being must take into account the double negation constituted by our solitude and our separation. Only in expressivity, in language, can one take up this experience of separation (later made famous by Levinas), unless pure thought would be nothing more than the intention to think. By saying that "one does not go beyond the world except by entering into it and that the spirit makes use of the world, time, speech, and history in a single movement and animates them with a meaning which is never used up" (EP 15/9), Merleau-Ponty is fully aware that he is trying to understand Lavelle better than Lavelle himself did. And adding that "It would be the function of philosophy, then, to record this passage of meaning, rather than to take it as an accomplished fact," he puts his finger precisely on a central phenomenon with which all hermeneutical thinking also concerns itself: understanding the labor of meaning through its contingent aspects signified in the idea of passage, rather than being satisfied with the sedimented aspects of meaning, crystallized in a "fait accompli."

We have just passed the centenary of the original publication of Bergson's *Matière et Mémoire*. This is a good time to admit that we are not yet finished with Bergson and in that respect, Merleau-Ponty's critical discussion of Bergson might become interesting once more. Much longer than the discussion of Lavelle, the presentation of Bergson's "ascending dialectic," interpreted along the line of Édouard le Roy, is much more important for our purpose. It places us exactly on the spot where the "junction between event and meaning" becomes inevitable. Once more, the taste for evidence and the feeling for ambiguity must be torn from a false philosophy of immediacy and fullness, which conceives intuition as a mere coincidence and pure contact (EP 18/12). In this fusionary conception, the simplicity of the philosophical act would consist in a "massive grip on being, without exploration, without interior movement of meaning" (EP 19/12). Exactly this conventional and superficial Bergsonism, for which everything is finally a matter of intuition, was one of the main targets against which Heidegger directed his attacks in his early Freiburg lectures.[7]

The Bergson whom Merleau-Ponty tries to save against the Bergsonians is totally different. His real problem is "the living and difficult relations of the spirit with the body and the world" (EP 20/13), that is, Husserl's and Merleau-Ponty's problem. In that case, the important thing is not intuition as such, but its interior movement. Thus philosophy becomes inventive in a twofold way: it is inventive in creating problems and in finding the appropriate solutions, for, says Merleau-Ponty, "the solution is also in us, and being itself is problematic" (EP 21/14); let us say that it is *fragwürdig* in Heidegger's sense.

Incidentally, we should note that the insistence on the inventiveness proper to philosophy is a characteristic feature of Gilles Deleuze's and Félix Guattari's book *What Is Philosophy?*[8] Deleuze too claims explicitly a very precise Bergsonian inheritance. In his case, one would even have to consider a threefold inventiveness: discovering problems, producing concepts, each one of which is "signed" by his author, and finally inventing "conceptual characters" ("personnages conceptuel"). This last notion could be of a great interest to a hermeneutical philosophy that tries to understand the processes of figuration, not only in literary texts, but also in the expression of philosophical thinking proper.

The metaphor of contact and fusion, that is, the metaphor of an "intuitive coincidence" (EP 38/30) must in this case be replaced by the metaphors of affection (*épreuve*), of solicitation, and of being haunted by the things themselves (this does not mean being persecuted by the other, as is the case with the late Levinas!). These metaphors make explicit the meaning of "the feeling for ambiguity." First of all, of course, we are haunted by the enigma of temporality. Without temporality there would be no ambiguity; in other words, to quote an astonishing formula, there would be no admission that at the heart of things, at the source of the *durée*, things appear to be "the adversity which makes us wait" (EP 23/15). Only if we quit the frontal relation of the spectator with the spectacle (the subject-object relationship) and if we enter into "a kind of complicity, an oblique and clandestine relationship" do we understand what "ambiguity" really means.

The phenomenological investigation of these three metaphors could be pushed even further. "Complicity," for instance, could be related to Heidegger's definition of the notion of *Befindlichkeit* (affection) in *Sein und Zeit*. This kind of complicity requires necessarily understanding (*Verstehen*) and some kind of explication (*Auslegung*). The category of obliquity plays an important role in Derrida's work, in particular, in *Marges*. As to the notion of clandestinity, it might be related to the phenomenological notion of "secrecy" elucidated in Jean-Louis Chrétien's book *La Voix nue*. What we can learn from Merleau-Ponty is the way to think those three phenomena together, instead of opposing them to each other.

In this context, Merleau-Ponty introduces another striking formula that announces his critique of absolute knowledge: "If to do philosophy is to discover the primary sense of being, then one does not philosophize in quitting the human situation; it is necessary rather to plunge into it. The absolute knowledge of the philosopher is perception" (EP 22/16). Much depends on how one sees the relationship between "plunging into the human situation" and the act of perception. Merleau-Ponty refers directly to Bergson's Oxford papers, which suggest "that instead of wishing to elevate ourselves above our perception of things, we immerse ourselves in it in order to bore into this perception and enlarge it." But in his comment Merleau-Ponty speaks also of the "human situation." Are these two notions strictly synonymous? If "situation" means the "hermeneutical situation," as Heidegger describes it in his early Freiburg teachings, the conclusion is unavoidable: perception, which means for Husserl the living givenness of things (*leibhaftig gegeben*), is not the primary source of givenness. A hermeneutical phenomenology like that of Heidegger transfers this privilege to care, as he claims explicitly in the Marburg lecture *History of the Concept of Time*.[9] Heidegger's rejection of "incarnation" (*Leibhaftigkeit*) as "a primary characteristic of the environing world" seems to indicate the major line of resistance that separates Heidegger's and Merleau-Ponty's description of being-in-the-world. Therefore I fully subscribe to Ricoeur's analysis in his article "Merleau-Ponty par-delà Husserl et Heidegger," where he shows through the example of Merleau-Ponty's analysis of temporality in the *Phenomenology of Perception*, why this conception of phenomenology resists a hermeneutics of care, because it refuses to replace the primacy of the present by that of the future.[10] Merleau-Ponty may search for a deeper hollowing ("creusement") and an enlargment of perception, as is shown in his later works, but nowhere does he replace it by something different.

A "generalized perception" that allows us to say "We are of it" ("Nous en sommes") (EP 22/17) is still a perception. Within the conceptual frame of a hermeneutics of facticity, which later develops into a hermeneutics of the destinal giveness of Being (*Geschick des Seyns, Zusage*, etc.), this "Nous en sommes" receives a different meaning. In Merleau-Ponty's eyes, it means first "that all beings are symbolic of our life, and that is what we see [or rather: we read "nous lisons"] in them" (EP 23/17). In this sense, notwithstanding the proximity with the philosophy of the later Heidegger, there is a fundamental difference between Heidegger's feeling for ambiguity and Merleau-Ponty's, or between Heidegger's understanding of the ontological difference and Merleau-Ponty's "Chiasm."

If our relation to Being is understood in the horizon of time, not only does it become oblique, moreover it leads to a "rapport obsessionnel." This expression must be taken in its etymological sense of being assieged. "We are of it": this also means that far from being reduced to one of the parameters of a genesis that could be described from the outside, "it is a history of ourselves which we tell to ourselves; it is a natural myth by which we express our ability to get along ("notre entente") with all forms of being" (EP 24/17). "A history of ourselves which we tell to ourselves": apparently this formula just tries to comment upon the true meaning of Bergson's *Creative Evolution*. However, it is also a formula that Merleau-Ponty applies to himself. Therefore, in the perspective of a hermeneutical philosophy, one will have to push further the analysis of this interconnection between the phenomenon of life and the act of storytelling, for instance, along the lines of Wilhelm Schapp's *In Geschichten verstrickt*.

In Merleau-Ponty eyes, what is most important is how the illusion of a perfect intuitive coincidence is dissolved in favor of the notion of coexistence. Once more, perception seems to be the essential mediating operator of this transformation, which makes "that this mute thing which, from the time it enters our life, begins to unfold its implicit meaning, which is revealed to itself through us" (EP 24/17). But does this not mean asking too much of perception? If we say with Heidegger that the world that surrounds us has a "significance" (*Bedeutsamkeit*) that indeed, leads from coincidence to coexistence (the latter term need not be reduced to its intersubjective meaning), does not perception come too late, because this transformation has already taken place?

Exactly, in this context of his critique of a certain Bergsonism, Merleau-Ponty introduces the topic of "the secondary, laborious, rediscovered naiveté" that "does not merge us with a previous reality, does not identify us with the thing itself, without any point of view, without symbol, without perspective" (EP 24/18). The use Ricoeur made of this topic of the transformation of the primary naïveté into a second naïveté, after having gone through the experience of suspicion, is well known. His debt to Merleau-Ponty is clearly admitted in his hermeneutical writings during the years 1965–1975. In the present lecture, it is Merleau-Ponty's thesis that "intuition needs to be understood, that it is necessary for me to appropriate a meaning in it which is held captive" (EP 25/18) that requires our attention. This thesis is crucial insofar as it raises the radical question "What precisely is intuitive in intuition?" This is almost literally the question that occurs in Heidegger's writings at the time when he introduces the notion of "hermeneutical intuition." Therefore it is legitimate to complete Merleau-Ponty's anti-Bergsonian question by asking: What is an intuition that, in order to be itself, needs to be understood, if not a hermeneutical intuition?

If we understand the concept of intuition in that way, maybe we can avoid an antinomy that dominates later philosophical debates: for instance, Derrida's opposition in *La Voix et le phénomène*, between the free play of signifiers, which gravitate around the pole of absence, and the nostalgic quest of a living and full presence guaranteed by intuition. This alternative is rejected by Merleau-Ponty when he declares that philosophical discourse occupies the place of an intuition that cannot be found, but "speaks also *to say it*, because it demands to be said, because it is not achieved before it has been said" (EP 25/19). In my opinion, this statement keeps a philosophy of ambiguity, as well as a hermeneutical philosophy, from becoming a *parole malheureuse,* an unhappy discourse. This could be illustrated through examples taken from literature, for instance, Sonnets XIII and XV of the first part of Rainer Maria Rilke's *Sonnette an Orpheus,* in which the poet too seems to speak "*for want of* being able to say the simplest sensual perceptions, but also in order *to say* them. Let me just quote the end of Sonnet XIII:

> *Wagt zu sagen, was ihr Apfel nennt.*
> *Diese Süße, die sich erst verdichtet,*
> *um, im Schmecken leise aufgerichtet*
>
> *klar zu werden, wach und transparent,*
> *doppeldeutig, sonnig, erdig, hiesig—:*
> *O Erfahrung, Fühlung, Freude—, riesig!*

FROM CONTACT TO READING

Even if in the poet's mouth formulas like "taste for evidence" and "feeling for ambiguity" receive another meaning than in the mouth of the philosopher, one cannot avoid noticing that on both sides the discourse makes uses of this double register. Is this enough to allow us to give an implicit hermeneutical dimension to this transformed concept of intuition that aims also to return to it "a component of negativity and ambiguity without which it would be blind"

(EP 29/22)? In my opinion, this interpretation is justified by the fact that the metaphor of contact is progressively substituted by that of reading. Although this metaphor too is directly borrowed from Bergson himself, it is obviously adopted by Merleau-Ponty. It is important to avoid assimilating at once the opposition *contact/reading* with the opposition *presence/absence*. The problem is not that of sacrificing the immediacy promised through intuition on the altar of absence. The problem is rather to allow intuition "to become what it is, because it contains a double reference to the mute being which it interrogates and the tractable [maniable] meaning which is derived from it" (EP 26/19). Is this not the fundamental gesture of phenomenology, expressed in the maxim: "Back to the things themselves"? This means, on the one hand, encountering them "through the appearances by which they are expressed," that is, in their specific mode of giveness, and, on the other hand, trusting "the words by which we express them" (EP 27/20).

For our purpose, we need not have a closer look at the three topics that illustrate Merleau-Ponty's interpretation of Bergson: the intuition of *la durée*, life, and God. Let us simply note that this threefold analysis confirms the importance of the metaphor of reading and the interpretation of "the consciousness of an agreement (d'un accord et d'un apparentement) between the philosopher and the phenomena" (EP 31/23, trans. mod.). "It is no longer a question of explaining life, but of deciphering it" (EP 31/23), says Merleau-Ponty, following Bergson. However, one must not assimilate this deciphering to the reading of a text. The multiple expressions of life are not deciphered as a text, but rather as a face, that is, as a physiognomy. This insistence, which goes together with the intention of leading Bergsonism from a "philosophy of impression to a philosophy of expression" (EP 36/28), is more in tune with a hermeneutical philosophy of expression like that developed by Georg Misch at the beginning of the thirties, than with a hermeneutic that privileges exclusively the paradigm of the text. In that sense one could say that hermeneutics leads from a philosophy of expression to a philosophy of understanding.

A NEW PLACE FOR TRUTH

Merleau-Ponty's statements regarding the notion of truth itself are also very important. Judgement alone is no longer the primary place of truth. When Merleau-Ponty says that for Bergson, "there is no place of truth to which one should go to search for it at any cost, even breaking human relationships and the ties of life and history. Our relationship to the true passes through others. Either we go towards the true with them, or it is not towards the true that we are going" (EP 39/31), he also defines his own position regarding the concept of truth. The philosophy of ambiguity, in contrast to other contemporary philosophies, does not dissolve the concept of truth altogether. It simply locates truth on another, more historical and intersubjective level. From now on, philosophical life will have to live up to the fundamental triangulation that is defined by three cardinal points: the true, the self, and the other. "The enigma of philosophy (and of expression) is that sometimes life is the same to oneself, to others, and to the true" (EP 40/32), says Merleau-Ponty in a beautiful formula. I would like to add that this is also the hope of reason and of understanding. In such moments of grace the tension between the taste for evidence and the feeling for ambiguity is no longer felt as being torn up, but as reconciliation.

THE LESSON OF SOCRATIC *A-TOPIA*

Avoiding the all too Hegelian term of "reconciliation," Merleau-Ponty sees this possibility as the expression of a "rebellious gentleness," a "pensive engagment," and an "intangible presence" (EP 41/33). This is why the philosopher is never a reassuring, but always a disturbing being. The three expressions just mentioned are not chosen at random; they are essential for understanding the figure of Socrates. Refusing to make philosophy a prison of books, that is, "an academic world where the choices of life are deadened and the occasions for thought are cut off" (EP 42/33), Merleau-Ponty certainly does not suggest that the best of all possible worlds is a world with no books at all. But there is a real danger that "The philosophy placed in books has ceased to challenge men" (EP 42/34). We could also say, referring to recent works of Pierre Hadot, Martha Nussbaum, and André-Jean Voelke, that this kind of philosophy no longer claims to heal the sicknesses of the soul and society.[11] Socrates, the patron of all philosophers was not yet "protected by literary immunity." Therefore, his *a-topia* remains the model of authentic philosophical existence, much more than the academic scholar or his contrary, the rebel. Thus, the praise of philosophy is first of all a praise of Socrates and his irony.

THE PHILOSOPHER CONFRONTING RELIGIOUS PHENOMENA

From my hermeneutical perspective, there is still another aspect of the "Praise" that has attracted my attention. It deals with the philosopher's attitude toward religion. Socrates, says Merleau-Ponty, believes *more* than any of his judges, "but he believes in another way, and in a different sense" (EP 43/35). However, does this mean that "Religion is therefore true, but true in a sense that it does not know"? Furthermore, does it mean that "it is in the world of the philosopher that one saves the gods and the laws by understanding them" (EP

46/37)? Does this statement not overestimate to some degree the philosopher's labor of understanding? In my opinion, this question concerns the very status of what we call "philosophy of religion." The strongest example of saving religion through philosophical reason is to be found in Hegel's *Religionsphilosophie*. This enterprise entirely relies upon the presupposition that religious thinking, which is bound to the element of *Vorstellung*, needs the assistance of the philosophical Concept (*Begriff*), in order to find access to its full truth. But is this promise fulfilled without a certain form of betrayal? Can it be reconciled with the definition of philosophy as an infinite investigation that prevents the newest and most living ideas from falling back into justifications and pretexts?

This question is important, because the most polemical part of "In Praise of Philosophy" is entirely dedicated to the struggle against two possible figures of absolute knowledge, the theological and the historical. To both, Merleau-Ponty opposes the contingency of history and finitude, a finitude whose counterpart is the perpetual beginning of the world. Finitude means also fragility, that is, "One explains nothing by man, since he is not a force but a weakness at the heart of being" (EP 52/44). Although I subscribe to this statement, I wonder whether it is enough to accuse theology of making use "of philosophical wonder only for the purpose of motivating an affirmation which ends it" (EP 53/44). This accusation underlies also Dominique Janicaud's argumentation in his polemical book on the theological turn of contemporary French phenomenology.[12] In his opinion, there is no doubt that Merleau-Ponty's position regarding theology represents the "good" answer, against the bad answers given by Levinas, Marion, Henry, and Chrétien. But is it enough to oppose simply Merleau-Ponty's metaphor of *enracinement* to Levinas's metaphor of *l'aplomb*?

I doubt whether hermeneutics can subscribe to the formula—it is not the same thing, it is almost the opposite, to understand religion and to accept it ("la poser") (EP 54/45). If this means just drawing attention to the difference between a positing and a reflective consciousness, it makes good sense. But in that case, there is no fundamental difference between the philosopher's attitude toward religion and his attitude toward other human phenomena, such as morality or politics. If, on the contrary, the real meaning is that religious consciousness as such, in its religious determination, is forever doomed to remain prisoner of the positivity of its dogmatic certitudes, it must be rejected, for the reason that it neglects the permanent effort of self-understanding and self-interpretation in which religious consciousness is engaged and that is reflected in the traditions and the texts through which it expresses itself. Later on in the Lecture, Merleau-Ponty rejects Hegel's thesis that "it is in the philosopher, and in him alone, that history makes sense" (EP 58/49–50). Why not do the same when the word "history" is replaced by "religion"? In fact, there never exists a zero-degree of religious consciousness, which would consist in a pure self-affirmative positivity and that would be totally opaque and blind as long as the philosopher has not helped it to rise to the level of the Concept, which in that case would mean indeed understanding it far better than it is able to understand itself.

Merleau-Ponty's discussion of the theological absolute is directed against Father (later Cardinal) Henri de Lubac and Jacques Maritain. He rejects the definition of philosophy as an atheism, which corresponds to philosophy as it is seen by the theologian, more precisely, by the theologian Henri de Lubac, author of the then famous book *Le drame de l'humanisme athée*. The statement that "we must admit that all thinking which displaces, or otherwise defines, the sacred, has been called atheistic, and that philosophy, which does not place it here or there, like a thing, but at the joining of things and words, will always be exposed to this reproach without ever being touched by it" (EP 55/46), could be compared to Heidegger's thesis in his *Natorp-Bericht*, which is taken up in numerous variations in his later lectures. For Heidegger, a philosophy that is exclusively dedicated to "letting see and apprehending factic life in its decisive ontological possibility" can only be "fundamentall atheistic."[13] Of course, neither Merleau-Ponty nor Heidegger mean by athe ism a theoretical or practical negation of the existence of God, which coul be reduced to the statement: "God does not exist; I have never encountere Him." This appears clearly in a note Heidegger added to the passage of th *Natorp-Bericht* just quoted: "Every philosophy which understands itself i what it really is must necessarily, as a factic modality of the explication c life, know—precisely when it has still some "feeling" of God—that thi tearing away through which life brings itself back to itself (*dieses von ih vollzogene zu sich selbst Zurückreißen des Lebens*) is, expressed in religiou terms, a way of raising one's fist against God (*eine Handaufhebung gege Gott*). But it is also in this way that it is loyal to God, in other words, tha it is at the height of its only possibility; to be an atheist thus means in thi case to be liberated from the need and the temptation to speak only in term of religiosity. Is not the very idea of a philosophy of religion, especially if i does not take into account human facticity, pure non-sense?"[14]

HOW TO THINK HISTORY AFTER HEGEL AND MARX?

Regarding history, which is the second figure of the absolute, Merleau-Ponty engages in a critical debate with Hegel and Marx. The important thing for me here is first the necessity of renouncing Hegel's conception of reason at work within history. Hegel is presented as a merchant of sleep who, in Alain's words, offers "us a sleep in which the dreams are precisely the world in which we live." In his opinion "it is in the philosopher, and in him alone, that history makes sense" ("rejoint son sens") (EP 58/49–50). On the contrary, Marx tries to "decrypt" the "historical rationality immanent in the life of men" (EP 59/50). But in that case also, the thinker must defend the immanent meanings of historical events and the contingency of the future against a rationality that sees historical development as "that of a river which under the influence of all-powerful causes, flows towards an ocean in which it disappears" (EP 61/52). Once more, ambiguity rhymes with fragility.

Has history still a meaning at the end of this double denial? It does so, if historical meaning is seen as "immanent in the interhuman event and as fragile as this event" (EP 60/51). Does this not require a hermeneutic of historical consciousness that replaces total mediation with an open interconnection of "spaces of experience" and "horizons of expectations"?[15] Following this hypothesis, historical narrative will play an essential role in the understanding of the "immanent meaning of interhuman events" (EP 64/53).

The fact is that in his lecture Merleau-Ponty never hints at such a possibility of narrative mediation of historical understanding. His only suggestion regarding the possibility of thinking history after Hegel and Marx alludes to the "living language" that makes possible the togetherness of thinking and thing. In living language, that is, in the act of speaking, the individual and the institution, event and structure cooperate. Thus, astonishingly enough, Merleau-Ponty sketches the hypothesis of a fecund encounter between a "theory of signs, as developed in linguistics" and a "theory of historical meaning" (EP 63/54). Will Saussure—the only linguist mentioned by name in the lecture—become the prophet of a philosophy of history of a new kind? The whole subsequent evolution has shown that he was not the right man for realizing Merleau-Ponty's dream. Indeed, what we are dealing with here is a dream and not with an elaborate theory; it is something like Socrates' dream of the theory of ideas in Plato's *Cratylus*. It is the dream that "An interconnection among all these phenomena is possible, since they are all symbolisms, and perhaps even the translation of one symbolism into another is possible" (EP 65/56).

This may be a dream, but it is a powerful one. The echo of this dream can still be found in 1965 in Ricoeur's book on Freud's *De l'Interprétation*, where he writes that "We are nowadays in search of a great philosophy of language which would take into account the multiple functions of human modes of signifying and their mutual relations."[16] However, Ricoeur was obliged to accept the evidence that there will never exist a unified philosophical theory of the multiple modalities of human expressivity, no more than there will be a general hermeneutics, which would cover all dimensions of the *ars interpretandi*.

LIMPING PHILOSOPHY AND THE "WOUNDED COGITO"

At the end of "In Praise of Philosophy," philosophy appears to be "an architecture of signs" (EP 66/57) that no longer can claim to be totally exterior to all the other systems of signs, of exchange, and of discourse. Precisely for this reason, its task—is this not the task par excellence of hermeneutics?—consists in the fact that "for the tacit symbolism of life it substitutes, in principle, a conscious symbolism; for a latent meaning, one that is manifest" (EP 66/57).

Not only does this task never come to an end, but also if we compare it to the confident steps of science, philosophy must confess its limping condition. To the spectator, to the outside observer, this limping is funny. Philosophy does not look like a very serious matter. Insisting on this lack of seriousness, Merleau-Ponty takes up Plato's clever idea in the *Theaetetus*, where he applies to Thales of Miletus, the ancestor of all philosophers, an Esopian anecdote concerning an astronomer who, contemplating the starry sky, fell into a hole. But, Plato would not be Plato, had he not read in this anecdote the tragical fate of Socrates.[17]

In his disconcerting conclusion, Merleau-Ponty still seems to have in mind Socrates' *a-topia*. A wise person (either a man or a woman) and a thinker are serious people. But, the philosopher is not just a "thinker." Even when he does not run away into "another world," or, we might say, into an "afterworld," he cannot avoid having "afterthoughts." Having such afterthoughts does not make him doubly serious; rather, the philosopher becomes someone "who is not altogether a real being" (EP 69/60). Does this comment turn him into a ghostly being? Not at all! Merleau-Ponty adds immediately that the division is not between two kinds of people, for instance, the Thracian servants on one side and the professional philosophers on the other. In each Thracian woman, there dwells a philosopher as yet unknown to her, for in her also burns the fire of the obstinate desire of understanding, a desire, which in the case of the philosopher, becomes a vocation. For the same reason, the superficial distinction between women and men of action and women and men of thinking, as well as the distinction between experts and nonexperts must be rejected.

I confess my admiration regarding the ultimate gesture through which "In Praise of Philosophy" opens out once more onto the extraphilosophical: "At the conclusion of a reflection which at first isolates him, the philosopher, in order to experience more fully the ties of truth which bind him to the world and history, finds neither the depth of himself nor absolute knowledge, but a renewed image of the world and of himself placed within it among others" (EP 79/63). In my understanding of hermeneutics each word of this sentence must be adopted. One could even say that hermeneutics must elaborate the theory of this interval between the philosophical and the extraphilosophical, which is also a meeting place.

Because our exploration of this in-between will never come to an end, we can say with Merleau-Ponty that "the limping of philosophy is its virtue" (EP 71/61). Hermeneutical philosophy too must acknowledge the fact that it will always be limping, not only because it renounces the idea of an absolute beginning and ending, but also because it rejects the idea of a *fundamentum inconcussum* that would forever guarantee an unshatterable evidence and certitude. Is it therefore enough to simply repeat Merleau-Ponty's lesson without further comment? Allow me to conclude my meditation by suggesting, in reference to the Bible story of Jacob struggling with the Angel, that sometimes this limping is not just a more- or less-heroic virtue, but can become a benediction.

NOTES

1. English translation: "Signs, that is, not a complete alphabet, and not even a coherent discourse. But rather, these signals, sudden like a glance, from which we receive events, books, and things."

2. Georg Misch, *Der Aufbau der Logik auf dem Boden der Philosophie des Lebens*. Göttinger Vorlesungen über Logik und Einleitung in die Theorie des Wissens, ed. F. Rodi et G. Bertram (Freiburg: Alber, 1994).

3. Cf. Theodore Kisiel and John van Buren, *Reading Heidegger from The Start: Essays in His Earliest Thought* (Albany, State University of New York Press, 1994).

4. "Éloge de la philosophie herméneutique" in: *Revue de l'Institut Catholique* 45 (janvier/mars 1993): 77–85.

5. Charles Taylor, *Philosophical Papers,* vol. I, *Human Agency and Language* (Cambridge: Cambridge University Press) 1985, chap. 2, p. 45.

6. Martin Heidegger, Gesamtausgabe, vols. 56 and 57. (Frankfurt: V. Klostermann, 1979), p. 116–17.

7. Cf. Otto Pöggeler, "Bergson und die Phänomenologie der Zeit" in: *Schritte zu einer hermeneutischen Philosophie* (Freiburg: K. Alber, 1994), p. 142–61.

8. Gilles Deleuze and Félix Guaattari, *Qu'est-ce que la philosophie?* (Paris: Ed. du Seuil, 1992), p. 170.

9. Martin Heidegger, *Gesamtausgabe*, vol. 20 (op. cit., 1976), p. 301.

10. Cf. Paul Ricoeur, *Lectures 2. La contrée des philosophes* (Paris: Ed. du Seuil, 1992), p. 170.

11. Pierre Hadot, *Exercices spirituels et philosophie antique* (Paris: Bibliothèque des Etudes augustiniennes) 1933; Martha C. Nussbaum, *The Therapy of Desire: Theory and Practice in Hellenistic Ethics* (Princeton, N.J.: Princeton University Press, 1994); André-Jean Voelke, *La philosophie comme thérapie de l'âme. Études de philosophie hellénistique* (Paris: Ed. du Cerf/Ed. Universitaires de Fribourg), 1993.

12. Cf. Dominique Janicaud, *Le tournant théologique de la phénoménologie française* (Paris: Ed. de l'éclat), 1992.

13. Martin Heidegger, *Interprétations Phénoménologiques d'Aristote,* trans. J. Fr. Courtine (Mauvezin, T.E.R., 1992), p. 27.

14. Ibid., p. 53.

15. Reinhart Koselleck, *Future Past: The Semantics of Historical Time,* trans. Keith Tiber (Cambridge: The MIT Press, 1985).

16. Paul Ricoeur, *De l'interpétation. Essai sur Freud* (Paris: Seuil, 1965), p. 13.

17. Cf. Hans Blumenberg. *Das Lachen der Thrakerin. Eine Urgeschichte der Theorie* (Frankfurt: Suhrkamp, 1987).

CHAPTER 6

The Thinking of the Sensible

MAURO CARBONE

THE PROBLEM OF THE CONCEPT

In a working note to *The Visible and the Invisible*, Merleau-Ponty writes that philosophy "shows by words . . . like all literature." He continues in the same note by saying that there is "no absolutely pure philosophical word" (VI 319/266).

The proximity of philosophy to literature—in this note, which attempts to "elaborate an idea of philosophy"—confirms what Merleau-Ponty claims in the last manuscript pages of *The Visible and the Invisible* (VI 200/153): the passage from the "ideality of the horizon" to " 'pure' ideality," from "sensible ideas" to "ideas of the intelligence," that is, from the "conceptless" to the "conceptual," does not imply a liberation from every visibility, but rather a *metamorphosis* of the flesh of the sensible into the flesh of language. This "metamorphosis"—a term that appears several times in these last pages—does not cancel the horizontal structures of the sensible. Indeed, the endless becoming of sense is due to these horizons. Thus, horizontal structures persist in the linguistic form that science considers as purified of horizons and therefore as "mature": the algorithm (PM 9/4; also PM 152/105–7, 175/125). The same final pages of *The Visible and the Invisible* in fact—and this comment is important for the developments this work would have had—maintain that "the system of objective relations, the acquired ideas [i.e., those "of the intelligence"], are themselves caught up in something like a second life and perception, which make the mathematician go straight to entities no one has yet *seen* [my emphasis], make the *operative* [Merleau-Ponty's emphasis] language and algorithm make use of a second *visibility* [my emphasis], and make ideas be the other side of language and calculus" (VI 201/153).

It is clear, therefore, that Merleau-Ponty qualifies the *sensible configuration* of the thing in the perceptual encounter as the "archetype" (VI 210/158) of a *carnal configuration* that likewise exists in the encounter with the language of the idea, of the concept, and of the algorithm.[1] In this sense, Merleau-Ponty also asserts that language participates in, is involved in onto-genesis (VI 139/102); it is *co-originating* with brute Being. This assertion does not mean, however, that there is no "world of silence," even negatively structured (VI 225/171); instead, it means that "the structure of [the] mute world is such that all possibilities of language are already given in it" (VI 203/155). In fact, language is not configured as a "second layer" that trans-lates a primordial layer (which, in turn, would be conceived as a positive "original text"); rather, language is conceived as the "metamorphosis" of the primordial layer, a metamorphosis that renews the carnal configuration of the mute world, but in "another flesh" (VI 200/153). Like the sensible (which, nevertheless, always still envelops language with its own silence), language itself is a "total part" (VI 271/218). It also functions "by encroachment (VI 200/153), and so—in its own being—it itself brings Being to expression. Language also, therefore, exceeds itself; it says "as a whole more than it says word by word" (PM 182/131). In this way, a ray of Essence shines through its nets (VI 273/220).

Concerning this question, a working note in *The Visible and the Invis-ible* devoted to the *problem of the concept* notes that "There is no longer a problem of the concept, generality, the idea, when one has understood that the sensible itself is *invisible*, that the *yellow* is capable of setting itself up as a level or a horizon" (VI 290/237; also VI 271–72/217–18). In fact, if the sensible can, in its individual visibility, outline its invisible generality, if the yellow is able to offer itself as an individual and as an element at the same time, then it manifests not only that the sensible immediately gives itself *with* an invisible, but also that it immediately can give itself *as* an "invisible," and not as its opposite.

What this passage means is that the concept is no longer a problem when it undergoes a "resignification" in the direction of the anti-Platonism that, according to Merleau-Ponty, Proust prefigures. In fact, Proust describes "ideas" that do not preexist independent from their sensible presentation (VI 195/149; also NC 191, 193, and 194); rather they are inseparable from and simultaneous with their sensible presentation, since the sensible presentation alone provides us with the "initiation" to them: ideas that are "there, behind the sounds or between them, behind the lights or between them, recognizable through their always special, always unique manner of entrenching them-selves behind them" (VI 198/151). In a similar sense, the same working note quoted above insists: "*every concept is first a horizontal generality, a gener-ality of style*" (VI 198/151; also VI 291/237).

It is precisely in this direction that Merleau-Ponty's thought seems to move in respect to what he indicates in "Everywhere and Nowhere" as "our"—epochal—"philosophical problem": "to open the concept without destroying it" (S 174/138). Here, by "to open"—not only the concept, but also all the other categories underlying the Western identity—Merleau-Ponty means an attempt to rediscover "the source from which they derive and to which they owe their long prosperity" (S 174/139). In this light, then, Merleau-Ponty tends, as we said, to "resignify" the concept, that is,—on the one hand—to reactivate its motivations in order to conserve its "rigor" (S 174/138), and—on the other hand—to abandon, as Proust's description of sensible ideas teaches (VI 198–99/151), the pretense to the "intellectual possession of the world" (S 174/138) that the concept seems always to exhibit.

Merleau-Ponty also criticizes such a pretense—in the exact same terms—in the working note we quoted initially. Here, in fact, on the basis of the very "idea of the *chiasm*," according to which "every relation with being is *simultaneously* a taking and a being taken," Merleau-Ponty explains that philosophy "cannot be total and active grasp, *intellectual possession* (my emphasis)" (VI 319/266). This implies, on the other hand, what Merleau-Ponty already maintained in "Indirect Language and the Voices of Silence" (1952): "No language"—not even that of philosophy—"ever wholly frees itself from the precariousness of mute forms of expression, reabsorbs its own contingency, and wastes away to make the things themselves appear" (S 98/78).

How, then, is this "showing by words" that, as we have seen, characterizes the proximity of philosophy to literature according to Merleau-Ponty configured? In order to clarify what *The Visible and the Invisible* calls, with a consciously inadequate term, the "object" of philosophy, Merleau-Ponty explains: "The effective, present, ultimate and primary being, the thing itself, are in principle *apprehended in transparency* through their perspectives, offer themselves therefore only to someone who wishes not to *have* them but to *see* them, not to hold them as with forceps, or to immobilize them as under the objective of a microscope, but *to let them be* and to witness their continued being—to someone who therefore limits himself to giving them the hollow, the free space they ask for in return, the resonance they require" (VI 138/101, my emphases). In this dense passage, the attitude of philosophy in relation to its "object" is qualified in terms of "seeing," which is understood, we could say, as "complying with," a verb that expresses the undistinguishability of activity and passivity. Characterized in this way, the attitude of philosophy implies the renunciation of the pretense to intellectual possession by the *Begriff*, and becomes instead a "letting-be." This last expression—which is not the only one inspired by Heidegger—is repeated a few lines later to designate perception itself, where the latter is significantly defined likewise as an "interrogative thought": "It is necessary to comprehend perception as this interrogative thought which lets the perceived world be rather than posits it, before which the things form and undo themselves in a sort of gliding, beneath the yes and the no" (VI 138/102).

Here, Merleau-Ponty's approach seems to extend, to the entire sensible domain, Kant's characterization of the limited domain of the beautiful, at least according to the interpretation of the first moment of the judgment of taste, proposed by Heidegger in his *Nietzsche*.[2]

LETTING-BE ACCORDING TO
HEIDEGGER AND MERLEAU-PONTY

In Heidegger's opinion, Schopenhauer "misinterprets" the first moment of the judgment of taste given by Kant in *The Critique of Judgment*: the beautiful as the object of a disinterested delight; Schopenhauer interprets this *absence of all interest* as the more common notion of "*indifference* toward a thing or person,"[3] and, consequently, claims that the aesthetic state occurs when "the will is put out of commission and all striving brought to a standstill."[4] Instead, Heidegger explains that "to take an interest in something suggests wanting *to have it for oneself as a possession, to have disposition and control over it. . . .* Whatever we take an interest in is always already *taken*, i.e., *represented*, with a view to something else."[5] Heidegger deems, on the other hand, that—in Kant's opinion—the behavior, by which we find something beautiful, "never can and never may" have an interest as its determining ground. "That is to say, in order to find something beautiful, we must *let* what encounters us, purely as it is in itself, come before us in its own stature and worth."[6] Thus, the behavior which initially Kant negatively defined as devoid of interest—the "comportment toward the beautiful"—manifests itself, according to Heidegger, as "*unconstrained favoring (freie Gunst)*." In the fifth paragraph of the *Critique of Judgment*, Kant in fact characterizes the disinterested delight toward the beautiful by that expression, on which Heidegger comments: "we must *freely grant* to what encounters us as such its way to be; we must *allow* and bestow upon it what belongs to it and what it brings to us."[7]

While in Schopenhauer's misinterpretation, the "unconstrained favoring" would mean indifference and suspension of will, thereby preventing every "essential relation to the object,"[8] in contrast Heidegger maintains that this very behavior—"letting the beautiful be what it is"[9]—would favor the essential relation to the object and would therefore be the first "magnificent discovery and approbation" of aesthetic behavior.[10] In fact, aesthetic behavior would be freed from the metaphysical stamp to which it has always been traditionally subject: "for the first time the object comes to the fore as pure object and . . . such coming forward into appearance is the beautiful. The word "beautiful" means *appearing* in the radiance of such coming to the fore."[11]

The disinterestedness characterizes, therefore, the real *openness*[12] to the world by the subject, who, in fact, frees himself from every interest, simultaneously liberating the object of the aesthetic contemplation, or, taking Heidegger's words up again, "letting the beautiful be what it is," *leaving it free* to *appear* as it is. Heidegger's comment, then, asks: "is not such unconstrained favoring rather the *supreme effort* of our essential nature, the *liberation* of our selves for the *release* of what has proper worth in itself, only in order that we may have it purely?"[13] In fact, the disinterestedness that, according to Kant, characterizes the delight toward the beautiful is, according to Heidegger, deeply connected to "letting the being be" in its disclosure, and—Heidegger believes—this "letting-be," in turn, defines freedom as the condition of truth understood as Un-concealment.[14] In addition, that "letting-be" has an essential connection not only with what Heidegger claims to be the meaning the term "logos" has— "letting-see" or "letting-appear" (*erscheinen lassen*)[15]—due to its derivation from the verb "legein," but also with the essence of thinking understood as *Gelassenheit* ("releasement" or "calmness").

Along these lines, in *The Life of the Mind*, Arendt offers a precious and synthetic recapitulation: "The mood pervading the letting-be of thought is the opposite of the mood of purposiveness in willing; later, in his re-interpretation of the 'reversal,' Heidegger calls it 'Gelassenheit,' a calmness that corresponds to letting-be and that 'prepares us' for a 'thinking that is not a willing.' This thinking is 'beyond the distinction between activity and passivity'."[16] Still, in the most important of Heidegger's writings about *Gelassenheit*— the "Conversations along a Country Path (*Feldweggespräch*)" written in 1944–45[17]—the letting-be of *Gelassenheit* that according to Arendt following Heidegger's intentions would have to be conceived as the opposite of purposiveness, seems to maintain, instead, a *purposiveness* in *Gelassenheit*. We find here, in fact, not a revocation of the will, but an echo of disinterestedness understood as "the supreme *effort* (*Anstrengung*) of our essential nature"— with its inevitable ethical resonances—that we already encountered in *Nietzsche*. Thus, in the "conversations"—significantly entitled *Zur Erörterung der Gelassenheit*—Heidegger, confirming yet again in this way the limits of his consideration of the sensible, indicates that *Gelassenheit* resides in the linguistic-ontological "place (*Ort*)" called the "Open" (*das Offene*), the place in which, according to his most famous discussions, the being manifests itself in the truth of its relationship with Being. But if, by virtue of this placement, *Gelassenheit* should then lie, as Arendt emphasizes, "beyond the distinction between activity and passivity," it seems to us instead that the *Gelassenheit* maintains the oscillation between activity and passivity. Indeed, the very definition of the essence of the *Gelassenheit* as "this restless coming and going between yes and no"[18] implies oscillation.

Earlier, we asserted that the "approbation" of the aesthetics based on what Heidegger traces in Kant's doctrine of the beautiful seems to be extended by Merleau-Ponty to the entire domain of the *aisthesis*: this extension appears to be the meaning of the "ontological rehabilitation of the sensible" discussed in the 1959 essay "The Philosopher and His Shadow" (S 210/167). We must then emphasize that Merleau-Ponty puts the "letting-be" in a place that, unlike that of Heidegger, lies—as we have already seen—"beneath the yes and the no." It is the aesthesiological-ontological place where original intentionality is ignited. Here we can see, therefore, the outlines of a thinking that does not operate "beyond," but *beneath* the distinction between activity and passivity. It is, in other words, a "logos of the aesthetical world," in which this genitive must be understood both in the subjective and in the objective sense, or rather *neither* subjectively *nor* objectively. In fact, this *logos* sprouts beneath the subject-object distinction, revealing itself as a thinking of the sensible itself (NC 186), as a thinking that is not, therefore, a kind of reflection on Being from the outside, but rather itself a phenomenon of this Being.

As we have seen, Heidegger's approach defines our disinterested openness to the world as "the supreme effort of our essential nature," and therefore it is not really able—in my opinion—to evade the distinction between activity and passivity. According to Merleau-Ponty instead, that openness is initiated by virtue of what Maldiney calls the "événement-avènement"[19] of appearing. Maldiney's "event-advent" is located beneath that distinction, or, in any case, it leads back beneath it, thus configuring itself as an *aesthetical shock*, which ignites the astonishment in our encounter with the sensible, suspends our habits, and causes the dispossession of the ability to distinguish between the active and passive poles reciprocally. Thus, echoing the last quote we took from *The Visible and the Invisible*, the interpretation of the unconscious given by Merleau-Ponty in conclusion of his last *résumé de cours* seems to move in this direction: "The unconscious is feeling itself, since feeling is not the intellectual possession of 'what' is felt, but a dispossession of ourselves in favor of it, an opening toward that which we do not have to think in order that we may recognize it. . . . the primordial unconsciousness would be the letting-be [*le laisser-être*], the initial yes, the undividedness of feeling" (RC 179/130–31).[20]

THE PHILOSOPHY OF A BAROQUE WORLD

In light of what has been said and taking up again the discussion of the passage of *The Visible and the Invisible* concerning the "object" of philosophy, we can therefore assert that, in the characterization of the philosophy as a "showing by words" (*faire voir*), the seeing implied here has to be understood as an "apprehending in transparency." This amounts to thinking of the sensible (the *logos* of the aesthetical world)—*letting it be* and thus returning to it, in a never ending phenomenological reduction (VI 232/178), "the resonance it requires." As a "showing by words," language is indeed the resonance of the silence in which the sensible dwells, and upon which the language itself feeds. Thus, the language does not have the pretense to observe from the outside, not to be implicated, because as we have seen, according to Merleau-Ponty, not even philosophical language "reabsorbs its own contingency, and wastes away to make the things themselves appear." Rather,

Merleau-Ponty assigns to philosophical language the duty "to accompany" (VI 165/124) the breakup of the originating. Therefore, we have to understand philosophy's "showing by words" in the sense which we have already mentioned, that of "complying with" (through the work of creation of those words) the showing of the sensible *logos* (VI 251/197). This implies, in turn, our taking part in this showing, our complying with it *from within*, and then pointing out our own *en-être* ("being of it"), "the passivity of our activity" of creation (VI 274/ 221), according to what Merleau-Ponty defines as "hyper-reflection" (*surréflexion*) (VI 61/38). But even what he says about painting in *L'oeil et l'esprit* (1960–61)—where, moreover, he emphasizes its *absence of interest* (OE 14/123)—and what he says about the *voyance* of modern literature in the course on "L'ontologie cartésienne et l'ontologie d'aujourd'hui" (NC 186 ff., 390–92) implies this taking part.

Precisely in these writings, Merleau-Ponty judges that modern art and literature—before and better than philosophy—have known how to express the "mutation" that is occurring in our epoch "within the relations of man and Being" (OE 63/139). In other words, he seems to be saying that modern art and literature (before and better than philosophy) have begun to *comply with*, from within, the showing of the sensible, *letting be* its peculiar "logic of implication or promiscuity" (RC 71/118) rather than superimposing upon it the antithetical logic of representation to which philosophy has been for the most part subordinate. In this way, as we have already been reminded, "every relation with being is *simultaneously* a taking and a being taken" (VI 319/ 266; also VI 177–78/134–35).[21] In fact, it is precisely the logic of seeing, conceived as "representing by frontally positioning," that underlies the configuration of the concept according to which the subject *grasps* in thought the universal representation of the object positioned in front of it.

In the last page of "The Philosopher and his Shadow," Merleau-Ponty provides the emblem of this logic of representation: the (supposed) representative frontality found in Renaissance perspective (S 228/181). On the other hand, he also assimilates the being of the sensible to a "Baroque world."[22] In this world, Merleau-Ponty sees a "configurational meaning that is in no way indicated by its 'theoretical meaning'" (or rather, by its *Kosmotheoretical* meaning), even if—as Merleau-Ponty emphasizes—it is precisely this "brute mind" that is going to be "asked to create culture anew" (S 228/181).

We must therefore think about what we called the "resignification" of the concept on the basis of the Baroque configuration of the sensible—in which every taking is simultaneously a being taken, and feeling is in reality a letting-be. We thereby renounce the pretenses of the *Begriff* to take "intellectual possession of the world" and are led conceptuality to speak, at last, about "the passivity of our activity," of which, Merleau-Ponty claims, "philosophy has never spoken" (VI 274/221). Perhaps, this is exactly what Merleau-Ponty meant by "open[ing] the concept without destroying it." Certainly, such a "resignification"—which takes into consideration, as hyper-reflection teaches, the bond between conceptuality and conceptlessness, between conceptuality and the sensible as itself *invisible*, as the always "carnal" configuration of sense (VI 319/265)—implies also the "resignification" of metaphoricity, which is traditionally opposed to conceptuality. Such a "resignification" of metaphoricity would lead us to recognize the deepest metaphorical, origin of the concept,[23] or better, to recognize a common source of the concept and metaphor as "styles of being,"[24] which therefore plant their roots in the polymorphism of Being itself, in the "oneiric world of analogy" (OE 41/132), in short, in the excess of the sensible, besides that of language.

Thus, at this point, it does not seem accidental that, precisely in a discussion about a theorist of the Baroque, we are reminded how the term "concept," in its Latin *etymon*, had a semantic halo that we can still trace in the direction of thinking in which Merleau-Ponty seems to be going: "Twentieth-century philosophy usually considers the term 'concept' as the translation of the German word 'Begriff.' This last word came to the attention of philosophical reflection because of the enrichment of a speculative complexity by German philosophers from Kant on. It happens, then, that we say 'concept,' but we think *Begriff*: what escapes us is that the word of Latin origin has an opposite semantic orientation to that of the German word. In the case of the latter, the act of apprehension is etymologically connected with *greifen*; in the Latin term *conceptus*, the act of apprehension is etymologically derived from *cum-capio*, which means 'taking' understood as 'welcoming.' In conclusion, to conceive does not mean taking possession of anything, but rather creating space for something."[25]

NOTES

This essay was translated from the Italian by Giacomo Carissimi.

1. See R. Barbaras, *Le dédoublement de l'originaire*, in M. Merleau-Ponty, *Notes de cours sur 'L'origine de la gémétrie' suivi de Recherches sur la phénoménologie de Merleau-Ponty*, ed. R. Barbaras (Paris: PUF, 1998), pp. 289–303. See also J. Taminiaux, *The Thinker and the Painter*, trans. M. Gendre, in *Merleau-Ponty Vivant*, ed. M. C. Dillon (Albany: State University of New York Press, 1991), p. 203.

2. See the paragraph entitled "Kant's Doctrine of the Beautiful: Its Misinterpretation by Schopenhauer and Nietzsche," in M. Heidegger, *Nietzsche*, Erster Band (Pfullingen: Neske, 1961), English translation by D. F. Krell as *Nietzsche: Volume I, the Will to Power as Art* (San Francisco: Harper & Row, 1979), pp. 107–14.

3. Heidegger, *Nietzsche*, vol. 1, p. 108, my emphasis.

4. Ibid.

5. Ibid., p. 109, my emphasis.

6. Ibid., my emphasis.

7. Ibid., my emphasis.

8. Ibid., p. 110.

9. Ibid., p. 109, my emphasis.

10. Ibid.

11. Ibid., p. 110, my emphasis.

12. On this subject, see both J. Taminiaux, "Les tensions internes de la Critique du jugement," in id., *La nostalgie de la Grèce à l'aube de l'idéalisme allemand. Kant et les Grecs dans l'itinéraire de Schiller, de Hölderlin et de Hegel* (The Hague: Nijhoff, 1967), p. 39; and P. Gambazzi, "La bellezza come non-oggetto e it suo soggetto," in *Azione e contemplazione* (Milano: IPL, 1992), p. 315.

13. Heidegger, *Nietzsche,* vol. 1, p. 107, my emphases.

14. See M. Heidegger, *Vom Wesen der Warheit* (Frankfurt am Main: Klostermann, 1943), section 4, now in id., *Wegmarken,* ed. F. W. von Herrmann (Frankfurt am Main: Klostermann, 1976), where it is also explained that the "letting-be" does not mean indifference, but rather trusting in the entity, and letting oneself be enveloped by it.

15. See respectively M. Heidegger, *Sein und Zeit* (Halle: Niemeyer, 1927, 1963), section 7b; id., *Der Satz*; id., *Vorträge und Aufsätze* (Pfullingen: 1954), Neske.

16. H. Arendt, *The Life of the Mind,* vol. 2 (London: Secker & Warburg, 1978), p. 178.

17. See M. Heidegger, *Zur Erörterung der Gelassenheit. Aus einem Feldweggespräch über das Denken* (Pfullingen: Neske, 1959), in id., *Gesamtausgabe,* band 13: *Aus der Erfahrung des Denkens 1910–1976* (Frankfurt am Main: Klostermann, 1983), pp. 37–74.

18. M. Heidegger, *Zur Erörterung der Gelassenheit,* p. 57: *"Das ist wieder dieses ruhelose Hin und Her zwischen Ja und Nein."*

19. H. Maldiney, *L'art, l'éclair de l'être. Traversées,* Seyssel: Éd. Comp'Act, 1993), p. 333.

20. For more about feeling as letting-be, see R. Barbaras, *La perception. Essai sur le sensible* (Paris: Hatier, 1994). For more about these questions, see Merleau-Ponty's course notes "Heidegger: la philosophie comme probleme" (NC 91–148). See also the commentary on these notes offered by F. Ciarmelli, "L'originaire et l'immediat. Remarques sur Heidegger et la dernier Merleau-Ponty," in *Revue Philosophique de Louvain,* vol. 34, 1998.

21. This confirms, moreover, how, unlike Heidegger, Merleau-Ponty's problem does not lie in revoking every will to possess, but rather in recognizing the original

and ineradicable reciprocity of the latter. See also R. Barbaras, "La puissance du visible: Merleau-Ponty et Aristote," in id., *Le tournant de l'experience. Recherche sur la philosophie de Merleau-Ponty* (Paris: Vrin, 1998), p. 19.

22. Christine Buci-Glucksmann has thematized the closeness between the aesthetical ontology of the "last" Merleau-Ponty and the ontological aesthetics of the Baroque. See C. Buci-Glucksmann, *La folie du voir. De l'esthétique baroque* (Paris: Galilée, 1986), esp. p. 73 and pp. 85–86.

23. As Arendt also does, with significant reference, in support of this thesis, to the relationship of "symbolical exhibition" between ideas of reason and aesthetical ideas, outlined by Kant and defined in section 59 of the *Critique of Judgment* (see "Language and Metaphor," in H. Arendt, *The Life of the Mind,* vol. 1, pp. 98–110).

24. Barbaras also reaches this conclusion in the paragraph entitled "La métaphorique du monde" of his *De l'être du phénomène. Sur l'ontologie de Merleau-Ponty* (Grenoble, France: Millon, 1991), p. 224 ff. That paragraph provides a valid examination of the working note of *The Visible and the Invisible* dated 26 November, 1959, which is devoted to the metaphor. Barbaras emphasizes how Merleau-Ponty criticizes the traditional conception Garelli, "Le lieu d'un questionnement," *Les Cahiers de Philosophie,* nouvelle série, n. 7, printemps 1989, pp. 131–33.

25. M. Perniola, "Presentazione" of B. Gracián, *Agudeza y arte de ingenio* (1648), It. trans. by G. Poggi (Palermo: Aesthetica, 1986), p. 19. See also the comparison between Merleau-Ponty and Gracián made by C. Buci-Glucksmann, *La folie du voir. De l'esthétique baroque,* p. 85.

CHAPTER 7

Is Merleau-Ponty Inside or Outside the History of Philosophy?

HUGH J. SILVERMAN

Putting together an anthology about famous philosophers may seem to be an inoffensive undertaking. Yet one does not attempt it without reservations. It raises the question of what idea one should have of the history of philosophy, and even of philosophy itself.

We know how uncomfortable a writer is when he is asked to do a history of his thoughts. We are scarcely less uncomfortable when we have to summarize our famous contemporaries.

Philosophy is everywhere, even in the "facts," and nowhere does it have a private realm which shelters it from life's contagion.

There is not *a* philosophy which contains all philosophies; philosophy as a whole is at certain moments in each philosophy. To take up the celebrated phrase again, philosophy's center is everywhere and its circumference nowhere.

—Merleau-Ponty, *Signs*

In 1956, Maurice Merleau-Ponty published a volume of essays on the history of philosophy. It was entitled *Les Philosophes célèbres*.[1] For this volume, he invited the contribution of colleagues and friends, many of whom at the time were hardly known. They included names such as Gilles Deleuze (on Bergson), Norberto Bobbio (on Croce), Anthony Quinton (on Russell), Alphonse de Waelhens (on Husserl, Heidegger, and Sartre), Alfred Schuetz (on Scheler) and on earlier centuries: Jean Beaufret (on Heraclitus, Parmedides, and Zeno), Maurice de Gandillac (on Nicholas of Cusa), Ferdinand Alquie (on Descartes and Malbranche), Raymond Polin (on Hobbes and Locke), Jean Starobinski (on Rationalism and on Montaigne), Gilbert Ryle (on Hume), Jules Vuillemin

131

(on Kant, Fichte, and Schelling), Eric Weil (on Hegel), Harold Rosenberg (on Marx), Karl Loewith (on Nietzsche), and others. This list itself—selecting only some of the principal names that became key to the development of twentieth-century thought in France, England, and the United States—is a kind of pantheon of figures of philosophical importance. Merleau-Ponty was himself of course already Professor of Philosophy at the Collège de France. And therefore he was able to gather together some of the luminaries or about-to-become-luminaries of his own age. There are also figures missing from the list—most notably Merleau-Ponty himself.

REASONS FOR THE SELECTIONS

Those who are absent from the list of major figures from the history of philosophy also signify. The "discovery" of Vico as a major figure from out of the eighteenth-century Italian rationalist tradition; Mill and Bentham might have been selected to account for nineteenth-century utilitarianism; but most remarkable is the complete absence of American philosophers from the list. James, Royce, Peirce, Santayana, Dewey, and even Whitehead are all noticeably absent. Of course, Renaissance specialists would have appreciated the selection of Pomponazzi, Ficino, and Pico della Mirandola and possibly even Machiavelli, Thomas More, and Erasmus. But the inclusion nevertheless of Bacon and Montaigne will be heartwarming to those who believe in Renaissance philosophy.

Apart from the absence of American philosophers—and he did ask Harold Rosenberg and Alfred Schütz to provide essays for the book—his shaping of twentieth-century thought will seem curious to some non-French historians of philosophy. Published in 1956, the oversized volume had been in preparation for several years. Now that four decades have passed since the book was published, the selections are worth some scrutiny. Continental philosophers today will note the dominace of some of its major figures: Bergson, Croce, Alain, Husserl, Scheler, Heidegger, Sartre. While Bergson, Croce, and Alain are not studied today as much as they might be, they were undoubtedly formative figures for Merleau-Ponty as he developed his philosophical identity. The inclusion of Maurice Blondel will be particularly surprising to many today. Some would have liked to see Ingarden, de Beauvoir, Levinas, Dufrenne, and even Camus in the list. And for those writing in the analytic tradition, the sole presence of Russell against the absence of Frege, Wittgenstein, Moore, Ryle, Austin, and Ayer will be annoying—as will the oversight of Lukacs, Benjamin, Horkheimer, and Adorno in the so-called Frankfurt school. There are also some contemporary Italian philosophers such as Enzo Paci and Luigi Payerson as with Ortega y Gasset and Unamuno in Spain who do not appear in the constellation of stars.

One cannot fault Merleau-Ponty for noninclusion of so many important philosophers who have subsequently become names to be reckoned with. Had a British philosopher produced a similar volume at the same time, it is doubtful that more than three of the nine philosophers: Russell, Husserl, and Heidegger (possibly also Sartre) would have survived the top hits list. And Bradley as well as Collingwood might even have been substituted for Croce. And I doubt that an American editor would permit the total omission of Emerson, Thoreau, James, Royce, Peirce, Santayana, Whitehead, Dewey, Mead, and so forth.

A catalog of names for different traditions is only a way of situating Merleau-Ponty in a particular location in the history of thought and in relation to the weight of national perspectives (if not national pride). Merleau-Ponty was in effect chronicling the very figures who marked his own philosophical development. Merleau-Ponty already occupied the Chair of Philosophy at the Collège de France, which Bergson had held years before him. Bergson, he says, "makes perception the fundamental mode of our relation to being" (S 195/155). And it should not be forgotten that Merleau-Ponty himself lectured on Bergson along with Malbranche and Maine de Biran in 1946 at the Ecole Normale Superieure. Furthermore, Alain, who was one of his teachers at the Ecole Normale Superieure, "described freedom upheld by the world's flux like a swimmer on the water which holds him up and is his force" (S 195/155). Croce was the dominant survivor of the Hegelian tradition in the twentieth century—apart perhaps from Bradley and Collingwood in Britain—and other than Kojève and Hippolyte who translated and lectured on Hegel in Merleau-Ponty's younger years in Paris. Of Croce, Merleau-Ponty says that he "put philosophy back into contact with history" (S 195/155). And there is no doubt about the role of Husserl and Heidegger in the phenomenological articulation of Merleau-Ponty's own position—even though Merleau-Ponty hardly thematizes Heidegger until a few years later in his 1960–61 lectures on "Philosophy and Non-Philosophy since Hegel." It is intriguing that when Merleau-Ponty describes Husserl's work, he says that he "took the carnal presence of things as the model of obvious fact." (S 195/155). In a sense then, the philosophers whom Merleau-Ponty has chosen for the twentieth century are the backdrops for his own development and thought.

Scheler is there not just because he provided a phenomenological theory of values and feeling but also because Merleau-Ponty had written a review of Scheler's study of *ressentiment* back in 1935. And then there is Sartre—Merleau-Ponty's contemporary, his fellow student, his collaborator at *Les Temps Modernes*, his coeditor at the Gallimard Bibliothèque de la philosophie, and his former friend. Probably when the project was undertaken, Sartre and Merleau-Ponty were still on good terms—the break occurred around 1954 when Sartre attacked Merleau-Ponty's student and friend Claude Lefort. And it is no accident that de Waehlens—who had already published a book on

Merleau-Ponty's philosophy and then one on Heidegger—was asked to write the essay not only on Husserl and Heidegger but also on Sartre. One might suspect that there was thereby some sense of security that Sartre would be "accurately" represented.

DISCOVERY AND INVENTION

Merleau-Ponty's own place in the history of philosophy is one that he has not only shaped through the selection of philosophers in the 1956 volume, but also through his own contributions to it. The volume is organized chronologically. He then wrote an introductory essay for the whole book and brief introductory remarks to each section. The sections included: "The Orient and Philosophy," "The Founders," "Christianity and Philosophy," "The Great Rationalism," "The Discovery of Subjectivity," "The Discovery of History," and "Existence and Dialectic." The introductory preface and five of the seven sections were gathered together and published as the chapter "Everywhere and Nowhere" in *Signs* less than a year before he died. The other two sections "The Founders" and "The Discovery of History" were published in English for the first time in 1992 in *Texts and Dialogues*.[2] It is curious that these two sections were not included since they are two of the most penetrating and insightful pieces in the volume.

Merleau-Ponty's selection of titles for each section is as significant as the philosophers deified by the book. For the last three sections, Merleau-Ponty clearly identified key themes from his own thought: subjectivity, history, dialectic, and existence—the discovery of subjectivity dealing with the question of the Self from Montaigne to Kierkegaard; the discovery of history having to do with the German idealists (Schelling and Hegel) to Marx and Nietzsche; and lastly "Existence and Dialectic" focusing on the twentieth-century developments from Bergson to Sartre.

Why Merleau-Ponty left out the section on the "Discovery of History" along with the one on "The Founders" from his essay in *Signs* is not fully clear. One might speculate that he was concerned about the repetition of "Discovery" in the two adjacent pieces—the discovery of subjectivity and the discovery of history. Although not reproduced in the English translation, he begins "The Discovery of History" with the expression "repetons que."— "repetons que les 'decouvertes' en philosophie sont toujours en meme temps des 'inventions' " (TD 126). Merleau-Ponty places considerable weight on the notion that discoveries in philosophy are also inventions. As he says with respect to "history": "When philosophers formed the concept of history, this 'realization' [*prise de conscience*] was a shaping [*mise en forme*] and not simply the observation or noting down of a prior fact" (TD 126). "Humanity," he says, "would not *live* a history if someone had not one day *spoken* of history" (TD 126). By this, Merleau-Ponty means that for history to be what it is it must be remarked, observed, noted down, articulated, in short, "said." It is not that there are events and then they are written down. Merleau-Ponty's understanding of history is that it is made, not observed after the fact. And his reading of the German idealists' position as well as that of Nietzsche is a rather radical view. It is not that history is inevitable or that history happens and then it is written down. On the contrary, in Merleau-Pontean fashion the lived is understood as lived through the descriptions and accounts that remark on it. Now although Merleau-Ponty writes the essay with the sense that this is his own view, he wants to show that Schelling, Hegel, Marx, Comte, and Nietzsche have not only held this position, but also that they *discovered* it. It is as though there were no *history* before these philosophers took it up, molded it, shaped it, rethought it, invented it. It is as though they "invented history" which, for Merleau-Ponty is also to say that they "discovered history." This is not to say that people did not experience history before the nineteenth century, that history, even the history of philosophy, did not take place. Rather, "at a certain moment, in a certain historical context history was first spoken of" (TD 126). The invention of history does not mean that things did not happen, or that there were not historians such as Thucydides, Herodotus, Plutarch, Livy, Commines, Joinville, Machiavelli, and others, long before Hegel and Marx, Comte, and Nietzsche, but rather that history came to be thought, invented in a way that it could not have functioned previously. It was now possible to experience history as it was written, to find truth by a "retrograde movement," in which history presents itself to us as existing prior to our act of knowledge. This is similar to Merleau-Ponty's own claim that when I walk into a room I experience it as "already there." Here it is a matter of history remarking what is already there, already experienced, already eventful. The philosopher, he says, will have to live with the history that history "discovers" as much as the history that the nineteenth-century philosophers have "discovered," that is, *invented*.

The repetition of the word "discovery" in the two essays is not insignificant. In the discussion of the "discovery of subjectivity," Merleau-Ponty asks why we should make into "stages of a single discovery" the different and discordant theories of subjectivity—from "the Self which Montaigne preferred above all and the one which Pascal hated" to Descartes's "thinking Ego" to Rousseau's abyss of innocence and guilt, to Kant's transcendental subject, to Biran's knowing subject in a world inhabited by a body, to Kierkegaardian "subjectivity." Merleau-Ponty's question is: "are we to believe that subjectivity existed before the philosophers?" (S 192/152).

And he goes on to ask: "What is this contact of self with self before the self is revealed?" (S 192/152–53). In this sense, for Merleau-Ponty the discovery of subjectivity is also the invention of subjectivity. The subjectivity that was already there was indeed already there when it came to be named, identified, articulated, expressed. But this is no more a realism than a nominalism. Subjectivity does not get its identity from being named (it is discovered) and subjectivity also comes into being (is invented) when it is encountered and named (in different ways). And it is not insignificant that Merleau-Ponty ascribes this notion of discovery to both subjectivity and history. For Merleau-Ponty both subjectivity and history were discovered in the modern age—they were already there waiting to be discovered, and yet they were also invented by the modern philosophers as well.

The discovery of history and the discovery of subjectivity were both preparatory—or perhaps better, prior stages to—the concerns with "Existence" and "Dialectic." The book ends with Sartre—and anyone who knows Sartre's work well is aware that Sartre's thought can be divided between a concern with existence—as in *Being and Nothingness* (1943)—and with dialectic—as in *Critique of Dialectical Reason* (1960). While Sartre had not yet published the latter, the methodology for it had appeared in 1956 as "Questions of Method" and that essay was in many respects a response to and reformulation of Merleau-Ponty's own *Adventures of the Dialectic* (1955).

Merleau-Ponty writes "we know how uncomfortable a writer is when he is asked to do a history of his thoughts. We are scarcely less uncomfortable when we have to summarize our famous contemporaries" (S 194/154). And the greatest discomfort for Merleau-Ponty was doubtless the need to summarize the work of Sartre. In 1936, he had reviewed Sartre's book *Imagination* and in 1943 he reviewed Sartre's remake of the Oresteia trilogy in *The Flies*. In the latter, he lamented the absence of the word "freedom" in most of the other reviews of Sartre's play: "Is freedom, then, devoid of dramatic value?" he asks. "Without homeland or family, made aware, by the Pedagogue and by travel, of the relativity of right and wrong, Orestes floated about in the air, impalpable, without convictions, open to any suggestion. But a moment comes when he wearies of that kind of freedom. He would like to really exist, feel the earth beneath his feet, and be a man among men" (TD 115). Now in 1956 when the sentiments had changed, Merleau-Ponty nevertheless gives Sartre a fair reading:

> Behind the idea of sovereign choice there was even in Sartre's thinking (as can be seen in *Being and Nothingness*) the different and really antagonistic idea of a freedom which is freedom only embodied in the world as work done upon a factual situation. And from then on, even in Sartre's thinking, "to exist" is not merely an anthropological term. Facing freedom, existence unveils a wholly new face of the world—the world as promise and threat to it; the world which sets traps for, seduces, or gives in to it. (S 196155)

Facing freedom, for Merleau-Ponty, is the fundamental element of Sartre's philosophy of existence. But what of the role of "dialectic"?

Merleau-Ponty says: "the dialectic our contemporaries are rediscovering is . . . a dialectic of the real" (S 196/156). It is also, through Bergson and Husserl, a "dialectic of time" and an "intuition of essences." He sees them linked together in a living unity whose contrasting dimensions are of a time that is ultimately coextensive with being. Time coextensive with being—this is the dialectic that (through Heidegger) Merleau-Ponty sees as the dialectic of his own age. He sees them as linked by temporality, perception, and our carnal being (S 197/156). This is hardly the dialectic of Hegel or even that of Sartre. Here Merleau-Ponty begins to inscribe his own account of dialectic and its imbeddedness in temporality, perception, and carnal being—three themes that have pervaded his thought from the time of the *Phenomenology of Perception* (in 1945). He sees this dialectic as one of mediation—a mediation in which in order to obtain access to the world, we must withdraw from it. Such a "concrete philosophy" requires that one stick close to experience. As Merleau-Ponty puts it:

> As difficult as it is . . . to imagine the future of philosophy, two things seem certain: it will never regain the conviction of holding the keys to nature or history in its concepts, and it will not renounce its radicalism, that search for presuppositons and foundations which has produced the great philosophies. (S 198/157)

Philosophy will not be able to be the scientific access to the secrets of nature and history as it once was; and philosophy will never give up being radical in its search for presuppositions and foundations. The former cedes to the natural and historical sciences what they have claimed for themselves. The latter reaffirms the necessity for philosophy to be radical in searching for what underlies judgments and positions, and in establishing foundations.

But what does it mean to seek to establish foundations? In the introductory section to the discussion of the Greek philosophers, Merleau-Ponty gives them credit with having "founded philosophy" while other societies simply encountered philosophy or brushed up against it briefly by chance. He claims that the Greeks had no sense of history and subjectivity (since that comes much later). But they did understand that "philosophy is the quest that brings to light all the presuppositions of life and knowledge, the desire for an unconditioned knowledge, absolute transparency" (TD 124). So the Greeks introduced, founded, part of the second radicalism that Merleau-Ponty sees as intimately and perhaps inextricably tied to philosophy. And further they "rediscoverd the abrupt upsurge of being prior to reflection, and that radical knowing rediscovers unknowing" (TD 124). As being presents or shows itself, there is also a kind of awareness of what is not known. This seeming paradox is basic to Merleau-Ponty's conception of founding—the kind of founding philosophy engages in, and the kind for which the Greeks were especially noted. Their *invention* of dialectic is crucial to the founding that they inaugurated. And for Merelau-Ponty that meant "overcoming skepticism," drawing out truth from paradox, recognizing that the power of truth cannot be separated from the power to go astray and that being-oneself means being-other (TD 124). This founding function that Merleau-Ponty attributes to the Greeks is also reaffirmed in his account of the future of philosophy at the end of "Everywhere and Nowhere." But these are also the elements that Merleau-Ponty himself values in philosophy, and that he himself will want to develop in his own philosophy. So what he sees in the Greeks is precisely what he sees in his own enterprises. Out of existence and dialectic is to come a new and radical founding of philosophy, founding again in the sense of discovery and invention, questioning and uncovering of an indirect language of experience.

INSIDE OR OUTSIDE?

Now we can return to our original question: is Merleau-Ponty inside or outside the history of philosophy? There is no question that in his account of the history of philosophy in *Les Philosophes célèbres*, he very much sees himself as part of a historical succession in which the discovery of subjectivity and the discovery of history turn into a dialectic of existence and dialectic. But again his dialectic is not of the Hegelian sort. His dialectic is such that he finds the philosopher encountering what is as already there; his dialectic is one of experience and philosophy becoming that experience, philosophy interrogating what is and finding itself there in what is interrogated. His dialectic is more of a tension between existence and dialectic, an ambiguity between the two.

But there is also a sense in which Merleau-Ponty is reflecting on the history of philosophy, placing himself outside it, somewhere in the future direction that he himself invokes. But Merleau-Ponty could not know in what sense he is already beyond the history that he introduces and interrogates. Merleau-Ponty could not know of the work of Foucault, Derrida, and Kristeva—to name three notable events that occur after Merleau-Ponty and that both draw him in and set him off from them.

When Merleau-Ponty reflects on the shape of the history of philosophy, he is asking what there is of this history that lives on in his own world: the founders (the Greek philosophers) were founders not because they introduced concepts or habits of thought and then receded into the past, but rather because "they practiced and defined the basic attitude that gave rise to everything subsequently known as philosophy" (TD 123). Hence reading the Greeks is reading philosophy today. Reading the Greeks is uncovering once again what we today—for whatever today—find to be already there in our own thought, attitudes, practices. In this sense, not only is Merleau-Ponty not fully inside the history of philosophy but also the Greeks are not simply historical figures but rather the very ongoing foundations of philosophical thought at any age since their time. Hence for Merleau-Ponty we are already Greek philosophers, we already think as they do because in founding philosophy, they are also present in our own thought.

The same is true of Merleau-Ponty as well. Merleau-Ponty specialists read Merleau-Ponty in detail, seeking to articulate the structures, the ambiguities, the dialectics, and the intertwinings in his thought. But there is also the sense in which the whole continental tradition since Merleau-Ponty thinks with him, in his terms, in his shadow. He himself spoke of the shadow that Husserl cast on European philosophy since his time—and yet every time Merleau-Ponty speaks of Husserl, he sounds more like Merleau-Ponty than Husserl. When Merleau-Ponty says that "Husserl took the carnal presence of things as the model of obvious fact" (S 195/155), would one associate that description more with Husserl or with Merleau-Ponty? As did Husserl before him, Merleau-Ponty finds in the history of philosophy what he himself has already discovered in philosophy itself, that is, what he himself has already invented in his own understanding of philosophy.

So what is it that is "partout and nulle part"—everywhere and nowhere? Merleau-Ponty says that it is philosophy that is everywhere and nowhere: "Philosophy is everywhere, even in the 'facts,' and nowhere does it have a private realm which shelters it from life's contagion" (S 163/130). Philosophy is public, but it is also in every nook and cranny of human life (and not just in those domains that people notice). Its business is to uncover these spaces—all of them, wherever they are, in whatever domain: whether it be in human society, in the natural world, in art and literature, in ideas and thoughts, in everything and everywhere. But can philosophy be located specifically, designated, framed, controlled? Merleau-Ponty's answer is a resounding "no." Philosophy has no "private realm," no space that is inaccessible, no safe haven away from the pain and pleasure of daily life, away from the worries and joys of human experience, away from the toil and turmoil of commerce and international exchange, away from peace and war, away from faith and conviction, away from any aspect of human experience. Philosophy is everywhere and nowhere is inaccessible to it.

But this does not mean that each and every philosopher has succeeded in uncovering every aspect of philosophy. And it does not mean that each and every philosopher provided insights into this entirely unlimited space of human experience. So the question to be posed is whether Merleau-Ponty himself has achieved this access. He certainly claims it for philosophy. And as we have seen, he has recounted how different philosophers or movements of philosophy at different ages have discovered (and invented) certain aspects of this unlimited nonprivate experiential domain, how some have founded it, how others have discovered the role of subjectivity, how others again have articulated the meaning of history, and how in his own day existence and dialectic have been found to operate throughout human spaces. Merleau-Ponty's own thought certainly opened up an understanding of perception that was not articulated previously—he would say that he found it there: the phenomenal field, spatiality, embodiment, the sexed body, temporality, the interworld, freedom, indirect language, expressivity, visibility, interrogation, and so on. But in what sense is Merleau-Ponty's own thought limited? In what sense is he "inside" the history of philosophy?

While he himself claims that the founding that some philosophers have achieved and the discoveries that others have accomplished are inside the history of philosophy, one could also say that Merleau-Ponty has played a similar role in the history of philosophy, and certainly for the middle of the twentieth century. But now we are at the end of the century. And in the continental tradition—the very same tradition that he himself identified in *Les Philosophes célèbres*—Merleau-Ponty himself as a philosopher is both every-where and nowhere. Very few of his successors in the European traditions of philosophy ever or hardly ever mention Merleau-Ponty. Today he is beginning to be studied as a figure in the history of philosophy in France, in Germany, in Belgium, in the Netherlands, in Austria, in Japan, in South America, and of course in North America by the scores and scores of both established and younger generation philosophers. But there are also those for whom Merleau-Ponty is a way of thinking, a way of philosophizing, a way of themselves entering into the history of philosophy—not just as those who teach it, com-ment upon it, interpret it, but who also become part of it.

But there was and is a whole generation of philosophers—particularly in France—who almost never mention the name of Merleau-Ponty and yet whose own philosophies are heavily marked with Merleau-Ponty's thought and contribution. It is as if Merleau-Ponty's own thought had become an indirect language—like the languages of painting, dance, music, architecture, and so on. It is there, present in the experience, and yet not spoken directly. A few examples include Michel Foucault, Jacques Derrida, Jean-François Lyotard, and Julia Kristeva. There is not time here to develop in detail how they articulate Merleau-Ponty's thought without naming it—and I have in many places elsewhere developed this theme in particular. However, I should like here to demonstrate the respect in which Merleau-Ponty is so wonder-fully situated somewhere between the history of philosophy and contempo-rary thought.

What Merleau-Ponty says about history in "Everywhere and Nowhere" set the stage for the kind of position that Foucault articulated in *The Order of Things* (1966)—ten years after *Les Philosophes célèbres*—even though Foucault himself had been publishing studies in psychology—on Binswanger, for instance—near the end of the five year period at the beginning of the 1950s. In *The Order of Things*, Foucault's idea that history is not just a fact to be remarked upon but that in each epoch there is a new understanding, a new formulation, a new identification of what counts as knowledge could be read back into what Merleau-Ponty says about history. It was not just that the nineteenth century discovered history, it is rather that the nineteenth century was a new knowledge formation with respect to the relation between words and things, thought and experience, perception and expression. The codes change, the structures of thought change, the semiotics change—and they replace what preceded. Foucault might not quite say that the new epoch discovers in what it sees what is already there, and yet the invention of a new epistemological practice, a new episteme, and a replacement of those that it succeeds is in a sense seeing the world differently, knowing the world differently, but also knowing differently—the discovery of another way of knowing is also another way of knowing that is found to be already there. Representation in the neoclassical age of the seventeenth and eighteenth centuries was not better than the *episteme* of "resemblance" in the Renaissance. It is another way of understanding, knowing, saying, interpreting its own codes and its own relations. It is as if Foucault were elaborating in much more intricate detail what Merleau-Ponty already understood to be the "ambiguity of history," "the intertwining of the visible and the invisible," "the expressivity of language" as an "indirect language."

Jacques Derrida—an avid reader of Husserl in his formative years at the end of the 1950s and early 1960s—could not have overlooked the importance of Merleau-Ponty. And there is a sense in which the very indecidability of Merleau-Ponty's position in relation to the history of philosophy was already stated there in Collège de France Professor of Philosophy's writings and teachings. Derrida was for many years *Maître de conferences* at the Ecole Normale Supérieure where his job was to teach the history of philosophy. Could he have not read *Les Philosophes célèbres*? Could he have not known Merleau-Ponty's work? And is there not a persistent sense that, while Merleau-Ponty wanted to open up the phenomenal field to "everywhere" and to find that it is not excluded "anywhere" he is marking off in effect the margins of philosophy—the limits of philosophical inquiry, the very question of what lies outside the philosophical? At what point is it not the next discovery to find that the field of philosophy is already the text of philosophy, the text of metaphysics? Merleau-Ponty calls the first section of his collected introductions to *Les Philosophes célèbres* "Philosophy and the 'Outside.' " With such a title, is he not also asking what it means to be "outside" philosophy, or we might even ask; outside the history of philosophy? Does this not raise the very question of the hinge between the inside and the outside of philosophy, the inside and the outside of the history of philosophy, and consequently Merleau-Ponty's own status as inside or outside the history of philosophy? Merleau-Ponty writes: "There is not *a* philosophy which contains all philosophies; philosophy as a whole is at certain moments in each philosophy. To take up the celebrated phrase again, philosophy's center is everywhere and its circumference nowhere" (S 161/128). Derridean decentering is already stated here in Merleau-Ponty's celebrated phrase. The very idea that philosophy should be at the center whether logocentric, phonocentric, egocentric, phallocentric, or ethnocentric has certainly been placed in question by Derrida. And yet each philosophy, even if all philosophy is in some sense located within it, will also be self-circumscribing, self-delimiting, and hence setting its own circumference. There is still the danger in Merleau-Ponty that philosophy might be regarded as a totality that inheres in each particular philosophy and that there may be some hope or understanding that philosophy has no circumference. Both Foucault and Derrida have shown that this cannot be the case—there are always limits to thought, limits to representation, limits to experience, limits to philosophy . . .

What Julia Kristeva has seen, and only later that it is already, in Merleau-Ponty is the role of the speaking subject. The subject speaks but always out of a corporeal containment—the *chora* is already incorporation, the semiotic is already indirect language, the symbolic is already an algorithm. And philosophy, for Kristeva, is only a phase, a type of symbolic or thetic expression. The psychoanalytic, the literary, the artistic, the religious, and so on, are also expressions of the semiotic and only when they become thetic do they miss the fullness of expression. But, for Kristeva, there is an ambiguity as to whether the symbolic can discover the movements, the bodily expressions, the poetic dimensions of the semiotic. If it can, then it is like Merleau-Ponty's philosopher who discovers what is already there in experience. If it cannot, then how can she theorize about the semiotic at all? The *chora* speaks poetically, psychoanalytically, religiously, and one would have to say, with Merleau-Ponty, *philosophically.*

And lastly, the postmodern thinking of Jean-François Lyotard—who published a little *Que sais-je?* volume on "Phenomenology" about the same time that Merleau-Ponty began his new position as Chair of Philosophy at the Collège de France in the early 1950s, could not—and he does not always deny it, be devoid of Merleau-Pontean philosophy. While there are some felicitous and illuminating comments on Merleau-Ponty in *Discours, Figure* (1972), Lyotard's account of the postmodern condition is quite Merleau-Pontean. The linking of Marx and Freud, of phenomenology and semiology, of politics and aesthetics, of art and experience are very much part of both Lyotard's and Merleau-Ponty's worlds. But when Lyotard describes the postmodern as the presentation of the unpresentable in presentation itself, he is reformulating in a postmodern way what was germinal in Merleau-Ponty. One could restate the account as the direct language of philosophy that seeks to name the indirect languages of art, poetry, architecture, and so forth, in philosophical expression. The problem that Merleau-Ponty continued to tackle was how indirect language can be articulated. Expression, gesture, speech, the chiasmic, visibility—these were all ways that Merleau-Ponty sought to uncover the discovery of what is already there in philosophical language.

It could be said that one phase of the postmodern is to thematize these elements of indirect language, these pieces of experience, these languages of art and to juxtapose them, interrogate them, and present them again and again in different ways, in different cultural forms. It could be said that while Merleau-Ponty was still excited by the new and the novel—and in that sense, he is still part of the history of modern thought, modern philosophy, modernity itself—he is also on the edge of what was about to make the postmodern turn, about to make a place for the indirect languages of culture and cultures. In this and in many other senses, Merleau-Ponty is a hinge, and indecidable moment, part of the space of desire that was about to be reformulated in postmodern terms, that was about to become embodied in culture, art, experience, politics, and society at the end of the twentieth century.

NOTES

1. Maurice Merleau-Ponty, *Les Philosophes célèbres* (Paris: Editions Mazenod), 1956.

2. Maurice Merleau-Ponty, *Text and Dialogues,* ed. Hugh J. Silverman and James Barry (New Jersey: Humanities Press, 1992). Hereafter TD.

PART II

Extensions of the Flesh

CHAPTER 8

The World at a Glance

EDWARD S. CASEY

[Mt. Ventoux] is the dominant feature of Provence . . . it has a presence; instinctively when within range, one looks at it the first thing in the morning to see what the weather will be like, glances at it during the day, looks again the last thing at night.

—Michelin guide for *Provence* (Paris, 1979)

[Landscape] is a portion of the earth's surface comprehended in a glance.

—J. B. Jackson, *Landscape*

At the same time, however, I can direct my glance at the perceived spatial world with its orientation. If I do that, the other [world] vanishes: And this vanishing is not a mere darkening, but a being pressed down to an "empty" presentation.

—Husserl, *Phantasie, Bild-Bewusstsein, Erinnerung*

THE PRIMARY PARADOX OF THE GLANCE

The glance—not the gaze or the regard (which is Sartre's territory) or studied scrutiny (the prescribed attitude of so much of Western philosophy, from Plato to at least Descartes) or even bare contemplation (an ascetic ideal). The glance has none of the gravity of these more austere and traditionally sanctioned kinds of looking. It is a mere featherweight by comparison. Instead of bogging down, the glance alleviates. Rather than petrifying things—as in the case of the Sartrian *regard*—the glance graces what it looks at, enhancing and expanding it. The glance does not make entities more "entitative"; rather than ballasting them with Being, it endows them with the lightness of Becoming.

The spirit of gravity, which seeks to fixate and to identify, is dissipated in the mereness of a glance.

Apophansis, that urge to predicate and judge that has held some two millennia of Western thought in thrall, is suspended in the glance. Instead of a logic of statement—of affirmation and confirmation—the glance returns us to the original and literal meaning of "apo-phansis": to *show* something *from* itself. From off its very surface. Which is precisely what the glance is uniquely capable of doing. Even the most penetrating glance stays on the surface rather than piercing it and going behind it. This is not to say, however, that the glance lingers on the surface. It would not be a glance if it did. From one surface—of one thing or group of things—it is deflected to another. *The glance moves on.* Contrary to what Husserl (cited by Derrida for a quite different yet ultimately parallel purpose) claimed, the look does *not* abide.[1] Not if the look is a glance.

But what is the glance? What happens in it? (What happens *to* it is all too clear; it is bypassed, outright neglected in almost all of Western philosophy, which assumes that the glance can only be concerned with trivialities. But to be concerned with the surface is not to be concerned with what is superficial.) What happens in the glance is this. A glance *takes in*—it takes a lot in, namely, all kinds of surface. In so doing, it *takes us places*, all kinds of places. For places are what hold surfaces together in more or less coherent congeries, giving them a habitation if not a (local) name: giving them a "layout."[2] If we can say of surfaces what Socrates says of shapes—namely, that they are "the limits of solids"[3]—they are not only the surfaces of things but of places as well. In these two regards, that is, by taking in surfaces and taking us places, a glance *takes us out of ourselves*, out of our customary egoic identity. It suspends this identity as surely as it dissolves the apophantic obsession with identification. In its egoless *ecstasis,* the glance refuses to succumb to the grasping that is so endemic to any settled sense of self and that is, for Buddhists, the essence of *samsara*, human suffering. By effecting this release, the glance can take us virtually anywhere—to almost any surface and place of the world. Indeed, it brings us to the world itself. The world at a glance: the world *in a glance.*

I said that the glance "takes *in*." I meant this rather literally. The glance not only goes out; it comes (back) in. It is in-formative. As performative of perspectives, it is informative of the world. For it is by glancing, just glimpsing, that we learn a great deal of what we know about the world. A great deal more than we are usually willing to admit in our official epistemologies. Not merely in the sense of many items of knowledge, much less an itemized sum of things. A glance reveals an entire situation, a whole scene of action. And it does so with surprising comprehensiveness and scope. Let me give some examples:

1. Being in a big city such as New York: I learn much by just glancing around at my surroundings: the glance suffices to tell me that "now I am in midtown," "I must be on the West Side," "Soho should be coming up," and so forth. I need not scrutinize the situation to pick these things up; they arise within my mere glance. (New York cabbies, it has been shown, know where they are by the mere momentary feeling of wind currents as they drive about.) It doesn't matter that the City is a very complex entity; the more complex, the better suited to being known at a glance: what Russell called "knowledge by acquaintance" here takes the form of knowledge by the glance.

2. The very different circumstance of traveling in Montana, where the landscape is often as complex as the New York cityscape; yet just by glancing about me as I hike in the woods or (for that matter) drive on Highway 90, I find that I take in an enormous amount: "amount" not as additive sum but as an amassed body of knowledge; I perceive six or seven different types of weather in different parts of the sky; I see the Crazy mountains suddenly rising from the plain on my right and the Absaroka on my left; having climbed twice before in the Crazies, I recognize them instantly; but even if I do not recognize the Absaroka, I take them in as south-central Montana mountains without pausing to scrutinize them one by one and without having to check my map. These outsize momentous Things, like the diverse weather over them, are *all there in the glance*—in one or two quick looks on my part.

3. The case of sexual identity: someone is walking toward me and I glance in that direction; usually, in most cases I know instantly that this is a man or a woman before me; even in cases of cross-dressing I can tell fairly soon if this is a male who is dressing as a woman, or vice versa; only if I cannot tell do I pause—if I am interested in this question—and examine the content of my perception; and even then the examination will tend to consist in a set of further glances, now from closer up and with a more particular disambiguating purpose than before.

4. Finally, ponder the circumstance of "sizing up a situation"; this happens all the time among human beings (indeed, it happens between human beings and animals, and among animals themselves); but it is effective and informative—often being all we need to understand what is going on, even if the circumstance is complicated (she is angry at how he treats her friend, who, however, has in certain ways provoked him); this is not to deny that some are more adept than others at quickly taking in a social situation; but virtually everyone possesses a modicum of such a skill—a skill that requires no more than a glance for its enactment.

Thus, in four different circumstances—two of them bearing on perceived "scapes" and two on social settings—the power of the glance is strikingly evident. In all four cases we witness *the primary paradox of the glance*: namely, the fact that something so diminutive in extent and bearing can provide such far-ranging and subtle insight. What the glance takes in greatly exceeds its meager means, whether these means be gestural or physiological (the glance is only one among many micromovements of which human beings and other animals are capable), spatial or temporal (the motion of the glancing eye is a matter of centimeters at best; and it lasts only for the very briefest moment). It is as if the glance were a fulcrum, a point of leverage, for quite massive being-in-the-world. In this respect, it is not unlike Heidegger's notion of *Befindlichkeit*, which also connects with whole worlds on comparatively slender emotional threads. The glance is, as it were, the perceptual analogue of Dasein's moodwise insertion into the world (the cognitive counterpart would be short-term memory, which within microseconds takes in an enormous amount of sophisticated data: a point on which very diverse contemporary cognitive psychologists are in substantial agreement).

Let us say, then, that the glance is the most poignant point of access, of immediate *intromission*, into the surrounding world. It is an incisive inroad into this world; it gets us there, even if we do not typically stay there by its means (though we have noted, in the case of disambiguation, that such staying may also occur). That is to say, it gets us to the surface of things, as many surfaces as we can bear—thus as many places as we can go. These surfaces and places are not bare or brute; they are telling; they say themselves, they show themselves, to the glance that takes them in.

LANDSCAPES, RAYS, AND GLIMPSES

> I already live in the landscape.
>
> —Merleau-Ponty, *Phenomenology of Perception*

Let me say how I have come to have these unwonted thoughts, a moment of philosophical autobiography as it were. For many years I have been struck by the unusual and usually unappreciated prominence of the term "paysage" in Merleau-Ponty's *Phenomenology of Perception*. The prominence is obscured in the English translation, thanks to the fact that this term is sometimes translated as "landscape" and sometimes as "countryside." I even wrote a paper some years ago that focused on a passage from the *Phenomenology* that describes two men looking at the landscape—a passage that raises interesting issues concerning the commonality of perception shared by different onlookers of the same scene:

> Suppose that my friend Paul and I are looking at a landscape. . . . When I think of Paul, I do not think of a flow of private sensations indirectly

related to mine through the medium of interposed signs, but of someone who has a living experience of the same world as mine, as well as
the same history, and with whom I am in communication through that
world and that history. . . . Paul and I "together" see this landscape, we
are jointly present in it, it is the same for both of us, not only as an
intelligible significance, but as a certain accent of the world's style,
down to its very thisness. (PP 464–65/405–6)

Already in the preface to the same book, there are a surprising number of
references to *paysage*: nine, by my current count. These (and a number of
later, also normally unnoticed mentions) often reflect the influence of Erwin
Straus's distinction between "landscape" and "geography."[4] The distinction is
important for Merleau-Ponty because landscape provides for him an adequate
intentional correlate for the richly ambiguous act of perception he is describing throughout the *Phenomenology*. Yet, surprisingly, Merleau-Ponty nowhere
singles out just what kind of perception, what perceptual mode, is appropriate
to the experience of landscape. The answer, I would propose, is the glance.
A second puzzlement stems from *The Visible and the Invisible*, where Merleau-
Ponty (especially in the "Working Notes") takes over Husserl's notion of
"rays of the world" without, once again, supplying the pertinent intentional
act for taking in such rays. Glancing is just such an act, I believe—as Husserl
had already hinted in the importance he accorded to the idea of *Blickstrahl*,
literally "ray of the look," a promising description of what happens in the
glance (as we notice in the case of locutions such as "he shot her a glance":
the glance as lance).[5]
    Then again, I have been intrigued for a long time with Bachelard's
L'intuition de l'instant, a strangely neglected book whose critique of Bergson
is brilliant and pointed and that parallels in many ways Derrida's (implicit but
I think powerful) rejection of Merleau-Ponty, whose sensibilities so strikingly
resemble those of Bergson to begin with. More recently, I have been struck
with Willem DeKooning's emphasis on the crucial character of the glance in
the evolution of his work. He regarded an entire series of paintings done in
the late 1960s as proceeding from glances he cast at the surrounding landscape in the Palisades and on Long Island as he streamed through in a car.
He wrote the following in an essay in verse form during this period: "Each
new glimpse is determined by many, / Many glimpses before, /It's this glimpse
which inspires you."[6] How, I asked myself, can such complex and monumental paintings as those of DeKooning stem from mere glimpses? There must
be, I thought, much more at stake in a glimpse (which I take to be tantamount
to a glance) than I had ever thought. What, then, is this stake? What makes
a mere glance so potent, allowing us to appreciate that it is not just another
act but something special in its own right?

THREE "PERI-PHENOMENA" OF THE GLANCE

Everything durable is the gift of an instant.

—Bachelard, *L'intuition de l'instant*

Let us now consider certain "peri-phenomena" (in William Earle's term) of the glance, features located at its edges as it were and making it possible: the now, the all-at-once, the here.

1. A glance takes place in the now; it puts places and their surfaces together in the immediate present—or better, it *captures them* in that present. Just now the glance darts out, and it does not last longer than its own momentary operation. The glance *alights*; it does not linger. It flickers off the surface of what is seen. For all this, an instant suffices. This instant is not the punctiform unit of chronometric time; it is Bachelard's instant of intuition, which does not merely mark time but constitutes the source of genuine novelty (Bachelard speaks, for example, of "the instant of the birth of knowledge"[*la connaissance naissante*]).[7] Like the glance, indeed as the temporal basis of the glance itself, the instant's importance and scope is belied by its diminutive duration. Indeed, if Bachelard is right, duration itself—thick, ponderous Bergsonian duration—is constituted by instants: "time is observed only in instants; duration is experienced only by instants."[8] *How else* are we to take in duration except in poignant moments of intense experience? Indeed, how else is the landscape world to be grasped but in momentary "cuts" into this world: cuts effected by glances? I glimpse this part of it, then that part, then another—all within the arc of the whole. To think that it happens otherwise in either case would require positing a special faculty of grasping either duration or world: a faculty that is nothing but a *deus ex machina* devised to solve a problem whose solution lies ready to hand in the instant, in the now.

By "now" I mean the immediate present that has its own duration—as Bergson and James both insisted. Crucial for our purpose is a special feature of the now most clearly articulated by Husserl: the now is a *moment of absolute flux*. It is the way such flux presents itself in the present, *as* the present. There is, as it were, a secret collusion between the now and flux—in contrast with "immanent" or "subjective" time, which is narrative and psychological in contrast. Thanks to this collusion, to experience the now is *at the same time* more than the now. It is also, thanks to experience, time in its radical mobility, its creativity, its depth, its Becoming. This is why Husserl can speak of the now as "absolute" and as "creative"—terms that Bachelard would welcome. For in undergoing an experience now, I am simultaneously experiencing myself in my deep temporality. As Wittgenstein would say, "the depths are on the surface."[9] For the now is the primitive form of the acccessible surface of time, just as flux is the primitive substance of its depth.

So too the glance is at once now and more-than-now. Now I see the Crazy Mountains, but in so seeing them I also see things that have lasted for hundreds of millions of years—an age I see on their very surface. Here the flux of Becoming is not in me but in the thing at which I glance. It is as if the lower portion of Husserl's celebrated time diagram were tipped up and over—projected out there as a peak in the landscape rather than being kept within me as "time-keeper." (So too we can imagine Bergson's equally celebrated pyramid of time inverted to much the same effect.) The difference, of course, is that my now returns to its *own* depth in flux, whereas the depth of the mountain's age is not mine but *its*, belonging to it alone. Of this depth I am only the witness. I do not have it within myself, nor can I (literally) incorporate it. But I can *take it in* nonetheless; and that's what matters most in matters of the glance. If the now takes in the flux of which it is a part, so the glance takes in the larger landscape to which it is directed.

2. In both of these cases as well, the taking-in has the character of the "all-at-once," a term I borrow from the third section of Husserl's 1905 lectures on internal time-consciousness. For Husserl, absolute flux is not merely successive (succession belongs properly to immanent time) but happens all at once. By this, Husserl does not mean strict simultaneity: were this latter to be the case, there would be no becoming at all. Instead, the different phases of flux overlap in an amalgam of loose assimilation, such that events can be said to happen at the same time without, however, happening at the identically same instant. Analogously, my glance takes in a diversity of things and events all at once by gathering the glanced-at in one more-or-less coherent perceptual mass. *The all-around is taken in all-at-once.* This is what glancing is all about: I see all at once what is happening in a social scene I size up; I perceive all at once the complex character of life at the intersection of Sixth Avenue and Ninth St. in New York City; the Montana mountainscape gives itself to me all at once as I glance at it along a trail I'm on or (in the manner of De Kooning) through the window of a speeding car.

It might seem as if we are dealing with something like a good Gestalt here, since we also perceive such a Gestalt all at once. As Nietzsche already said in the *Birth of Tragedy*, "we enjoy an immediate grasp of figure (*Gestalt*); all forms speak to us; there is nothing indifferent and unnecessary."[10] Merleau-Ponty's continual reversion to *Gestalt* as a paradigm for perception bespeaks much the same sense of it as something whose parts we assimilate all at once as parts of a single whole. Yet this paradigm, for all its indisputable value, has the disadvantage of implying homogeneity among the parts, their mutual fittingness if not their outright similarity. The glance, however, can draw things of the greatest diversity together in an instant: this is the very source of its uniqueness. (Similarly, the now assimilates virtually anything that happens in the flux whose epiphenomenon it is; what Bachelard says of duration holds true for flux: "we shall never succeed in conquering the character of duration's prodigious heterogeneity."[11] In short, we do not need a good Gestalt in order to glance at something, even the most complicated and diverse something, and to take it in all at once.

3. And the here? Here is where my body always is, and from this here I take in an indefinite number of theres in my surroundings, my literal *Umwelt*. Sound familiar? "You betch'a"—as they say in Montana. Once more a delimited defile gives access to an astonishing richness of content: this time in terms of basic orientation. From just here I take in a very great deal of what is there. To be here is not just to be limited to my pinpointed position, my site in space, it is to be implaced in such a way as to reach out, *already*, to a world of theres (a "there-world," as it were) to which I find myself multiply related. There is no such thing as being *merely here*. To be here at all is also to be there . . . and there . . . and there.

What is a privilege of the body (hence Husserl speaks of it as possessing, or better *being*, an "absolute here") is *a fortiori* a privilege of the glance as well. In glancing, I am conscious of glancing *from here*, the place of my bodily situatedness. More exactly, I glance *from here to there* (though not back again: except in the case of glancing at myself in the mirror, glancing lacks the reflexivity of time-consciousness). I take myself out of myself in order to let my here find its complement in the there-world arrayed around me: in order to land my glance over there, it must stem from the here where I am. The rapidity and ease of this glance reflects the fact that glancing, albeit a bodily act, lacks the dense corporeality of touching or walking or hammering. But it shares with them the intense ineluctability of the here/there dialectic.

When I introduced this section, I spoke of the now, the all-at-once, and the here as "peri-phenomena associated with the glance." But we have seen that more than association is at stake here—for instance, in my claim that the glance not only resembles the now and the here in certain basic ways but actively implicates them in its own operation. Now I would go further and say that the three things I have been discussing are constituent features of glancing. A glance cannot but occur in the now and, in so doing, include duration and flux in its very performance; nor can it not happen here, or fail thereby to relate to a set of pertinent there's; and it cannot help but exhibit the structure of the all at once in its own manifestation. All three are essential traits of glancing. Yet, even when taken together, they are not sufficient for glancing to arise; other acts, for example, attention, possess the same three traits, albeit in variant degrees. What, then, is special about glancing: what, together with the three things just discussed, makes it into glancing and not some other act?

SURPRISE AND THE GLANCE

Je ne cherche pas, je trouve.

—Picasso

The missing matter is *surprise*. To glance is to be open to surprise. It is to enter an Open where surprise is not only possible but highly probable. Why else would we glance unless we were willing to be surprised? (This is so even when we are fearful, furtively glancing at precisely what we fear the most.) Were we not so willing to be surprised, we would restrict the circle of vision to what is already fully known—or so well known as to exclude surprise. Rather than looking *out*, we would look *in*: either inside the perimeter of the familiar or within ourselves, where we think we know the way. (It is revealing that we rarely speak of "glancing inside ourselves.") The characteristic vector of the glance is outward, which is just what *Blickstrahl* connotes: the eye's ray moves from the eye to the world. This outward directionality includes upward and sidewise as internal variations: we "glance up" and we steal "sidewise looks."

Whatever the variation, in glancing we move into an arena of open possibility where we must, as Heraclitus put it, "expect the unexpected."[12] It is the unexpected, or at least not fully known, that we take in with the glance: to this reverse directionality from the world to us there corresponds the *Weltstrahlen* posited by the later Husserl (though already present in Greek theories of vision as a two-way emission of visual rays).[13] By our glance we are drawn—or more exactly, we draw ourselves—into a region where many things can happen and thus where we may be surprised: where we may well have to take in what we did not expect to encounter. If a mere glance can take in so much, this is only because we have risked something to begin with: nothing ventured, nothing gained. The venture, the adventure, of the glance is to go out into a domain of the unfamiliar and unknown, whether hoped for or feared, and to witness what happens there—come what may.

To venture out in this way is to be curious as to what lies out of direct vision. In contrast with Heidegger's caustic and dismissive analysis of curiosity as on a par with gossip—both being forms of everyday fallenness—the curiosity at stake in the glance is a positive epistemic matter. It is not a matter of being cognitively "nosy" or seeking the new for the sheer sake of the new, that is, a matter of mere "idle curiosity." The glancer is genuinely curious as to what may be the case around her, and wants to find out even at the expense of being disappointed or shocked by what meets the glance. (One thinks of Plato's example in the *Republic* of being overcome by spirit, by *thumos*, when a person is impelled to look at a corpse on the roadside even though his reason tells him not to. The morbid, as well as the erotic, are virtually irresistible objects of the glance.) On the other hand, the curiosity in question is not to be assimilated to *wonder*, that prototypical philosophical emotion. Wonder implies a sense of mystery that is missing in the curiosity appropriate to the glance, and it calls for a very different looking—a slow, contemplative gazing that includes an element of longing: *pothos* and *thaumazein* are closely affined in early Greek thinking. The longing is to know the ultimate truth of the way things *are*—the metaphysical truth of being, as Aristotle makes clear[14]—whereas glancing is content to know the truth of what happens on the surface of things: that is, what is first in the order of seeming. (The glancer thus reverses the counsel of Wallace Stevens' iceman: not "let be be finale of seem"[15] but "let seem be the content of be.")

The active curiosity of glancing is expressed in the simple desire to know *what is going on over there where I'm glancing.* To enact this curiosity in a glance I cannot be too apprehensive—or else I will be closed to what the glance reveals. I must be willing to expose myself to what my glance itself exposes. I must be, in every sense of the word, *open-eyed* to what I do not yet know for sure is the case—to what is concealed from the glance as it starts to send its ray outward. And it is just because the world conceals so much of itself—gives itself only by partial profiles, as Husserl says—that the glance is drawn to discover what I do not yet know about my physical or social surroundings. I take in the world at a glance only because the world itself withdraws so radically from full revelation. It does not give itself all at once, but for this very reason the glance is inspired to light on appearances that do present themselves all at once, here and now—even if these appearances, and their status as *totum simul*, cannot claim to be the ultimate truth of things.

The price of this gift of the world's seeming—this discovery of what appears to be the case in terms of the surfaces of particular places—is comparatively small. The price is simply surprise. To glance into the world is to let oneself be surprised by the world. "Surprise" is regarded by theorists of emotion as one of the seven basic emotions (happiness, fear, anger, sadness, disgust/contempt, and interest being the other ones).[16] According to one leading researcher, the aim of surprise, especially in its primitive form of "startle," is "to help prepare the individual to deal effectively with [a] new or sudden event and with the consequences of this event."[17] Surprise is the emotional *response* to the discovery of the unexpected, and it is often the result of glancing. To glance is to expose oneself to surprise, and it is to do so in the mode of the *sudden*.

The importance of the sudden (already noted by Parmenides) was brought back to Western attention by Kierkegaard, for whom it represented the exception to the Hegelian system—in which nothing happens suddenly but only according to the slow labor of the negative.[18] The sudden interrupts and disrupts the Juggernaut of continual dialectical synthesis. Like the instant, it is a factor of discontinuity.[19] Hence its disconcerting character: human beings generally and not only logocrats such as Hegel, prefer the continuous and predictable. But they also know that all is not continuous and predictable. Thus they glance out around themselves in order to anticipate and encounter the sudden before it arrives wholly unbidden and blindsiding.

The sudden always cuts into the customary, arriving seemingly from nowhere. To meet it halfway, rather than being its mere victim, is to beat it at its own game. Thus we go out to meet the sudden—in a glance, often defined as "a hurried [or quick] look."[20] Our glance's characteristic celerity, its darting, matches that of the sudden it is prepared to confront: one suddenness calls for another. This is why it is never too soon to glance (though it can certainly be too late: as Orpheus learned tragically, glancing backward at Eurydice). The more suddenly we glance the more adequate we are to the world's waywardness, its quirky happening, its effervescent eventfulness. In the face of this cosmic uncertainty, we are saved by a glance. Or almost so: for we have to do here with what Jankélévitch calls the "presque rien," the almost nothing that matters greatly in the scheme of things.

Kierkegaard, speaking out of the temporocentrism that kept him tied to Hegel despite his animadversions against the system, considered the sudden to be a temporal category—thus allied exclusively with the instant or moment (*Augenblick*). But if the sudden is a truly radical interruption *of time*, then it cannot be just another temporal notion—something to be swallowed up by time at large. On the contrary: part of being sudden is to resist temporal, indeed causal, analysis: to appear, not just from nowhere but more particularly from *nowhen*. If anything, the sudden accrues more closely to place than to time. Typically, we experience it as attaching to a given scene of action: "the forest is aflame!" we say, pinning the sudden on a patch of fuming woods that constitutes a concrete place. Although we can have sudden thoughts or memories, the sudden belonging to the glance seeks material exemplification—and thus a place in which to appear (as well as surfaces in which to be manifest). This follows from the fact that we glance from here to there, that is, from one place to another. The now in which we do so is not the exclusive partner of the glance but the temporal medium for its transpositional work. It is, indeed, an *Augenblick*, literally "look of the eyes" and not merely a "moment" as the word is often translated into English; and it is a look that happens immediately (as *augenblicklich* connotes), "in the blink of an eye." The moment of the glance is an immediate look (outward) of the eyes—a look that is equal to the sudden way the world emerges differently from what we had expected, thereby surprising us.[21]

It is not because of time-consciousness, then, that we must "admit the other into the self-identity of the *Augenblick*; nonpresence and nonevidence . . . into the *blink of an instant*."[22] These words of Derrida's—intended to deconstruct Husserl's phase "*im selben Augenblick*" ("at the same time," "simultaneously") as employed in the *Logical Investigations*—could also apply to the glance. For it is by the glance that what is other to/than what we expect is allowed to interrupt our self-certainty and self-presence—that the nonpresent and the nonevident enter into us as lifelong curiosity seekers.

The glance, in sum, allows us to savor the world as a surprising affair— as something that happens suddenly. It lets us see the world on its cosmetic sleeve: a slender sleeve of seeming whose surface surprises us in its suddenness. It lets us see so much in so little—so much surface and place, so little time and space. If the poetic image is, according to Bachelard, "a sudden salience on the surface of the psyche,"[23] the content of the glance is an equally sudden salience on the surface of the world. It is the world at a glance.

THE RHETORIC OF GLANCING

... to strike a glancing blow

—An English idiom

And the *language*—as well as the rhetoric—of the glance? The history of the word "glance" is revealing. The four main historical usages noted in *The Oxford Dictionary of English Etymology* all correspond to senses still alive in the phenomenon as I have described it: "gliding *off* an object struck" is the oldest usage and is already extant in the fourteenth century; critical here is the "off," a word underlined earlier in this paper and one that implies a surface *off which* the gliding is done; by extension, the surface deflects an incoming beam or object, as in the current definition of "to glance" as "to strike a surface or object obliquely."[24] Hence: "a glancing blow," still in common parlance and capturing the outgoing intentionality of purely visual glancing, which I have emphasized. The second oldest usage, "to move rapidly," is closely akin to the factor of the glance's intrinsic speed, which was at stake when I discussed the need for the glance to anticipate the possible depredation of the sudden. Third in historical succession is "to make a flash of light," to which corresponds the way glancing extends into an Open—*Lichtung* in German—in which the unexpected can be taken in more fully and freely than if we were closed in upon ourselves. And the fourth usage, stemming from the sixteenth century, "to flash a look," reminds us of the visual ray that darts from the eye to the object beheld—a ray with fateful consequences, as we are warned in mythological recountings such as those of Actaeon and Diana, and in Hermes' darting look.

Etymologically regarded, "glance" signifies gliding or sliding off a slippery surface. Hence its origin in Old French *glacier*, "to slide, slip," also the root of the English word "glacier," whose polished surface betokens a threatening glide downward to an unknown fate. It is speculated that "glance" also derives from Old Northern French *lancher*, the source of "launch," meaning "to set in rapid motion; [or] to cause (a vessel) to move from land,"[25] that is, from the known to the unknown. Critical here is the idea of the slippery slope (including the slope of a boat launcher), hence the cross-cousin *glacis*, that is, a sloping bank such as that employed in fortifications to discourage enemy advances upon battlements, as well as *glacé*, signifying "smooth and highly polished" (hence modern French *glace*, "ice," "ice cream"), with Latin *glaciare*, "to freeze" lying behind these latter two words. Glaciers combine all these traits: slippery slopes, smooth surfaces, frozen substance; they are the most adequate analogues from the natural world, and they exemplify the logic of glancing in that they come to something immense from a modest source. In the cultural world, paintings are the closest correlates of the glance: here, too, smooth surfaces contain colors and shapes that have become congealed into place. DeKooning, that master of the painted glance, once called himself a "slipping glimpster."[26]

"Glance," as a verb, can also mean "to allude briefly to a subject in passing."[27] Here one darts to a topic in conversation instead of quickly looking at something; one "touches on" the topic lightly, exhibiting that *light touch* of glancing to which I drew attention in opening this essay. But this does not entail that glancing touches superficially, without insight; the lightness at issue also signifies the light of illumination, bringing the topic into the lighting of the Open—if not "the brightly lit circle of perfect presentation"[28] as Husserl put it optimistically in *Ideas*, then the clarified consciousness of deepened insight.

This is doubtless why an extant common meaning of "glance" is "gleam."[29] By glancing, I enter into a gleaming realm. I look from the darkness of not knowing into the light of knowing: knowing places and surfaces that gleam sufficiently to attract my glance, placial surfaces off from which the glancing rays of dawning ken may bounce. I move from being *here* and *now* into the glistening horizon of being *there* and *then*—into the glint of space and duration. In merely taking a glance, I come all at once into the glitter of the world, a cosmos bedecked in its own proper cosmetics.

The rhetoric of phrases such as "at a glance" and "in a glance" as well as "a mere glance" and "a sideways glance" is of special import. As is often the case, the rhetoric mimes the phenomenon. For all four phrases—each composed of three basic English words—are diminutives that act to conceal the larger significance of glancing itself: a significance I have been at pains to bring out in this essay, which can be regarded as itself nothing but a glance at a very slippery phenomenon. Such phrases downplay what is, covertly considered, quite momentous. The rhetorical ploy is: it's only just *this*, something trivial, while in fact it is precisely by this means that the larger prey is to be found. In short: a game of decoy, throwing the listener or reader off the track of an insight not otherwise attainable than through this devious route. Off the *obvious* track, the straight road of the spirit of gravity, the *via regia* of sober science; off, too, the primrose path of the egoic self and off the highway of despair of which Hegel speaks in the *Phenomenology of Spirit*.

The gay science of the glance proceeds otherwise. It proceeds by what Kant calls disdainfully *herumtappen*: "random groping."[30] The "swift oblique movement"[31] of a mere glance glides quickly off the glabrous back of the thing or topic—the *Sache*. It glides off precisely in order to attain a more

informative and copious insight into the *Sachen selbst*, just as my glance
steals off the surfaces of the Crazy Mountains—off these "mere appearances"
(*blosse Erscheinungen*) and *thereby* sees them as a complete phenomenon
(complete but not total: reminding us of Cézanne's claim that a painting is
complete at every stage even if never finished at any).

My glance, I say, *sees* the mountains as a whole without my having to
say anything about this whole. The *apophansis* happens not in statements but
in showing off the surface by my mere glance. It is all, you see, a matter of
deflection: the phrases' own rhetorical deflection, their self-deprecation,
mimicks the deflection of the visual ray off the slippery surface of what we
glance at. We look around this surface as we look at it, thus taking it in all
at once. Here and now—though outside the self. The shortest way around is
the most effective way home. The glance may not abide, but it does deliver
the depths that only surfaces can afford. And it does so with a suddenness and
sense of surprise that should make philosophers wake up and take notice of
this lambent, much too long neglected act.

THE POWER OF THE GLANCE

I see by glimpses now.

—William Wordsworth, *The Prelude*

If this discussion of the glance seems to you unduly oculocentric, I can only
reply that looking of all sorts remains one of the indispensable inroads into
the surrounding world; we cannot do without it; the only question is how we
assess it and, in particular, which forms of looking we choose to valorize. In
the West, there has been an overvalorization of certain sorts of sight at the
expense of others. Steady scrutiny, disciplined contemplation, mystical vision, eidetic insight, the "natural light": all of these have been given primary
attention. Each of them, however, comes with a heavy price to pay; each is
a mode of making presence determinate, overdeterminate, a matter of
Anwesenheit, typically in the guise of the present-at-hand, and always reflecting
a particular hegemony of political, social, and academic power. The result has
been a rejection out of hand, or even more tellingly a never taking seriously,
of other, nondeterminate, nonheavy kinds of looking. We have noted Derrida's
attention to the blink of the eye. Heidegger has analyzed the importance of
making a sign by a mere gesture such as winking at someone.[32] Lacan has
explored the psychoanalytic sense of looking at oneself in the mirror, especially in the infantile stage of human development. Merleau-Ponty has said
suggestive things about the mirror stage, too, and still more crucially about

the crossing of vision, in its chiasmatic form and in the exchange between human beings and natural things (e.g., the tree that is not only seen but in a certain sense *sees us*) (VI 183/139).

But no one, to my knowledge, has looked into the unsuspected significance of the glance. Not surprisingly: the glance is too often taken as the epitome of the shallow in human perception, something that merely flits over the *superficies*—literally the "outer face," the bare "outward appearance"—of things, like a butterfly playing on the surface of a glacier. My argument has been that precisely in such flitting, such fickle and flirtatious glimpsing, the glance proves to be of inestimable value in coming to know the world as a full phenomenon. Not unlike the *papillon*, by indirections we find the world's directions out—as well as, perhaps better than, in conventional modes of visual address. And in so doing we gain a special gift: the alleviation of the heavy-spirited ways of doing philosophy that have dominated the discipline since Zeno first rose to speak in the dust of Elea. Our self-chosen yoke in philosophy has been heavy; but our burden can become light if only we accord to the glance—and to other light-fingered phenomena of brevity and transience—a new respect and a new interest.

We shall also gain thereby the advantage of finally having in hand the spatial (or more exactly, placial) equivalent to Kierkegaard's and Heidegger's *Augenblick* and to Bachelard's "instant"—to what Wordsworth calls "spots of time" in the *Prelude*, a poem contemporaneous with Hegel's *Phenomenology of Spirit*. Wordsworth had this to say:

> There are in our existence spots of time,
> Which with distinct pre-eminence retain
> A vivifying virtue, whence, depressed
> By false opinion and contentious thought,
> Or aught of heavier or more deadly weight,
> In trivial occupations, and the round
> Of ordinary intercourse, our minds
> Are nourished and invisibly repaired;
> A virtue, by which pleasure is enhanced,
> That penetrates, enables us to mount,
> When high, more high, and lifts us up
> when fallen.[33]

Just as moments and instants in their pointed and spotty ways *cut up time*, so glances *sever space*. The oppressiveness of all that bears "heavier or more deadly weight" is pierced by the glance as much as by the now-point: Just as the now-point is at once a punctate entity and a creative source, the glance lacerates as well as comprehends. Each effects a *via rupta* through the complacency of contented, continuous time and space.

And as the *Augenblick* represents the possibility of retrieving an authentic relation to Dasein's temporality—a way of cutting through the rigors of merely successive time (which Husserl called "the march of death")—in order to discover how human beings truly prosper and perish in time, so the glance allows us to cut through the encrustations of space—its *rigor mortis* in the sclerosis of site—in order to find a more suble and suitable relation to our spatiality. At the same time, the glance enables us to cut through the cant and dogma of "false opinions and contentious thought," through the unduly stratified layers of all too settled and sedimented thought in order to reach a lively mother lode of new possibilities of interpersonal life. A single glance suffices to detect the corruption or pretention of a social scene, and with this glancing blow an entire new vista of a less hegemonic, more organic sociality may open up. The unsuspected power of the glance is nowhere better displayed than in this liberating moment, in which space and time collude and collapse as separate parameters. It is, however, a moment all too quickly forgotten or overlaid by heavy, stultified actions—or dismissed as trivial.

I consider the glance to be an important part of thc arsenal we need to assemble in the ongoing struggle against temporocentrism, the philosophical cancer of late modernity. The glance restores to the placial and spatial its rightful due by giving it back its cutting edge—that which can, "with one blow" as the French like to say (*tout d'un coup*), instantly insinuate itself into the heart of things, into the things themselves even. (Indeed, the French for "glance" as a noun is *coup d'oeil*, a phrase that conveys the force of a blow struck by the eye, a blow reinforced by the verb phrase *jeter un regard*.) The direction, the intentionality, of the glance is straight into things and people and situations. Or we should say *onto* them, gliding across their proffered surfaces, athwart them as it were, striking them, thus rendering them striking to the glancer: surprising both parties.

All of this happens in a moment, a mere thrice. In this moment the now and here rejoin the glance, reinforcing it from below and bringing space and time back together all at once in one gleaming moment.

All of a sudden the glance occurs, an event stands out, something significant happens on a shoestring. I look at you, you at me. We have met in the glance. A brief encounter, but a most momentous one.

Glance out. Glance back. Glance out again. There is a world to win.

NOTES

1. Jacques Derrida, *Speech and Phenomena,* trans. D. Allison (Evanston: Northwestern University Press, 1973), p. 104.

2. I borrow "layout" from J. J. Gibson, *The Ecological Approach to Visual Perception* (Mahwah, N.J.: Erlbaum, 1987).

3. Plato, *Meno* 76 a.

4. On the distinction between landscape and geography, see Erwin Straus, *The Primary World of Senses: A Vindication of Sensory Experience,* trans. J. Needleman (Glencoe, Ill.: Free Press, 1963), pp. 318–23. For Merleau-Ponty's rather lame acknowledgment of the distinction, see PP 332/287.

5. On rays of the world, see VI 271/218, 184–87/140–42, 318/265. Concerning the *Blick* of the ego, see Husserl's *Ideas,* vol. 1, trans. W. R. B. Gibson (New York: Macmillan, 1975), sections 36, 38.

6. Willem De Kooning, *Sketchbook I: Three Americans* (New York: New York Times, Inc., n.d.), p. 6. Reprinted in *The Collected Writings of Willem DeKooning* (New York: Hanuman Books, 1990), p. 177.

7. Gaston Bachelard, *L'intuition de l'instant* (Paris: Gonthier, 1966 [Stock, 1932]), p. 6.

8. Ibid., p. 33. Cf. also p. 34.

9. Ludwig Wittgenstein, *Zettel,* ed. G. E. M. Anscombe and G. H. Wright (Berkeley: University of California Press, 1967).

10. Friedrich Nietzsche, *Birth of Tragedy,* trans. W. Kaumann (New York: Random House, 1967), p. 34.

11. Bachelard, *L'intuition de l'instant,* p. 32.

12. Heraclitus frag. 18, trans. P. Wheelwright, *Heraclitus* (New York: Atheneum, 1968), p. 20.

13. On the Greek view of vision, see F. M. Cornford, *Plato's Cosmology* (New York: Liberal Arts Press, 1957), pp. 151–54.

14. Aristotle cites "wonder" as the basis of doing philosophy at the very beginning of his *Metaphysics,* bk. I, chap. 2: "it is owing to their wonder that men both now begin and at first began to philosophize" (W. D. Ross translation).

15. Wallace Stevens, "The Emperor of Ice-Cream." *The Collected Poem of Wallace Stevens* (New York: Alfred A. Knopf, 1968), p. 64.

16. On the seven basic emotions, see Paul Ekman, ed., *Emotion in the Human Face,* 2nd ed. (New York: Cambridge, 1982), esp. chap. 3.

17. Carroll Izard, *Human Emotions* (New York: Plenum, 1977), p. 281. I owe this reference and that in the previous footnote to Jenefer Robinson, "Startle," *Journal of Philosophy* 92 (February, 1995): 53–74.

18. Soren Kierkegaard, "Interlude," *Philosophical Fragments,* trans. D. Swenson and H. Hong (Princeton, N.J.: Princeton University Press, 1962), pp. 89–110.

19. Bachelard, *L'intuition de l'instant,* pp. 15, 23, 38, 67, 81, 103.

20. "Hurried look" is from the *Oxford English Dictionary;* "brief look" is given in the *American Heritage Dictionary.*

21. For a discussion of several points in this paragraph, and for reflections on the importance of the bodily "here," I am grateful to Irene Klaver in conversation.

22. Jacques Derrida, *Speech and Phenomena,* trans. David Allison (Evanston, IL: Northwestern University Press, 1993), p. 65; his italics.

23. Gaston Bachelard, *The Poetics of Space,* trans. M. Jolas (New York: Orion, 1964), p. xi.

24. *The Random House College Dictionary* (New York: Random House, 1968), p. 559. The historical usages are cited from *The Oxford Dictionary of English Etymology* (Oxford: Clarendon Press, 1983), p. 400; italics as in the text.

25. *Oxford Dictionary of English Etymology,* p. 518. On the double origin of "glance," see ibid., p. 400. Most major dictionaries agree that "glance" derives ultimately from *glacier* and the earlier forms in English include *glench, glence, glanch.*

26. DeKooning, *Sketchbook I.*

27. *Random House College Dictionary,* p. 559.

28. Edmund Husserl, *Ideas,* I, section 69, p. 181.

29. "Gleam" is cited as the second or third meaning in all major dictionaries, including *Merriam-Webster* and *American Heritage* as well as *Random House* and the *Oxford English Dictionary.* Note that "glimpse," which is a weakened form of "glance," connoting faint or partial vision, derives from the same base as "glimmer," which shares with "gleam" a common origin in Middle High German *glimen,* "to shine, glow" (*Oxford Dictionary of English Etymology,* pp. 400–401).

30. Immanuel I. Kant, *Critique of Pure Reason,* trans. Norman Kemp Smith (London: Macmillan Press, 1929), preface to the second edition.

31. *Oxford Dictionary of English Etymology,* p. 400.

32. For Heidegger's assessment of *winken* ("to make a sign"), see "The Nature of Language," in *On the Way to Language,* trans. P. D. Hertz (New York: Harper, 1971), pp. 95–96. Earlier, in note no. 22, I have referred to Derrida's treatment of the *Augenblick* as a form of nonpresent blinking. Whereas Derrida's blink closes and cuts—makes a mark or trace—gesture of *winken* makes a sign *toward,* thus opens discourse (*Sprache*). My own assessment of the glance also opens: opens so as to comprehend an entire situation, for example, a whole landscape, but not exclusively or even mainly in the realm of words.

33. William Wordsworth, *The Prelude* (version of 1805–1806), bk. 12, lines 258–68.

CHAPTER 9

Blind Man Seeing:
From Chiasm to Hyperreality

EDITH WYSCHOGROD

Once in a great while a play opens that should have irresistible appeal to afficionados of Maurice Merleau-Ponty. Such a play is *Molly Sweeney*, Irish playwright Brian Friel's extraordinary drama about the crisis in the sensory and affective life of a woman born blind who, through surgery, supplants a world of darkness with one of limited sight. Where does sensory richness lie, the play inquires, in the mingled conformation of sound, feeling, taste, and smell in which language and percept are commingled or in the ability to experience the world as spectacle? Consider the preliminary account of Molly's predicament as interpreted by her husband, Frank, a Gaelic hippy, an autodidact of fluctuating enthusiasms. He explains that bereft of touch and smell, "[Molly] wouldn't know a flower from a football." He goes on succinctly to summarize the history of the question:

> This problem was debated three hundred years ago by two philoso-
> phers, William Molyneux and his friend John Locke. I came across this
> discussion in a do-it-yourself magazine of all places! Fascinating stuff
> philosophy. If you are blind . . . said Molyneux . . . you can learn to
> distinguish between a cube and a sphere just by touching them, by
> feeling them. Right? . . . Now supposing your vision is suddenly re-
> stored, will you be able to tell which object is the cube and which the
> sphere? Sorry, friend said Locke . . . you will not be able to tell which
> is which.
>
> Then who comes along [seventeen years later] to join in the debate but
> another philosopher, George Berkeley, with his essay entitled "An Es-
> say towards a New Theory of Vision.". . . When the problem was put to
> the Lord Bishop he came to the same conclusion as his friends. But he

went even further. He said there was no necessary connection *at all* between the tactile world . . . and the world of sight . . . that any connection between the two could be established only by experience. . . .[1]

Molly's surgeon corroborates this claim: the world built up by vision is not pre-given but constructed by memory and by the creation of categories and relations.

THE SITING OF THE SIGHTLESS

The surgeon has got it right, if by seeing he means a specific mode of world-habitation. For Merleau-Ponty in *The Phenomenology of Perception*, the world is both preconstituted and made. To be sure, nowhere in this work does he mention Molyneux or even Locke. Let us nevertheless follow his recasting of their legacy in his general account of sensation and in his interpretation of blindness and of later becoming sighted to see whether we can learn from him and from Molly Sweeney something about the experience of blindness that provides an entering wedge into the hyperreal and the world of virtual reality.

As described by Merleau-Ponty sensation inundates; it is total and overwhelming, comparable to the experience of the sacrament of Communion on the part of the believer. The communicant, he tells us, expects and apprehends not a symbol but the real presence of God that has come to be localized in bread and wine so that "sensation, is literally a form of communion." For Molly, astonishingly, blindness provides the open sesame of sensation. Speaking of swimming she reflects:

> Just offering yourself to the experience every pore open and eager for that world of pure sensation, of sensation alone—sensation that could not have been enhanced by sight—experience that existed only by touch and feel; and moving swiftly and rhythmically through that enfolding world . . . such liberation, such concordance with it.[2]

Molly has provided a description of sensory experience that dispenses with what Merleau-Ponty calls the standpoint of "intellectualism" from which there are only determinate objects that present themselves through a series of possible experiences, objects that exist for a subject that recognizes them. But, contrary to intellectualism, he states that individual colors are experiences that are incommunicable and that become my own when I coincide with color. I do not "lay siege" to impressions by means of thought so that, for the sake of turning them into knowledge, I cease to be a living being immersed in a world but am changed into a subject of cognition. For the knower, expressions such as "I see with my eyes" are rendered meaningless for the eye ceases to be me, an instrument of bodily excitation, and can only be viewed as another object in the world (PP 246/212). Had he been able to foresee the Derridean double genitive, Merleau-Ponty might have attributed a twofold meaning to the expression "sensation of blue": for intellectualism, blue belongs to the *subject* of sensation; in actual experience it is blue itself that takes over and "owns" sensation. It is the latter meaning that is intended when Merleau-Ponty writes:

> As I contemplate the blue of the sky, I am not set over against it as an acosmic subject. . . . I abandon myself to it . . . plunge into this mystery, it "thinks itself within me," I am the sky itself as it is drawn together and unified, and as it begins to exist for itself; my consciousness is saturated with this limitless blue. (PP 248/214)

Lest we depict Merleau-Ponty as a phenomenological Schleiermacher or Novalis or, to update this genealogy, a Timothy Leary, he does not think of ordinary sensation as a drugged trance; we are not as a matter of course awash in sensation. This return to the richness of the sensed is qualified by my body's participation; "it is my gaze that pairs off with color and my hand with hardness and softness" (PP 248/214). I am, after all, my body, that prepersonal "system of anonymous 'functions' which draw every particular focus into a general project," that is the delineation of my place in the world (PP 294/254). This subtle interaction of sentient and sensible fits easily into a Madhyamika Buddhist perspective, which claims that there is no self as an ego or independent consciousness apart from our positing of continuity; there are only the fleeting dhammas, events that arise, persist for a moment and pass away in endless succession.

   If we are left merely with the thought that sensory experience consists of discrete sectors of being that succeed one another and moreover exist as unrelated sensory fields we have not gone beyond the statue described by Condillac, that inert maniken who receives each of the senses one by one like successive layers of a costume and who is finally ventriloquized into speech. But Merleau-Ponty has no such sorry view of corporeality. Nor does he posit a *sensus communis* as a master coordinator of the individual senses in the manner of Aristotle. Instead, he constructs a view of space in which space is no longer a form of sensory intuition as Kant believed or a container that holds things that are laid out *partes extra partes*, but a kind of universal power that allows them to be linked. This is not a distinction without a difference in that now the unity of space both comes to be and is discovered in the interplay of contingent sensory interactions. Neither a priori nor a posteriori, each sense is endowed with its own mode of world exploration but it is only as a modality of spatial configuring that the coexistence of things becomes possible.

It is just here that Merleau-Ponty's interrogation of the experience of blindness followed by sight becomes significant both for his theory and for our theme, the hyperreal. The blind person is constantly challenged to imagine what sight must be like, to attach significations to descriptions of shape and color as they must appear to the sighted. These indications are however intellectual constructs so that if sight is later acquired the seen world differs radically from the one anticipated. But intelligence cannot achieve the synthesis of touch, the blind person's way of encountering the world, with sight, a synthesis that is only possible in the realm of the sensory itself.

The removal of cataracts from the eyes of those blind from birth may unlock the experience of sight but not that of space, which already inheres in tactility, Merleau-Ponty contends. If the patient denies the spatiality of the tactile experience, it is only because it appears impoverished when compared with that of visual space. True, the newly sighted patient fails to identify objects and may speak, for example, of the hand as a white patch. Her eye may follow the contours of the object in the way that the hand palpates but the very gestures of reaching and feeling presuppose spatiality, a site. The patient must learn what it is to see, what it is that makes seeing distinct from the exploration of a haptic field. Yet despite this difference between touch and sight, there is a connectedness, even a unity to our world encounters. In showing this, Merleau-Ponty would seem to have entered terrain where poststructuralists fear to tread: the quest for the origin, the place where both things and ideas come into being out of a more primordial oneness. But the world that analysis uncovers, even if it is one that is always already there, is "an open totality, the synthesis of which is inexhaustible and of an I that is demolished and remade in the course of time" (PP 254/219). A world that reposits itself in this way is one that is masked in Nietzsche's sense of the term, not as camouflage for a concealed foundation but rather as attesting undecidabilty, the ambiguity of phenomena that deconstruct and refigure themselves and are thus fissured by primordial difference.

The relation of tactility and sight in Merleau-Ponty may be thought of as working in the manner described in Husserl's famous example of apprehending a cube: tactility entails a circumnavigation of an object to obtain a sense of the whole whereas vision supplies the whole on the basis of the aspect it sees. At the same time, vision is also panoptical encompassing a field determined by a horizon, whereas the tactile sense can explore the world only as far as the body's mobility allows. Merleau-Ponty does not fail to bring out the difference in experienced temporalization: the successiveness of tactility, one feel after another, and the simultaneity, the panoramic expansiveness, of vision. Thus undecidability is built into temporalization, being and becoming are perspectives intrinsic to sensory world apprehension for which, it could be argued, Derrida's later account of undecidabilty and difference, a present that is always already ruptured by delay, provides an elaborate adumbration.

Never hesitating to cull rich phenomenological deposits from the physiological research of the day, it is likely that, without cossetting the materialists, Merleau-Ponty would have engaged Daniel Dennett, Patricia Churchland, and Roger Penrose with interest, perhaps even conceding that consciousness does not exist having already expressed the view that experience is a better term for the complex of activities attributed to consciousness (PP 299 n/ 258 n). If forced to take sides, he might have found himself most in accord with Penrose who builds temporal undecidability into the deepest level of neuronal activity. Thus Penrose:

> Indeed it would be unwise to make too strong an identification between the phenomenon of conscious awareness, with its seeming "flowing" of time and the physicist's use of a real number parameter to denote what would be referred to as a "time coordinate." . . . Can we be specific about the relation between conscious experience and the [real number] parameter that physicists use as the "time" in their physical descriptions? Can there really be any experimental way to test "when" a subjective experience "actually" takes place in relation to this physical parameter? Does it even mean anything in an objective sense to say that a conscious event takes place at any particular time?[3]

Penrose's account depends on an as yet unexplained difference between the quantum level of neural activity and that accessible to classical physics, one that disturbs the standard picture of such activity so that replicated at the level of brain processes is a self-dividing difference. There is no way of pinpointing the "when" of a neural process in its coinciding with experience. Writing in the same vein, Merleau-Ponty insists that in considering the experience of depth there is in the brain "a functional structure homologous with it" but the experience itself cannot be correlated with retinal images (PP 294/258). This impossibility is registered in Molly Sweeney's frustrated outcry when psychologists attempt to correlate neural activity with her visual experience: "Test, tests, tests. . . . Those damned tests with photographs and lights and objects . . . endless tricks and illusions and distortions."[4]

Merleau-Ponty takes for granted that "visual experience is truer than tactile" (PP 270 n. 1/234 n. 1) without worrying about ancient skepticism's account of the deceptions of sight "does not a straight stick appear bent in water?" or Berkeley's claim that the moon looks small but touch more truly reveals its immensity. Far outweighing these considerations for him is the fact that sight provides a plethora of detail absent in touch. A further advantage is that difference in size marks off difference in distance: the smaller the object is in relation to its actual size, the further away it is. Thus richness and complexity characterize the findings of sight. For the sighted person who becomes blind we may think of the process described by Merleau-Ponty as a kind of etiolation, a thinning of the visual field, a regress from sense experience to pure being: colors lose their saturation; the spectrum is simplified so that fewer and fewer colors remain until at last a grey monochrome stage is reached (PP 16/9).

Conversely, for a blind person who acquires sight, the richness of the newly acquired spectacle would seem to afford great affective dividends. Merleau-Ponty contends that the patient marvels joyously at the experience of space that has been acquired. Yet when the first exhilaration wears off, Molly Sweeney laments that the familiar is gone and that the immense effort required to recompose the world are too much for her. She reaches a point where she can absorb no more sensation and is forced to shut her eyes in order to recapture darkness. Sensation was holding her in its thrall impinging upon her freedom. The visual is there for her but she prefers it as an absence. It is such an absence that Merleau-Ponty finds in a blind boy's characterization of vision as enveloping him from a distance, yet penetrating him and holding him in subjection (PP 259/224).

THE CHIASM

In *The Visible and the Invisible*, a subtle shift occurs from the privileging of vision to a greater focus upon tactility and from the relative independence of each sense's world apprehension to their reciprocal imbrication. In stressing tactility, it is as if sense experience refracted that of blindness: vision looms as an absence. On this view, the world is palpable not only when touched but when seen: "What is this prepossession of the visible. . . . We would perhaps find the answer in the tactile palpation where the question and the questioner are closer, and of which the palpation of the eye is, after all, a remarkable variant. . . . Vision is a palpation with the look" (VI 177/134). In the *Phenomenology of Perception*, the tactile is concentrated into manual activity, into the hand that feels and does, agile, prehensile, busy with the world. But in *The Visible and the Invisible*, another concept, one frequently discussed, that of the flesh, emerges:

> The flesh is not matter in the sense of corpuscles of being which would add up or continue on one another to form beings. . . . To designate it we should need the old term element in the sense it was used to speak of water, air, earth, and fire, that is in the sense of a general thing. (VI 183/139)

Neither a spatiotemporal individual nor an idea, flesh is something between the two. Just as the one hand touching the other suggests the reversiblity of sensation, so too the world is not only touched by us but, as flesh, touches and loops around us. Not the Word, as in Christian doctrine, but the world has been made flesh as if, in a gesture of pantheism, Spinoza's substance had become animated and its modes converted into individual expressions or styles. No longer is it possible to construe blindness as though it were a form of Husserlian bracketing that put the visual out of play in order to illuminate a certain essential relation of the world to the senses but rather, in accordance with Merleau-Ponty's own best insights, existent and world are disclosed *in situ* so that sensory experience materializes in all of its plenitude. Still, there is something missing even in this later view of the senses. Although Merleau-Ponty is not unaware of the affect that permeates sensation, emotion does not play a prominent role in his interpretation of sensory fields. It is Derrida who carries us *un pas au-delà* (to borrow Blanchot's phrase), a step beyond yet not beyond the visible. In the catalogà for an exhibit that Derrida organized at the Louvre (26 October 1990–1 January, 1991), *Memoires memories and memoirs d'Aveugle*,[5] he demonstrates that sight enters into an economy of exchange: a sacred mission is bestowed upon the blind in return for their having relinquished sight, an exchange rendered vivid in the tales of the lives of Homer, Tiresias, and Oedipus. Of the blind poet Milton, Derrida writes: "the blind man . . . recoups and compensates for what the eyes of flesh have to renounce with a spiritual or inner light."[6] It is worth noting that when Molly's newly acquired sight begins to fail and the world becomes hazy, she enters into a medical condition called gnosis, which her husband identifies with mystical knowledge.

The exchange of outer for inner light brings to the fore what transcends sight and cognition, the act of weeping, a point upon which one would have welcomed comment from Merleau-Ponty. The joy and mourning attendant upon the revelation given to the blind seer are, Derrida maintains, veiled by tears. Whereas animals can see and sleep, only human beings can weep. Derrida cites Andrew Marvell's wonderful lines from "Eyes and Tears": "How wisely nature did decree/ With the same eyes to weep and see! . . . Thus let your streams o'erflow your springs,/ Till eyes and tears be the same things:/ And each the other's difference bears; those weeping eyes/ those seeing tears."[7]

THE HYPERREAL AND THE VIRTUAL

What then can be gleaned from the experience of blindness, more specifically from the blind who are newly sighted, that may be of use for the age of the hyperreal and the virtual (VR)? Perhaps it is the manner in which flesh is coiled around flesh, not in a unifying synthesis but in an interpenetration in which world and self have become something other than they were, something as yet undetermined and perhaps inherently indeterminable.

With the information revolution, something extraordinary has happened, something that has reduced the visible world to codes with the genetic code as the prototype of coding generally and, in that sense, a drying up of sensation. What Guy Debord had referred to as the culture of the spectacle has, according to Jean Baudrillard, disappeared: "We are witnessing the end of perspective," what Merleau-Ponty thought of as the depth of the world, as well as the disappearance of panoptic space, its breadth and range. Instead, images, like language, are reduced to binary formulations so that they "circulate not, any longer, in our memories, but in the luminous, electronic memory of the computers."[8] In what might be thought of as a remarkable parallel, Merleau-Ponty cites a case of "number blindness," the pathology of a man who has memorized a sequence of numbers and can perform certain operations with them but for whom "number has no meaning as a fixed quantity, as a group or as a determinate measure" (PP 154/133). A proponent of strong Artificial Intelligence (AI) might sneer, "But that's all there is: number is operational; the only thing that is missing is a more complex retrieval system." Without entering into intricate AI debates, I want to suggest that Merleau-Ponty's point is that what has been lost in number blindness is the power of "physiognomic perception," the fluid ever changing relation with the world in which number is encoded.

This sensory blindness occurs as a decoupling of image and information. What makes the transmission of information possible is the conversion of a signal into numerical atomic constituents or bits, each bit having, for practical purposes, the numerical value of 1 or 0. Rather than encoding information analogically in which case there is some resemblance between code and the phenomenon encoded, information has been digitized breaking with any physically discernible relation between object and percept. "A bit, has no color, size or weight, and it can travel at the speed of light."[9] Digitization's advantage is that it achieves high levels of data compression thereby increasing the amount of data that can be transmitted. With the increased bandwidth, the "number of bits that can be moved through a given circuit in a second" of fiber optic (glass or plastic) cable, the transmission of information is expected to expand even further.[10]

The world of digitization that is depicted in Baudrillard's critique, can be said to resemble the physiological condition known as blindsight as it afflicted Molly Sweeney. Claiming that she could see nothing, Molly nevertheless responded to visual cues, reaching for objects as seen rather than touched, but she could not process the received signals in the usual way: information was indeed received and somehow used but without the intervention of a conscious image.

What is missing in Baudrillard's account of information is the sense in which images "televised, computer simulated or auditory" are generally the *raison d'être*, the final product of the shipping of information. "Digitizing a signal is to take samples of it, which if closely spaced, can be used to play back a seemingly perfect replica."[11] What is more, the interface, the point of interaction between user and computer, relies increasingly upon images, upon iconic or graphical rather than character-based commands.

Baudrillard seems to concede the point when he depicts the triumph of the information culture as a transformation of the real into the hyperreal, the duplication of the real through some medium of reproduction resulting in a hallucinatory doubling of a real that resembles itself. To be sure, there is a volatilizing of events as if the Pythagorean claim that the world is actually made of number had at last been realized. But far from remaining static, a world of formal mathematical relations as Pythagoras envisioned it, modernity's speeding up of all aspects of existence has "propelled us to 'escape velocity,' with the result that we have flown free of the referential sphere of the real[12] releasing a plethora of images.

We may still ask to what does the real that the hyperreal has dissipated refer? Had meaning not been leached from the term "reality" by philosophers from Derrida to Donald Davidson? Here we may appeal to the anti-foundationalist account of Merleau-Ponty: "Reality is not a crucial appearance underlying the rest, it is the framework of relations with which all appearances tally" (PP 346/300). It is this framework in its temporal and spatial density that speed has destroyed.

Are there any psychic gains that accrue in the world of the hyperreal? In Milan Kundera's novel *Slowness* ecstasy is the spillover of speed. The cost however is high: the loss of the pleasure of slowness. But what is to count as slowness? If we are to avoid falling into quantification, let us think with Merleau-Ponty of tactility as succession that is always already slow paced: one feel after another cannot be accelerated beyond a certain point. Perhaps evolutionists would say the slowness of tactility in which the whole body is the sensorium is the heritage of one-celled animals. By contrast, vision is simultaneity. Speed is the effort to simulate this all-at-onceness, a kind of regulative ideal, approached but never attained, for once complete coexistence is achieved, motion and, with it, the ecstasy of speed, would vanish.

Accelerated movement has yet another affective consequence: speed turns tragedy into farce so that the eye ceases to be the organ of tears. Thus, for example, in Chaplin's film, *Modern Times,* the plight of the assembly-line worker when seen as the inability of lived time to keep up with the speed of the machine, becomes comical. More recently, in Oliver Stone's *Natural Born Killers,* the murder spree of its Bonnie and Clyde protagonists is marked by accelerated filmic images, a fast forwarding that parodies the successive murders they commit. Whatever social commentary may have been intended is offset by the destruction of the affective ranges of sadness and mourning "the tears of which Derrida spoke" now supplanted by indifference to suffering expressed in derisive laughter and hard-edged ecstasy.

In expanding his narrative of the information culture as an unsaying of the real, Baudrillard proclaims that the individual is no longer the progenitor of another, but clones him or herself, metastasizes the genetic code. "Cloning is the last stage of the history of modeling the body, the stage at which the individual having been reduced to his abstract and genetic formula is destined for serial propogation."[13] Such procreation, he thinks, is an act of incest minus the tragedy. What is more, in the industrial age, extensions of the body were mechanical, rebounded upon the body image and modified in a way that allowed the image to be internalized. But today, Baudrillard continues, there is a point of no return in simulation; prostheses invade the micromolecular core of the body so that it is not the prosthesis that replicates the body but rather the body that reproduces the prosthesis, just as in the age of the hyperreal the map determines the territory rather than the converse. Consider a *New York Times Magazine* report of the woman who asked for cosmetic surgery that would replicate the face of a Barbie doll.[14]

VIRTUAL WORLDS

Virtual reality (VR) is an effort to reproduce actual experience in all of its *Leibhaftigkeit*. It would therefore be a mistake to regard it as a subset of the hyperreal in which the notion of mimesis has disappeared. Just as the newly sighted Molly Sweeney tried to regain the world of touch, VR is an effort to recapture the world as it had once been known by replicating it in order to reinstate the old epistemology of representation. VR can be thought of as a move of epistemic fundamentalism, so that the virtualized subject can say: "This is what sights and sounds, feels and smells really are." Software is programmed to create what is seen and to respond to new information; instruments are developed for the transmission of this information as sensory input. Headphones adjusted to locate the direction of sound convey auditory stimuli. Visual simulation is achieved through the use of goggles whose lenses are adjusted to a computer display for each eye. Movements of the head are tracked by a sensor that adjusts what is seen in conformity with those movements so that the computer can synthesize the visual field. It has been theorized that bodysuits with sensors could reproduce tactile sensations.[15] When VR is regarded as a simple phenomenon of bilocation so that we are in two places at the same time, Merleau-Ponty's account of the chiasmatic provides a useful description. We have seen that the flesh, for him, is not matter, a formless substratum of the real but rather a commingling of world and sense and of the senses with one another. The body is always already in several places at the same time:

> It is a coiling over of the visible upon the seeing body, of the tangible upon the touching body, which is attested in particular when the body sees itself, touches itself seeing and touching the things, such that si-

multaneously as tangible it descends among them . . . it draws this double relationship from its self, by dehiscence or fission of its own mass. (VI 192/146)

The body does not bifurcate in the manner of one-celled life but bilocates, splitting and resynthesising itself in every perceptual act. Yet VR is not *simply* a phenomenon of bilocation but is entrapped in the hyperreal that it tries unsuccessfully to escape, an elsewhere that shifts in conformity with one's actions that, in turn, are determined by the parameters of software programming and instrumentation. The effect of this technology is not to destroy bilocation but rather to virtualize the "actual" spatiotemporal locale of the viewer so that there is no stationary point of reference. Science fiction envisages programming that would overcome this doubleness by becoming part of an individual's neurophysiological processes. Although such programming is highly unlikely, new technologies reflect an effort to create simulations in which there would be no fissure between simulation and the real, no "there" as Heidegger conceives it other than the spatiotemporal coordinates of virtual reality.

With virtualization, the epistemic difficulties connected with knowlege as representation are rendered far more complex and require fundamental reconceptualization that is only now beginning. Paul Virilio observes: "From now on everything will happen without our even moving, without our even having to set out."[16] Although VR is parasitic upon the transposition of the visual into information, the illusion of reality is contingent upon replicating not only the body's sensory capacities but also its kinesthetic experiences. Merleau-Ponty's discussion of the kinestheses or body movements points proleptically to their ultimate virtualization. Although not regarded as a sense, the kinestheses determine the horizon of perception. I move my body from one place to another without looking for it; it is always already there, he contends. The decision to move and the felt movement itself are inseparable. Once movement and the will to move are simultaneous or, to make an even stronger claim, once the conatus to move follows upon the activity of moving as William James had declared, we are only a step away from proclaiming that all the accoutrements of movement, "sensations in the limbs, altered horizons," can simply be the dehiscence of a body that remains at a standstill. Presence and absence until now discriminable by location—when I am here, I am not there—cannot be told apart, not only at the level of neurophysiology but phenomenologically. Can the world of VR not then be summed up in Molly's account of her postsurgical life:

My borderline country is where I live now. I'm at home there. . . . It certainly doesn't worry me anymore that what I think I see may be fantasy or indeed what I take to be imagined may very well be real . . . external reality. Real imagined "fact" "fiction" "fantasy" "reality" there it seems to be all right. And why should I question any of it anymore?[17]

NOTES

1. Brian Friel, *Molly Sweeney* (New York: Plume Books, Penguin, 1994), pp. 11–12.

2. Ibid., p. 15.

3. Roger Penrose, *The Emporer of the New Mind: Search for the New Science of Consciousness* (Oxford: Oxford University Press, 1994), p. 385.

4. Friel, *Molly Sweeney*, p. 53.

5. Jacques Derrida, *Memoirs of the Blind: The Self-Portrait and Other Ruins*, trans. Pacale-Anne Brault and Michael Naas (Chicago: University of Chicago Press, 1993).

6. Ibid., p. 109.

7. Ibid., pp. 128–129.

8. Jean Baudrillard, *Simulations,* trans. Paul Foss, Paul Patton, and Philip Beitchman (New York: *Semiotexte,* Columbia University, 1983), p. 2.

9. Nicholas Negroponte, *Being Digital* (New York: Alfred A. Knopf, 1995), p. 14.

10. Bill Gates, *The Rhoad Ahead* (New York: Penguin, 1996), pp. 30–31.

11. Negroponte, *Being Digital,* p. 14.

12. Jean Baudrillard, *The Illusion of the End,* trans, Chris Turner (Stanford, Calif.: Stanford University Press, 1994), p. 1.

13. Jean Baudrillard, *The Transparency of Evil,* trans. James Benedict (London: Verso, 1993), p. 118.

14. Charles Siebert, "The Cuts that Go Deeper," *New York Times Magazine,* 7 July 1996.

15. Gates, *The Road Ahead,* pp. 131–32.

16. Paul Virilio, "The Last Vehicle," in *Looking Back on the End of the World,* ed. Dietmar Kamper and Dieter Lenzen (New York: Semiotext(e), 1989), p. 112.

17. Friel, *Molly Sweeney,* pp. 69–70.

CHAPTER 10

Merleau-Ponty and the Origin of Geometry

MARJORIE HASS AND LAWRENCE HASS

> We are trying to show not that mathematical thought rests upon the sensible but that it is creative.
>
> —Merleau-Ponty, *The Prose of the World*

> We touch here the most difficult point, that is, the bond between the flesh and the idea. . . .
>
> —Merleau-Ponty, *The Visible and the Invisible*

It is clear from "An Unpublished Text" that after completing *Phenomenology of Perception* Merleau-Ponty became committed to elaborating what he calls "a theory of truth" (PRI 6–9). It is also clear from his writings and notes that he understood this to be a fully developed account of the relationship between "the perceived world [and] the field of knowledge, i.e., the field in which the mind seeks to possess truth" (PRI 6). Given the abandonment of *The Prose of the World* and the abbreviation of *The Visible and the Invisible*, this project, in some sense, went unfulfilled. Nonetheless, Merleau-Ponty's writings contain passages that shed considerable light on this "most difficult point": we believe, specifically, his passages on the nature of mathematics. Thus, our project in this paper is to explore these passages, arguing that they yield a genuinely nontranscendental account of the nature and force of mathematical truth. This account, we will argue, is important in its own right offering promising possibilities for contemporary philosophy of mathematics. But we will also suggest that it illuminates certain important dimensions of Merleau-Ponty's thought an exemplar, perhaps, of the relationship between "flesh and idea."

Merleau-Ponty's richest discussions of the nature of mathematics occur in "The Cogito" chapter of *Phenomenology of Perception* and in *The Prose of the World.* In both instances the context is his developing critique of transcendental metaphysics: in the latter text it is a critique of transcendental theory of language and meaning; in the former text, it is an extended argument to undermine the view of a pure, self-possessed thinking subject whose categories are constitutive of worldly experience. Either way, transcendental thinkers such as Plato, Kant, and Husserl have typically made their most forceful arguments for transcendental cognition by appealing to mathematical truth. How else are we to explain the apparent necessity, certainty, and universality of such truth? No philosophy, the arguments go, that is committed to the *fundamentality* of worldly, historical, and cultural experience can account for this. In these passages Merleau-Ponty works to rebut this central argument of transcendental thought to show that one can account for the *force* and *origin* of mathematics without reverting to transcendental subjectivity or categories.

Merleau-Ponty begins both passages by examining the process of mathematical proof.[1] He invites us to consider, for instance, a proof for the theorem that a line drawn through the apex of a triangle results in three angles equal to the angles in the triangle (PP 440/383–84). We prove this geometrical theorem, Merleau-Ponty says, by drawing "on paper or in our imagination" first the triangle, then the extension of one of the sides, and the line drawn through the opposite vortex parallel to the extended line: The resulting image, he says, contains lines and angles organized in such a way that we see the truth of the theorem and regard it as proven.

But *how* do we *see* and *regard* it as proven? Merleau-Ponty answers this question by arguing that the activity of the geometer is fundamentally *expressive,* that arriving at the conclusion of a proof (or essential steps along the way) is a process of *expression.* Let us say, at the outset, that this phenomenon, "the phenomenon of expression," is central to much of Merleau-Ponty's thought after *Phenomenology of Perception.* It is, for example, at the heart of "Cézanne's Doubt" (1945) in *Sense and Non-Sense,* serving as the explanation of Cézanne's task. It is thematic in "Metaphysics and the Novel" (1945), also in *Sense and Non-sense,* and a "horizon" of *Humanism and Terror* (1947). In "An Unpublished Text" (1950), Merleau-Ponty not only explicates behavior in terms of expressive activity ("[the body] is our expression in the world"), but also suggests that expression is the key to working out his theory of truth (PRI 6–7). And indeed, it is clear that *The Prose of the World* (1951) is a concentrated attempt to elaborate the phenomenon of expression as central to that theory.

This is not to say that expression is absent from *Phenomenology of Perception*: already in the chapter on "The Spatiality of the Body" Merleau-Ponty suggests, however briefly, that behavior is "expressive movement itself" (PP 171/146); already he has argued at length that gestures and language must be understood as acts of expression. But we believe that the passages on mathematical proof in "The Cogito" chapter offer what is in many ways his best example of expressive activity:

> When I [prove a conclusion], I commit the first structure [i.e., the image of a triangle] to a second one, the "parallels and secant" structure. How is that possible? It is because my perception of the triangle was not, so to speak, fixed and dead, for the drawing of the triangle on the paper was merely its outer covering; it was traversed by lines of force, and everywhere in it new directions not traced out yet possible came to light. In so far as the triangle was implicated in my hold on the world, it was bursting with indefinite possibilities of which the construction actually drawn was merely one. The construction possesses a demonstrative value because I cause it to emerge from the dynamic formula of the triangle. It expresses my power to make apparent the sensible symbols of a certain hold on things. . . . It is an act of the productive imagination. (PP 443/386)

There are a number of things to be elaborated here. First, for Merleau-Ponty, "causing the conclusion to emerge" is not a deductive process of restating what is already given in the initial figure of the triangle. Rather, it "goes beyond" or "transgresses" that initial figure. And this happens, he says, not because the initial triangle is "fixed and dead," that is, meaning*less*, but because of the opposite: because the triangle is "fecund," "traversed by lines of force," shot through with "indefinite" meaning possibilities. It is, Merleau-Ponty argues, precisely because the geometer confronts the initial triangle as a *Gestalt*, as an "open and incomplete situation" (PM 176/126) that she needs, somehow, to discover and articulate a particular meaning that "makes sense" of it along some line of development. Thus, for Merleau-Ponty, reaching the conclusion of a proof, or grasping some essential step along the way, "an act of expression" both "transcends and transfigures" the initial situation. Following no known law, it involves "crystallizing" insight where suddenly some meaning-possibility "reorganizes" and "synchronizes" what was before a *con*-fusion of meaning, a problem to be solved. In short, Merleau-Ponty argues that mathematical proof as expression is a fundamentally "*creative act*" (PP 448/391).

A second thing to see is Merleau-Ponty's view that the process of mathematical proof presupposes an embodied subject. "The subject of geometry," he says, "is a motor subject" (PP 443/387). This means, first, that the body involves stable vectors of organization that guide and inform the process of proof at every step, vectors such as "up," "down," "left," "right," "in," "through," "intersect," "extend." There can be no proof without tacitly drawing on the meaning these terms and operations get from corporeal experience, without working on pictorial or imagined triangles that retain these vectors.

In *The Prose of the World*, Merleau-Ponty argues that algebra equally presupposes that there are corporeal vectors of temporality (PM 142–60/100–13). But the above passage by Merleau-Ponty also means that the body in its perspectival relation to things opens up the *con*-fusion of spatial meaning-possibilities that the geometer aims, through her proof, to creatively synchronize. It is, he argues, precisely because I am *not* a transcendental subject, precisely because I am a fundamentally embodied being—open to a world that means more than it says and more than I know—that I find myself trying, creatively, to express certain possible dimensions of it, to "make sense" of it. There are, a priori, no mysteries, puzzles, or mathematical problems for a thought in full possession of itself. As Merleau-Ponty puts it: "Our body, to the extent that it moves itself about, that is, to the extent that it is inseparable from a view of the world . . . is the condition of possibility, not only of the geometrical synthesis, but of all expressive operations." (PP 445/388).

The third thing to see about Merleau-Ponty's account of mathematical proof as an act of expression is that it has "demonstrative value,"—that is, although genuinely creative, such expressions have the force of necessity. There are, he explicitly argues, two interrelated dimensions to this. In the first place, the additional lines in a developing proof are not successively random images. The process, he argues, is fundamentally unlike a child's drawing in which each new line completely transubstantiates what has come before ("its a house, now a boat, now a man") (PP 440/384; PM 167–68/119–20). In a proof, the initial triangle *perseveres* throughout the additional stages of development; those stages—including the conclusion—don't erase the initial figure, but rather illuminate that *Gestalt* along one possible line of development. The geometer then is yielding new insight about *that* figure, demonstrating something new about *it*. But it is also the case that this new insight "transcends" and "transfigures" that figure, synchronizing what was before "bursting with indefinite possibilities." So while the geometer, in the midst of the process, might well have proceeded down other "lines of force," this particular "solution" has the retrospective feeling of necessity. It is, one might say, just like the experience one has in reading an excellent mystery novel: along the way everyone seems a likely suspect, but after the dénouement it feels as though it couldn't have been any other way—"Of course!" "It had to be the butler!" "I knew it!"

And so Merleau-Ponty's view of mathematical proof as embodied creative expression accounts for the force and necessity of mathematical theorems. And it does so without compromising the fundamentality of worldly experience—that is to say, without reverting to transcendental subjectivity and without making mathematical truths *representations* of transcendental objects. Mathematical truths, he argues, are better understood as *expression*—meaning giving transformations of our worldly experience that are nonetheless of *it*. Thus, Merleau-Ponty insists, such truths are historically and geographically located; they are "cultural acquisitions." They might never have come to be expressed; they could in fact disappear if the tradition and milieu that sustains them were suddenly destroyed. But once created, once articulated, they are necessary in that they powerfully synchronize what was a *con*-fusion of meaning, they make sing what was before a babble. Indeed, further expressive transformations may well "go beyond," but it is not clear to us how they could ever be revoked. As Merleau-Ponty puts it, once a mathematical theorem has made its first appearance, "subsequent 'appearances', if successful, add nothing and if unsuccessful subtract nothing, [and it] remains an inexhaustible possession among us" (PP 447/390).

Having seen the main contours of Merleau-Ponty's theory of mathematics as embodied, creative expression, we would like to briefly explore its relation to twentieth-century philosophy of mathematics. A first thing to be said is that it speaks to a central issue in that domain: namely, the search for a nontranscendental foundation for mathematical thought.[2] But it is also the case that Merleau-Ponty's account is markedly different from the most prominent of such current theories, and, we believe, holds particular promise in relation to them. Given the purposes of this paper we cannot treat these exhaustively, but by considering three such theories—the analytic view, formalism, and intuitionism—we hope to both illustrate the force of Merleau-Ponty's thought in this domain, as well as clarify important dimensions of it.

A particularly influential explanation of mathematical force has been the claim that mathematical statements are *analytic*. Laid out by Hume in the first *Enquiry*, this thesis was revived in the twentieth century by both positivists (such as Ayer and Carnap) and logicists (such as Frege, Wittgenstein in the *Tractatus*, and Russell). This has been an attractive thesis because it accounts for the apparent necessity of mathematical theorems (in that their denial is contradictory) without having to posit transcendental mathematical objects. But the view demands that anything we ever say about triangles and integers is already contained in them, and this is precisely what Merleau-Ponty has argued against. Far from being a rearticulation of what is already known, the process of mathematical proof as an act of expression involves the "miraculous" human ability to "go beyond" what's given, to transgress the *con*-fusion posed by the initial figure and make sense of it in a crystallizing insight: it is, to repeat what we have already shown, a genuinely creative labor. As Merleau-Ponty explicitly puts it in "The Cogito" chapter:

> The necessity of the proof is not an analytic necessity: the construction which enables the conclusion to be reached is not . . . contained in the essence of the triangle, but merely possible when that essence serves as a starting point. There is no definition of a triangle which includes in advance the properties subsequently to be demonstrated. (PP 441/385)

Implicit here is a second criticism of the analytic understanding of mathematics: namely, it presumes that the essence of a mathematical "concept," such as triangularity, is constituted by its formal definition. But for Merleau-Ponty, the triangle cannot be reduced to its formal definition since "no logical definition of the triangle could equal in fecundity the vision of the figure" (PP 441/385). Mathematics, Merleau-Ponty has argued, begins with our *lived interaction* with a triangle, not with the formal definition of triangularity. The triangle's essence is thus concrete and informal, consisting as he says in an attitude, a style, "a certain modality of my hold on the world" (PP 442/386).

This second response to the "analytic" attempt by empiricists and logicists to explain mathematics carries with it implications for the theory known as formalism. Formalism, as articulated by the mathematician David Hilbert, is the view that a mathematical system contains statements about the manipulation of certain uninterpreted symbols. Since, the formalist argues, those symbols refer to nothing outside of themselves, that is, they are just "marks on a page," such a system is grounded by *nothing other than its internal formal consistency*. But, as we have just seen, for Merleau-Ponty formal thought is secondary to expression in that the journey from premises to conclusion can be formalized only once it has first been expressed. Formalization is thus always retrospective, Merleau-Ponty argues, always in this sense *abstract*; it brings clarity to our thought, and perhaps an apparent rigor, but it is not itself the creative operation that gives rise to truth. In short, the formalist treats what is merely an *upshot* of mathematical activity as its "condition of possibility."

But perhaps the most illuminating of these comparisons is with intuitionism. Prefigured by Kant, fully developed by Brouwer, and rearticulated, somewhat idiosyncratically by Michael Dummett, intuitionism is the view that mathematical statements are synthetic, self-evident representations of the pure intuition of space/time. The character of these pure intuitions determines the kind of mathematical proofs that can be constructed and hence the mathematical theorems we can assert. Since, according to intuitionism, formal statements of mathematical theorems are constructed in keeping with these internal intuitions, we must be careful not to mistake the *linguistic* representation of the proof for the internal process of constructing the proof. Intuitionists argue that it is because we allow our mathematical talk to go beyond what can actually be constructed that leads us to think that mathematical objects exist independently of and prior to those constructions. Hence, they insist upon restricting mathematics to the study of actually constructable mathematical entities. And this has dramatic and limiting consequences upon the procedure and contents of legitimate formal mathematics. For instance, intuitionistic mathematics is *finitistic*, rejecting any talk of actually existing infinite sequences.

There are, to be sure, certain resonances between Merleau-Ponty's theory and intuitionism—both maintain that mathematical truths are the upshot of a human operation, that the operation is historically located, and that it *precedes* all formalization. And given Merleau-Ponty's use of the term "intuition" in certain passages in "The Cogito" chapter, it might seem natural to conclude that his theory of mathematics is intuitionistic. But, in fact, the difference here could not be more profound. And that is because the theories understand the "human operation" that is involved in radically different ways. For the intuitionist, mathematical construction is about *representing* these internal, self-evident, a priori intuitions about space/time, and so unfolds along deductive lines of *necessity*. But for Merleau-Ponty mathematical proof happens amidst a field of proliferate possibilities and takes shape through genuinely creative, transgressive insights—insights that once formalized, actually disguise the *open* character of the activity and the dramatically *other* potential lines of development. One important point to make about this distinction is that Merleau-Ponty's account can explain and allow for a genuine multiplicity of formal systems. Far from having to treat (*à la* Kant) non-euclidean geometry as a threat to the whole system of self-evident intuitions and law-abiding representations, Merleau-Ponty's account grasps such geometry (or any nonintuitionistically justifiable system) as just an *expression* of say, triangularity, along some significantly other "line of possibility." Indeed, the ability to *celebrate* rather than suppress a multiplicity of formal systems is one of the most powerful and promising dimensions of his theory of mathematics. While considerably more could be developed here, for instance, about how Merleau-Ponty's account avoids the intuitionist's commitments to subjectivism and finitism, we have perhaps seen enough to say that the difference between "in-tuition" and "ex-pression" is *all* the difference.

Beyond these implications for contemporary philosophy of mathematics, grasping Merleau-Ponty's account of mathematics as expression can illuminate, we believe, other important dimensions of his thought. A first thing is that we can appreciate his understanding of the *rapprochement* between mathematics and art (PP 447–48/390–92). There is, Merleau-Ponty insists, "no essential difference" between them: neither can claim privilege as the fount of truth in itself; both are expressive activity—"different ways of singing the world's praises" (PP 218/187). Giving due weight to his claims here seems important. First, given our own culture's apparent adherence to a dichotomy between classical modes of thought privileged as "hard" and "rational," and romantic modes demoted as "intuitive,"[3] his view does justice to the genuinely *creative* dimension of mathematical (and *a fortiori* logical) activity. But it also helps us appreciate the *force* and *necessity* that art, literature, and poetry can have: it was in fact *possible* for the Mona Lisa to have had some other facial expression, but for us *now* "it wouldn't be the Mona Lisa" if it did. Seeing this analogous relation between mathematics and art also helps explain why Merleau-Ponty so frequently appeals to Cézanne and Proust just when he is supposed to be discussing truth. Art isn't, for Merleau-Ponty, something *other* than truth, but one of its fundamental modalities. Indeed, defying conventional categories, Merleau-Ponty's writings on art are integral to his epistemology.

Merleau-Ponty's account of mathematics as expression also has implications for his theory of language. For it is clear that he grasps language itself as expression—an activity, he says in the *Phenomenology* chapter on language, in which "available meanings suddenly link up in accordance with an unknown law, and once and for all a fresh cultural entity [takes] on existence" (PP 213/183). This and other descriptions of language are strictly analogous to what he says in "The Cogito" chapter about mathematical proof, and it is indeed no accident that the discussion of mathematics there directly *precedes* and informs an extended passage on language.

Having said that, it is also important to note Merleau-Ponty's view that language is not *merely* one modality of expression among others; it is not *merely* analogous to mathematical truth, but rather intimately connected with it—providing necessary conditions for its formulation as such. Indeed, Merleau-Ponty argues that just as Descartes can only establish the cogito as an apparently eternal, transcendental, and noncontingent truth by drawing upon and then forgetting the field of language, so too does the mathematician draw upon linguistic expression and its sedimented upshots. It is, he says, because the field of language (and the world) disappear behind the expression (PP 459/401), because once given voice such expressions in their synchronizing force seem both obvious and necessary, that mathematical thought appears transcendental and eternal. But again what is obscured are the corporeal, linguistic, and prior mathematical activities that helped them come to light. In "The Cogito" chapter, Merleau-Ponty does not reassert this important dimension—that is, that language (among other things) is essential for thought-become-truth—and so Merleau-Ponty's discussion of language there is incomplete. And yet the *Phenomenology* chapter on language is missing the exemplar of expression that mathematical proof provides. It would seem that Merleau-Ponty's theory of language in *Phenomenology of Perception* is best understood by bringing these two chapters into close relation.

We have, however, already seen enough to grasp how radically different Merleau-Ponty's account of mathematics is from Husserl's. In no text is this more evident than Husserl's "The Origin of Geometry."[4] There are, to be sure, certain superficial similarities in language: both thinkers talk of mathematical truth as "acquisition" and "expression"; both talk about "tradition" and "history" in relation to such truth. But far from understanding mathematical expression as a genuinely embodied, *creative* act that crystallizes "a certain hold on things," Husserl here (as elsewhere) casts the origin of mathematics in terms of "explication": in terms of "extracting" and "reactivating" self-evident, primal truth-meanings "*within* the subject" against the "passivity" of the empirical, historical, and cultural field. As such, the whole question for

Husserl is about how what is *inside* can become *outside*. In the end, Husserl's view of the force of mathematical truth really amounts to an *analytic* understanding, that is, laying out what we already know, and his project becomes one of *retrieving*, "univocally" *representing*, and *protecting* this inside from the outside—the oldest of metaphysical gestures. Nothing could be more foreign to Merleau-Ponty. Acts of expression, he insists, are always "empirical," that is, always—while they creatively "go beyond" and "transfigure" what is opened up through our corporeal immersion in the world, they happen in and amid it; they are inextricably *of* the world. As Merleau-Ponty explicitly says of our expressions: they "sublimate rather than suppress our incarnation" (PRI 7)—"they are the inside of the outside and the outside of the inside" (OE 23/125).

While much could be developed here about this radical difference between Merleau-Ponty and Husserl, one thing we can see is that Derrida's powerful deconstruction of Husserl in *Speech and Phenomena* really has no bearing against Merleau-Ponty.[6] This observation seems important because, first of all, Derrida's argument centers squarely on Husserl's account of *expression*, and it might thus appear by association that Merleau-Ponty's philosophy of mathematics (and art and language) is equally compromised. But it is also relevant because Derrida's text seems to make this equation—to imply that the argument bears upon "all phenomenology," "phenomenology itself." Consider, for instance, the following passage:

> [Our] whole analysis will thus advance in the separation between de facto and *de jure*, existence and essence, reality and intentional function. . . . [W]e would be tempted to say that this separation . . . defines the very space of phenomenology.[7]

Recurrent in the text, such locutions and passages obscure two points relevant for our contemporary work at the interface between phenomenology and poststructuralism. The first is that Merleau-Ponty's writings—"The Cogito" chapter in particular—already "deconstruct" this alleged "separation"; Derrida's concluding distinction between his own project and a "phenomenology of perception" is deeply questionable.[8] The second point is a more constructive one: that Merleau-Ponty's account of mathematics (and *a fortiori* logic) as creative expression opens up the possibility of both understanding and practicing these activities beyond the framework and limits of logocentrism.

It is true, however, that an important dimension of Merleau-Ponty's account is a distinction he makes between *expression* (on one hand) and *sedimented* language or thought (on the other)—between what he sometimes calls "originating" and "secondary" or ("acquired") speech. Does not this betray what contemporary writers are calling a *nostalgia* for origins and "primacies"? The difficulty here, natural though this objection may appear, is that it really misses Merleau-Ponty's understanding of the specific relationship between these modalities. Far from some hierarchical, genealogical, or foundational account that roots or grounds "the secondary" in "the originating," Merleau-Ponty insists on their complex intervolvement. "Secondary," "ready-made" meanings are, he argues, upshots of expressive activity. But it is also the case that expression, that is, the creation of some new, transformative, and forceful sense, always takes shape in relation to secondary thoughts, meanings, or language (PP 227/194). And since expression genuinely "goes beyond" that ensemble, it cannot be reduced to it. In sum, Merleau-Ponty grasps the relation between these modalities as a mutually dependent, nonreductive one. As he puts it in *The Prose of the World*:

> We must therefore say about [sedimented] language in relation to meaning [i.e., expression] what Simone de Beauvoir says of the body in relation to mind: it is neither primary nor secondary. . . . There is no subordination . . . between them. What we have to say is only the *excess* of what we live over what has already been said. (PM 111–12, our emphasis)

For Merleau-Ponty then, expression is neither external nor foundational in relation to the sedimented, nor is it, alternatively, *derived* in any linear or causal sense from those "givens." The relationship is something other—marked not by reduction, but *excess, creativity, freedom*: "We are not reducing mathematical evidence to perceptual evidence. We are certainly not denying . . . the originality of the order of knowledge vis-à-vis the perceptual order. We are trying only to loose the intentional web that ties them to one another, to rediscover the paths of sublimation which preserves and transforms the perceived world into the spoken world" (PM 173/123–24).

In sum, this nonfoundational, nonreductive, internal relationship seems to be what Merleau-Ponty has in mind between the "flesh" and the "idea." And it *is* a "difficult" one. But, we might add, it was already rendered as just such a relationship in "The Cogito" chapter of *Phenomenology* under the paradoxical heading of *fundierung*—elaborated there explicitly in relation to mathematical proof and expression (PP 451/394). There is, Merleau-Ponty says there and elsewhere, no *explanation* for our ability to creatively transfigure the world through our expressions; it is "an ultimate fact," a "mystery." And by its very nature there is no *end* to it. Rather, it is up to us, he argues in *The Prose of the World*, to keep our ready-made thoughts open to their limits, to remain alive, through expressive questioning and activity, to the enigma of creative expression amid our truths (PM 117–18/164–65). Perhaps this very possibility is what Merleau-Ponty creatively expresses in *The Visible and the Invisible* as "Interrogation." And perhaps, in the end, this also explains what otherwise might seem disparate: that is, how a text that argues for a view of philosophy as "Interrogation" is able to offer, in the same gesture, a "theory of truth."

NOTES

1. It is worth noting that Merleau-Ponty's account in both texts is virtually identical. One important difference, however, is that in *Phenomenology* he develops it in relation to geometry, and in *The Prose of the World* to algebra. Seeing his account in these two different domains makes clear that he is not engaged in familiar practice of reducing algebra to geometry (or vice versa). But also, seeing his account worked out in relation to algebra, that is, to number is for him to show that his account can be made out with what most people would consider the difficult case.

2. This is not to say there haven't been attempts to defend transcendental accounts of mathematics. For a contemporary defense of methematical Platonism, see Penelope Maddy, *Realism in Mathematics* (Oxford: Clarendon Press, 1990).

3. A distinction developed and criticized by Robert M. Pirsig in *Zen and the Art of Motorcycle Maintenance* (New York: Bantam, 1974).

4. Edmund Husserl, "The Origin of Geometry," in Jacques Derrida, *Edmund Husserl's Origin of Geometry: An Introduction,* trans. David Carr (Lincoln: University of Nebraska Press, 1989), pp. 157–80.

5. Ibid., p. 161.

6. Jacques Derrida, *Speech and Phenomena,* trans. David B. Allison, (Evanston: Northwestern University Press, 1973).

7. Ibid., p. 21.

8. Ibid., p. 104.

CHAPTER 11

Embodying Perceptions of Death: Emotional Apprehension and Reversibilities of Flesh

SUZANNE LABA CATALDI

Perceptions of death are extremely evocative, intrinsically affective experiences. Unless we are coroners or undertakers, our knowledge of the significance of death is not based on dispassionate observation. An advantage of Merleau-Ponty's philosophical approach to perception is that perceptions and emotions can be thought as together, as copresently implicated.

In this chapter, I implicate two emotions relevant to our understanding of the death of others, the emotions of horror and grief, to show how the reversibility thesis of Merleau-Ponty's *flesh* ontology may be applied to emotional perceptions of death. I think that some account of our emotional responses to perceptions of death may help us to affirm that there is something right both about Merleau-Ponty's reversibility thesis and about his bodily based sense of the elementally intercorporeal aspects of our perceptions. I hope to show how even live and dead bodies can be brought together, thought together, in the folds of *flesh*.

When I speak of "reversibilities" or "crossovers," I have in mind certain reversals of meaning that can take place between "sides" of phenomena that are ordinarily thought in opposition; and I point out how these "sides" can switch places—"reverse" and "become" each other. Here of course I follow Merleau-Ponty's intuition, which he applied in the area of perception, that so-called opposites can reverse only because they are not so opposite after all—only because they do in fact share some common ground.

He called this common ground that "identifies incompossibles"—*flesh*. The in-sensible places "in" *Flesh* where these crossovers or "reversibilities," as he called them, are thought to take place are conceived as "chiasms."

As a philosophical expression, *flesh* includes but means something more than human embodiment or human flesh. Elementally, it is thought as a generalized surface of sensibility, a "skin" or fabric into which our own enfleshed sensitivities—the sight of our eyes, the taste in our tongues, the touch in our hands—are indivisibly interwoven or enmeshed. As perceptible-perceiving fabric, *flesh* is two-sided; and its two sides—the sensitive and the sensed—are not thought *entirely* as apart from each other. The sides of perceptibility are reversible—as a jacket or the windings of a Mobius strip, so that, as "insides" and "outsides" are reversibly confused, "one no longer knows," as Merleau-Ponty says, who is perceiving and who is being perceived (VI 318–19/264–65). According to Merleau-Ponty, such reversibilities are the way of all "flesh."[1]

It is also the way of all live flesh to die, eventually, and decay. Inasmuch as this process is *ir*reversible, seemingly linear and unidirectional, perceptions of this process, of dead bodies, do not, at first blush, appear to fall within the compass of the reversibility thesis—at least in its interpersonal or intercorporeal applications, since dead others, who no longer perceive, appear to be incapable of returning our perceptions in requisite ways—to revert our perceiving to a sense of being perceived or to model Merleau-Ponty's belief in the transitivity of human experience—transitivities of meaning "from one body to another" in the intercorporeal body of *flesh*.

Perceptions of death may also be thought as part of a larger, more general problem with reversibility, namely, how to convincingly extend it to perceptions of inanimate objects. (The problem to which I refer here has to do with the ascription of the "activity" of perceiving to the "passively" perceptible. This side of the thesis is not as compelling as its converse—the claim, i.e., that perceiving has perceptible dimensions.)

In terms of my project, one aspect of this problem is that the insensible gap between life and death, between living and dead bodies, may not appear to be as fruitfully chiasmatic as is the "gap" between, say, touched and touching hands, the emblem of reversibility. For while we do, or may, perceive life crossed, or crossing over into death, we are not so cognizant of the ways in which we may perceive death, crossed or crossing over into life. Thus we might be led to believe that the boundary between life and death is not chiasmically reversible, and that Merleau-Ponty's provocative contention that all perceptions are is simply wrong.

But we know that Merleau-Ponty meant his reversibility thesis to apply even to perceptions of inanimate objects (trees returning the gaze of an artist is the infamous example here [OE 31/129]), and while I do agree that its interpretation is troublesome—especially since this example falls outside of the circle of tactility, I do not think that the problem is insurmountable—not because I think it is so easy to describe reversibility outside of this circle, but because I think that more experiences fall within its purview than we might ordinarily suppose.

I hope that my descriptions will speak for themselves, but in case they don't, I want to prop them up with the following suggestion: I believe that much of this problem might be circumvented by incorporating the affective aspects of our perceptions into our studies and theories of them—as the history of philosophy's work on perception has not traditionally done. If we were to do this, I suspect that we would not so frequently find ourselves *outside* of the scope of the circle of tactility. Since touch and emotions overlap, perceptually, in the domain of feelings, and if we recall Merleau-Ponty's claim that "every visible is cut out in the tangible" so that we remember to think of sight, for example, as a form of eye *contact*, then we may regard our emotional apprehensions *as* ways *of being touched*, of being affected, by some perceptible object or other. And if we do opt this path of least resistance, then it simply does not or would not matter so much if the perception that is "actively" touching us is that of an animate or inanimate object, since we can be emotionally touched or "moved" by both. The "objective" or perceptible sight of a dead body, for example, can be said to be horrify*ing* or heartbreak*ing*. And if a perception—a sight, a sound, a smell—is emotionally "touching" us,—is emotionally *appealing* to us in some manner, then I believe that it is *activ*ated enough to occasion the reversibilities of significance and transitivities of meaning about which Merleau-Ponty spoke, transitivities of meaning from one body to another—*even if* one of these bodies happens to be dead.

In the course of my research for this project,[2] I came upon a number of funny epitaphs. My favorite was a hypochondriac's, whose tombstone read: "I *told* you I was sick."[3] As you will see, my text is concerned with how—through reversible crossovers of significance, perceived others may "tell us" that they're dead.

WHAT'S SO HORRIBLE ABOUT DEATH

My first apprehension of death as horrible was through a tactile experience I had as a child when I touched the folded-over hands of a corpse.

I was motivated to do this after observing that that was what others were doing, at a funeral, to "pay their last respects" to this distant relative of mine. As we lined up in church to circle around her open casket, I decided that I would touch her hands too. Might as well, right? No big deal.

Well, of course, my hand was in for a shock. I was taken totally off guard—NO PERSON I had ever touched felt like THAT—so hard, so cold, so stiff, so lifeless. My horrified hand instinctively withdrew itself from this lifeless piece of flesh (I immediately left off touching it), and I remember being very shaken by the experience as I walked back to my pew, trying, I'm sure, to be

mature about all of this—to look appropriately cool and sombre and respect-
ful. I was old enough to know that I couldn't, under the circumstances,
scream—but I think I would have if I could have; and I was also old enough
to know that it would have been bad form to discuss with anyone how horrible I felt/it felt. Perhaps this is because, however inchoately or immaturely
I sensed it, I realized that whatever I was feeling was nothing compared to
what had happened to the woman in the casket. *She* wasn't feeling *anything.*
And, of course, *that's* exactly what I felt (that she wasn't feeling anything);—
and that is what horrified me, my hand.

Somehow, in momentarily mingling with my own, this lifeless hand
was able to communicate the sense of itself, not simply as dead, but horribly
and repulsively dead. How dead flesh can do this is an interesting question
from a Merleau-Pontyean perspective. It cannot, I think, unless we share
some common ground, unless there is some overlapping "element" between
us serving as a medium of exchange. And of course there is. Live and dead
hands are both perceptible, as objects; they "overlap" in this regard. They are
both caught up in the same fabric or skin—the same *flesh* of perceptibility.
The difference between them is that one is entirely and only perceptible; the
other, because it is still able to perceive, is not. This difference between the
two sides of *flesh,* this bifurcation, if you will, can itself, be perceived; and
when it is, splayed out in this fashion, the perception is horrifying. It is
horrible to sense a hand stripped of its sensitivity—a hand so like yet so
unlike our own.

When we touch a lifeless hand, we feel it as something "cut off"—
something amputated, *in*complete—something we can't quite connect with,
can no longer attach or annex to our own—the way we do or can when we
hold or shake another's hand, for example. This experience is quite obviously
of a different order than the experience described by Merleau-Ponty in his
famous circle of the touched and touching hands. We sense a limitation there—
a horrifying stoppage of sensation—when we touch a lifeless hand.

The sensation of this limitation is not irreversible, however; that is, it
does not put Merleau-Ponty's reversibility thesis out of play. For as this
horrifying significance of death is conveyed to us, certain "crossovers" do
take place.

The first is a reversal or transitivity of meaning having to do with the
way in which the sense of that hand's being amputated or stripped of something "crosses over" onto me. For notice that I apprehended the sense of the
dead hand as something "cut off" from sensitivity by reversibly "cutting it
off" from my own, by releasing it. This embodied gesture of mine goes to
show that I somehow have contagiously "caught onto" its meaning, in a
moment of shared significance, despite the differences between us. It's almost
as if in sensing the dead hand of another one is actually, at the same time,
experiencing a sensation of how one's own hand would feel, if it were dead

or otherwise "cut off," through amputation or paralysis, for example. It is almost as if our own live hand momentarily "crosses over" to a (living) sensation of its own extinction. My touching reverses to a sense of being touched, of being "cut off"—by the Hand of Death, which momentarily has *me* in *its* grasp. The sidedness of the perception is confused, crossed over, so that, absorbed in the horror of this "gripping" experience, one no longer knows who is perceiving and who is being perceived. That's reversibility.

Apart from this strange sensation, another sort of crossover takes place when we encounter dead flesh "in the flesh." Although we may momentarily identify with it, we do not remain so for long. After this invasion, this grafting of dead flesh onto live, our spontaneously letting it go is induced by a surgence—a flush—of feeling, a feeling of horror. In this instance, it is as though the complete lack of feeling on its part, momentarily crossed over onto me, crosses over again, into a permeation of feeling on mine—a compensating infusion of feeling that fills in or feels into what is felt, to be missing—that completes its sense of incompleteness (or, in "reverse," incompletes its sense of completeness). I may have stopped touching, but I don't stop feeling. My skin is still creeping, still "crawling"—away. These "tremors" or "shudders" of horror *assure* us (both in the sense of comforting and in the sense of guaranteeing) that we are, *our* flesh is, still alive.

Horror is a combination of fear and repulsion. According to some theorists, horror takes place when objects are perceived both as threatening (in either a physical, moral or social sense) and as impure. Impurity is defined like this:

> an *object* or *being* is impure if it is categorically interstitial, categorically contradictory, incomplete [as a representative of its class] or formless. . . . Things that are interstitial . . . cross the boundaries of the deep categories of a culture's conceptual scheme.[4]

My reaction of horror is understandable in this context: in the first place, in my perceiving on an emotional level some threat to my identity (my identity as a living, sensitive being); and, in the second place, as an experience of "impurity"—both in my grasp of that hand's "cut-off" incompleteness and in our "interstitial" comingling (our breach of a boundary) a categorical distinction, between the living and the dead.

In terms of reversibility and Merleau-Ponty's view of *flesh* as an intercorporeal body, there are two moments to notice in my emotional apprehension of horror: An initial identification with the hand—its "encroachment" on me, to use a Merleau-Pontyean expression, which *subsequently* and reversibly and strikingly "becomes" differentiated from it through gestures and feelings of repulsion. I think that unless we do suppose some intercorporeal identity already existing or operating between us—something like what

Merleau-Ponty meant by *flesh,* we could not make sense of these sorts of horrific perceptions of dead flesh or the passion with which our own live flesh strives to stem, to curb its encroachment. And so, I think, the gap between live and dead bodies is really not so wide; the barrier between the living and the dead, between ourselves and even these "others," is really not so impermeable, not as uncrossable, as we might initially suppose. Jacques Roubaud's poetry, from his collection entitled *Some Thing Black,* is rich in intercorporeal and reversible imagery. Merleau-Pontyean themes can be read into several of its lines.

Roubaud speaks indirectly of some horrifying aspects of death as he recounts the violent recurrence of a memory, a memory he does not try to remember—an image of his wife's dead hand:

> Heavy blood under your skin   in your hand   sunk to
> the fingertips I couldn't see it as human.
> This image again   for the thousandth time with the
> same violence can't help replaying forever. . . .[5]
> Blood coagulated at the fingertips, like dregs of Guinness
> in a glass.[6]

"Like dregs of Guinness in a glass," her coagulated blood is there, at the tips, the fingertips—her extremities . . . marking the spot . . . pointing in two directions . . . indicating the conclusion, the congealing, of her life and the dawning of his realization that she is in fact, and transparently, dead. Only this residue, this vestige, remains. This superfluous sedimentation. A certain irreducible materiality. "Settled"—to the bottom, forming the basis of his knowledge of her death and his understanding of death as "Some Thing Black."

This image of settling, the recurring reminder of this "remainder," of something left—over—is unsettling. Unsettling in its certainty—a certainty he cannot "budge" and at which he arrives, through comparison:

> Having seen, having recognized death, that it didn't just
> seem, but was, there was, certainly, no sense doubting it.
> I couldn't see it as human. 'there's blood in any human
> hand.' I understood this proposition very clearly. because I
> was seeing it confirmed by its negative.
>   . . . the blood
> here obviously not flowing. I could not doubt it. I had no reason to.[7]

There is no sense doubting it, doubting the difference between live and dead hands. As he says,

Everything depends on the point when the unlike appears.
and thence something, but some thing black.[8]

Some thing black is something silent, something inarticulate. Although there is something obscurely perceptible about it, there is also some perceived sense of limitation, some perceived lack, of communication. Her mouth, he notices, is "closed, absolutely,"[9] and his contact with death means, to him, "admitting that there is in language, in all of its constructions, something over which" he has "no control."[10] Some thing black is something like a "dark light"—a "radiation"—entering his "sleep as X-rays do the flesh."[11] Like a shadow or a shade of existence, some thing black is something like an exposure, an overexposure—some thing like the whole unraveled—into its "loathsome fabric."

> Through simple repetition of *there is no more* the whole
> unravels into its loathsome fabric: reality.
> Some thing black which closes in. locks shut. pure, un
> accomplished deposition.[12]

So, some thing black is something deposited, laid down—a natural accumulation. Some thing black is a declaration, a pronouncement, of death: A death sentence. An incomplete sentence. A sentence with nothing—with "no more"—to say.

Death as a closure, as something closed in and locked shut (coffinlike) represents the death of temporality and subjective sensation. It is this "flavor" of his wife's life that is no more, which is drained—out—of it; and which "crosses over" onto his body, in the form of sensible memories.

> ... what life you've left, if any, is imprinted on
> me, your shroud, fused with me and refuses to be sorted out.
> ... This life which is:
> Your smell, your taste, the feel of you.[13]

Death as a closure is also temporal. It represents a loss or an "incompletion" of time. Part of his observation of his wife's dead hand is that of a watch, strapped to her wrist—the place where her own pulse should be, but is, no more. Instead, the hands of the watch keep on moving,[14] as he does, mechanically, senselessly, along. The motion of the watch's hands signals the appearance of another "unlike."

In our ordinary experience of time, as it is lived, the past and the future reversibly cross over into each other in the [chiasmic] medium of the present. Our pasts open up onto a future that in turn crosses over into a past, which again opens up onto a future and so on. Until we die. Death interrupts this circulation of time. Obstructs its flow. It blocks off the future.

And not simply on the part of the deceased, but also on the part of those who grieve their loss, their passing, entirely and irreversibly, into the past. Like the stamp of her senses, impressed on his body's memory, her sense of lost time also crosses-over onto him, is "fused with him and refuses to be sorted out."

> I live in nearsighted times don't tell me
> look at the grass over there ten years hence go
> that way[15]

He can't, you know. His view is blocked; "cut off." With unforgettable memories; and as he relives them, over and over, he is temporarily stuck, with her, in the past.

Our senses die when we do, when we run out of time. The sensitive side of our flesh, seamlessly woven into and dependent on but nevertheless not reducible to its sensible other side, gives us the sense of ourselves, our lives, as more or less radically gaping—open—and our sense of death as a consummate closure. To see or feel a body, dead, is to perceive that the interior, sensitive side of *flesh* has entirely and irreversibly "crossed over" to its other, exterior, sensible side—a side in which these "openings" no longer re-side. To see or feel a body, dead, is to see or feel it as a piece or a part of a world from which it is no longer separated, through openings of perceptions. As Roubaud pugnaciously puts it, in death our eyes are "smashed into the view."[16]

> A view for the viewing. Seeing crossed-over, collapsed, into
> the seen/scene.

The perception of this crossover, the perception of the way in which death "unravels" the living fabric of our lives, our enfleshed sensitivities, is what is so horrible about perceptions of death. The perception of this reality, the eventuality of our bodies reversibly turned "inside-out," of openings closed, our reduction to "dregs" is, as Roubaud observes,[17] "loathsome."

But a perception of an aspect of reality as "loathsome" is an emotional apprehension; it is something that is tangibly felt in the experience of horror—when we perceive a body, dead, and realize through its absence how delicately interlaced, inextricably interwoven, caught up, in *flesh* the embodied life of perception actually is, was; and that there really is, as Merleau-Ponty might say, an "indivision" between the sides of perceptibility—an indivision that subtends our repulsions and our fright, at the site/sight of perception crossed—over the threshold of death.

EMBODIMENTS OF GRIEF AND MOURNING

Perceptions of death are not always horrible. They sometimes cause us to grieve and mourn. By relating these emotional feelings and behaviors to Merleau-Ponty's ontology, I think that we can further our understanding of them as well as our understanding of intercorporeal reversibilities.

Grief is the felt sense of separation, the emotional distress we feel in response to loss or deprivation. Grieving is a process, and the difficulty of this process is that of accustoming ourselves to an absence.

To me, what is most interesting, profound, and painful about the grieving process is the way in which it reveals how intimately woven, incorporated others are, into the fabric of our own lives. We cannot even begin to make sense of the pain of grief, which is a pain of parting, a pain of separation, unless we do suppose, in advance of it, some intercorporeal bonds—some enfleshed attachments we may have been unaware of, until we experience their loss, and to which even then we may persistently "hang on," through memories, behavior, and a juncturing of shared significances, transitivities of meaning, from one body to another.

Paradoxically, it seems to me that we only begin to sense the ultimacy of death's separations through processes of (embodied) identification with the dead. For example, however a loved one's death is communicated to us, we may initially feel shock, and a numbing sense of unreality. Shock is another interesting feeling—another "strange sensation." It is a feeling of not feeling, a feeling of being perceptually and emotionally shut down, closed off. Again, it is as though the inability to perceive (or the ability to not perceive) temporarily infiltrates our own perceptions. Our bodies, our brains may blank out, become insensible, unfeeling—as the dead are. We may feel "thick" in a certain sense, like we're "dense,"—like "numb-skulls"—like the reality of their parting hasn't really gotten "through" to us. But, of course, we see that it has gotten through, that it has begun to sink in. We see this when we see our grief-stricken selves walking around "like zombies"—our appetites gone; our senses dulled. Perception is the source of meaningfulness in the world, and as we "catch on," in the process of identifying with the dead, to the *senseless*ness of death, the senselessness of life may also become more apparent. As our ordinary occupations and observations take on alien and unreal aspects, lose their import, and confront us as meaningless activity, the connection between perceptions of death and perceptions of meaninglessness becomes less and less obscure.

Grief is a deeply disorienting emotion. "The act of living is different all through."[18] As we temporarily identify with the deceased, we may be disturbed, transformed, on very fundamental levels—not only on the levels of sense and meaning, but also at the levels of space and time. As I mentioned earlier, our sense of time may warp, be bent out of its usual shape, so that we may feel stuck or suspended in the past, unable to look ahead, as though our future is closed-off. Spatially, we are affected too. Dislocated. We may become withdrawn, appear to be "removed" from life. We may feel like we're "in a fog"—as though the atmosphere of our life is changing, has changed. It has, of course. It has lost this particular bearing, this particular "mooring." In "losing" a loved one, we have the sense of being "lost," without them— a sense of being left, without direction.

In writing about the death of his wife, C. S. Lewis depicts this sense of lost direction as a sense of frustration, the frustration of loving impulses, of live attachments, as part of the pain, of grief.

> I am beginning to understand why grief feels like suspense. It comes from the frustration of so many impulses that had become habitual. Thought after thought, feeling after feeling, action after action had Helen, for their target. Now their target is gone. I keep on, through habit, fitting an arrow to the string, then I remember and I have to lay the bow down.[19]

One of Merleau-Ponty's models for the intimate ways in which the sides of perceptibility are related is that of the concave and the convex, and one of his images of reversibility is that of "the finger of the glove that is turned inside out." In this instance, he says,

> There is no need of a spectator that would be *on each side*. It suffices that from one side I see the wrong side of the glove that is applied to the right side, that I touch the one *through* the other . . . the chiasm is that, the reversibility—. (VI 317/263)

Actions as simple as reaching for the telephone or starting to set a place at the table in a moment of forgetfulness are telling, illustrative here. They tell us, they force us to review the significance of the death of loved others—at the same time as they show us that there are still some traces of them left, on us, *and* intentionally inscribed on the "other side" of our bodies, the side to which our actions refer—the worldly side of *flesh* where they did once physically exist, in space and time. But now, since they no longer do, our relationship to them is obviously and definitively altered, and we come to realize this too, in working our way through the grieving process, as we are stopped short in our gestures, our conducts, unable to complete our actions or really connect with, open onto loved others in the ways that we were accustomed. For there, again, is that gap—that stoppage of sense, that *sens* of direction, the direction of our actions, backed up, backing up in us, back-ing us up, so that we are left, feeling "at a loss"—left feeling "incomplete."

But it is precisely that sense of being stopped short, of incompleteness, that is so revealing here. For it is through that very incompleteness, that gap, that chiasm, that sense*less*ness, that we can apprehend that we do, in a sense, remain "in touch" with the dead—and that to do this there really is "no need of a spectator that would be on each side."

Grief can be imaged, embodied in various ways. It has been compared to the fracturing of a bone, that requires time to mend. It is sometimes thought as an amputation—not in its "horrible" sense of incompleteness exactly, as I discussed earlier, but as a missing we're not so sure, not so certain of. In grief, we are not so instantaneously "cut off," from our family members, and we do not, so spontaneously, "let them go"—a major difference between the experience of grief and the experience of horror. The strange sensation here is emotionally analogous to the strange sensation of a phantom limb. We can see that in the thwarting, the subversions and misdirections of our actions, in our being continuously pulled back from our attempts to go ahead, to go forth, as we were. The backfiring of impulses that occur as we are becoming accustomed to the loss may be felt, as a counteraction—between sensing their presence and realizing their absence; as a conflict between accepting and denying the reality of the loss.

I image grief as an injury; as a type of open wound: torn tissue. I came to this sense of grief through reflecting on how I felt as a teenager, when my father died, completely, unexpectedly all at once. I felt as though he was ripped away, and that I was ripped apart from him.

For this reason, the conception of *flesh* as a fabric—flesh as the perceptible skin, the living tissue of a reality in which we are all profoundly and indivisibly enmeshed—has a deeply felt meaning to me. So I was fascinated to discover the image of grief as torn tissue—precisely as a tearing of fabric—embedded in a Jewish mourning custom called *kriyah*.

Upon learning of the death of their loved ones, Jews rend their garments. They rip their clothing, to symbolize the ruptured relationship and the pain of grief. What is felt, on the inside, crosses over onto the outside and is expressively exposed: the external tearing of fabric dramatically symbolizing a stabbing finality—"the internal tearing asunder that mourners feel in their relationship with the deceased."[20]

This ritual tearing of garments apparently stems from an earlier practice and one that is still, infrequently, carried on—the tradition of actually "tearing the flesh and the hair which symbolizes the loss of one's own flesh and blood in sympathy for the deceased."[21] Moroccan Jews "still scratch and cut their faces as a sign of mourning, notwithstanding their rabbis' denunciation of it"[22]; and female mourners in the Tigre province of Ethiopia may pull out much of their hair, in the process of their grieving.[23]

This tearing of tissue is, to be sure, a violent expression of mourning. But there is a certain violence, and a severity of emotional pain to be expressed, in the experience of grief. We can see this violence, this sense of being "ripped" away from a loved one, reflected in our ordinary language—when we speak, metaphorically, of a person who is grieving as being "all torn up." We could not feel this way at all—so hopelessly dispossessed or deprived, of a side of our selves, of our own flesh and blood, unless we are, as Merleau-Ponty supposed, existentially bound to significant others in the sensitive depths, the fabric, of our own embodied being.

In time of course these wounds are mostly mended, as the temperament of grief draws some of the sting out of the horror of death as a closure, and some of the pain out of separation, by leaving itself some opening—some room—so that its tears may still seep through, so that its "tears" may still be felt—now and again. When memories blur and blot our vision, when we swallow that "lump" in our throat, or hear that "crack" in our voices, we can emotionally perceive that loved ones are behind it, that they are still there, still intermingled, intermingling with us, as they must have been—all along. As a friend said to me recently, in a way that made us laugh—how sad it would be if we couldn't cry. For what if no *body*, no "living soul" remembers them in and through death's inevitable and perceptible stoppage of life? Then that gap, that chiasm, between us really would be uncrossable, irreversible . . . and they really *would* be dead—wouldn't they?—*completely* separated from, and unable to "actively" affect the living that still goes on in us.

NOTES

1. See Richard A. Cohen's article, "Merleau-Ponty, the Flesh and Foucault," *Philosophy Today* (winter 1984).

2. I take this opportunity to thank the Detroit Institute of Arts and Isabela Basombrio particularly for inviting and encouraging me to work on the topic of death in connection with their March 30, 1996 conference on "Death: An Etiquette of Cultural Memory."

3. Sharon Scholl, *Death and the Humanities* (Cranbury, N.J.: Associated University Presses, 1984), p. 36.

4. Noel Carroll, *The Philosophy Of Horror* (New York: Routledge, 1990), pp. 31–32.

5. Jacques Roubaud, *Some Thing Black,* trans. Rosemarie Waldrop (Elmwood Park, Ill.: Dalkey Archive Press, 1990), "Meditation of 5/12/85," p. 9.

6. Ibid., "Meditation on Certainty," p. 11.

7. Ibid., pp. 11–12.

8. Ibid., "Meditation on the Indistinct, on Heresy," p. 73.

9. Ibid., "Real and Steadfast Death," p. 116.

10. Ibid., "Envoi," p. 91.

11. Ibid., "Meditation on Comparison,." p. 82.

12. Ibid., "Meditation on the Indistinct, on Heresy," p. 74.

13. Ibid., "History Knows No Souvenirs," p. 111.

14. Ibid., "Real and Steadfast Death," p. 116.

15. Ibid., "Meditation of 5/12/85," p. 9.

16. Ibid., "Real and Steadfast Death," p. 116.

17. And as Kristeva also theorizes in her account of horror. See *Powers Of Horror: An Essay In Abjection* (New York: Columbia University Press, 1982).

18. C. S. Lewis, *A Grief Observed* (Greenwich, Conn.: Seabury Press), p. 13.

19. Ibid., p. 7.

20. Audrey Gordon, "The Jewish View of Death: Guidelines for Mourning" in Elisabeth Kubler-Ross, *Death: The Final Stage Of Growth* (Englewood Cliffs, N.J.: Prentice-Hall, 1975), p. 48.

21. Maurice Lamm, *The Jewish Way in Death and Mourning* (New York: Jonathan David Publishers, 1969), pp. 38–39.

22. Jack D. Spiro, *A Time to Mourn: Judaism and the Psychology of Bereavement* (New York: Bloch Publishing Co., 1985).

23. Robert W. Haberstein and William M. Lamers, *Funeral Customs the World Over* (Milwaukee, Wis.: Bulfin Printers, 1960), p. 211.

CHAPTER 12

Écart:
The Space of Corporeal Difference

GAIL WEISS

[U]ltimately, it is only the strange which is familiar and only difference which is repeated.

—Gilles Deleuze, *Difference and Repetition*

It is not clear who makes and who is made in the relation between human and machine.

—Donna Haraway, *Simians, Cyborgs, and Women*

Taken together, these two claims challenge clear-cut divisions between the familiar and the unfamiliar, the natural and the unnatural. Inverting the Platonic understanding of mimesis in which copies not only depend for their existence upon a prior origin(al), but derive their own (moral) value and aesthetic merit through the preciseness with which they imitate that origin(al), Deleuze argues that the new and the different can only arise through repetition; as he says: "We produce something new only on condition that we repeat."[1] Repetition, he maintains, cannot be understood as a recurrence of the same, rather, "repetition is the power of difference and differentiation: because it accelerates or decelerates time, or because it alters spaces."[2]

Although Deleuze and Haraway have markedly different projects and methodologies, as well as different conceptions of both humans and machines, I would argue that both are indebted to the notion of reversibility articulated in the later Merleau-Ponty. While for Deleuze, this connection is more obvious given that Deleuze acknowledges Merleau-Ponty as a formative influence on his thought, I would maintain that Haraway's own understanding of the cyborg as "a hybrid of machine and organism, a creature of social reality as well as a creature of fiction"[3] is itself a chiasmic notion that fore-grounds the reversible, mutually constitutive relationship between the human and the nonhuman.

The place where Merleau-Ponty most eloquently (and enigmatically) articulates what he means by reversibility is in the chapter "The Intertwining-The Chiasm" of his final, unfinished work, *The Visible and the Invisible*. Feminist theorists, in particular, have focused on this particular essay, critically examining the examples of reversibility Merleau-Ponty offers there, challenging the limitations of this "metaphysical principle," and exploring its radical possibilities. Most of the recent work feminist theorists have done on this essay has involved approaching this chapter through Luce Irigaray's mimetic reading of it: "The Invisible of the Flesh: A Reading of Merleau-Ponty," *The Visible and the Invisible*, "The Intertwining—The Chiasm."[4] In this essay, Irigaray repeats the Merleau-Pontian text, challenging its omissions, exploring its fissures, in order to produce an alternative account of reversibility that could be said to precede Merleau-Ponty's prior articulation of it.

Passing in and out of Merleau-Ponty's essay, picking up certain themes only to drop them and move on to related issues, Irigaray folds her own essay into his, intertwining them to produce an account of corporeality that extends back before birth (Merleau-Ponty's starting point) and forward to an imagined future in which the reversible relations that continuously unfold within women's own bodies are recognized and appreciated sites of knowledge, pleasure, and desire. Before examining Irigaray's subversive strategy and the critique of Merleau-Ponty's understanding of reversibility that issues from it more closely, let me begin by discussing those aspects of reversibility that are crucial for both thinkers as well as for Deleuze and Haraway.

First, and foremost, it should be noted that the image of reversibility Merleau-Ponty provides in *The Visible and the Invisible* and in his earlier essay, "Eye and Mind," is extremely spatial. Reversibility, as depicted by Merleau-Ponty, might best be described as a metaphysical principle that functions on both a micro and macro level to characterize the body's interactions with itself, with others, and with the world. On a micro level, reversibility breaks down the (conceptual) boundaries between what have traditionally been understood as discrete bodily sensations, performing what Butler has called a kind of "transubstantiation" of vision into touch, movement into expression, whereby I see by "touching" and move by "speaking" with my body.[5] On a macro level, reversibility describes an ongoing interaction between the flesh of the body, the flesh of others, and the flesh of the world, a process in which corporeal boundaries are simultaneously erected and dismantled. Bringing these two levels together, Grosz maintains that:

> Flesh is being as reversibility, being's capacity to fold in on itself, being's dual orientation inward and outward, being's openness, its

reflexivity, the fundamental gap or dehiscence of being that Merleau-Ponty illustrates with a favorite example—the notion of "double sensation," the capacity of one hand to touch another that is itself touching an object."[6]

If reversibility indeed is, as Merleau-Ponty implies, an operative principle that makes perception, thought, and language possible, the paradox involved in interrogating it is both temporal and spatial. The temporal dimension of the paradox can be understood as analogous to the paradox that Judith Butler identifies in attempting to provide an account of the becoming of the subject, a becoming that constitutes the subject as such, but which can only be interrogated from a given subject position which it both anticipates and repeats:

> The temporal paradox of the subject is such that, of necessity, we must lose the perspective of a subject already formed in order to account for our own becoming. That "becoming" is no simple or continuous affair, but an uneasy practice of repetition and its risks, compelled yet incomplete, wavering on the horizon of social being.[7]

To trace the process of becoming that forms the subject is itself a transformative enterprise. As Butler argues, the becoming of the subject cannot be described through a linear trajectory, but involves a disparate series of backward and forward movements in which the subject repetitively, reflexively, turns back upon itself, and moreover, this self that the subject returns to is not a fixed self but a self that is phantasmatically projected as a stable site of significance. Butler's chiasmic account of a subject turning back upon itself, forming itself through its subjection to this compulsive desire for repetition of an original moment that it can never reproduce, is indebted not only to Freud and Lacan, Nietzsche and Foucault, figures whose work she analyzes and critiques at length, but also to Merleau-Ponty's articulation of the phenomenon of reversibility.

To foreground the spatial dimensions of the chiasm, one must recognize that the intimate interrelationships that reversibility makes possible between humans and humans, between humans and nonhumans and between nonhumans and nonhumans, are themselves grounded upon what Merleau-Ponty calls *écart*, a space of noncoincidence that resists articulation. More specifically, in order for human beings to "interface" with machines, in order for us to become one with our familiar, mass-produced or even "one-of-a-kind" prostheses (e.g., glasses, clothes, artificial limbs, moussed-up hair, cars, watches, etc.), there must be, as Deleuze affirms, a strange space of disincorporation that makes incorporation possible. While Merleau-Ponty never explicitly addresses the relationship between humans and machines, Deleuze argues that human beings are themselves machines, desiring machines that "work only when they break down, and by continually breaking down."[8]

The body's sudden rejection of a transplanted organ that hitherto had been working "just fine" reminds us that the crossover between human and machine is never seamless or untroubled. Discussing her experience of hearing renowned physicist Steven Hawking give a "talk" through a Vortrax, a computer-generated speech device, Allucquère Rosanne Stone asks:

> Who is doing the talking up there on stage? In an important sense, Hawking doesn't stop being Hawking at the edge of his visible body. There is the obvious physical Hawking, vividly outlined by the way our social conditioning teaches us to see a person as a person. But a serious part of Hawking extends into the box in his lap. In mirror image, a serious part of that silicon and plastic assemblage in his lap extends into him as well . . . not to mention the invisible ways, displaced in time and space, in which discourses of medical technology and their physical accretions already permeate him and us. No box, no discourse; in the absence of the prosthetic, Hawking's intellect becomes a tree falling in the forest with nobody around to hear it.[9]

According to Stone, Hawking is not Hawking without his prosthetic voice. His Vortrax is inextricably tied to who "he" is in a complex, boundary-defying relationship in which the machine is the person and the person is the machine. And yet, to ask "who is doing the talking up there on stage?" itself gestures toward a space of disincorporation, a virtual site that sets the terms for the reversible relationship between man and machine.

It is this site, the unrepresentable space of differentiation that makes reversibility possible that interests me. The seductiveness of the chiasmic intertwining that Merleau-Ponty invokes to describe reversibility has led many to focus on how corporeal reversibility is lived rather than on the invisible "hinge" that both makes reversibility possible and, simultaneously, prevents it from being fully achieved. For Irigaray, this invisible, yet indispensable place is what she calls the "maternal-feminine," the site of all sexual difference.[10] While Irigaray is clearly drawing upon Merleau-Ponty's own understanding of reversibility in tracing out the chiasmic relationship between mother and fetus as the ground for all future instances of reversibility that we experience in our lives, she uses this paradigmatic experience to illustrate that Merleau-Ponty has not taken reversibility far enough. According to Irigaray, he does not extend it far enough because he begins with bodies that are already sexually individuated and talks about the reversible relations that play out within those bodies (e.g. one hand touching the other), and between those bodies and other, equally individuated bodies. In doing so, she argues, Merleau-Ponty offers us a "labyrinthine solipsism" whereby all touching, all looking, all hearing, reverberate back upon an individuated subject who experiences herself as touched, looked at, heard. By gesturing toward that originary, maternal, phantasmatic site we all once inhabited but to which we can never return, Irigaray points out that reversibility is already operative before the subject is differentiated as such, and that it involves, from the outset, a relationship between bodies that are nondiscrete, one enveloped within the other.[11]

While this is itself a trenchant critique that I believe Merleau-Ponty, with his interest in early childhood development, may have been responsive to, Irigaray also claims that Merleau-Ponty takes reversibility too far, in that he describes a harmonious, flowing, two-way interaction between the tangible and the visible whereby, as noted earlier, we "see" through touching and "touch" through seeing, a process that involves not merely these two senses alone but all the other senses that constitute our "aesthesiological" bodies. Although, historically, vision has been accorded primacy over all the other senses, and although Merleau-Ponty himself seems to subvert this primacy by placing touch (and later on hearing) on an equal footing with vision, Irigaray maintains that Merleau-Ponty nonetheless refuses to grant the primacy of touch, a primacy that she claims can be seen once we acknowledge our previous, intrauterine experience in which we touched before seeing and were touched before being seen.

For Irigaray then, Merleau-Ponty takes reversibility too far because he does not acknowledge that certain, tactile experiences (e.g., intrauterine existence, and female sexuality more generally) cannot be rendered visible nor does he recognize that the reversible relationships that are nonetheless occurring (e.g., the fetus' relationship with its mother and a woman's relationship with her own body) are ruptured through attempts to specularise them.[12] Rather than opening up the body to other bodies, to the world and to itself, Merleau-Ponty's notion of reversibility, Irigaray asserts, closes off these rich corporeal sites because it weaves them too tightly together, and, in so doing, fails to acknowledge differences that are nonreversible, such as the sexually specific differences between maternal and nonmaternal, female and male bodies.[13] Thus,

> According to Merleau-Ponty, energy plays itself out in the backward-and-forward motion of a loom. But weaving the visible and my look in this way, I could just as well say that I close them off from myself. The texture becomes increasingly tight, taking me into it, sheltering me there but imprisoning me as well.[14]

To view Irigaray's own critique as a decisive repudiation of Merleau-Ponty is itself an act of foreclosure that refuses to take the notion of *écart* that is so foundational to his thought seriously. While one may argue that this is precisely what Irigaray herself is accusing Merleau-Ponty of doing, it is also

possible to take Irigaray to task for offering an idealized account of intrauterine existence characterized by fluid interactions between mother and fetus,
in which each resonates, aggressively as well as lovingly, to the movements
and demands of the other (the same could be said of her depiction of female
sexuality). In her well-known essay, "And the One Doesn't Stir without the
Other," Irigaray articulates the reversibility between the fetus/mother relationship and the daughter/mother relationship and, in both cases, views the intervention of "third-parties" such as the father, as disruptions to the flow of their
exchange. "Nourishing," she claims:

> takes place before there are any images. There's just a pause: the time
> for the one to become the other. Consuming comes before any vision
> of her who gives herself. You've disappeared, unperceived-imper-ceptible
> if not for this flow that fills up to the edge. That enters the other in the
> container of her skin. That penetrates and occupies the container until
> it takes away all possible space from both the one and the other, re-
> moves every interval between the one and the other. Until there is only
> this liquid that flows from the one into the other, and that is nameless.[15]

Passages such as these, leave no room for any other parties to this symbiotic
relationship between the one and the other. Indeed, Irigaray portrays the
(invisible) father as someone who is turned to when the daughter seeks to
escape the all-encompassing intensity of the mother/daughter relationship, an
escape that is an illusion because rather than provide the daughter with the
space needed to develop her own identity, he disregards her needs and continues on his own path, graciously allowing her to follow behind him. Repu-
diating the imaginary mother for attempting to fix the fluidity of their
relationship by adhering to established patterns of exchange, Irigaray's daughter
threatens:

> if you turn your face from me, giving yourself to me only in an already
> inanimate form, abandoning me to competent men to undo my/your
> paralysis, I'll turn to my father. I'll leave you for someone who seems
> more alive than you. For someone who doesn't prepare anything for me
> to eat. For someone who leaves me empty of him, mouth gaping on his
> truth. I'll follow him with my eyes, I'll listen to what he says, I'll try
> to walk behind him.
>   He leaves the house, I follow in his steps. Farewell, Mother, I shall
> never become your likeness.[16]

The mother, however, is not so easily left behind. She appears in the mirror
as the daughter's "double" and haunts the daughter's attempts to establish her
"own" identity.

What concerns me about this account, is Irigaray's failure to acknowledge the numerous and often positive ways in which the mother/daughter and
mother/fetus relationships themselves are always already mediated by others,
even at the moments when they are most intense and seemingly all-encompassing. These "third-party" interventions are not established with birth and
the cutting of the umbilical cord, rather, the interventions occur before, during, and after the pregnancy and profoundly affect the woman's and the fetus'
relationship to one another.

A woman who becomes impregnated through rape for instance, sustains
a reversible relationship with her fetus that is often mediated by hatred,
resentment, shame, and disgust, feelings that the fetus' responsive movements
may actually enhance rather than overcome. Although Irigaray might respond
that these interventions come from the "outside," from a phallocratic society
that has historically blamed women for their rape, blamed the child for being
born "out of wedlock" and, through a calculated act of *invisibility*, absolved
the man from accountability for his violence against them both, the point is
that even when sex and pregnancy are actively chosen, the interactions that
unfold between mother and fetus are never just a matter of "the one and the
other." Nor, and this is the more important point, should these interventions
be viewed negatively as they often seem to be in Irigaray's work, disturbing
the maternal-fetal dyad with their specular intrusions.

Irigaray's position is complicated, for while she does seek a space of
disidentification between mother and daughter that will allow the daughter to
recognize her maternal debt without seeking to collapse her own identity into
her mother's, she will only depict this space positively insofar as it emerges
from *within* the mother/daughter relationship and not from the contribution
that others make to it. More generally, Irigaray's intensely antispecular approach, an approach that Martin Jay has shown is itself part of a larger,
twentieth-century French critique of ocularcentrism, leaves her in a position
where she seems forced to view all visible interventions into women's sexuality and procreative potentiality negatively. On her account, the reversibility
of looking freezes the looker and the looked-at in a mirrorlike relationship
that has historically reflected, not the genuine otherness of she who is looked
at, but the seer's own narcissistic desires. By contrast, Irigaray celebrates the
tactile domain as a potential sphere of self-knowledge and genuine intimacy
that will allow bodies to interact with one another in a manner that preserves
their differences apart from the "leveling" gaze that reduces irreducible difference to sameness in difference.

Écart, for Irigaray, is tied to multiplicity: two lips that never become
one, two sexes that will never be one. While affirming these differences,
Irigaray also articulates a hope for a new chiasmic relationship between them,
one that is predicated on an incorporation of difference *as* difference rather
than a transubstantiation of difference into sameness. Strangely, her resistance

to visibility, despite her own attempts to make these differences visible in her work, does not enhance but restricts her own understanding of difference and the potentiality for corporeal incorporation of difference.

The speculum, ultra-sound, laporoscopies, are all technologies of the visible that reveal women's bodies to others and to themselves. That these invasive technologies are often uncomfortable, embarrassing, painful, and alienating, is undeniable, but what also must be affirmed is the way in which they open up women's bodies to experiences and possibilities that would not be available otherwise. To endorse uncritically these technologies is as problematic as uncritically rejecting them: both maternal and fetal lives have been saved through their use but their easy availability (in the Western world in particular) has also greatly complicated the decisions women, their families, and those crucial intermediaries, the doctor and the insurance companies, have had to face regarding if, when, where, and how to have children.

Merleau-Ponty's conception of flesh, flesh that is not just of bodies but a "flesh of the world," allows us to see the intercorporeal possibilities inherent in the chiasmic relationship between humans and machines. "For if the body" he asserts,

> is a thing among things, it is so in a stronger and deeper sense than they: in the sense that, we said, it *is of them,* and this means that it detaches itself upon them, and, accordingly, detaches itself from them. (VI 181/137)

While Irigaray argues that Merleau-Ponty leaves no room for silence, because "[t]he structure of a mute world is such that all the possibilities of language are already given there,"[17] she also deliberately ignores the ways in which these possibilities are, on his account, predicated on "a presentation of a certain absence" that remains inexplicable. This inexplicable absence that in different ways makes visibility, language, and perception possible, constitutes a paradox that Merleau-Ponty begins to articulate in the following passage:

> our body commands the visible for us, but it does not explain it, does not clarify it, it only concentrates the mystery of its scattered visibility; and it is indeed a paradox of Being, not a paradox of man, that we are dealing with here. This paradox of Being arises insofar as visibility can only emerge from the ground of invisibility, language from silence, and perception from that which is imperceptible. (VI 180/136)

While Irigaray objects to the image of an invisibility that awaits visibility to be recognized and a silence that attains significance through being regarded as pregnant with linguistic possibilities, it is passages such as the one above that remind us that Merleau-Ponty savored the irresolvable mysteries of visibility, language, thought, and perception, mysteries that both defy and are constitutive of reversibility.

In the introduction to their edited collection, *Posthuman Bodies*, Judith Halberstam and Ira Livingston articulate the paradoxes that arise out of the interface between technology and the human body through the trope of the posthuman body. "The posthuman" they argue:

> does not necessitate the obsolescence of the human; it does not represent an evolution or devolution of the human. Rather it participates in re-distributions of difference and identity. The human functions to domesticate and hierarchize difference within the human (whether according to race, class, gender) and to absolutize difference between the human and the nonhuman. The posthuman does not reduce difference-from-others to difference-from-self, but rather emerges in the pattern of resonance and interference between the two.[18]

The posthuman body, they suggest, is both a present reality and a future possibility. It is a present reality insofar as any conception of the human depends upon the active positing of that which it is not, the nonhuman, of which machines are both the most paradigmatic and most contested example (e.g., artificial intelligence as well as artificial life have served as primary cases for and primary challenges to the nonhumanness of machines). It is a future possibility as well since there is a significant difference between living this complicated interface between the biological, the psychical, the cultural, and the technological, an interface that is inscribed and expressed in our body images, and recognizing the transformative potential it makes possible both within and across these interdependent dimensions of our existence. Opposed even to a *phantasmatic* ideal of coherence, wholeness, or completeness, a phallic fantasy that structures the symbolic domain and plays such a crucial role in the construction of the psyche in Lacanian psychoanalytic theory, Halberstam and Livingston argue, in Deleuzian fashion, that the posthuman subject has no telos to cling to:

> Unlike the human subject-to-be (Lacan's "l'hommelette"), who sees his own mirror image and fixed gender identity discrete and sovereign before him in a way that will forever exceed him, the posthuman becoming-subject vibrates across and among an assemblage of semi-autonomous collectivities it knows it can never either be coextensive with nor altogether separate from.[19]

Reinforcing and simultaneously deconstructing the importance of the prenatal ties that link us to our mothers, Halberstam and Livingston stress that: "Posthuman bodies never/always leave the womb. The dependence or interdependence of bodies on the material and discursive networks through which they operate means that the umbilical cords that supply us (without which we would die) are always multiple."[20] Whether these multiple umbilical cords take the form of medical technologies such as feeding tubes, respiratory apparati, and dialysis machines, or electronic and mechanical technologies such as computers, telephones, and cars, the body's chiasmic relationship with them has resulted in their incorporation in our body images, an incorporation that is continually renegotiated through the space of disincorporation that makes new linkages possible, a space that Merleau-Ponty calls *écart*.

Discussing the ways in which mobile technologies such as the railway system allow relatively unmoving bodies to be moved across great distances (i.e., as passengers sit in their compartments watching the landscape unfold outside their windows), Mark Seltzer argues that "[w]hat these mobile technologies make possible, in different forms, are the thrill and panic of agency at once extended and suspended."[21] Virtual reality devices also offer the promise of moving without being moved, and their increasing popularity testifies to an increasing desire to challenge the very terms that traditionally established what it means to be a bodily agent. This, in turn, forces a reconceptualization not only of movement and agency, but also of desire.[22]

According to Deleuze and Guattari, "[d]esire constantly couples continuous flows and partial objects that are by nature fragmentary and fragmented. Desire causes the current to flow, itself flows in turn, and breaks the flows."[23] Through the intensification of desire that comes from pursuing some linkages over others, new assemblages are formed. These assemblages are also fragmentary, contingent, and multiple, and their intercorporeal transformations are registered in a series of body images linked together through their own chiasmic interchanges.

As a space of disincorporation, *écart* marks the fissures and gaps that allow us to separate bodies from what they were, what they are not now, and what they may or may not become. It is this space of differentiation, I would argue, that holds out the promise for new linkages between bodies and machines and that therefore guarantees that our own body images will always be multiple.

To take the Merleau-Pontian notion of *écart* seriously is crucial as well for the Irigarayan project of coming to terms with sexual difference in its materiality and corporeality. Irigaray depicts this possibility through the image of a double desire, the desire of two who can never be reduced to one. "If," she argues,

> there is no double desire, the positive and negative poles divide themselves between the two sexes instead of establishing a chiasmus or a

double loop in which each can go toward the other and come back to itself.[24]

On Deleuze's and Guattari's model, these double desires unfold not only between bodies but also within bodies, bodies conceived as micromachines producing a multiplicity of (often conflicting) microdesires. While Elizabeth Grosz calls attention to Deleuze's and Guattari's problematic tendency to "utlize models and metaphors that have been made possible only at the expense of women's exclusion and denigration,"[25] Grosz also argues that:

> Deleuze and Guattari's notion of the body as a discontinuous, nontotal-ized series of processes, organs, flows, energies, corporeal substances and incorporeal events, intensities, and durations may be of great relevance to those feminists attempting to reconceive bodies, especially women's bodies, outside of the binary polarizations imposed on the body by the mind/body, nature/culture, subject/obect, and interior/exterior oppositions.[26]

Interestingly, Deleuze and Guattari depict the body's excessive, multiple desires as functioning fairly independently on a micro or local level even while they are, on a macro level completely interconnected. Just as parts of a car such as a battery, engine, transmission, and radiator, perform their different functions in relative isolation from one another but these performances are coordinated with other necessary operations into the running of the car, intracorporeal desires ennervate local bodily regions and these ennervations reverberate, in surprisingly consistent ways, throughout the body.[27]

Haraway, in contrast to Deleuze and Guattari, is much more concerned with the political implications of models of multiplicity as well as with the power of metaphors such as that of the cyborg. Indeed, the figure of the cyborg, Haraway suggests, expresses both the dangers as well as the possibilities of multiplicities that transgress ideologically established boundaries. According to Haraway:

> The home, workplace, market, public arena, the body itself—all can be dispersed and interfaced in nearly infinite, polymorphous ways, with large consequences for women and others—consequences that themselves are very different for different people.[28]

Without these reversible relationships, communication itself would become impossible. And yet a predictable effect of our branching network of communication technologies (like that of our reproductive technologies) is that it has spawned new cyborgian constructions (e.g., the internet), cyborgs that exceed and disrupt the multiple discourses out of which they have emerged.

Écart, as the moment of disincorporation that makes all forms of corporeal differentiation possible, is also precisely what allows us to establish boundaries between bodies, boundaries that must be respected in order to respect the agencies that flow from them. From a Merleau-Pontian perspective, these boundaries can best be respected not by artificially viewing bodies as isolated from one another but by acknowledging the reversible relationships that are exhibited within and across them. Thus, to demonize any form of technology as an alien force "out to get us," can cause us to lose sight of technology's own fleshly existence. More specifically, I would argue, we may fail to recognize that: (1) technology is itself embodied and not simply a means of transforming bodies and (2) that to demonize technology or even certain technologies on the basis of their artificiality is to demonize the body that is continually being reconfigured through them. On the other hand, to defend these claims does not entail uncritically affirming each and every technology or each and every bodily practice that incorporates those technologies; indeed one way of assessing the promise of new technologies and the new bodies and body images produced by them should be the extent to which they promote and preserve the space of differentiation that makes our intercorporeal exchanges possible (cf. VI 178/135).

For, as Jonathan Benthall notes, "[u]ntil we become more aware of the body's power and resourcefulness, we will not feel a sufficiently educated outrage against its manipulation and exploitation."[29]

NOTES

This essay is reprinted from *Body Images* by Gail Weiss. © 1998. Reproduced by permission of Routledge, Inc.

1. Gilles Deleuze, *Difference and Repetition,* trans. Paul Patton (New York: Columbia University Press, 1994).

2. Ibid., p. 220.

3. Donna Haraway, *Simians, Cyborgs, and Women: The Reinvention of Nature* (New York: Routledge Press, 1991), p. 149.

4. Examples of prominent feminist theorists who have offered readings of Irigaray's reading of Merleau-Ponty include Elizabeth Grosz ("Merleau-Ponty and Irigaray in the Flesh"), Tina Chanter ("Wild Meaning: Luce Irigaray's Reading of Merleau-Ponty, collected in this volume), and Judith Butler (two lectures offered to the 1994 National Endowment for the Humanities (NEH) Institute on *Embodiment: The Intersection between Nature and Culture* at the University of California, Santa Cruz).

5. Comments from the 1994 NEH Institute on Embodiment at the University of California, Santa Cruz.

6. Elizabeth Grosz, "Merleau-Ponty and Irigaray in the Flesh," *Thesis Eleven* no. 36 (1993): 44.

7. Judith Butler, *The Psychic Life of Power: Theories in Subjection* (Stanford: Stanford University Press, 1997), p. 30.

8. Gilles Deleuze and Félix Guattari, *Anti-Oedipus: Capitalism and Schizophrenia,* trans. Robert Hurley, Mark Seem, and Helen R. Lane (Minneapolis: University of Minnesota Press, 1983), p. 8.

9. Allucquère Rosanne Stone, *The War of Desire and Technology at the Close of the Mechanical Age* (Cambridge: The MIT Press, 1995), p. 5.

10. Luce Irigaray, *An Ethics of Sexual Difference,* trans. Carolyn Burke and Gillian C. Gill (Ithaca, N.Y.: Cornell University Press, 1993), *passim.*

11. Ibid.

12. These include the cutting of the umbilical cord that connects mother to fetus, and the specular gaze of the traditionally male medical establishment that mediates women's understandings of their own bodies and bodily potentialities.

13. A serious and presumably deliberate omission in Irigaray's own account is an explanation of the differences between what she calls the "maternal-feminine" and the oxymoronic but nonetheless experienciable "non-maternal-feminine." Her strategic coupling of the maternal and the feminine while perhaps successful in offering a more positive, powerful image of woman as mother, also assumes the risk of leaving women who are not and will not be mothers out of account altogether, except as daughters to their own mothers. (Ibid.)

14. Luce Irigaray, *An Ethics of Sexual Difference,* trans. Carolyn Burke and Gillian C. Gill (Ithaca, N.Y.: Cornell University Press, 1993), p. 183.

15. Luce Irigaray, "And the One Doesn't Stir without the Other," *Signs* 7, no. 1 (autumn): 63.

16. Ibid., p. 62.

17. Luce Irigaray, *An Ethics of Sexual Difference,* trans. Carolyn Burke and Gillian C. Gill (Ithaca, N.Y.: Cornell University Press, 1993), p. 180.

18. Judith Halberstam and Ira Livingston, "Introduction: Posthuman Bodies," in *Posthuman Bodies,* ed. Judith Halberstam and Ira Livingston (Bloomington: Indiana University Press, 1995), p. 10.

19. Ibid., p. 14.

20. Ibid., p. 17.

21. Mark Seltzer, *Bodies and Machines* (New York: Routledge Press, 1992), p. 18.

22. Several feminist theorists, in particular, have focused on this latter project including Teresa de Lauretis who reconfigures lesbian desire from within a psychoanalytic framework in *The Practice of Love: Lesbian Sexuality and Perverse Desire,* and Elizabeth Grosz who, in her collection of essays, *Space, Time, and Perversion:*

Essays on the Politics of Bodies, rejects the psychoanalytic model of desire based on lack and instead works from a Deleuzian perspective, which emphasizes the multiplicity of desires, subjects of desire, and objects of desire.

23. Gilles Deleuze and Félix Guattari, *Anti-Oedipus: Capitalism and Schizophrenia,* trans. Robert Hurley, Mark Seem, and Helen R. Lane (Minneapolis: University of Minnesota Press, 1983), p. 5.

24. Luce Irigaray, *An Ethics of Sexual Difference,* trans. Carolyn Burke and Gillian C. Gill (Ithaca, N.Y.: Cornell University Press, 1993), p. 9.

25. Elizabeth Grosz, *Space, Time, and Perversion: Essays on the Politics of Bodies* (New York: Routledge Press, 1995), p. 190.

26. Ibid., pp. 193–194.

27. In his essay, "The Body in Consumer Culture," in *The Body: Social Process and Cultural Theory,* ed. Mike Featherstone, Mike Hepworth, and Brian S. Turner (London: Sage, 1991), p. 182, Mike Featherstone argues that this analogy between bodies and cars is rendered explicit through the contemporary call for increased "body maintenance," a term that "indicates the popularity of the machine metaphor for the body."

28. Haraway, *Simians, Cyborgs, and Women,* p. 163.

29. Jonathan Benthall, *The Body Electric: Patterns of Western Industrial Culture* (London: Thames and Hudson, 1976), p. 92.

PART III

Limitations of the Flesh

CHAPTER 13

Wild Meaning: Luce Irigaray's Reading of Merleau-Ponty

TINA CHANTER

Merleau-Ponty calls for a new beginning, a recommencement of philosophy, a return to a place that will allow us to form "new instruxments" to replace those of "reflection and intuition." Instead of the fixed subject-object opposition, or the rigid distinction between existence and essence, he wants to "rediscover . . . some of the living references" that sustain the "mystery" and enigma of the exercises that we call "seeing and speaking" (VI 172/130). Just as he was in *Phenomenology of Perception*, he is concerned in *The Visible and the Invisible* with the way in which language "promotes its own oblivion," how the power of expression "exceeds language" (PP 459/401). He recalls in *Phenomenology of Perception* a children's story about the "disappointment of a small boy who put on his grandmother's spectacles and took up her book in the expectation of being able himself to find in it the stories which she used to tell him." But the boy finds no story, "nothing but black and white." Merleau-Ponty says "For the child . . . the story is a world which there must be some way of magically calling up by putting on spectacles and leaning over a book." The power of expression that resides in language to bring "the thing expressed into existence' " to "ope[n] up to thought new ways, new dimensions and new landscapes, is, in the last analysis, as obscure for the adult as for the child" (PP 459–60/401).

Merleau-Ponty consistently emphasizes both the enigmatic quality of perception and language, seeing and speaking, and the need to find new instruments of thought, to open up new dimensions and landscapes. He wants to "recommence everything" (VI 172/130), refusing to settle for the comfort of preconceived and sedimented oppositions between subject and object, I and world, vision and the visible, or the visible and invisible. With the notion of "flesh" he unsettles these distinctions, situating them in a medium that resists the fixity of mutually exclusive categories, an in between, "a sort of

220   TINA CHANTER

incarnate principle that brings a style of being" (VI 184/139). Thus at the end
of the chiasm chapter he can invoke what he calls "two aspects of
reversibility"—a reversibility that he says is "the ultimate truth" (VI 204/
155). First, there is the purpose of philosophy according to Husserl: the
restoration of "a power to signify, a birth of meaning, or a wild meaning" (VI
203/155) and secondly there is the fact that "as Valéry said, language is
everything, since it is the voice of no one, since it is the very voice of the
things, the waves, the forests" (VI 203–4/155).

For Irigaray, the reversibility of Merleau-Ponty's *The Visible and the
Invisible* constitutes a "closed system"[1] (ES 161/172), a "closed economy"
(ES 161/173), a "closed world" (ES 163/174). "What Merleau-Ponty seeks"
she says "is something that closes the circuit" (ES 163/174), that totalizes and
encloses (see ES 163/175), that reduces the tactile to the visible (ES 164/
175). His "way of talking about the flesh . . . already cancels its most powerful components, those that are moreover creative in their power" (ES 164/
175). In his discourse there is "nothing new, nothing being born. . . . No new
speech is possible here" (ES 166/178). "Nothing new can be said. . . . Everything is unceasingly reversible" (ES 167/180). "Nothing new happens, only
this permanent weaving between the world and the subject. Which supposes
that the subject sees the whole" (ES 170/182). "It is always the same"—"The
phenomenology of the flesh that Merleau-Ponty attempts is without
question(s). . . . [There is] no Other to keep the world open" (ES 170/183).
"Everything is given" (ES 171/184). Is it possible, asks Irigaray finally, "to
restore a power to signify, a birth of meaning, or a wild meaning . . . without
changing the foundations of language? Without lifting the hypothesis that
reversibility is the final truth?" (ES 171/184)

How can Irigaray maintain that there is room for nothing new in Merleau-
Ponty's phenomenology of the flesh, that nothing new can be said, that there
is no room for the other? How can she insist on the closure and "solipsism"
(ES 159/169) of his system, on its lack of questioning, and its failure to
preserve otherness? Does not Merleau-Ponty precisely call for a new beginning, a recommencement, new instruments of philosophy? Does he not tell us
that the philosopher is "obliged to reinspect the most well-grounded notions,
to create new ones, with new words to designate them, to undertake a true
reform of the understanding" (VI 17/3)? Does not Merleau-Ponty break new
ground with his notion of the flesh, introducing a new philosophical term, that
hitherto had "no name in any philosophy" (VI 193/147)? Isn't his attempt
more radical than Irigaray is willing to acknowledge? I want to address this
question by showing both that there is a sense in which what Merleau-Ponty
catches sight of in the notion of the flesh presents philosophy "and feminist
philosophy in particular" with a genuinely radical alternative to traditional
categories, and that there is a sense in which Irigaray is right to criticize him
for not going far enough.

In a recent interview Luce Irigaray divides her work into three phases. The first stage, which she identifies as the most critical one, constitutes an attempt to show "how a single subject, traditionally the masculine subject, had constructed the world and interpreted [it] according to a single perspective."[2] The second stage was "to define those mediations that could permit the existence of a feminine subjectivity" that is to say, another subject" (JLI 97). The third and final stage is to "define a relationship, a philosophy, an ethic, a relationship between two different subjects" (JLI 97), to construct "an intersubjectivity respecting sexual difference" (JLI 96). The essay by Irigaray that I will focus on today, "The Invisible of the Flesh," is a close reading of Merleau-Ponty's chapter "The Intertwining—The Chiasm" in *The Visible and the Invisible*. Irigaray first presented this interpretation of the chiasm chapter at Erasmus University in Rotterdam in 1982 as part of a series of lectures she gave there under the title "The Ethics of the Passions." It was subsequently published as the penultimate chapter of *Ethique de la différence sexuelle* (*An Ethics of Sexual Difference*). This book is situated on the cusp of the first and second phases of Irigaray's corpus. It participates in both what Irigaray proclaims to be the most critical phase of her work, the earliest period in which she exposes the "auto-mono-centrism of the western subject," and the second more positive phase, in which she defines "a second subject," a feminine subject.

Irigaray's essay on Merleau-Ponty can be productively read as combining the critical project that she undertakes in *Speculum of the Other Woman* and *This Sex Which Is Not One*, with the constructive project of defining woman as a subject in her own right, an endeavor also pursued in such texts as *Parler n'est jamais neutre* and *Sexes and Genealogies*.[3] I want to present these two interlocking aspects of Irigaray's reading of Merleau-Ponty, but some context is needed in order to appreciate the role and importance of, on the one hand, her critique of the singular masculine subject that has been the linchpin of Western philosophy and, on the other hand, her attempt to create a space for a new feminine subject.

Just as it is no accident that feminists are increasingly engaging with the psychoanalytic scene, in which the problem of bodies is confronted, rather than elided, so it is no accident that Merleau-Ponty—whose work of course demonstrates a constant preoccupation with the problem of bodies—among phenomenologists enjoys perhaps the singular distinction of engaging psychoanalytic thought from an early stage of his philosophical career. In a statement that is remarkable both for its stark simplicity, and because it manages to fly in the face of the entire philosophical tradition of the West, Merleau-Ponty says, "It is the body and it alone, because it is a two-dimensional being, that can bring us to the things themselves" (VI 179/136; also VI 25/10). The Cartesian privileging of the mind over the body is a legacy that can be attributed, without too much oversimplification, both to Husserl's search for the "things themselves" and Heidegger's development of that search in his elaboration of the question of Being. If Merleau-Ponty is almost single-handedly responsible,[4] among phenomenologists, for giving the body its due, his position is no mere reversal of Descartes. Not wishing simply to replace the priority of thought with that of the body, he concedes that it is "not entirely my body that perceives" (VI 24/9). Merleau-Ponty's great contribution lies precisely in his refusal to settle for easy reductionist answers, be they intellectualist or idealist on the one hand, or materialist/realist on the other. In his nuanced and subtle investigation of what it means to perceive the world with our bodies, Merleau-Ponty offers feminism a way out of the impasse of mind/body dualism. There is no doubt that his abiding interest in embodiment has played a major part in drawing theorists of sex and gender to his reflections. In fact, even to use the term embodiment, while it conveniently indicates the area of inquiry I want to pursue, is to call up images that in the final analysis must prove inadequate—as if the body is "in" the world and we are "in" our bodies, as the water is in the glass (VI 182/138). As if the proverbial ghost were in the machine.

FEMINIST REVISION OF SEX AND GENDER

I take it that among the most compelling tasks confronting contemporary feminist theory is the need to rethink the relationship between sex and gender. Feminist theorists as diverse as Braidotti, Butler, De Lauretis, Fox-Keller, Gatens, Haraway, Harding, Tuana, Williams—to mention only a handful of the most decisive figures—have seen the need to revisit and redefine what we mean by the terms sex and gender. While I cannot do justice here to the multiple issues at stake in the project of redefining the relationship between sex and gender, let me indicate first why there is a need to redefine sex and gender, secondly how Irigaray's project develops this trend of feminist theory, and finally how Merleau-Ponty's notion of the flesh intersects with, and contributes to, this project.

As typically conceived, the relationship between gender and sex is besieged with the same set of problems as naive solutions to the Cartesian mind/body problem would be. Accounts of how gender works tend toward two opposed but equally reductive views. Traditionally, gender was seen as something genetically programmed into us, or caused in some way by our physical natures. As such, gender seems unavoidable and unchangeable. Anyone interested in achieving equality between the sexes will be disturbed by the fatalist implications of this view. The view that gender is a direct result of our physical natures tends to translate into an equation of women with bodies, and men with minds. At the very least, as Beauvoir saw, women are represented as subject to their bodily cycles, as unable to transcend their immanence in order to realize their projects.[5] Female reproductive capacities are said to dictate women's alleged nature as maternal, and nurturant.

In reaction to this traditional picture, in which sex governs and determines gender, those who want to emphasize the impact of gender over sex—as feminists have wanted to do—are liable to end up conceiving of gender as a fairly free-floating construction, in part produced by society, and in part freely chosen by the subject. The relations between these "parts" often stands in an uneasy tension that is inadequately theorized, so that the view can ultimately be reduced to two equally problematic theses. On the one hand there is social determinism or behaviorism, and on the other hand voluntarism, or intellectualism.

If we assume that "society" or "culture" (usually taken to be an amorphous and largely unspecified monolithic entity) produces gender, little headway is made over the biologically determined point of view that sex (understood as vaguely equivalent to "biology" or "nature") causes gender. In place of "biology" or "nature," one simply invokes "society" or "culture" as the cause of gender, merely reproducing the problem of determinism at another level.

The advantage of establishing that some combination of social, cultural, and individual forces are at work in creating gender roles, rather than accepting the more traditional view that women are feminine because it is in their genes, written in the stars, or writ large by the hand of destiny is, of course, that this emphasis of gender over sex paves the way for change. But if culture merely replaces nature as the cause of femininity and masculinity, then there is little room for change—unless some account can be given whereby cultural forces can be transformed, such that women and men can be free to adopt, respectively, more masculine and feminine roles and identifications without impunity.

The problem for theorists of sex and gender is to avoid the pitfalls of social determinism/behaviorism without being driven to the other extreme of individual choice, thereby lapsing into a form of voluntarism, which assumes the ability to adopt and manipulate gendered behavior at will—if you don't like who you are, then change it. This ignores the fact that one's gender does not occur in an uncontextualized vacuum but against the very specific background of an individualized female or male body. Girls are encouraged to be feminine because they have female bodies, and boys are encouraged to be masculine because they have male bodies—and any of the grey areas in between (transvestism, transsexualism, hermaphroditism, bisexuality, and so on) are actively discouraged. Gender is not just an abstract category—it must be explained not merely as a cultural overlay of sex, but as an ongoing dynamic interaction with sex, as an interpretation of social signals about how our bodies should look, behave, and constitute themselves. Gender might be seen as a certain style of being, to borrow Merleau-Ponty's terminology.

Not only does the excessive and philosophically naive emphasis on gender in abstraction from sex replay the Cartesian privileging of mind over sex, ignoring the fact that whether one is a boy or a girl, one's body matters, but it also ignores the fact that the body can have material effects that cannot be intellectually or prescriptively circumscribed. Judith Butler's title succinctly states the double valence of this issue: *Bodies That Matter*.[6] Bodies signify—they encourage the development of one gender identification rather than another—but they also exceed signification, by refusing to be contained by the thoughts with which we try to think them. Bodies are irreducible to thought. They overflow and defy philosophers' attempts to express them, in much the same way that for Merleau-Ponty the world remains obstinately enigmatic in the face of our attempts to explain it and account for our experiences of it and in it.

We can see, then, the inadequacy of positing a uniform cause, be it biology or society. In either case, an uncomplicated causal relationship between sex and gender is assumed. Whether sex or society is assumed to cause or produce gender, not only do things look pretty bleak for those of us who would like to see more flexibility in sexual roles, this model also fails to explain the fact that there is already a good deal of variation. If women are programmed or hardwired by their sexed bodies, or by their social settings, then how do we account for individual variations among women? It is unsatisfactory to assume a volitional account of gender in order to respond to this problem, since this only introduces a new order of problems. It ignores the fact that gendered behavior does not occur or develop irrespective of our sex, but in relation to it. There is an intricate exchange between the fact that one is female and the fact that one is expected to behave, and expects oneself to behave in a feminine way.[7]

The body is not a neutral ground upon which the script of gender is constructed by society and played out by individuals. But what are the positive implications of this thesis? We cannot be content with pointing out the inadequacies of elevating sex over gender, or merely reversing the strategy and emphasizing gender at the expense of sex. We have seen that if the former strategy tends to embrace a determinist materialist position, the latter either reiterates this determinism but replaces biological reductionism with social psychologism or else—in an effort to avoid positing any deterministic or originating cause of gender, it lends itself to an idealist voluntarism. Since these two extremes are just what Merleau-Ponty seeks to avoid, it is no accident that theorists such as Gatens and Butler have drawn on his work in order to articulate revised conceptions of sex and gender. Gatens draws on the body-image, or the corporeal schema, an imaginary system that organizes, and makes possible my bodily coordination, but that is reducible neither to bodily materiality, nor to the mind, thought, or ideas. It is precisely against the background of one's sexed body that gender is produced and created. The imaginary body is the site of an interpretation of gendered existence, a medium that stages an interplay between cultural possibilities and bodily sedimentations.

If Merleau-Ponty's corporeal schema is one of the tools Gatens employs in order to find a way out of the impasse presented us by causal or voluntaristic models, Butler's account of gendered subjectivity is informed by the idea of Sartre's pre-reflective cogito, which arguably parallels Merleau-Ponty's notion of the tacit cogito (VI 224/171). Following Beauvoir, Butler says "We become our genders, but become them from a place which, strictly speaking, cannot be said to exist." By drawing on the idea of "project," Butler brings into question the idea that gender is a simple choice. "Becoming a gender" is she says "a subtle and strategic project, which only rarely becomes manifest to reflective understanding;" it is a "process of interpreting a cultural reality laden with sanctions, taboos, and prescriptions. To choose a gender is to interpret received gender norms in a way that organizes them anew." It is a "tacit project to renew one's cultural history in one's own terms."[8]

Both the notion of the tacit cogito, and that of the corporeal schema are revised by Merleau-Ponty in *The Visible and the Invisible*. Merleau-Ponty devotes a good deal of time distinguishing his position from what he calls "philosophies of reflection," an effort that is directed in large part against Descartes, and that (particularly in the working notes) takes up and reworks the question of the tacit cogito (VI 224–25/170–71). As Lingis acknowledges (VI liv), and as is clear from the text (VI 259/205, 243/189), the notion of the flesh in *The Visible and the Invisible* develops the idea of corporeal schema of *Phenomenology of Perception*.

THE SIGNIFICANCE OF REVISING THE
SEX/GENDER DISTINCTION

Underlying feminist attempts to revisit the sex/gender distinction is the recognition that there is a need to disrupt the oppositional categories of nature versus culture and body versus mind. In order to have a meaningful account of the mechanisms and processes by which bodies become gendered, one that does not resort to dualisms that rest—explicitly or implicitly—on Cartesianism, feminists have had recourse to some third term (corporeal schema, tacit cogito), one that does not merely mediate between sex and gender in a dialectical way that would leave intact the concepts themselves, as if sex and gender were independent of one another and untouched by the relationship that constitutes them. To envisage a genuinely interactive relationship would be to give ultimate priority to neither term, but to see each as constituting and affecting the other in an ongoing dynamic. In such a scenario neither gender, nor sex, would make sense by itself, in abstraction from the creative relationship between them, since what has to be understood is that one term constitutes the other while it is being constituted by it. A constituting-constituted relationship, one might say. A relationship such as Merleau-Ponty envisages as that which allows us to articulate the touching-touched, the chiasmic inter-twining of the flesh.

I have focused on the problem of recasting the sex/gender distinction in order to point to the continuity between this effort in feminist theory and Merleau-Ponty's effort to avoid the traditional dualisms that inform the sex/gender distinction. I now want to show how Irigaray inflects the need to revise this distinction in a particular direction, and that she does so by turning her attention to the notion of the flesh, thereby taking up Merleau-Ponty's elaboration of the issues he explored in terms of the corporeal schema.

Irigaray is concerned that feminist efforts have been misdirected toward an ideal of equality that tends to obliterate sexual difference. This concern can be expressed in terms of the language of the sex/gender distinction. In seeking equal opportunity, equal pay for equal work, and so on, feminists have empha-sized gender similarities, and played down the importance of sex—an arena in which the differences between men and women come to the fore. By accepting that the project of feminism is to represent the sexes as essentially the same as one another, feminist theory itself becomes implicated in the neglect of sexual difference. It harbors a tacit bias toward masculinity, and away from femininity, such that the ideal of equality is taken to be neutral, and universal, but is in fact governed by traditionally masculine goals and aspirations. In striving for equal-ity, feminists have inadvertently represented themselves as if they were poten-tially as good as, equal to, and therefore—the implication is—the same as, men. By thematizing the neglect of sexual difference Irigaray draws attention to the reluctance of feminist theory to deal with women's bodies, and calls for a thorough engagement with female sexuality—a call to which Grosz, Butler, Gatens, and others are now responding.

Rather than construing feminism as a quest for equality, which tends to assume the essential similarity of the sexes, Irigaray exposes an error that she takes to be not only symptomatic of feminism construed as a struggle for equality, but endemic to philosophy as a whole. Irigaray sees the occlusion of the feminine in the discourse of philosophy as a reflection of a more pervasive tendency characteristic of the philosopher's endeavor, namely its effort to homogenize, to totalize, or to refuse to tolerate otherness. This eradi-cation of alterity has the effect of excluding the feminine. The feminine has been seen as complementary to, inferior to, or as a variation of masculinity, but not thought on its own terms.

THE REDUCTION OF THE TACTILE TO THE
VISIBLE, OF FEMININE TO MASCULINE

As readers of *Speculum of the Other Woman* will know, the priority of the one is a major theme for Irigaray.[9] Her critique of the monistic tendency of Western metaphysics is as fundamental as her objection to its specularisation. The two problematics are intimately related. The mind's eye—as we say—has always been accorded priority over the body's eye, and the urge for unity and systematicness goes hand in hand with the subordination of certain faculties over others—thinking over feeling, rationalizing over emoting, and so on. The ordering of principles in hierarchical terms has, since the Greeks, favored mental capacities over physical, form or mind over matter. Perhaps it is not, as we might first think, that the privileging of sight over the other senses derives from a prior elevation of mental sight, or thought over bodily sensation, but rather the other way around. As Merleau-Ponty says in the lectures on "The Child's Relation with Others": "Our images are predominantly visual, and this is no accident; it is by means of vision that one can sufficiently dominate and control objects" (ENF 58/138). If the metaphor of vision is used not only for imaging but also for thought, in what way does the body inform this language? For traditional philosophy, Irigaray would argue, the body subtends thought in a way that has been neglected and unappreciated by philosophers. Without the body, no thought would be possible, yet the place, locale, and role of the body has not been theoretically elaborated. The body's systematic alignment with women, and the mind's systematic association with men is not incidental.

Philosophy's traditional denigration of the body, and its accompanying disdain for women, will not be alleviated—as is clear from the foregoing discussion of sex and gender—by merely reversing our habitual elevation of mind over body. Such a gesture would merely reinstate the dichotomy, reversing the hierarchy but failing to displace its dualism. Irigaray wants both to disrupt the rigid mind/body dichotomy, and to reveal the sense in which phenomenological or ontological attempts to do precisely that remain tied to a one-sex model. The first of these aims, the disruption of traditional dualism, is continuous with Merleau-Ponty's project, but Irigaray departs from his trajectory to the extent that Merleau-Ponty's articulation of the flesh privileges a traditionally male point of view. Irigaray's term "maternal-feminine" performs a critique of Merleau-Ponty's term "flesh," borrowing from its resources even as it takes a distance on its alleged neutrality. We should bear in mind that the French word *féminin* does not carry with it the largely cultural connotations of the English "feminine," but rather designates at the same time the female sex. The maternal-feminine, like the notion of the flesh, can therefore be understood neither exclusively in terms of culture, nor entirely in terms of nature. It precisely brings into question the ease with which such categories take on their meaning. Along with several other terms that Irigaray deploys—the figure of the lips, mucous, the elemental, and the sensible transcendental for example—the maternal/feminine resists and disrupts the dualisms toward which post-Cartesian philosophy still tends to gravitate. As such it has close affinities with what Merleau-Ponty presents as the chiasmic intertwining of the flesh. But beyond this, there is a critical edge to Irigaray's deployment of the term "maternal-feminine." Before commenting further on this critical deployment let's remind ourselves of the work that the notion of the flesh accomplishes in *The Visible and Invisible*.

Merleau-Ponty wants to avoid the dualisms that he does not think he managed to get away from in *Phenomenology of Perception*. In the working notes he says "The problems posed in Ph.P are insoluble because I start there from the 'consciousness'-'object' distinction" (VI 253/200). Not content to posit "an activity-passivity *split*" (VI 288/235), a distinction between culture and nature (VI 306/253), or a subject-object dichotomy (VI 268/214), Merleau-Ponty searches for a new language. He seeks a language that will allow him to say that "the whole of 'consciousness' is a function of the objective body" (VI 253/200), or that "everything is cultural in us" and at the same time "everything is natural in us." Even "our perception is cultural-historical" and "even the cultural rests on the polymorphism of the wild Being" (VI 307/253). It is "flesh" that provides him with this new language, it is chiasm that takes the place of the subject-object split.

Irigaray remarks the failure to acknowledge the multiple roles that women serve for men with the term "maternal-feminine," a term she introduces near the beginning of her essay on Merleau-Ponty, but that she has already put to work in earlier essays. With this term, Irigaray means to throw into relief the extent to which women have been identified with and restricted to maternity, to call attention to the perjorative and negative connotations motherhood typically carries with it, and to restore the maternal to a positive role. By naming together—as if they were inseparable—the maternal and the feminine, Irigaray indicates the traditional understanding of women as mothers. Like Lacan, Irigaray does not think that the distinction between mother and woman can be made within the order of the symbolic.[10] One of her tasks then is to make such a differentiation possible, by reflecting on precisely what the figure of the mother contributes, what she gives, and how this giving can be represented as irreducible to what it means to be a woman.

The novelty of Irigaray's essay lies not merely in the fact that while other feminist discussions (such as Butler's and Young's) have tended to focus on the *Phenomenology of Perception*, Irigaray takes *The Visible and Invisible* as her central text. What is decisive about Irigaray's approach is that she fuses her objections to his privileging of male sexuality with a thoroughgoing critique of another perhaps unwitting privilege that she finds at play in his writing: that of vision. Despite the fact that *The Visible and the Invisible* has been described as offering "an ontology of the tactile,"[11] according to Irigaray "Merleau-Ponty accords an exorbitant privilege to vision. Or else, once again, he expresses the exorbitant privileging of vision in our culture. Must [asks Irigaray] my aesthesiological body be completed by vision?[12] Why completed? Why vision?" (ES 163/174).

Merleau-Ponty understands that the sensible world underlies, and makes possible any kind of vision, mental or otherwise, but that its role in seeing with the mind has not been adequately thought through. He says that "every thought known to us occurs to a flesh" (VI 191/146). The notion of flesh cannot be understood simply as equivalent to "body," as he reiterates several times. "We must not think flesh starting from substances, from body and spirit—for then it would be the union of contradictories" (VI 193/147). Flesh must rather be seen as "the formative medium of the object and the subject," as an "element, as the concrete emblem of a general manner of being" (VI 193–94/147, also 184/139). Again, it is an "anonymity innate to Myself" (VI 183/139).

Whereas Irigaray's account of the elemental prepares the way for a philosophy of alterity in which the other is radically other, asymmetrical in relation to the I, Merleau-Ponty's account, according to Irigaray, emphasizes reciprocity, reversibility, and exchange. Is Irigaray's rendering of Merleau-Ponty borne out? To be sure Merleau-Ponty calls flesh "an ultimate notion" (VI 185/140), and reversibility "the ultimate truth" (VI 204/155); he finds a "reciprocal insertion and intertwining" of the "seeing body" and the visible body" (VI 182/138); "the seer and the visible reciprocate one another" (VI 183/139). But he also affirms the "constitutive paradox" of our body as "sensible sentient" (VI 179/136), and approaches what he calls the "paradox of Being" (VI 180/136) by acknowledging that it is "not as the bearer of a knowing subject, that our body commands the visible for us, . . . it does not explain it, does not clarify it, it only concentrates the mystery of its scattered visibility" (VI 180/136). Not only does he emphasize this paradoxical mystery, but he also takes back the completion that is indicated when he confers on reversibility the status of "ultimate truth." It is "a reversibility always imminent and never realized in fact" (VI 194/147). In short, Merleau-Ponty's philosophy seems to advance only by maintaining an interrogative stance, by persistently putting back into question what in another moment he offers as a description of what there is. If on the one hand he endorses visibility as "cohesion" and "principle," as that which "prevails over every momentary discordance" (VI 184/140) on the other hand this "principle of visibility" invites further explanation, awaits "a more exact vision and a more exact visible," so that its very cohesion is "'crossed out'" (VI 184/140, also 65/41–42), forever in question. Merleau-Ponty says,

> we are asking precisely what is that central vision that joins the scattered visions, that unique touch that governs the whole tactile life of my body as a unit, that *I think* that must be able to accompany all our experiences. We are proceeding toward the center, we are seeking to comprehend how there is a center, what the unity consists of, we are not saying that it is a sum or a result. (VI 191/145–46).

With the notion of the "reversibility of visible and the tangible" (VI 188/142–43), Merleau-Ponty wants to establish not only "the unity of my body" (VI 187/142), but also that the "generality" of the "sensible sentient" (VI 180/137) is "open . . . to other bodies" (VI 187/142). The unity of my body is the sense in which "my two hands . . . open upon one sole world . . . making of my hands one sole organ of experience" (VI 186/141) just as "my two eyes" are "channels of one sole Cyclopean vision" (VI 186/141). Beyond this "experience of one sole body before one sole world" (VI 186/142) he stresses the concordance of my vision with that of someone else, because "it is not *I* who sees, not *he* who sees, because an anonymous visibility inhabits both of us, a vision in general, in virtue of that primordial property that belongs to the flesh" (VI 187/142). Again, "what I see passes into him, this individual green of the meadow under my eyes invades his vision without quitting my own, I recognize in my green his green . . . " (VI 187/142).

Above all, it is the absence of any opening in what Merleau-Ponty takes to be the "concordant operation of his body and my own" (VI 187/142) to which Irigaray objects. Whose bodies are in agreement here, and at the expense of whose absence, occlusion, or eradication? With the term "maternal-feminine" Irigaray reintroduces a "sameness" that "has been assimilated before any perception of difference" (ES 98/98). It designates the maternal and material cause that, out of which each of us is formed, but that which is also forgotten, repressed, excluded from the account of flesh. The maternal body is that which brings to birth, makes viable, creates each individual, and as such it contributes the initial home, dwelling, vessel that renders life possible. This intrauterine space that gives rise to life, this invisible flesh that makes possible visible flesh is a theme that structures Irigaray's reading of Merleau-Ponty.[13] Her point is that the "primary maternal-feminine" (ES 153/162) is both that which makes life possible, and that which has remained unthought, or subjected to a "certain forgetfulness" (ES 153/162). By bringing to thought, putting into language, what she calls the invisible *"prenatal sojourn"* (ES 155/165), Irigaray both introduces a way of thinking the "singularity of the body and the flesh of the feminine" (ES 156/166) that she sees as absent from Merleau-Ponty's discourse, and articulates a dimension that she thinks is called for by his own descriptions. While Merleau-Ponty does not refer to the intrauterine as such, he does refer to "the current making of an embryo a newborn infant" (VI 193/147), to "pregnancy" (VI 195/149) and to "invagination" (VI 199/152). In fact, Merleau-Ponty often makes use of the image of the newborn child. For example, in the cogito chapter of *Phenomenology of Perception*, he says "The consciousness which conditions language is merely a comprehensive and inarticulate grasp upon the world, like that of the infant at its first breath, or of the man about to drown and who is impelled towards life" (PP 462–63/404). In the same chapter, Merleau-Ponty describes the effect on the home of the birth of a child:

In the home into which a child is born, all objects change their significance; they begin to await some as yet indeterminate treatment at his (sic) hands; another and different person is there, a new personal history, short or long, has just been initiated, another account has been opened. (PP 466/407)

While Merleau-Ponty sees the newborn child as capable of bestowing meaning upon the objects of the world, Irigaray thinks that he neglects the maternal giving that makes this possible. At one point, Merleau-Ponty says,

I believe that I have a man's senses, a human body [*j'ai des sens d'homme, un corps d'homme*]—because the spectacle of the world that is my own, and which, to judge by our confrontations, does not notably differ from that of the others, with me as with them refers with evidence to typical dimensions of visibility, and finally to a virtual focus of vision. (VI 192/146)

Of course we could read over the sexual specificity of the assertion "I believe that I have a man's senses," read it as neutral, read it as a term that means human being in general, as is usually done. But Irigaray's critique precisely consists in taking seriously the sexual marking of the discourse of philosophy, in asking what it leaves out, refuses, subordinates, sublimates, and yet depends upon. What difference does it make that this philosophical discourse is produced by a man? She says,

If I wanted to apply some terms here which I do not really like to use outside of their strictly clinical setting—where, moreover, I do not use them as such—I might say that Merleau-Ponty's seer remains in an incestuous prenatal situation with the whole. This mode of existence or of being is probably that of all men, at least in the West." (ES 162/173)

This incestuous situation allows Merleau-Ponty to entertain the illusion of completeness, covering over the gap, fissure or opening that marks the place of the "woman-mother," the other from which the I issues and is born. Irigaray finds in Merleau-Ponty a refusal of otherness and openness.[14] What he "seeks is something that closes the circuit" (ES 164/174). "Vision is a sense that can totalize, enclose" (ES 163/175). This is why he can gloss over differences, believing that "the spectacle" of my world "does not notably differ from that of the others" (VI 192/146), and that the "landscapes" of different organisms "interweave, their actions and their passions fit together exactly" (VI 187/142). It is the urge for synchrony, the search for an "ultimate truth" (VI 204/155) to which Irigaray objects. "He tries to establish a *continuum* . . . but he cannot manage it" (ES 145/154). Irigaray is worried that there is no room for the other.

She thinks that the "touch(ing) between the world and the subject" is "solip-sistic," that Merleau-Ponty's "whole analysis is marked by this labyrinthine solipsism. Without the other, and above all the other of sexual difference, isn't it impossible to find a way out of this description of the visible, doubled with that of the tactile of the touching hands?" (ES 148/157). The other, more specifically the other of sexual difference is left out of account.

CONCLUDING REMARKS

What Irigaray objects to is the status that Merleau-Ponty wants to accord to reversibility as "the ultimate truth" (VI 204/155), and the reciprocity that she thinks Merleau-Ponty establishes with this "ultimate notion" (VI 185/140). Irigaray calls for change. And it is in her demand for change that she finds Merleau-Ponty wanting. The change in question is the opening up and rec-ognition of an as yet unheard of meaning, "that of a language which is sexuate and which encounters through speech and in the world a sex which is *'irreducible'* to it, and with which it is impossible to have relations of reversibility without remainder" (ES 171/184). This sexing of language would not reduce the one to the other, the feminine to the masculine, mapping one on to the other as if they were essentially the same—a problem that charac-terizes not only philosophy that is typically conducted from a male perspec-tive, but that extends to feminist thought too insofar as it has been conceived as a struggle for equality, and to the extent that this struggle has been played out in the demand to be represented as the same as men.

The change that Irigaray calls for is at the level of rediscovery that Merleau-Ponty elicits in his reference to those "living references" that can help us to form new instruments of philosophy that would avoid situating themselves in the realm of reflection. "This operation" says Irigaray, "is absolutely necessary in order to bring the maternal-feminine into language" (ES 143/152). Such an effort is to be undertaken neither quickly nor easily. Irigaray is well aware of the enormity and difficulty of the task that she proposes, of "why it is so difficult to effect any changes" (ES 165/176):

> The entire speaking body of the subject is in some way archaeologically structured by an already spoken language. To signify to him that this language must be modified amounts to asking him to modify body, his flesh. Which cannot be done in a day. Or in a year. Resistance to all the discoveries that convulse language can be understood in this way. Also the impossibility of accepting, without a detachment that is truly difficult to conceive for one who does not feel its carnal necessity, the idea that discourse is *monosexual* and that it is necessary to make room, leave a place, for another discourse, one that is put together differently. (ES 165/176–77)

In acknowledging the extreme difficulty—especially for male subjects—of recognizing the urgency of the operation of change that she nonetheless calls for, Irigaray takes seriously the corporeality and carnality of our experience that Merleau-Ponty does so much to elucidate. In this sense, she takes him at his word. It would be a mistake to take her undeniably critical stance toward his philosophy as signaling an unappreciative reading, just as it would be shortsighted to understand her interpretation merely as an isolated attempt to demonstrate the shortcomings of a particular philosopher. I have suggested both that Irigaray's work is best understood as partaking in a productive exchange with Merleau-Ponty's text (and as such it anticipates the third stage of her work as she outlines it), and that it partakes in an ongoing project to demonstrate the failure of philosophy as a whole to address the feminine. Seen as an exploration of the effects of this lacuna on the shape of philosophy as a whole, her work both draws on the resources of that philosophy, and exposes its own blindspots, indicating where it stops short of an articulation of the feminine, and how it is unaware of doing so.

In Merleau-Ponty's defense, it should be said that Merleau-Ponty does try to leave room for the other—although not the other as sexually marked—and is wary of the lures of solipsism. For example, he says that the visible—"as the surface of inexhaustible depth—is "open to visions other than our own" (VI 188–89/143) and that these other visions "bring out the limits of our factual vision" and "betray the solipsist illusion that consists in thinking that every going beyond is a surpassing accomplished by oneself" (VI 189/143). It should also be said that Irigaray's strategy of reading allows her to pass over such passages without comment.[15]

Irigaray selectively retraces steps of the original essay, absorbing its trajectory almost parasitically, and reproducing the textual moves of her host, while supplementing his steps with others that she sees as having been left out, expelled from the overt content of the text. If she restores the unacknowledged gaps and crevices, the blanks, the repressed alterity of the text she reads, bringing into presence that which subtends Merleau-Ponty's discourse but that is also barred access, at a more fundamental level, the movements that she sketches are in one sense already present. These absences that she remarks are those that nourish and sustain the arguments and reflections of the text—in much the same way that the invisible subtends the visible in Merleau-Ponty's text. Irigaray's textual procedure is one in which she enables, facilitates, or brings to birth the concealed truth underlying Merleau-Ponty's project—a procedure that must overturn and transform that project, making it into an unrecognizable legacy even as she draws out its own presuppositions. A chiasmic reading, one might say—one that returns to the unthought ground of Merleau-Ponty's thinking, in a gesture that both imitates his own attempt to subvert the distortions that are permitted by a philosophical arrogance that does not question its own reflective authority in relation to what it would explain, and challenges the limitations that such an attempt

imposes upon itself. Merleau-Ponty seeks to repair the damage of philosophies of reflection, not in order to restore some pristine foundation that would
be untouched by thought—which would be an impossible task—but rather in
order to acknowledge the paradox of trying to do so, a contradictory attempt
that is named in the phrase "wild meaning." Irigaray asks whether any attempt to restore wild meaning does not already always in advance tame the
very wilderness it seeks to restore by having contained it in a language that
takes itself to be neutral, universal, and common to all, but is in fact a sexed
language, one "which encounters through speech (parole) and in the world a
sex which is *irreducible* to it" (ES 171/184). The irreducibility of sexual
difference will not be tamed. Rather it must be acknowledged as a difference
whose effects cannot be canceled by having been anticipated in advance by
a language that is "everything" (Valéry).

We may wish to question the audacity of Irigaray's reading at certain
points, its wild meaning. Does Merleau-Ponty really effect a reduction of the
tactile to the visible, and is it fair to represent the reversibility of the flesh,
the chiasm, as reciprocal? But what remains persuasive is Irigaray's insistence upon raising the question of sexual difference. Merleau-Ponty wants to
"catch sight of the *problem of the* world" (VI 21/6). Irigaray wants to formulate the question of sexual difference. Like time for Augustine, the world,
according to Merleau-Ponty, is "perfectly familiar" to each of us, but as soon
as we try to "explain it to others . . . the evidence of the world, which seemed
indeed to be the clearest of truths" (VI 17/3) withdraws into an "enigma" (VI
18/4). For Irigaray it is the enigma of sexual difference that demands our
urgent attention, since it is in danger of being eclipsed before it has properly
been brought to the level of philosophical reflection.

NOTES

1. Luce Irigaray, *An Ethics of Sexual Difference,* trans. Carolyn Burke and
Gillian Gill (Ithaca, N.Y.: Cornell University Press, 1993); *Ethique de la différence
sexuelle* (Paris: Minuit, 1984). Hereafter cited as ES with reference first to the French,
then to the English translation.

2. Luce Irigaray, " 'Je-Luce Irigaray': A Meeting with Luce Irigaray," interview by Elizabeth Hirsh and Gary A. Olson, *Hypatia* 10, no. 2 (1995): 93–114, see
esp. p. 97. Hereafter cited as JLI in the text.

3. Luce Irigaray, *Parler n'est jamais neutre* (Paris: Minuit, 1985). *Sexes and
Genealogies,* trans. Gillian C. Gill (New York: Columbia Press, 1993); *Sexes et Parentés*
(Paris: Minuit, 1987).

4. One might want to argue that not only Merleau-Ponty, but also Sartre
acknowledges the importance of the body, but, if Levinas is right—and I think he is—
ultimately the depth of Sartre's understanding of the role of materiality is canceled out

by freedom. See Emmanuel Levinas, *Time and the Other,* trans. R. Cohen (Pittsburgh: Duquesne University Press, 1987), p. 62; *Temps et l'autre* (St. Celment: Fata Morgana, 1979), p. 44. Originally published in Jean Wahl's *Le Choix, Le Monde, L'Existence* (Grenoble-Paris: Arthaud, 1947). Levinas himself might be credited for having addressed the difficulty that phenomenology has had in accommodating the body, but his way of correcting the problem consists of going beyond phenomenology itself.

5. See Simone de Beauvoir, *The Second Sex,* trans. H. M. Parshley (New York: Knopf, 1954). On the relationship between Simone de Beauvoir and Merleau-Ponty, see Beauvoir, "Merleau-Ponty and Pseudo-Sartreanism," *International Studies in Philosophy* 21, no. 3 (1989): 3–48; "Merleau-Ponty et le Pseudo-Sartrisme," *Les temps modernes* 10, no. 115–115 (1), 1955(1): 2072–2122. See also Merleau-Ponty, "Metaphysics and the Novel," *Sense and Non-Sense.*

6. Judith Butler, *Bodies that Matter* (New York: Routledge, 1993).

7. See Iris Marion Young, "Throwing Like a Girl: A Phenomenology of Feminine Body Comportment, Motility, and Spatiality," *"Throwing Like a Girl" and Other Essays in Feminist Philosophy and Social Theory* (Bloomington and Indianapolis: Indiana University Press, 1990), pp. 141–59. esp. p. 145.

8. Judith, Butler, "Sex and Gender in Simone de Beauvoir's *Second Sex,"* *Yale French Studies* 72, 1986, p. 40.

9. Luce Irigaray, *Speculum of the Other Woman,* trans. Gillian C. Gill (Ithaca, N.Y.: Cornell University Press, 1985); *Speculum de l'autre femme* (Paris: Editions Minuit, 1974).

10. See Margaret Whitford, *Luce Irigaray: Philosophy in the Feminine* (London and New York: Routledge, 1991), p. 46.

11. Judith Butler, "Sexual Ideology and Phenomenological Description: A Feminist Critique of Merleau-Ponty's *Phenomenology of Perception,"* in *The Thinking Muse: Feminism and Modern French Philosophy,* ed. Jeffner Allen and Iris Marion Young (Bloomington: Indiana University Press, 1989), pp. 85–100, see esp. p. 97.

12. Irigaray is responding to Merleau-Ponty's statement that "vision comes to complete the aesthesiological body" (VI: 154; 202).

13. See, for example, ES 152/144, ES 159/150, AND ES 162/153.

14. It is worth noting that Lacan, like Irigaray, objects to Merleau-Ponty's emphasis on homogeneity, totality, unity, synthesis, and understanding. See Jacques Lacan, *The Seminar of Jacques Lacan,* ed. Jacques-Alain Miller, bk. 2, trans. Sylvana Tomaselli (New York: W. W. Norton & Company, 1991), pp. 77–78.

15. Irigaray structures her essay by following very closely the first few pages of the chiasm chapter, and then jumping to the last few pages in order to resume her commentary. This enables her to pass by several passages that, while they should not entirely undermine her reading, would certainly complicate it. As is typical of her textual readings, her strategy is to quote a passage, and then comment on it, in a commentary that will sometimes include other words that are direct quotes from

Merleau-Ponty, but that are not marked as such—are not enclosed within quotation marks. This strategy can be frustrating for first-time readers of Irigaray, but it does have certain advantages. It compels her readers not only to read her own texts carefully, but also to return to the text she is commenting upon with equal care. Irigaray's "mimicry" is one of the strategies for which she has become renowned. She established it in *Speculum,* and she employs it again in *An Ethics of Sexual Difference.*

CHAPTER 14

Recursive Incarnation and Chiasmic Flesh: Two Readings of Paul Celan's "Chymisch"

JAMES HATLEY

" . . . to feel my eyes is to feel that they are threatened with being seen."

—Merleau-Ponty, *The Visible and the Invisible*

CHIASMIC FLESH AS GOODNESS

Merleau-Ponty's elaboration of the chiasmic body in *The Visible and the Invisible* leaves the self articulated through that body, at least in the passage quoted above, in a state of "threat" or "menace." The other's gaze, Merleau-Ponty notes, often burns my own body at the point seen. This burn, this wounding of my flesh, is not a trauma induced through a violation of my own embodied gaze, as if the gaze of the other overtook me at this very moment in order to rob me of my self-integrity. Certainly, in encountering another, I can find my body reduced to a mere surface of appearing, an object shorn of all interiority and utterly exposed to manipulation by the other's powers. But to characterize the generic gaze of the other in this manner is to have already forgotten yet another, even more disturbing, one might say, more traumatic sense of trauma, although one in which goodness and generosity are at issue rather than violence and disintegration.

The gaze of the other burns for Merleau-Ponty because it reveals my body as what he calls in another passage a "fundamental divergence, a constitutive dissonance" in which the "invisible contact of self with self" (VI 287/234) is exposed as a myth I never could have lived, even though I perhaps have convinced myself otherwise. At the basis of human identity is no base at all, no fundament pure and simple, but an elemental reversibility, a playing of one side against another that Merleau-Ponty terms chiasmic.

Because the structure of my identity is chiasmic, the trauma of the other's gaze in its deepest sense is not imposed upon me through an act of domination from a without utterly outside of me, but is already articulated in very depths of my own visibility. In feeling my eyes, I already feel as well the other's eyes implicated in them: to see is already to be seen. The very contact of self with itself, of a gaze with its own visibility, finds in its articulation of this contact to be a decentering, a reversibility, that continually returns my gaze to me in a perspective that questions not only the primacy of my own outlook, not only the inviolate nature of my own intimacy with myself, but the essential goodness of any attempt to live out my existence as an intimacy of the same with the same. "We *must* [italics mine] accustom ourselves," argues Merleau-Ponty in a tone that is redolent of an ethical command, " . . . that thought [as well as perception] lives outside of intimacy with oneself, *in front of* us, not in us, always eccentric" (VI 287/234).

Thus, the threat of the other's gaze is not imposed from without but works its disruption from a within that is always already an *otherwhere*, a decentering of the within to precincts unanticipated and yet always implicated in my own flesh. In my vulnerability to this gaze, I discover that I already am *for the other* (VI 299/245), not because he or she exposes me to a power utterly external to my own, but because I and the other are, in Merleau-Ponty's words, *"Ineinander"* or *"entrelacé."* As an embodied identity, I am always already caught up in an intimacy with or toward the other that displaces any notion of intimacy thought as a pure return of the same to the same. In Merleau-Ponty's words, "to feel ones body is also to feel its aspect for the other" (VI 299/245).

Although the language of ethics plays no overt role in the ontological project of Merleau-Ponty's late thought, his notion of chiasmic flesh is implicitly ethical. As the analysis above indicates, insofar as I "feel my eyes," that is, insofar as I find myself already submitted to my body as a chiasmic opening upon the world, a seeing that is also a seen, I *am commanded* (*"il faut"*) to "rediscover" the "reality" of a world that is primordially "interhuman" and "historical." I encounter this world as the "surface of separation between myself and the other which is also the place of our union, the unique *Erfüllung* of his life and my life" (VI 287/234).

One should be careful here to keep in mind the chiasmic nature of this separation between oneself and the other that is also a union. Because the self of each particular chiasmic body is already articulated as a multidimensional differentiation of itself with itself, the encounter of the other in one's field of bodily awareness becomes inextricably intertwined with one's encounter with oneself. In Merleau-Ponty's words, the world is inserted "between the two leaves of my body," even as my body is inserted "between the two leaves of each thing and of the world." The self of such a body is neither an identity nor a nonidentity but the articulation of a "difference of difference." The other is that chiasmic differentiation that is in turn different than my own self-differing. My own self then is most primordially "the other than the other." The revelation of this other, as well as the revelation of myself as the other to this other occurs through a body subjected to "encroachment, thickness, *spatiality*" (VI 318/264). My body's opacity, its resistance to its own self-intimacy, renders it as well the scene of the other's appearance, an appearance that occurs as an encroachment to which my body was already vulnerable before it could ever have been articulated simply as my own flesh, my own self.

Sue Cataldi in her book *Emotion, Depth, and Flesh,*[1] gives innumerable examples of how the chiasmic nature of one's own body leaves one necessarily vulnerable to the encroachment of other bodies. While these incursions become the very manner in which self-identity is sedimented and articulated, they also serve to undermine the stability of that identity once it has been elaborated.

In my view, Cataldi's argument implies that this undermining is in principle the very expression of ethical goodness. Chiasmic embodiment already resists any posture on my part that would assume an invulnerability, or an indifference to the implication of the other within me. I am, so to speak, already beset by the other before any resistance on my part might have been offered: her or his gaze burns within me. But this undermining of self does not imply an emptying out of self. For Merleau-Ponty the traditional gesture of *kenosis*, of humility characterized through self-abnegation, is replaced by a humility caught up in the overfilling, the overdetermination of one's identity by the others surrounding oneself: goodness is articulated as a *hyperplethora*. Given the chiasmic structure of one's identity, one cannot be oneself without already being the site of the interfolding of other bodies, of other beings into one's own embodied existence. In finding one has always already welcomed all the others into one's own body, one can no longer pretend that one is or ever was capable of excluding the other. In this realization, one's flesh is revealed as the very elaboration of a goodness signified through an intractable involvement with the other.

This involvement undermines all attempts to draw any secure boundary or limit between oneself and the other. In yet another implied moral maxim Merleau-Ponty writes in his working notes for *The Visible and the Invisible*: "Chiasm, instead of For the Other: that means that there is not only a me-other rivalry, but a co-functioning. We function as one unique body." (VI 268/215) The chiasmic nature of the flesh undermines any straightforward antithesis between "for oneself" and "for the other," any antithesis implying a "rivalry," that is, a *polemos*, a differing whose incompossibility divides and sets at odds. At odds with being at odds, goodness implies a "co-functioning" in which my being is first a Being without restriction, a being in which I and the other exist in a coexchange, in which the boundaries between one and the other are both diffused and reversible.

One's identity in such a situation is both promiscuous and contagious: continually undergoing an introjection of the flesh of others into one's own flesh in order to be who one is, one also inevitably finds one's flesh projected into the very others whose flesh is already so deeply implicated in one's own identity. This introjection and projection are not simply active, nor do they occur in relation to a distinct node of identity—I am not already there disposing of my flesh as I freely choose. Rather, out of the intercrossings of flesh with flesh provisional identities emerge only after encroachment has already occurred. At the very core of my identity is something more radical than a "cofunctioning," what one might better term an erring, an encroaching, a confusing: "It [the body] is neither thing seen nor seer only, it is Visibility sometimes wandering and sometimes reassembled" (VI 181/137–38). The reversibility of my flesh into and among the flesh of others does not imply a stately dance of give and take, of your move and then my move. The reversibility of the chiasm submits me to an "overdetermination," (VI 294/240) an intensity and redoubling of intertwining whose innumerable crossings overwhelm any attempt to figure the boundary of one's self unequivocally.

To move Merleau-Ponty's implicit characterization of goodness in this direction is to place him in the vicinity of Kristeva's notion of abjection, in which an initial *jouissance*, a continuity before identity provides the matrix, the womb, by which identity itself can be gestated. I am implicated in the other and the other in me in such a manner that the boundaries by which our respective self-identities are configured are plunged into one another. The goodness of such an implication of oneself in the other would be, in Merleau-Ponty's terms, "wild," that is, a *welcoming* so surreptitious, so uncanny, that its very articulation undoes any norm that would grasp and control its movement toward the other.

Cataldi's analysis, as well as Merleau-Ponty's own words, also implies that evil can be characterized as the repression of the chiasmic elementality of one's body. Referring to Iris Marion Young's discussion of xenophobia and abjection in her *Justice and the Politics of Difference*,[2] Cataldi analyzes how the attempt to cleanse my own body of the other's implication in it is an ongoing although regrettable feature of political life. Paradoxically, the very articulation of justice, insofar as it is based upon preserving a notion of self-identity characterized as an intimate contact of self with self within itself, inevitably becomes an attack upon that other who most unsettles, interferes with, interrupts the unquestioned struggle for self intimacy. The evil-doer, in an attempt to undo the *goodness* of her or his flesh, represses its chiasmic vulnerability, its wildness, by erecting political and social borders around the body in an attempt to control all access to it. These borders constitute an official lie by means of which one forgets the uncanny permeability of one's own body to the bodies of others. One sets up a classification, a "scaling" of bodies (in Young's terms) so that those found to be "different" from one's own can be identified and segregated. In this manner, the segregation of oneself from the other is instituted under the rubric of a politically defined or socially constructed norm that in actuality is the very perversion of the elemental goodness of chiasmic flesh. Those classified as "different" find their bodies labeled as dangerous and disgusting. In this situation, one's very body is transformed into "an object of coercion and an instrument of oppression" (ED, 140).

RECURSIVE INCARNATION AS GOODNESS

All too often set in the margins of the ongoing discussion of his thought, Emmanuel Levinas's characterization of embodiment, particularly as it is set out in *Otherwise than Being*, deserves more attention. The incarnation of the subject is for Levinas the sufficient condition of a human *kenosis*, a call to humility in which one's most singular self is revealed as the emptying out of one's identity into another. In one's submission to the priority of the other is found the very goodness of the good. In Levinas's own words, the for-the-other that instigates all ethical action "has meaning only among beings of flesh and blood."[3] Yet, in elaborating his notion of embodiment, Levinas not only avoids Merleau-Ponty's notion of chiasmic flesh but exercises an implicit critique of it as being too caught up in an ontology rather than an ethics of goodness.

Levinas speaks of the embodied self, the ethical subject, as being "a materiality more material than all matter" (OB 108) such that "irritability, susceptibility, or exposedness to wounds and outrage characterizes its passivity." More material than a matter that merely waits, whose passivity can be characterized as "the capacity to undergo the cause that would bring it out of that state [the passivity of inertia]" (OB 75), incarnation for Levinas is revealed in one's sensitivity, one's pain. In pain, the materiality of incarnation is not prime matter, a stuff without determinacy, but an undergoing that not only finds itself exposed but also finds its very exposure exposed. In the sensitivity of the body to pain, what Levinas terms "sensibility," is given "a having been offered without any holding back," or "vulnerability itself" (OB 75). Thus, "the body is neither an obstacle opposed to the soul, nor a tomb that imprisons it but that by which the self is susceptibility itself" (OB 195 n. 12).

In having been offered without any holding back, the body is "bound to others before being tied to [itself]" (OB 76). Alphonso Lingis points out in his introduction to *Otherwise than Being*, that for Levinas, the weight of one's materiality is not found in one's own being mired in oneself but in "the gravity of having to bear the burden of an alien existence" (OB xxi). As in Kristeva's notion of abjection, the Levinasian body is already tied to others before the issue of its own or the other's identity can even be raised. But the meaning of this abjection is ethical rather than ontological. What is at issue is not the generation of bodies but the giving up of one's bread, one's matter, for the good of the other, even before that other has actually emerged into existence. In Lingis's words, in one's corporeality one finds "one's substance [is] required and one's support demanded" (OB xxvii). In Levinas's own words, one is involved in the giving of "a gift that costs" (OB 195 n. 12).

In a passage echoing but also subverting the discourse of Merleau-Ponty's evocation of chiasmic flesh, Levinas develops the ethical implications of incarnation as vulnerability. Contact with the other's skin, according to Levinas, places him (i.e., Levinas) against a "divergency between the visible and the invisible, quasi-transparent, thinner than that which would still justify an expression of the invisible by the visible" (OB 89 f.). Here, Levinas speaks of a divergency between his self and the other that excludes any chiasmic reversibility, any crossing over from one leaf of the opposition to the other. Unlike the chiasmic divergency discussed earlier by Merleau-Ponty, Levinas's divergency is so thin that it excludes any thickness, any spatial separation, whatsoever. For Levinas, no room is given in the other's divergency from my touch for that "co-functioning," that erring, encroachment, confusion typical of a chiasmic reversibility. No side, layer, leaf, or hinge can appear on the other side of the impossible, nondimensional thinness of this divergency. Instead of a cofunctioning, the touch reveals an utter lapsing of the approach and the approached. The depths of my body are not implicated in my touch of her or his skin, as if the other side of my flesh was the other's flesh, as if the significance of goodness could be exhausted in the inexhaustible erring of a being continually decentered into the other's body in order to be within its own body.

For Levinas, the divergency of the other's skin from my own in my touching of her or him is instead characterized as "poverty exposed in the formless, and withdrawn from this absolute exposure in a shame for its poverty" (OB 90). Insofar as the other's exposure to my touch is revealed to me, I encounter the nudity of that exposure, its utter capitulation to the powers my touch imposes upon her or his skin. But in the wake of this capitulation, I feel shame for the vulnerability of his or her nudity to my touch. In this shame, which reveals an ethical rather than ontological articulation of my corporeality, the other's body provides no place at all for my own erring, my own search for a return to myself from no matter how far a distance. No longer simply body, the skin I would touch is revealed as a face, which is to say, a vulnerability that instigates my address toward it rather than my implication in it. In my shame before the face of the other, I find my incarnation imposed upon me as an infliction. Granted no locus of repose, I become a restlessness beyond any possible satiation, any possible moment of reprieve.

In this restlessness, what Levinas later calls a "cellular irritability" (OB 143), is given the inwardness of my ethical subjectivity. This inwardness is articulated as "a *recurrence* to oneself out of an irrecusable exigency of the other, a duty overflowing my being, a duty becoming a debt and an extreme passivity" (OB 109). Such a passivity actually would accentuate the separation of my body from the other's body insofar as I find myself addressed by the other's body as the site of a gaze that refutes any possibility that its vulnerability to my touch might be grasped or enfolded into my own body, as if I could feel the other's pain *as if* it were my own. The other's passivity would also emphasize in one sense my utter singularity—I am the one whose responsibility to the other can find no stand-in for me. But this singularity utterly forecloses the issue of my own identity, since the recursion to myself that is my inwardness occurs as a restlessness for the other's nudity. The other's transcendence of my own body claims me before my body could even begin to be articulated as an identity. Thus, the gaze of the other's face claims me, not because through it the other already dwells in me and I feel anxiety about this, but because the gaze is a sign of how the other's vulnerability to suffering and death is infinitely not my own. Such a vulnerability inspires my address, my giving of a sign that would proclaim my restlessness before that vulnerability (OB 56, 143).

In this vein, Levinas argues that incarnation, "far from thickening and tumefying the soul, oppresses it and contracts it and exposes it naked to the other to the point of making the subject expose its very exposedness, which might cloak it, to the point of making it an uncovering of the self in saying" (OB 109). In so doing, the incarnational body "makes one *other* without alienating" (OB 109). This making *other* of oneself does not involve what á la Merleau-Ponty might be termed the encroachment of one's body with the feelings, thoughts, perceptions of the other's flesh. Rather, before one feels one as one's self, one finds one's body is already "obsessed" with the other "prior to all reflection, prior to every positing" (OB 111).

In a manner, the openness of Merleau-Ponty's chiasmic body to the insertion of the other into it, an openness that claims my self before my self can ever be articulated as my own, is reminiscent of Levinas's notion of a passivity to which I am submitted before any possibility of my acting as my own self could even arise. But the passivity articulated in the chiasms of touching-touched and seeing-seen always implied a diffused migration of the other into my own body (as well as my own body into the other's body). Levinas's account of the face resists such a migration. In the face, the other's flesh is revealed as a "tenderness" to violation whose history and presence utterly eludes my own. In it all notions of intentionality break down and I am submitted to an "irreversible diachrony." On the other side of the other is a past [and a space?] that is "unrecuperable" (OB 90).

Because the otherness of the other is so absolutely other, the incursion of the other into myself is not "alienating" or "threatening" but shameful; I do not find the other as an ontological trace of the strange inhabiting my own being but as an ethical trace of the stranger for whose vulnerability to my own violence I find myself in obsession.

As in Cataldi, the opening of the Levinasian body *upon the other* gives the good as such. One is claimed by the good not through the incurring of a variety of benefits for oneself or the reasoned consideration of a universal imperative but by one's relationship with the other pure and simple. But, this being said, one observes that the very categories that signaled a collapse of the good for Cataldi become the elaboration of the good for Levinas. Separation, persecution, and obsession—categories that would imply border anxiety and repression of the chiasmic body for Cataldi—are given entirely unexpected interpretations in the Levinasian account of incarnation. This occurs because Levinas insists on characterizing the incarnated body as an ethical subject whose uniqueness is not to be found in the chiasmic play of its enfoldments, of its reversibility into the other, but in "the very fact of [its] bearing the fault of the other" (OB 112).

CREMATED BODIES, CREMATED LANGUAGE

> Silence, cooked like gold, in
> charred, charred
> hands.
> Fingers, insubstantial as smoke. Like crests of air
> Around—[4]

During the reign of National Socialism in Germany, Jewish individuals were insistently recategorized by an ongoing manipulation of political processes into stateless persons to be deported and ultimately into genetically flawed bodies to be eradicated. In the lines quoted above, Paul Celan remembers this annihilation of the other, this destruction without reserve, this Shoah, which the policies of National Socialism instituted and then carried through.

The obsessive attention given to bodies and their categorization by the Nazis certainly squares with Cataldi's and Young's notion of a boundary anxiety run amuck, of a politically instituted series of norms that are in fact the repression, the perversion of goodness. The bodies of those exterminated in the Shoah became threatening and threatened because the Nazis were so insistent on repressing the wildness, the promiscuity of chiasmic flesh. As developed above, the outcome of this process of political repression, of the setting up of boundaries vitiating chiasmic promiscuity and encroachment, was the transformation of a set of bodies "into objects of coercion and instruments of oppression."

But the outcome of Nazi policies, at least in the case of Jews, Gypsies, homosexuals, and the mentally infirm, involved not only the coercion and oppression of those bodies found to be abnormal but also their ultimate eradication. The bodies of the oppressed were not simply segregated, manipulated, or tortured, acts that presuppose the survival of the body, at least for a specified time. They were also, as Celan's lines above emphasize, burned and vaporized. As a result, these bodies no longer remained after their victimization to provide some possibility for a renewed struggle for justice, or even for reflections upon the outrage of their victimization. The bodies, in their annihilation, were rendered utterly silent.

The memory of these annihilated bodies, of these fingers as "insubstantial as smoke," obsess the address of Celan's poem. In his memory of them, Celan summons the annihilated from out of a silence, an absence, whose abysmal withdrawal exceeds that silence associated with the merely dead. Within the silence of the annihilated seethes the moral chaos, the indifferent brutality to which the annihilated were submitted in their being annihilated. They did not merely die—they were also degraded.

The paradoxical meaning of Celan's summons deserves a careful and nuanced consideration. In summoning the silence of the annihilated to an alchemical transformation, in letting it be "cooked like gold," the poet hints at that sort of conversion (in its several meanings) that would bestow upon the silence, in Werner Hamacher's words, "a face or a mask," a "Gestalt."[5] One might add in the wake of our considerations of Merleau-Ponty—a body. This alchemical face or body, which would be in part the poem itself, would convert the loss of the annihilated into a speaking, a poeticizing, that would no longer refer to something absent but would in its struggle to articulate the absent make that very articulation what is significant about the absent. Hamacher refers to Hegel for whom "this tarrying with the negative" becomes "the magical power that converts it into Being."[6] In this manner, the poem would give the annihilated a life beyond their own in the ongoing struggle of a surviving subjectivity to live out the meaning of those deaths.

But the alchemical transformation of silence in Celan's poem is in actuality a repudiation, a *widderruf*,[7] of what alchemical transformation might be traditionally thought to be. In Celan's address of the annihilated, the figure of alchemy only underlines the failure of memory, or even more radically, the obscenity of a memory that would redeem the silence left in the wake of the annihilation of bodies by means of the living bodies of those who survive to read the poem. The attempt to transform the silence of annihilation into gold, to become the alchemist of the Shoah's memory, only ends up in the outrageous repetition of what cannot be undone. For this reason, the *"charred,*

charred hands" from the poem are doubly charred, that is, the charred hands are charred once again in their very figuration in the poem.

These doubly charred hands not only resist Hegel but also trouble a chiasmic reading via Merleau-Ponty of their visibility that would focus attention on the body as the site of an ontological trace, of an interfolding of one flesh into another. The very gesture that would counter oppression for Young and Cataldi, that is, the social and political rearticulation of the flesh's chiasmic promiscuity, fails to have an effect in this instance. The hands of the annihilated resist chiasmic visibility, resist an interfolding of flesh into flesh, because their vulnerability to annihilation leaves them without flesh. The silence of the cremated hands is the silence of a flesh whose life was crushed out precisely as its embodiment was obliterated. As Young and Cataldi point out, the wildness and fecundity of the flesh is betrayed in the coercion and manipulation of the body by social institutions. But beyond coercion and manipulation lies the possible impossibility of annihilation, of a manipulation so radical that nothing is left to manipulate. In the submission of flesh to annihilation, the victim's vulnerability to oppression utterly exceeds the power of flesh to recuperate what is betrayed, to heal what is wounded. In annihilation, the flesh is utterly lost both to itself and to others.

This vulnerability leaves the poet, or anyone else who would remember annihilation, in a state of impotent distress. What the poet witnesses is that the other's flesh can be charred, can be "disappeared," but the vulnerability of the other's incarnation cannot be possessed, cannot be articulated, cannot be embodied. In fact, the very attempt to memorialize the annihilated by giving them a body beyond their own within this poem or this essay would be a betrayal. Such a gesture would repress the very significance of the other's vulnerability by acting as if the other's nudity were somehow capable of even the most cursory translation, the most tentative appropriation, as if one could feel the pain of the other for her or him. In such an appropriation empathy for the other is substituted for the vulnerability of the other. In this substitution, the uniqueness of the other, her or his utter separation, is repressed. For this reason, rather than restoring these hands to a chiasmic viability, to a flesh that would give them yet another chance to be, Celan's poem fumbles through an alchemical catastrophe, the very turning into gold of these fingers only chars them again.

How then might one be true to the vulnerability, the desolation of the annihilated? Here, the Levinasian notion of a body whose goodness is announced in separation, persecution, and obsession can be of some help. In Levinas's recursive incarnation what is emphasized is not the invisible visibility of the hands, their shadowy life beyond their death in the bodies of others, but the responsibility of the reader and writer of the poem to these hands that recur to but can never dwell within one. In the wake of this responsibility, the bodies of both poet and reader would find themselves traumatized, already "accused of what the others do or suffer" (OB 112).

In a similar manner, the language of Celan's poem also finds itself traumatized. As Veronique Foti has argued:

> Whereas Heidegger in "Language," reads Trakl's verse *"Schmerz versteinerte die Schwelle"* as an articulation of the painful yet firmly sustaining rift of the Differing, Celan's hardening into language does not gather, apportion, or sustain. It petrifies the chaotic desolation of violence, letting its traces lie outcast, tangled, exposed like the victims, bereft of any inherently meaningful order.[8]

Here language becomes ethical precisely by its being submitted in the manner of its very writing to an accusation that it has ceased to be the opening upon an interhuman world, a world of chiasmic flesh, in which one can gaze upon those others whose gaze in return provides an access to one's own being. In this charred language, the presence of the flesh of one's own body and the play of covering and uncovering that presence implicates, becomes irrelevant. Instead, language articulates in its very destitution and shame, the indignities visited upon the bodies of the exterminated. Here the reader's soul, far from being "thickened and tumefied," finds itself so oppressed by and exposed to the other that all recursion to oneself becomes a yet more troubling questioning of how one is not those others, those who were exterminated.

Thus, the address of the poem reveals a restless subjectivity, a grappling with the silence of the exterminated that cannot be stilled, that cannot find its place. The poem is the reinscription of trauma as the only ethically acceptable sign of a victimization that cannot be undone. And yet this very restlessness for the other is also a human *kenosis*, an emptying out of identity, that articulates the very goodness of goodness. In the silence of the Shoah, the vulnerability of those charred fingers, that nonlocus beyond any touch, remains to haunt those who would address and be addressed by the annihilated.

In the second half of the poem's verse, the "charred charred hands" become "fingers, insubstantial as smoke." They become, the poet has written,

"like crests, crests of air around—"

In so ending, the verse seemingly turns from the morbidity and devastation of hands doubly charred to the grace of fingers somehow transformed, made insubstantial but enduring, breathed into the heavens perhaps in the very breath of the poet who would speak these lines. As if to reinforce this impression, the verse's ultimate line empties into a nonsaying, a pause indicated by two dashes suspended over a small white space intervening between the poem's penultimate and ultimate verses. Hovering in the paper's white silence, the figure of the fingers, already insubstantial as smoke, already a silence rendered as a crest of air, a "breath for no one," now eddies around yet another silence, a pause beyond any figuration, any breathing, except that innocuous dash where no word might enter, where the poem's address waits in breathless insomnia, in poverty.

One could imagine that silence beyond silence figured in the dash as the utter agitation of an address too moved, too remorseful, too in pain for any word to emerge. The whiteness of the page a white noise beyond knowing, a noise so full of absence that only every word and no word can suffice to give it breath.

But even this imagination of the other's loss is both too much and too little. The fingers of smoke are also the fingers of the exterminated, eddying into the heavens, invoking in their very gesture of dissolution yet another *widerruf*, another repudiation of a transformation that would mask this silence in jewels and gold, or in the poet's breath, or in the whiteness of a page.

The line cedes itself to no one. No one waits its beyond. No one waits. Waits . . . "like crests of air around—"

Only now can Celan whisper the poem's final verse. Only now might the figure of goodness be given some colorless indication of a meaning forever sacrificed, forever in exile, yet forever "Kingly":

> Grosse. Graue. Fährte-
> lose.
> *K*önig-
> liche.

NOTES

1. Suzanne Cataldi, *Emotion, Depth, and Flesh* (Albany: State University of New York Press, 1993). Henceforth cited as ED.

2. Iris Marion Young, *Justice and the Politics of Difference* (Princeton, N.J.: Princeton University Press, 1990). See chapter 5: "The Scaling of Bodies and the Politics of Identity."

3. Emmanuel Levinas, *Otherwise than Being,* trans. Alphonso Lingus (The Hague: Martinus Nijhoff, 1981), p. 74. Henceforth, OB.

4. Paul Celan, *Poems of Paul Celan,* trans. Michael Hamburger (New York: Persea, 1988), pp. 178–81.

5. Werner Hamacher, "A Second of Inversion: Movements of a Figure through Celan's Poetry," in *Word Traces,* ed. Aris Fioretos (Baltimore, Md.: John Hopkins University Press, 1994), p. 221.

6. G. W. F. Hegel, *Phenomenology of the Spirit,* trans. A. V. Miller (New York: Oxford University Press, 1977), p. 19.

7. For a discussion of *Widderruf* see Götz Wienold, "Paul Delan's Hölderlin Widderruf," *Poetica* 2 (1968): 216–28.

8. Veronique Foti, "Paul Celan's Challenge to Heidegger's Poetics," (paper presented at the 1988 meeting of the Heidegger Circle), p. 8.

CHAPTER 15

Merleau-Ponty and Feminist Theory on Experience

LINDA MARTÍN ALCOFF

Feminist philosophy, if it is to aid in the empowerment of women, must develop a better account of the relationship between reason, theory, and bodily, subjective experience.[1] To quote Rosi Braidotti, we need to "elaborate a truth, which is not removed from the body, reclaiming [our] body for [ourselves]. . . . [We need] to develop and transmit a critique which respects and bears the trace of the intensive, libidinal force that sustains it."[2] If women are to have epistemic credibility and authority, we need to reconfigure the role of bodily experience in the development of knowledge.

It is within the context of this project that some feminist theorists have been interested in Merleau-Ponty's work as the best attempt thus far to transcend mind-body dualism and start philosophical thinking from an embodied perspective. Although Merleau-Ponty himself tended to universalize embodiment in his existential phenomenology, his ontology is so attentive to the concrete and the corporeal that it offers great potential for feminist philosophy, as has been noted by Iris Young, Elizabeth Grosz, Judith Butler, and others.

But it is striking that in Anglo-American feminist theory in general, phenomenology is today only rarely invoked or utilized and Merleau-Ponty's influence is all but nonexistent. I believe that this is mainly because feminists have been skeptical that phenomenology's belief in the epistemological centrality of experience can incorporate or be made compatible with the critique of the ideological content of corporeal experience that has been the cornerstone of feminist social criticism. Although feminist work in the academy began with the project of "making women's experience visible" in light of phallocentric distortions and erasures, since the 1980s this project has been largely displaced out of a concern that experience itself is the site of ideology rather than the source of truth. Given this, Merleau-Ponty's emphasis on the epistemological primacy of perception has seemed to some an outdated, unusable approach, despite its improved ontology of embodiment.

While the worry about uncritical treatments of experience is understandable, I will argue that the repudiation of phenomenology is a mistake, and that current feminist theory could benefit especially from Merleau-Ponty's treatments of experience. Poststructuralist feminism has largely negated the *cognitive* importance of experience on the grounds that experience and subjectivity are produced through the interplay of discourses. On this view, the ultimate source of knowledge about social meanings cannot be "experience," or, worse, "perception," but language and textuality. Experience plays a role in knowledge only in so far as it is articulated, and some even go so far as to deny the ontological validity of an inarticulate or inarticulable experience. I believe that, although poststructuralism has provided critically useful elaborations of how social meanings are produced and circulated, the pendulum has swung too far toward the elimination of experience's formative role in knowledge, and that a renewed attention to Merleau-Ponty's work can provide a helpful corrective.

I will begin with an explanation of the evolving treatments of experience in feminist theory, highlighting one recent example of a poststructuralist approach. I will then turn to Merleau-Ponty's work and show the advantages of his approach by working through an example taken from Foucault.

EXPERIENCE AND LANGUAGE

The rising influence of poststructuralism has worked to discredit phenomenology on the grounds that it takes subjectivity and subjective experience as cause and foundation when in reality they are mere epiphenomenon and effect. Phenomenology is sometimes portrayed as developing metaphysical accounts of experience outside of culture and history. Though in reality phenomenology and poststructuralism are not wholly opposed, too often they operate as if they are mutually exclusive, and this has helped to spawn a growing divide between feminist work in the social sciences influenced by phenomenology and feminist work in the humanities influenced by poststructuralism.

One of the critical motifs that dominated feminist scholarship throughout the 1970s was the idea of making women's experience visible and validating it against the multitude of "scientific" theories that worked ultimately to delegitimate many of our own responses and feelings, even calling into question our reports of events and incidents. From its inception, feminist scholarship and research in such fields as psychology, sociology, and anthropology was dedicated toward basing a new area of study on women's own understanding and interpretation of our experience. Consciousness-raising groups created a model of individual empowerment through collective sharing, validation, and reflection on personal experience. And women's studies departments emerged from the idea that the identity and experience of researchers had epistemological effects, and thus that the study *of* women should come to be done primarily *by* women. The focus on identity itself, politically manifested in identity politics, is not justified on the grounds of an intrinsic significance of identity but on the belief that identity is a marker, however imperfect, for a certain body of shared experiences.

But experience itself, or the subjective understanding of one's own personal experiences including affective experiences, is the object and site of gender ideology. When women report feeling contentment and happiness only in the domestic sphere, when women feel revulsion toward our own bodies, or when women experience sexual violence as deserved, it is clear that these experiences are the product of structural forces that shape the meanings of events. Complex social structures construct subjectivities as sets of habitual practices that create dispositions toward certain affects and interpretations of experience. Subjective experiences, or women's own accounts of our lives and its meaning, cannot be accepted uncritically without relinquishing our ability to challenge the gender ideologies embedded in these structures. And this has raised questions about the project of feminist social science to make visible and to validate women's experiences.

The feminist turn toward poststructuralism was motivated by the felt need for a deeper methodological and metatheoretical critique of the roots of sexism and patriarchal assumptions in all existing domains of knowledge than an experiential-based feminism could provide. Discourse theory, poststructuralism, psychoanalysis, and literary forms of analysis offered a means to problematize gender formations as a contingent rather than necessary system of practices. They helped to reveal the ubiquity of gender systems operating within every domain of social practice and system of meaning. And they offered a way to analyze misogyny as part of the very formation of subjectivity, thus explaining how reasoned argument and good intentions could continue to peacefully coexist with sexist practices and beliefs in the lives of millions of both men and women.

However, this "turn" has left unresolved the issue of experience's role in cognition. Feminist theory has swung from the extreme of taking personal experience as the foundation for knowledge to discrediting experience as the product of phallocentrism. This latter position is clearly articulated in a recent anthology edited by Judith Butler and Joan Scott entitled *Feminists Theorize the Political*.[3] In Joan Scott's contribution to this volume, which she entitled "Experience" in quotes, she critiques a view that would "appeal to experience as uncontestable evidence and as an originary point of explanation [or] a foundation upon which analysis is based." (EXP 24). This is the sort of view I characterized as dominant in 1970's feminism. Her critique of this pre-Hegelian account of experience focuses on its political limitations; she argues that it can only produce liberatory theories whose project is centered around "making experience visible," that is, making visible that experience of heretofore invisible identities, but that such a project precludes an analysis of the way in which ideological systems construct identities and experiences as well as differences. Thus, Scott says, the project of making experience visible renders invisible the historicity of experience and reproduces the very terms and conditions upon which that experience is in fact founded; and therefore it cannot contribute to a *transformation* of experience.

Scott's alternative account of experience is articulated as follows: "It is not individuals who have experience, but subjects who are constituted through experience. Experience in this definition then becomes not the origin of our explanation, not the authoritative (because seen or felt) evidence that grounds what is known, but rather that which we seek to explain, that about which knowledge is produced" (EXP 26). "Experience is," in short, "a linguistic event. . . . The question then becomes how to analyze language" (EXP 34).

Scott thus turns the naive account of experience on its head; on her account, experience is an epiphenomenon, originating outside of the individual in linguistic structures, and its explanatory value is therefore eclipsed by the theorization of language. We are asked thus to choose between an epistemology of experience, in which experience serves as the unproblematized authoritative foundation for knowledge, and an epistemology of theory, in which theory interrogates and seeks to explain experience. Clearly this is a false dilemma, and one that replays tired modernist debates between empiricism and idealism. One need only have recourse to Hegel's concept of *Erfahren* to develop an alternative account that understands experience as epistemically indispensable but never epistemically self-sufficient. But Scott's essay and the view it presents is widely influential and partly responsible for the eclipse of phenomenology within feminist theory. And it follows from a Derridean tendency to focus exclusively on texts and discourses as sites of cultural representation and knowledges, a focus thought to be justified, as I shall discuss in a moment, by the view that *all* experience and knowledge operates within a linguistic terrain.

But let me return first to Scott's formulation of the task of theory. Convincingly, Scott notes the importance of recognizing the knower's stake in the production of knowledge, and she argues that we need to explore the relations between discourse, reality, and cognition. But this of course goes for the theorist herself who is analyzing the production of experience: *her* own experience is operative in the development of the analysis. No theoretical work is uninformed by the theorist's experience. If experience is not considered cognitively reliable, the ubiquity of it's influence will lead to skepticism. So either Scott holds a view of theory as potentially transcendent of experience, or she must acknowledge its formative influence, in which case her repudiation of its ability to justify knowledge will entail skeptical conclusions.

Not surprisingly, Scott does end up with a Rortyan-type epistemological skepticism. As an illustration of her argument that experience is constitutively dependent on orders of meaning that originate outside of the individual and that its explanatory value is thereby eclipsed by the theorization of language, Scott offers two readings of an autobiographical passage from Samuel Delaney's *The Motion of Light in Water*. In this passage Delaney recounts a powerful experience he had in 1963 when he visited a bathhouse and saw for the first time a large room full of openly gay men. In her first reading of this passage, Scott presents Delaney's experience (following Delaney's own account) as one that changed Delaney's comprehension of the political potential of gay sexuality. Paraphrasing Delaney here, Scott develops this first reading to postulate that "The 'apprehension of massed bodies' gave him (as it does, he argues anyone, 'male, female, working or middle class') a 'sense of political power' " (EXP 22).[4] In other words, Delaney's perceptual experience of seeing gay men en masse led him to new conceptions about actual possibilities or, in short, to new knowledge. However, Scott ultimately rejects this reading of Delaney's account, and substitutes instead a reading to the effect that Delaney's experience was not "the discovery of truth (conceived as the reflection of a prediscursive reality)" but "the substitution of one interpretation for another" (EXP 35). If there is still knowledge gained from experience on this second reading, it is not a representational knowledge, but a Rortyan-type or constructivist knowledge characterized as the ability to imagine new language and new interpretations rather than the ability to discern new truths about a shared reality.

In offering these comparative readings, Scott assumes that any acknowledgment of Delaney's experience as grounding knowledge would be a kind of naive realism. Thus, her rejection of the first reading is based on its (purported) assumption that "vision is a direct, unmediated apprehension of a world of transparent objects" (EXP 23). The only apparent alternative to this naive realism is a view in which experience is the product of structural, linguistic systems and never the source of truth. Given this, Scott denies that rendering experience visible can disrupt dominant knowledges and resist ideological interpellations, as 1970s feminists assumed.

Clearly, however, the project of "making experience visible" *has* sometimes had the effect of disrupting dominant discursive formations. Consider the current flurry of controversy over the term "date rape" and the ongoing inability of U.S. state laws to recognize rape within marriage. Why are these terms, based on the simple experiential reports of rape victims, so resistant to being processed or incorporated? Obviously because the very existence of such an "experience" as rape within the context of a heterosexual date or marriage must necessarily call into question the primary ways in which such institutions are understood, as well as such concepts and practices as man, woman, and heterosexuality itself. The principal tactic of the survivors' movement in North America has been to break the silence, to render visible the reality of sexual violence and its effects. It is true that survivors' descriptive reports of their experience have also been recuperated within the media to solidify patriarchal institutions, but this tactic of breaking the silence has unquestionably had a profound political impact and has tremendous subversive potential. Such subjective descriptions have often had subversive political effects, when they challenge existing epistemic hierarchies concerning what kinds of embodied speakers have credibility and authority, and when they raise questions about the benign status of institutionalized heterosexuality.

This example is particularly useful to explore the role of experience in relationship to discursive formations. What is the relationship between the discourse and the experience of sexual violence? We have more than adequate reason to believe that rapes occurred on dates and in marriages before terms such as "date rape" and "marital rape" were invented and before these issues became widely discussed. On the other hand, it is also clear that the changes in discourse have effected changes in at least some of the experience of such traumas. But a position that links experience to discourse too securely might hold that, prior to the discourse of date rape, the experience itself could not occur, or at least not the sort of experience with such traumatizing aftereffects as we now associate with rape (and such a view is today being promoted in "postfeminist" articles in the United States, e.g., by Katie Roiphe). Thus date rape is said to be a fiction invented by feminists that is now having material effects in needlessly traumatizing young impressionable women. Such a view could gain credence from the claim that experience and language are coextensive.

In my view, this claim is a metaphysical error. Experience sometimes exceeds language; it is at times inarticulate. Feminism has not invented sexism out of whole cloth; it has provided new language by which to describe and understand old experiences and that then alters present and future experience. Certainly discourse permeates and affects experience, but to say as Scott does that "experience is a linguistic event," or that discourse is the condition of intelligibility for all experience, is to erase all of those kinds of experiential knowledges unsusceptible to linguistic articulation. If meaningful experience must pass the test of discursive formulation, we will preclude the inarticulate from the realm of knowledge and risk erasing forms of oppression that cannot be expressed under reigning regimes of discourse. A better view would be one that understood experience and discourse as imperfectly aligned with locations of disjuncture.

Here is where phenomenology and Merleau-Ponty's work in particular can play a critical role in feminist theory today. Feminist theory needs a better account of the relationship between theory and experience, one in which theory is understood as itself embodied rather than simply formative of, without being formed by, bodily experience.[5] We need also to start from descriptions of specific bodies, with their own specific individual histories and inscriptions, rather than an abstract concept of the body or one that exists only in textual representation. If we begin to tie theory to specific bodies, however, we must also rethink what it is theory can claim to know, that is, its metaphysical scope, or the ontological status of its claims to truth. The phenomenological tradition, extending from Hegel's project to theorize knowledge as it appears to consciousness, and developed further through the work of Husserl and especially Merleau-Ponty, has itself struggled to formulate an account of knowledge and the cognitive aspect of experience without separating mind from embodiment or reifying the object world as over and against subjective, corporeal experience.

MERLEAU-PONTY AND THE
COGNITIVE VALUE OF EXPERIENCE FOR FEMINISM

Husserl's project was to base philosophical knowledge on indubitable grounds by going back to the things themselves. But he understood this as an original intuition or immediate vision that manifests itself in bodily presence.[6] Thus Husserl claimed "That every originarily given intuition is a legitimate source of knowledge, that everything which presents itself to us originarily in 'intuition,' so to speak in its bodily presence, has to be taken simply as what it presents itself to be, but only within the limits in which it presents itself."[7] Despite this epistemic legitimation of intuition, however, for Husserl consciousness is not a passive receptor as it was for many modern philosophers; consciousness is positional, intentional, inherently and incessantly open to the world and yet constitutive of the meaning of that world and of our experience within it. Perceptual experience is indubitable not as a means to know an object world separate from human existence, but as a means to know the lived world and to disclose the necessary structures of consciousness.

Thus, despite its focus on immediacy of perception, Husserlian phenomenology does not accept without challenge the naturalness of what consciousness encounters; one of the purposes of the transcendental phenomenological reduction is to suspend the natural existence of what I perceive, to distance myself from the familiarity of the world, and to transform the world from the realm of the actual to the realm of the phenomenal, that is, that whose validity is not yet determined. Despite Husserl's heavy investment in the Cartesian project of providing a foundation for certainty, experience is not a clear datum, as it was for the logical positivists, but a complex of elements in need of clarification and reflection. Thus, for Husserl, "experience" is a complex object that exceeds sensory perception to include cognitive and interpretive faculties as well.

Husserl's epistemology remains, however, too wedded to the goal of establishing certainty and too confident about the value of the reduction. And his concept of the transcendental ego remained in important respects disembodied, with its valorization of critical detachment as the route to a reasoned assessment of immediate experience. Merleau-Ponty's development of Husserlian phenomenology more successfully transcends the legacy of mind-body dualism that still operates in Husserl's epistemology, and shifts emphasis away from a foundationalist project and toward acknowledging the fact that knowledge is always unfinished and incomplete, precisely because of the open-ended nature of experience and of meaning. Merleau-Ponty also developed an important criticism of Husserl's approach to experience that applies in some respects to Scott's formulation.

For Merleau-Ponty, the purpose of existential phenomenology is not to ground absolute knowledge but to describe human existence as it is lived at the between point of world and consciousness. In this space what exists is a dynamic and developing synthesis incapable of total consistency or closure precisely because of our concrete, fleshy embodiment. Pretenses toward abstraction or a transcendental perspective are inappropriate and inadequate starting points for describing this space.[8]

Thus, the centrality that Merleau-Ponty accords to perceptual experience in no way leads him toward positivist conclusions. Because the cogito is founded on the percipio, it is both undetachable from bodily experience and incapable of achieving absoluteness or permanence. It is only because being is always being in the world, and not apart or over the world, that we can know the world. But it is also because being is always being in the world that our knowledge is forever incomplete, caught as it is inside, carried out within the temporal flux, and incapable of achieving a complete reduction (PP ix/xiv). Thus, acknowledging the cognitive centrality of experience, far from producing pretensions of indubitability as in naive realism, actually has the reverse effect. "The world is not what I think, but what I live through. I am open to the world, I have no doubt that I am in communication with it, but I do not possess it; it is inexhaustible" (PP xi–xii/xvi–xvii). Bringing bodily experience into the center of epistemology has the precise effect of dislodging any hope of certainty or an indubitable foundation.

Whereas poststructuralism bases its claims about the inevitability of incomplete understandings, about the absence of closure, and about the deferrals of meaning on the nature of language, phenomenology bases its account primarily on a reflective description of lived human experience as a corporeal being in the world. Lived experience is open-ended, multilayered, fragmented, and shifting not because of the play of language, but because of the nature of embodied, temporal existence. The world is laden with a depth of meaning without total closure or consistency, not because deferral is the inevitable structure of linguistic meaning, but because the temporal texture of experience folds the absent and the past into the present moment.

Moreover, Merleau-Ponty's account of experience is irreducible to an account of language because in his view experience is not supervenient or ontologically dependent on language. It is for this reason that he considers it possible to offer a conceptualization of animal experience, an unthinkable project for a theory that denies the possibility of cognition outside of language. The critical difference then between his account and Joan Scott's concerns language: what is the best way to conceptualize the relationship between language, perception, and phenomena? Is there a ground to language? If experience is necessarily a linguistic event, then experience cannot be thought about except through language, and it makes sense to say, as Scott does, that language should be the focus of analysis. However, if language does not exhaust the meaningful world, then experience, involving always the perception of phenomena, needs to be attended to. Two questions surely arise here: what can it mean to attend to experience except through language, and is this unarticulateble experience outside of culture and history? I will answer the second question first.

For Merleau-Ponty, the meaning of an experience is produced within an embodied synthesis of consciousness in the world. Meaning exists in the interworld of history, and thus refers to a world that is always already there before I come upon it and yet a world in which I live, whose meaning is always a meaning for me (and thus whose meaning necessarily includes values).

> We therefore recognize, around our initiatives and around that strictly individual project which is oneself, a zone of generalized existence and of projects already formed, significances which trail between ourselves and things and which confer upon us the quality of man, bourgeois or worker. Already generality intervenes, already our presence to ourselves is mediated by it and we cease to be pure consciousness, as soon as the natural or social constellation ceases to be an unformulated *this* and crystallizes into a situation, as soon as it has a meaning—in short, as soon as we exist. (PP 513–14/450)

The world is not an object at a distance from me nor is it that which I construct or form; "it is the background from which all acts stand out . . . the natural setting of, and field for, all my thoughts and all my explicit perceptions" (PP v/xi). As Iris Young explains, for Merleau-Ponty:

> Consciousness has a foundation in perception, the lived body's feeling and moving among things, with an active purposive orientation. Unlike a Cartesian materialist body, the lived body has culture and meaning inscribed in its habits, in its specific forms of perception and comportment.

Description of this embodied existence is important because, while laden with culture and significance, the meaning embodied in habit, feeling, and perceptual orientation is usually nondiscursive.[9]

Thus, experience is never capable of being understood or represented as if prior to specific cultural and historical locations. In my view, Merleau-Ponty did not fully grasp all of the implications of this analysis, particularly as these impacted his own descriptions of bodily comportment. Nonetheless, his most general characterizations of experience reiterate their constitutive relationship to the specificity of social location.

The passage from Iris Young just quoted also helps to explain how we might answer the first question raised above concerning how one might approach experience other than through language. As Young explains, meaning is nondiscursive in the sense that its ground is not language nor does it refer ultimately (only) to language. Merleau-Ponty develops this claim in his analysis of gesture, which he understands as neither a transparent reference to something external to it nor as something predetermined by linguistic practice, and he hypothesized that language originally evolved from gestural forms of communication (PP 203–32/174–99). The meaning of a gesture is not produced or discerned entirely via a system of internal references as in Saussurean diacritics, such that one gesture gains its meaningfulness through its system of relations to other gestures. Smiles are "natural" in the sense that they are universal to the species and thus evidently characteristic of our form of embodied existence; they are not completely dependent on an internal system of references for their intelligibility. Another difference from the Saussurean account is that the meaning of gestures is displayed directly rather than inferred by the one(s) to whom it is directed. In this sense their meaning is intrinsic rather than relational. On the other hand, the meaning of any given smile is also conventional in the sense that the specificity of its meaning, its appropriateness within the context, and so on, varies by culture. Thus, in one sense it could be said that for Merleau-Ponty bodily gestures are both natural and conventional, natural in the sense of exhibiting forms of embodiment general to human beings and conventional in the sense of attaining specificity through cultural codes. Such an account does not understand the meaningfulness of gesture as supervenient on linguistic practice nor as positioned outside of culture and history. Rather, meaning is produced through the embodied actions of consciousness in the world, some of which involve linguistic practices and some of which do not. Social practice, and thus experience, is not the *result* of discourse, but the *site* where meaning is developed.[10]

But what can it mean to know the features of experience, and to offer an epistemologically adequate description, without reducing experience to language? One might argue that even if experience exceeds linguisticality, our knowledge of it cannot. Therefore, insofar as experience has a relation to knowledge, it is necessarily subordinated to the realm of articulation. If, as M. C. Dillon puts it, "we are always already in language . . . if expression is always the coherent deformation of already available forms of expression, if it is impossible to penetrate the layers of sediment "then it would seem that we are imprisoned in linguistic immanence and that there is no stratum of meaning that is not already mediated by signifiers."[11] Merleau-Ponty rejects this Heideggerian-inspired belief in the "prison house of language," not because language is unnecessary to establish truth, but because language itself is not a closed system. He says:

> Signs do not simply evoke other signs for us and so on without end, and language is not like a prison we are locked into or a guide we must blindly follow; for what these linguistic gestures mean, and gain us such complete access to that we seem to have no further need of them to refer to it, finally appears at the intersection of all of them. (S 101/ 81)

Thus Merleau-Ponty is not suggesting that experience provides determinate and transparent knowledge outside or beyond the meaning-laden depth of the world, which would amount to a positivist form of empiricism. The mistake in the prison house of language view is that *language is a prison.* Meaning and knowledge are not locked into language, but emerge at the intersection between gesture, bodily experience, and linguistic practice.

Scott's concern is essentially with positivism, with a view that would take experience as "uncontestable evidence" and as "an originary point of explanation" or "foundation upon which analysis is based." The nuances of multiple meanings, the multidirectionality of connotation, and the influence of convention would be lost in such an account. However, she assumes that any nondiscursive experience will be taken as uncontestable, like the logical positivists notion of datum, and this assumption itself presupposes that a world not imbued by language is determinate and coherent, without layers of conflicting meanings already embedded in it. Such is not the case, given the depth of the world in a temporal unfolding. The phenomenal world constantly folds back on itself, adding to what has come before and what remains still in the background of the present moment; the past is that which has been surpassed, yet remains within. There are no complete breaks or total separations, only folds within a continuous cloth, pregnant with latent meaning.

> When we speak of the flesh of the visible, we do not mean to do anthropology, to describe a world covered over with our own projections, leaving aside what it can be under the human mask. Rather, we mean that carnal being, as a being of depths, of several leaves or several faces, a being in latency, and a presentation of a certain absence, is a

prototype of Being, of which our body, the sensible sentient, is a very remarkable variant, but whose constitutive paradox lies in every visible. . . . What we call a visible is, we said, a quality pregnant with a texture, the surface of a depth, a cross section upon a massive being, a grain or corpuscle borne by a wave of Being. Since the total visible is always behind, or after, or between the aspects we see of it, *there is access to it only through an experience* which, like it, is wholly outside of itself. (VI 180/136; emphasis added)

Such an ontological picture does not yield determinacy or consistency; it does not produce evidence that is "incontestable."

Experience is then not a series of data with transparent meaning, and does not provide "incontestable evidence" for a single interpretation. However, it is and must be the basis of explanation. There is no conceivable alternative basis or ultimate justification for knowledge other than experience of my body in the world. If we refuse this fact, and attempt to define explanation as a self-referring system without source or ground, we are in effect espousing a form of epistemological skepticism as well as incorrectly understanding the phenomenal features of language itself.

Scott's account gains its plausibility from the powerful contemporary currents of what Dillon names "post-hermeneutic skepticism" and "semeiological reductionism."[12] Post-hermeneutic skepticism is a version of epistemological skepticism that repudiates the possibility of knowing the world on the grounds that all knowledge-claims are tainted by bias and interpretation, and has emerged from a reading of Heidegger's claim that Being is forever imprisoned in the house of language. Semiological reductionism, taken from Saussure, holds that signifiers can only refer to other signifiers. Together these positions have yielded support for a belief that experience has no intelligibility outside of language. However, within the phenomenological tradition, experiences are not perfectly coextensive or coincident with the realm of discourse or language. There is a pre-predicative experience that can be referred to but never fully articulated. As Young says, "Meaning subsists not only in signs and symbols, but also in the movement and consequences of action; experience carries the connotation of context and action."[13] On the other hand, experience is understood as fundamentally historicized, rather than comprised of Kantian-based stable constituents. Experience can therefore never be understood outside of its full material context. If we reduce this context to the sphere of language, we will miss the ways in which meanings, and thus the historical motion of cultures, can be imparted and transformed through nondiscursive modes of practice. For this reason, in his search for philosophical truth, Merleau-Ponty relies even more heavily than Sartre on nuanced descriptions of the subjective perspective for various phenomena and life events.

Like structuralism and poststructuralism, and to a much greater extent than Sartre, Merleau-Ponty's account of subjectivity allows us to understand how it is constituted by and through historically specific cultural practices and institutions. However, he is consistently critical of the objectivist descriptions of the self found in some versions of structuralism. He says that in a phenomenologically based descriptive psychology, "I am not the outcome or the meeting-point of numerous causal agencies. . . . I cannot conceive myself as nothing but a bit of the world, a mere object of biological, psychological, or sociological investigation" (PP ii/viii). At the same time, contra Descartes and Kant, phenomenological description also shows that my subjectivity is never detached from the world, never standing free and clear, capable of providing its own foundation, or merely "housed" in a mechanical body. Because subjectivity is not an object or mere epiphenomena of something more basic, it cannot be theorized apart from its lived, embodied experience. Thus he attempted to walk a line between structuralist accounts that recognize the importance of social influence and individualist accounts that allowed for meaningful intentionality. Toward this end, he strived to develop a new language of ontological description that could avoid invoking the dualisms of subject and object, body and world, past and present, perception and imagination.

Flesh was one such word, which Merleau-Ponty used to describe the general mode of being. Just as whenever I touch an object so I too am touched by it, flesh is the experience of the world in me, a doubled sensation imperfectly represented by dualist language. This account holds great potential for feminist philosophical reconstructions of the traditional transcendental accounts of the self imbued with masculinized autonomy and exaggerated self-control. There are (at least) four features of his account in which this is the case.

First, the capacity of the body to see, which has been centered in Western epistemology as the basis for mastery through a detached, objectifying gaze, is for Merleau-Ponty grounded in the body's own visibility. "To say that the body is a seer is, curiously enough, not to say anything else than: it is visible. When I study what I mean in saying that it is the body that sees, I find nothing else than: it is 'from somewhere.'. . . More exactly: when I say that my body is a seer, there is, in the experience I have of it, something that founds and announces the view that the other acquires of it or that the mirror gives of it" (VI 327/273–74). Thus, in one sense, it is our own objectification, our embodiment in the world, and thus the very opposite of mastery that grounds the possibility of our seeing.

Second, if our capacity to see is grounded in being seen, or being seeable, then the metaphysical picture of knowing needs to be rethought, which must in turn affect the expected scope or reach of epistemology. Consider this passage from Merleau-Ponty's unfinished notes:

the idea of *chiasm*, that is, every relation with being is *simultaneously* a taking and a being taken, the hold is held, it is *inscribed* and inscribed in the same being that it takes hold of. Starting from there, elaborate an idea of philosophy: it cannot be total and active grasp, intellectual possession, since what there is to be grasped is dispossession. It is not *above* life, overhanging. It is beneath. (VI 319/266)

Would that he had lived to elaborate further on such an idea. But clearly, even in these illusive notes, one can find a way to begin an epistemology on very different grounds. From underneath, rather than above, one might develop the new feminist methodological counsel to bring the researcher into the research product more explicitly and to incorporate the subject location of the knower into the ontology of truth itself. It is not the case that one cannot *know*, in the absence of a total possession, but that both knower and known are altered in the process. Knowing is a kind of immanent engagement, in which one's own self is engaged by the world—touched, felt, and seen—rather than standing part and above.

The third and fourth aspects involve what the absence of mastery over the visual field implies for intersubjective relations. To some extent Merleau-Ponty is developing his account in opposition to Sartre, who was famously pessimistic about human relationships. Sartre's pessimism was based on his ontological picture of the configuration between selves and world, in which each consciousness posits its own system of meanings and values and posits the Other as a mere value to be configured within this schema. Conflict arises inevitably over whose system will prevail, in effect, over whose mastery will dominate to organize the social field. In Merleau-Ponty's picture, in contrast, neither consciousness can effect such mastery, either over the meaning of the world or of the other. "The other is no longer so much a freedom seen *from without* as destiny and fatality, a rival subject for a subject, but he is caught up in a circuit that connects him to the world, as we ourselves are, and consequently also in a circuit that connects him to us" (VI 322/269). There are two points made here. One is that we cannot objectify the other any more successfully than we can objectify the visible world, the world that sees us in our seeing of it. There is no position of mastery that can be won or lost, and it is probably our assumption of such mastery that creates an imaginary position that is then fought over. The other is not an "object" for us, as a thing over and against us that we can see as if from above; we are, rather, beneath the other, in the same way that we are beneath being generally. A second point is that we are primordially, ineradicably, connected to the other. In both Hegel and Sartre's ontology of self-other relations, it is possible to theorize the self prior to the other, prior to that moment of encountering and being shaken by the other's competing existence. For Merleau-Ponty, our connection to the other is inscribed in our being, our capacity to see, to touch. We are fundamentally an "openness," he says, a "stage" where something takes place (VI 317/263). Our consciousness of this fact may not be explicit in our spoken characterizations of our existence, and in our pronouncements, for example, of our "autonomy" and our "freedom"—but is revealed in our comportment in the world, our gestures or what might be called "body language." Thus, the feminist critiques of exaggerated claims about autonomy gain support from Merleau-Ponty's phenomenological description of intersubjectivity.

Still, there are significant limitations and problems for feminists in Merleau-Ponty's philosophy. As Young, Butler, and Grosz have all shown, Merleau-Ponty's existential subject, particularly in *The Phenomenology of Perception*, is masculine, his account of sexuality is patriarchal heterosexuality, and he naturalizes current gender relations.[14] However, neither Young nor Grosz attribute these problems to phenomenology's metaphysics, nor see phenomenological description as positing a foundational experience outside of culture and history. Rather, on their view Merleau-Ponty's shortcomings result mainly from the fact that his analysis of embodiment did not specify sexual difference, and thus male embodiment was allowed to stand in for the whole.[15] Still, much of Merleau-Ponty's categories of embodiment can be put to the service of specific analyses of the ways in which gendered subjectivity emerges from sexual practices.

Thus, despite its limitations, Merleau-Ponty's phenomenology offers an ontology that is more open to the assimilation of corporeality within epistemology than the Kantian and neo-Kantian traditions. This marks an important break from the philosophical articulations of patriarchy, which devalued the female element alongside matter, the body, and the emotions. Phenomenology thus can offer to feminist theory the beginnings of an expanded conception of reason and knowledge, one that is not predicated upon the exclusion of the feminine, the concrete, or the particular, and one that will not require women to become manlike before they can participate in the sphere of philosophical thought. In my view, such a transformation in our conception of knowledge must attribute a cognitive value to experience: not just that through experience knowledge is communicated, but that experience produces knowledge. As Grosz says, feminist theory has relied on "lived experience and experiential acquaintance as a touchstone or criterion in the evaluation, not only of theoretical paradigms and propositions but also of day-by-day and mass politics." While it is true that "experience cannot be understood as the unproblematic criterion for the assessment of knowledges, . . . without some acknowledgment of the major, indeed, formative, role of experience in the establishment and functioning of theoretical systems, socio-political and aesthetic constructs and moral and political values, feminism has no grounds for disputing patriarchal norms. Merleau-Ponty as one of the few more or less contemporary theorists committed to the primacy of experience is thus in a

unique position to help provide a depth and sophistication to feminist understandings, and uses, of experience in the tasks of political action."[16]

The position we take on experience's role in cognition thus has a special relevance for feminist theory. In the final section I will use an example
taken from Foucault to suggest what is at stake in this debate for feminists.

THE IRREDUCIBILITY OF EXPERIENCE
AND PHENOMENOLOGICAL DESCRIPTION

Attempts to explain experience as solely constituted by macro structures fail
to take seriously or adequately into account lived, personal, individual experience. Merleau-Ponty is right when he says that I do not, nor can I, experience myself as the mere meeting point of causal agencies, or as a mere
construct of structures. My lived experience includes such things as choices,
intentions, and a range of inarticulate affects that exceeds discourse. Such
experiences as rape cannot be reduced to linguistic effects, nor is the meaning
of the experience as ambiguous as any statement in a language. To theorize
rape adequately we must have recourse to the description of embodied experience, and not merely the various possible and actual discursive representations of that experience. This does not imply that a rape experience is
unsusceptible to discursive constructions. I can experience a rape as deserved
or undeserved, as shameful for myself or as shameful for the perpetrator, as
an inevitable feature of woman's lot or as an eradicable evil. But when I
supplement the analysis of the discourses of rape with the phenomenologies
of rape experiences from the perspectives of survivors of rape, I will be much
less likely to suppose that rape itself might be the product of an interpretation,
either a misdiagnosis of an event or an experience whose traumatizing effect
is created by a particular political stance.

Without phenomenological descriptions, discursive analyses of sexual
practices are more likely to be distorted. A telling example of this can be
found in Michel Foucault's account of sexual experience in volume one of the
History of Sexuality. Foucault is often grouped among the poststructuralists,
but his variance from their excessive focus on textuality is well known. His
work has contributed a great deal to the material conceptualization of power,
history, and subjectivity. And yet, in regard to sexuality, Foucault's account
accords to discourse the unique ability to attach meanings and values to our
feelings and sensations.[17] This can have disastrous effects on how we understand sexual violence.

Foucault introduces a case from 1867 France, which serves to mark that
moment in the history of sexuality when sex is brought under the jurisdiction
of expert discourses in the human sciences. The case involved a "simple-
minded" farmhand who was turned in to the authorities after having

obtained a few caresses from a little girl, just as he had done before and seen done by the village urchins round about him; for, at the edge of the wood, or in the ditch by the road leading to Saint-Nicolas, they would play the familiar game called 'curdled milk.' . . . [and] this village half-wit . . . would give a few pennies to the little girls for favors the older ones refused him.[18]

But this time, Foucault relates, the familiar, ordinary incident in the life of the village, the "everyday occurrence [of] inconsequential bucolic pleasures" became the subject of judicial and medical intervention. The farmhand was subjected to detailed, invasive questioning about his "thoughts, inclinations, habits, sensations, and opinions."[19] The "experts" inspected his anatomy to the point of studying his "facial bone structure" and measuring his "brainpan" for signs of "degenerescence."[20] In the end, he was shut away at a hospital.

Foucault's objective in discussing this case is to suggest that it marked a discursive turning point in the construction of sexual experiences between adults and children, a change from a situation in which such relations were "inconsequential bucolic pleasures" to the object of "collective intolerance" and "judicial action." Evidently for Foucault, before the intervention of an expert discourse on sexuality, the meaning of the sexual act in 1867 between the farmhand and the girl was, simply, pleasure. His narrative of the event suggests a picture in which pleasure stands on one side, in a kind of pure form, innocent and harmless, and on the other side stands discourse, power, and domination. He makes this argument through illuminating what he takes to be a disparate juxtaposition between the insignificance of this event and the portentous response it received from the authorities, what he refers to as the overlay of an "everyday bit of theatre with their solemn discourse."[21] In this way, the overlay of expert discourses on sexual events produces what Gayle Rubin has called an excess of significance.[22]

On the basis of this analysis we are led to posit pleasure as antithetical to power. Foucault does not think that pleasure is always disconnected from discourse and power, and in much of this volume he is at pains to reveal the ways in which pleasures can get used and taken up by institutional discourses. His view is, rather, that when properly disinvested of dominant discursive associations, pleasure is innocent and harmless, and even the privileged site of resistance. Thus he ends the volume with the claim that the "rallying point for the counterattack against the deployment of sexuality [as a form of power/ knowledge] . . . ought . . . to be . . . bodies and pleasures."[23]

But is it the case that pleasures, in and of themselves, when disinvested of discursive categorization and valuation, are resistant to power? Let us look again at the case from 1867. It hardly need be said that Foucault lacked sufficient evidence to warrant his claims about the girls' participation in or feelings about the event. If such relations were reciprocally initiated and pleasurable for both parties, why did there need to be an exchange of a "few pennies" to insure the girls' participation? Given this, on what does Foucault base his claim that any pleasure at all existed on the side of the children? His quickness to assume such knowledge manifests unfortunately typical male and adult patterns of epistemic arrogance.

Consider a phenomenological description of such an encounter from the child's subjective point of view. I have reconstructed such a description using current writings by adult survivors of sexual abuse, as well as my own experiences. In these accounts, trauma is often masked as confusion, for as a child one has no names to identify the ordeals endured or the sensations one feels. In encounters similar to the one Foucault described, the child exhibits a need to be held or hugged, to have affection or attention, or perhaps to obtain some basic good like money for food or shelter. The adult complies but on the condition of genital stimulation. This misresponse produces in the child pain and fear mixed with compulsion and intimidation, a duress created by uncertainty and the disparity between soothing words and painful, uncomfortable invasions, by the command to be silent and the assurance that all that is happening is ordinary and based on affection. One is told by a trusted adult to take the thing in one's mouth, to allow groping explorations, to perform distressing enactments that feel humiliating and foreign. While the child gags and whimpers (or screams and cries), the adult sighs and moans, holding tightly so that the child cannot get away. Pleasure here is dimly perceived by the child as somehow dependent on one's own anguish, the product of intimately experienced terrors. Afterward, the child fears trusting anyone again, feeling that everyone who expresses concern ultimately only wants sex. The child also feels a shame marked on the body itself, as a thing to be used, a kind of living spittoon. The flesh of one's own body envelops and incorporates the dreaded other, with its disregard for oneself and its capacity for psychic or physical violence. No wonder these events often produce a psychic dislocation from one's own corporeal present and one's ability to accept inhabiting this body, which is the continued site of the other. One's body now will forever retain a layer of remembered experience as the colonized space for a monstrous subjectivity.

Such phenomenologies of sexual violence would suggest, I believe, a very different political ontology of pleasure than the one Foucault offers. During a rape, locked in the pantomime of an embrace, consumed by feelings of fear, pain, and anguish, one sees or feels the signs of pleasure in the other. Perhaps one feels an erect penis, or hears a moan, or sees the glassy eyes and flushed face of postorgasmic ecstasy. Even while one's hands are bound, one's mouth is covered, even while all of one's muscles feel tight, sore, and bruised from straining to get free, one can perceive the frenzied pace of desire in the hurried, impulsive movements of the other. Even while one wonders silently how it will be possible to survive this torment, how much more violence is in store, and how death itself might be a comforting end, one can detect the sexual enjoyment experienced by the other, in his rapid thrusting, his incessant groping, his sexual energy. Pleasure here is corporeally perceived as the product of one's own pain and torment.

It is one of the most central features of patriarchy that pleasure can be received through the humiliation and physical harming of another. This is exemplified not only in rape, but in the cruel and hostile humor that produces entertainment through ridicule and derision, and the aggressive competitions that produce pleasurable sensations of satisfaction and contentment through acts of conquest and mastery over others. The association between pleasure and violation in such practices is more than mere juxtaposition; it is closer to a relationship of ontological dependence.

Now I have juxtaposed a phenomenological description culled from contemporary accounts with a narrative from a very different cultural period, and this may well seem an invalid move. But my purpose is to call into question Foucault's claim that discourses can alter the experience of events like sexual relations between adults and children to such a degree that they can become "inconsequential pleasures." This claim is belied by the phenomenology of sex itself, which involves uniquely sensitive, vulnerable, and psychically important areas of the body, a fact that persists across cultural differences. If rationality and knowledge are embodied, then it becomes clear how and why sexual experiences are cognitive: why, that is, they have the capacity to impart critically important meanings specifically concerning one's body, one's self, and the limits and possibilities of one's relationships with others. This does not establish that sexual acts have uniform meanings, but that they have in any case significant subject-constituting meanings.

My suggestion is that we need to supplement discursive accounts of the cultural construction of sexual experience with phenomenological accounts of the embodied effects on the subjectivity of certain kinds of practices. The meanings and significance of sexual events inhere partly in the embodied experiences themselves, whether or not they can be rendered intelligible within any discursive formation.

Much more needs to be said about the complicated issues surrounding the relations between discourse, meaning, and sexual experience. But the point I wish to make in conclusion is that such phenomenological descriptions should be a critical part of any attempt to explain experience, and not merely as endpoints or data that require theoretical illumination, but as capable of shedding light on theory itself. This will be vital if we are to reconfigure the role of bodily experience in the development of knowledge.

NOTES

1. This chapter is a revised and expanded version of "Phenomenology, Post-structuralism, and Feminist Theory on the Concept of Experience," in *Feminist Phenomenology,* ed. Linda Fisher and Lester Embree (Reidel, forthcoming). It also contains passages from my "The Politics of Postmodern Feminism, Revisited," *Cultural Critique* 36 (spring 1997): pp. 5–27.

2. Rosi Braidotti, *Patterns of Dissonance* (New York: Routledge, 1991), p. 8.

3. (New York: Routledge, 1992); hereafter cited as "EXP."

4. See also Samuel R. Delaney, *The Motion of Light in Water: Sex and Science Fiction Writing in the East Village, 1957–1965* (New York: New American Library, 1988).

5. In two recent books, Susan Bordo both offers strong arguments defending this claim and provides an exemplary model of how to do it: *Unbearable Weight: Feminism, Western Culture, and the Body* (Berkeley: University of California Press, 1993); and *Twilight Zones: The Hidden Life of Cultural Images from Plato to O. J.* (Berkeley: University of California Press, 1997).

6. See *Phenomenology: The Philosophy of Edmund Husserl,* ed. Joseph Kockelmans (Garden City, N.Y.: Doubleday, 1967).

7. Ibid., p. 29–30.

8. See Vincent Descombes, *Modern French Philosophy* (New York: Cambridge University Press, 1980), p. 57.

9. Iris Young, *"Throwing Like a Girl" and Other Essays in Feminist Philosophy and Social Theory* (Bloomington: Indiana Press, 1990), p. 14.

10. My thanks to Fred Evans for helping me develop this analysis, though he may still disagree with some of my formulations.

11. M. C. Dillon, *Merleau-Ponty's Ontology* (Bloomington Indiana University Press, 1988), p. 198–99.

12. See ibid., pp. 177–86.

13. Young, *"Throwing Like a Girl,"* p. 13.

14. See ibid., Judith Butler, "Sexual Ideology and Phenomenological Description: A Feminist Critique of Merleau-Ponty's *Phenomenology of Perception"* in *The Thinking Muse,* ed. Jeffner Allen and Iris Young (Bloomington: Indiana University Press, 1989); and Elizabeth Grosz, "Merleau-Ponty and Irigaray in the Flesh," *Thesis Eleven* no. 36 (1993): 37–59.

15. Butler perhaps offers ths sharpest criticism, not only of his generic accounts of bodies and sexualities, but of the way in which he takes misogyny to be an intrinsic feature of perception, and of his reification of masterslave relations in the structure of sexual desire. On these points I find her analysis compelling.

16. "Merleau-Ponty and Irigaray," pp. 3–4.

17. Michel Foucault, *The Use of Pleasure,* trans. Robert Hurley. (New York: Random House, 1985). pp. 3–4.

18. Michel Foucault, *The History of Sexuality: Volume One,* trans. Robert Hurley (New York: Random House, 1980), pp. 31–32.

19. Ibid., p. 31.

20. Ibid.

21. Ibid., p. 32.

22. See her "Thinking Sex: Notes Toward a Radical Theory of the Politics of Sexuality," in *Pleasure and Danger,* ed. Carole Vance (Boston: Routledge, 1984), p. 279.

23. Foucault, *The History of Sexuality,* p. 157.

CONTRIBUTORS

LINDA MARTÍN ALCOFF is Professor of Philosophy and Political Science at Syracuse University. She is the author of *Real Knowing: New Versions of the Coherence Theory* (Cornell, 1996), coeditor of *Feminist Epistemologies* (Routledge, 1993), and editor of *Epistemology: The Big Question* (Blackwell, 1998). She is working on a new book called *Visible Identities*.

RENAUD BARBARAS is Professeur at Université Blaise Pascal Clairment-Ferrand and a member of the Institut Universitaire de France. He is the author of many books, *De l'être du phénomène* (which will soon appear in English from the Humanities Press); *La perception*; *Le Tournant de l'expérience*; and *Merleau-Ponty*; he is also the author of many essays on phenomenology.

MAURO CARBONE is a researcher, primarily in the area of aesthetics, with the Department of Philosophy at the University of Milan. His publications include the second revised Italian edition of *Le visible et l'invisble*, the Italian translations and editions of *Résumes de cours*, *Philosophie et non-philosophie depuis Hegel*, and *La natur*; he has also published *Il sensibile e l'eccedente* (1996), concerning Merleau-Ponty, Cézanne, and Proust, and a number of essays in Italian and French.

EDWARD S. CASEY is Chair and Professor of Philosophy at the State University of New York, Stony Brook. Among his many accomplishments, he has published the following books: *The Fate of Place: A Philosophical History* (University of California, 1997); *Getting Back into Place: Toward a Renewed Understanding of the Place World* (Indiana University Press, 1993); *Remembering: A Phenomenological Study* (Indiana University Press, 1987); *Imagining: A Phenomenological Study* (Indiana University Press, 1976).

SUZANNE LABA CATALDI is an Associate Professor of Philosophy at Southern Illinois University at Edwardsville, and the author of *Emotion, Depth, and Flesh: A Study of Sensitive Space*. Professor Cataldi has published essays in ethics, feminism, and existential phenomenology. Her current research focuses on feminist implications of Merleau-Ponty's thought.

TINA CHANTER is Associate Professor of Philosophy at the University of Memphis (Tennessee). Her publications include *Ethics of Eros: Irigaray's Rewriting*

273

of the Philosophers (Routledge, 1995), and *In the Time of Death: Levinas with Heidegger* (forthcoming), in addition to a number of articles published in journals such as *Philosophy and Social Criticism, Research in Phenomenology,* and *Differences.*

FRANÇOISE DASTUR is Professor of Philosophy at the Université de Paris XII. She is the author of many books: *Husserl: des mathématiques à l'histoire* (1995); *La mort: essai sur la finitude* (1994); *Dire le temps* (1996); *Heidegger et la question du temps* (1994); and *Holderlin: le retournement natal* (1997). She is also the author of essays on phenomenology. In 1993, she founded L'Ecole Francaise de Daseinanalyse of which she is the president.

FRED EVANS is Associate Professor of Philosophy and Coordinator of the Center for Interpretive and Qualitative Research at Duquesne University. He is the author of *Psychology and Nihilism: A Genealogical Critique of the Computational Model of Mind* (State University of New York Press, 1993) and has published articles on contemporary continental philosophy, political philosophy, the philosophy of psychology, and the philosophy of technology. He is currently working on a book entitled *The Multi-Voiced Body: Society, Communication, and the Age of Diversity.* He is a member of the editorial board of *Chiasmi International: Tri-lingual Studies Concerning the Thought of Merleau-Ponty.*

JEAN GREISCH is Professor of Philosophy at the Institut Catholique de Paris and member of the research group "Phenomenologie—Hermeneutique" at the Centre Nationale de Recherche Scientifique. He is the author of *Hermeneutique et grammatologie* (1977); *L'age hermeneutique de la raison* (1985); *Hermeutik und Metaphysik* (1984); *La Parole heureuse* (1986); *Ontologie et Temporalite* (1994). A new book entitled *The Tree of Life and the Tree of Knowledge* will appear in 2000.

MARJORIE HASS and LAWRENCE HASS are both Associate Professors of Philosophy at Muhlenberg College (Pennsylvania). Lawrence Hass has published essays in Twentieth Century Continental philosophy in *Man and World, Symploke,* and in several edited collections; he is the coeditor of the forthcoming *Re-Reading Merleau-Ponty: Essays Beyond the Continental-Analytic Divide* (Humanities Press, 2000); and he is currently writing a book on Merleau-Ponty's theories of language, thought, and knowledge. Marjorie Hass has published articles on topics in the philosophy of logic and in feminist philosophy.

JAMES HATLEY is Associate Professor of Philosophy at Salisbury State University (Maryland). He is the author of a forthcoming book on the Holocaust entitled *Suffering Witness: The Quandary of Responsibility in the Aftermath of the Irreparable* (State University of New York Press, 2000). He has also published articles and given papers on Levinas, Kristeva, Arendt, Lyotard, Merleau-Ponty, Heidegger, Paul Celan, and Leslie Marmon Silko revolving around the issue of ethical responsibility. He is currently at work on a phenomenology of backpacking to be titled: *The Silence in which Silence is Walking.*

LEONARD LAWLOR is Associate Professor of Philosophy at the University of Memphis. He is the author of several essays on recent French and German philosophy as well as a book entitled *Imagination and Chance: The Difference between the Thought of Ricoeur and Derrida* (State University of New York Press, 1992). He co-translated Jean Hyppolite's *Logic and Existence* (State University of New York Press, 1997) and Merleau-Ponty's notes on Husserl's "The Origin of Geometry" (Northwestern, 2001). He is coeditor and cofounder of *Chiasmi International: Tri-lingual Studies Concerning the Thought of Merleau-Ponty.* He is in the process of completing three books: *The Basic Problem of Phenomenology: An Essay on Derrida's Interpretation of Husserl*; *The Being of the Question: Essays on Ontology Today;* and *The Challenge of Bergsonism: Phenomenology, Ontology, Ethics.*

HENRI MALDINEY is a retired Professor of Philosophy in France. He is the author of many books, including *L'art, l'éclair de l'être* (1993); *Aux deserts que l'histoire accable* (1996); *Le Vouloir Dire de Francis Ponge* (1996); *Regard, Parole, Espace* (1994); and *Traversées* (1993).

HUGH J. SILVERMAN is Professor of Philosophy and of Comparative Literature at Stony Brook University (State University of New York Press). He is the author *of Inscriptions: Beyond Phenomenology and Structuralism* (1987; reissued 1997) and *Textualities: Between Hermeneutics and Deconstruction* (1994), as well as numerous articles, essays, and book chapters in Continental philosophy, aesthetics, and literary theory. Silverman is editor or coeditor of eighteen volumes including *Merleau-Ponty: Texts and Dialogues* (1992).

BERNHARD WALDENFELS is a Professor of Philosophy at Ruhr-Universität at Bochum and has lectured as a visiting professor at universities in Rotterdam, Paris, New York, Rome, Louvain-la-Neuve, San Jose (Costa Rica), and Debrecen. He is the author of *Das Zwischenreich des Dialogs* (1971); *Der Spielraum der Verhaltens* (1983); *In Den Netzen der Lebenswelt* (1985); *Ordung in Zwielicht* (1987) (English translation as *Order in the Twilight*, 1996); *Der Stachel des Fremden* (1990); *Antwortregister* (1994); *Deutsch-Franzosiche Gedankengange* (1995); *Studien zur Phaenomenologie des Fremden: Topologie des* Fremden (4 volumes, 1997); *Grenzen der Normalisierung* (1998); *Sinneschwellen* (1999);

and *Vielstimmigkeit der Rede* (1999). He is the German translator and editor of several books by Merleau-Ponty, and, in collaboration with A. Metraux, edited a volume of essays on Merleau-Ponty *Leibhaftige Vernunft: Spuren von Merleau-Pontys Denken* (1986).

GAIL WEISS is an Associate Professor of Philosophy and of the Graduate Program in the Human Sciences at The George Washington University. She is the author of *Body Images: Embodiment as Intercorporeality* (Routledge, 1998) and the coeditor of *Perspectives on Embodiment: The Intersections of Nature and Culture* (Routledge, 1999). Her teaching and published work focuses on the interconnections between phenomenology, feminist theory, and literature.

EDITH WYSCHOGROD is the J. Newton Rayzor Professor of Philosophy and Religious Thought at Rice University. Her most recent books are *An Ethics of Remembering: History, Heterology, and the Nameless Others* (1998), and *Saints and Postmodernism: Revisioning Moral Philosophy* (1990).

AUTHOR INDEX